alfred HITCHCOCK'S

Tales to Make You Quake & Quiver

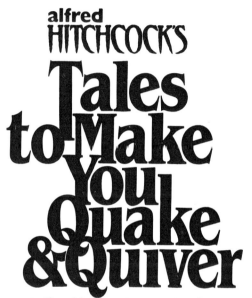

alfred
HITCHCOCK'S
Tales to Make You Quake & Quiver

Edited by Cathleen Jordan

THE DIAL PRESS
Davis Publications, Inc.
380 Lexington Avenue,
New York, N.Y. 10017

Grateful acknowledgment is hereby made for permission to include the following:

That Monday Night by Pauline C. Smith; copyright © H. S. D. Publications, Inc., 1971; reprinted by permission of the author. *Big Tony* by Jack Ritchie; first published in ADAM READER #25; copyright © 1966 by Knight Publishing Corp.; reprinted by permission of Larry Sternig Literary Agency. *Martin for the Defense* by Jaime Sandaval; copyright © H. S. D. Publications, Inc., 1971; reprinted by permission of the author. *The Waiting Room* by Charles W. Runyon; copyright © H. S. D. Publications, Inc., 1969; reprinted by permission of Scott Meredith Literary Agency, Inc. *Scream All the Way* by Michael Collins; copyright © H. S. D. Publications, Inc., 1969; reprinted by permission of the author. *Thieves' Bazaar* by W. L. Heath; copyright © 1956 by H. S. D. Publications, Inc.; reprinted by permission of Ann Elmo Agency, Inc. *The Keeper* by Clark Howard; copyright © H. S. D. Publications, Inc., 1971; reprinted by permission of Alex Jackinson Literary Agency. *Nice Guy* by Richard Deming; copyright © H. S. D. Publications, Inc., 1969; reprinted by permission of the author. *A Funny Place To Park* by James Holding; copyright © H. S. D. Publications, Inc., 1971; reprinted by permission of Scott Meredith Literary Agency, Inc. *The Jade Figurine* by Bill Pronzini; copyright © H. S. D. Publications, Inc., 1970; reprinted by permission of the author. *A Small Down Payment* by Stephen Wasylyk; copyright © H. S. D. Publications, Inc., 1971; reprinted by permission of the author. *Coffee Break* by Arthur Porges; copyright © 1964 by H. S. D. Publications, Inc.; reprinted by permission of Scott Meredith Literary Agency, Inc. *The Volunteers* by Reynold Junker; copyright © 1966 by H. S. D. Publications, Inc.; reprinted by permission of Lenniger Literary Agency, Inc. *Death at Stonehenge* by Norma Schier; copyright © H. S. D. Publications, Inc., 1969; reprinted by permission of the author. *Call Me Nick* by Jonathan Craig; copyright © H. S. D. Publications, Inc., 1968; reprinted by permission of Scott Meredith Literary Agency, Inc. *One November Night* by Douglas Farr; copyright © 1960 by H. S. D. Publications, Inc.; reprinted by permission of Scott Meredith Literary Agency, Inc.; *Arbiter of Uncertainties* by Edward D. Hoch; copyright © H. S. D. Publications, Inc., 1969; reprinted by permission of the author. *Witness* by Lee Chisholm; copyright © H. S. D. Publications, Inc., 1971; reprinted by permission of the author. *Breakfast in Bed* by Maeva Park; copyright © 1965 by H. S. D. Publications, Inc.; reprinted by permission of the author. *Summer in Pokochobee County* by Elijah Ellis; copyright © 1964 by H. S. D. Publications, Inc.; reprinted by permission of Scott Meredith Literary Agency, Inc. *Variations on an Episode* by Fletcher Flora; copyright © 1967 by H. S. D. Publications, Inc.; reprinted by permission of Scott Meredith Literary Agency, Inc. *Finders-Killers* by Ed Lacy; copyright © 1957 by H. S. D. Publications, Inc.; reprinted by permission of Howard Moorepark Agency. *The Pin-Up Boss* by Georges Carousso; copyright © 1966 by H. S. D. Publications, Inc.; reprinted by permission of McIntosh & Otis, Inc. *Rainy Wednesday* by Thomasina Weber; copyright © H. S. D. Publications, Inc., 1967; reprinted by permission of the author. *The Short And Simple Annals* by Dan J. Marlowe; copyright © 1964 by H. S. D. Publications, Inc.; reprinted by permission of the author. *Bite of Revenge* by James McKimmey, Jr.; copyright © 1958 by H. S. D. Publications, Inc.; reprinted by permission of Robert P. Mills, Ltd. *The Pearls of Li Pong* by W. E. Dan Ross; copyright © 1957 by H. S. D. Publications, Inc.; reprinted by permission of Robert P. Mills, Ltd.

Introduction

The first issue of *Alfred Hitchcock's Mystery Magazine,* from whose archives all but one of the stories included here were taken, was published in December, 1956, the year Alfred Hitchcock had produced the new version of *The Man Who Knew Too Much* (the James Stewart-Doris Day remake of the 1934 original). Before that, in the 1950's alone, Hitchcock had brought us movies like *Stage Fright, Strangers on a Train, Dial M for Murder, Rear Window,* and *To Catch a Thief,* among others. In 1955, his popular television series, *Alfred Hitchcock Presents,* had first been aired, the start of nearly a decade's run. Mr. Hitchcock was keeping those of us who were around in those years very scared and very entertained, and we knew, with pleasure, that he was going to continue to do so.

From the beginning, *AHMM* continued that tradition. And this past December, it celebrated its 26th birthday. Over the years, the magazine has published thousands of tales, by a great many notable writers. In 1977, its editors began compiling some of those stories into anthologies, of which this is the eleventh volume. One third of it has been contributed by writers from the early days of the magazine, and in some cases the stories included here are their first ones. Fletcher Flora was published in the first issue of *AHMM;* Richard Deming, Jack Ritchie, and W. L. Heath (with the story below, "Thieves' Bazaar") in the second; W. E. Dan Ross (with "The Pearls of Li Pong") in the third; Ed Lacy (with "Finders-Killers") in the fourth. Before the 1950's were out we had welcomed James McKimmey, Jr. (with "Bite of Revenge"), Douglas Farr, and Arthur Porges.

Most of the writers represented in this book are very practiced hands at the mystery story (and mystery novel) business, and most, as well, have done numerous stories for *AHMM*. (Some, however, we've seen too little of. Heath, for instance, sent in only that one tale, Ross only one other; Reynold Junker sent us only "The Volunteers.") Readers of the magazine and mystery aficionados in general are likely to need little introduction to such names as Bill Pronzini, Edward D. Hoch, Clark Howard, James Holding, Elijah Ellis, Dan J. Marlowe (who also writes under the name of Jaime Sandaval), Pauline C. Smith, Charles Runyon, Jonathan Craig, and Michael Collins, in addition to those mentioned above. Newcomers to their work have a feast of many courses to choose from—and they may be interested in knowing, for instance, that Elijah Ellis's story, "Summer in Pokochobee County," is one of a series in *AHMM* about that county and its sheriff, Ed Carson, that began with his first story for us in November, 1963 ("To Stop a Fire"); that Bill Pronzini's story "The Jade Figurine" was rewritten into a novel by that name in 1972; that Arthur Porges' "Coffee Break" is one of a series of stories about Professor Middlebie, who first appeared in 1962; that a number of novels recount the further adventures of Dan Fortune, Michael Collins's one-armed detective; that Ed Lacy, Michael Collins, Clark Howard, Dan Marlowe, and Edward D. Hoch are all winners of the Mystery Writers of America's Edgar Allan Poe Award.

And we hope that, in the best Hitchcock custom, whether you are returning to old friends or making new ones, the whole collection will keep you very scared and very entertained.

Cathleen Jordan

Contents

That Monday Night

by Pauline C. Smith

That Monday night at nine o'clock, as soon as "Laugh-In" was over, Jim Copeland remembered to get up and turn on the porch light. His daughter, Michele, should be home from the store by nine thirty. She always was.

He yawned, stretched, and looked at the TV news. Discarding the movie on Channel Four that would take too long, he switched to Channel Two. Then he went into the kitchen, opened a can of beer, returned, settled down to the television set, and was sound asleep by nine fifteen.

The screen finished its Mayberry problems and began a Doris Day entanglement, continuing then with Carol Burnett's comedic exaggerations. . . .

Jim Copeland slept on.

Mrs. Carrie Mason, the middle-aged widow next door, was also watching television, from her bed. Her bedroom window looked out upon the Copeland porch so that she saw the light when it went on at nine o'clock. For Michele, she thought, knowing that the girl worked on Monday nights at Harper's department store in the Plaza shopping center. She would be home at nine thirty right on the dot, because she always was, then the light would go off.

Carrie became absorbed in the movie, not noticing that the porch light remained on, not until after the movie was over at eleven. Her first thought, then, was that Jim Copeland had forgotten to turn it off after Michele's arrival home. "Just like a man," she muttered, knowing that Mrs. Copeland, Sue, was in Tremont, babysitting for that married daughter of hers, the one with three children. With Sue gone, wouldn't Jim Copeland keep the porch light on until all hours!

Carrie switched off her TV set, went to the kitchen, swallowed a jigger of bourbon to help her sleep, returned to the bedroom, turned off her light, and opened the window a scant three inches. Just before she slanted the blind slats enough so that the morning sun would not awaken her with the terrible start of remembering that she was alone and a widow, she looked out upon the Copeland driveway where Michele always parked her car and found it empty.

Her heart squeezed and her mind formulated four thoughts in rapid succession. The first: *That eighteen-year-old child who had seemed so dependable, so studious and conscientious was, perhaps, like the rest of this young college generation, out whooping it up heaven-knows-where.* The second: *That father, who seemed so nice for a man, was letting her whoop it up while he sat goggle-eyed in front of his television set, which she could see grayly flickering in the Copeland living room.* Her third thought was that there was some kind of trouble: *Michele never stayed out after her evening at the store and her father never stayed up on a week night.* Fourth: *She should go over and find out, being a woman and with Sue gone.* Then she remembered that she was a forty-year-old widow . . . well, all right, forty-five . . . and her act of Samaritanism might be misinterpreted, especially with a jigger of liquor on her breath.

She lay down, but uneasily, and slept restlessly, the empty space in the Copeland driveway on her mind.

It was one o'clock when she was awakened by the rumble of Jim Copeland's car as it backed with noisy abandon from the garage.

She peeked out between the slats of the blind. The Copeland driveway was empty and fog-washed. The Copeland garage was open and dark. The porch light still shone, as did a lamp dimly from the living room.

Something was wrong.

The town lay between the ocean and the mountains, quietly serene. With a sprawling megalopolis to the south and a tightly aloof city to the north, it was left out by the AP and the UPI news reports and ignored during the television weather forecast; a forgotten town.

At nine thirty that Monday night, a co-worker, Linda Fischer—("I'm in jewelry, but Michele moved around from department to department because she went to college, you see, and only worked two nights a week plus Saturday . . .")—saw Michele in the brightly lighted parking lot. "Of course I know it was Michele Copeland. She was standing there by her car, that little green bug she drives, and she waved when my husband and I drove by. My husband picks me up about nine twenty. He parks in the A section, and when I'm through we drive down to the D section which is near the coffee shop, and we go in there for coffee and a snack."

The coffee shop, Linda Fischer explained to the police on Tuesday when they questioned her, stayed open until ten. She and her husband left just before it closed. There was only one car in the D section when they left, probably the coffee shop owner's car, and the owner explained to the police when questioned that, yes, he took off five minutes after the last customers, but he drové out the other side. Out through D, he meticulously explained, to the turnoff on Sargent and, as far as he could remember, there wasn't a car in the parking lot. As far as he could *see* there wasn't a car; but then, of course, he hadn't looked back toward A, the Harper parking lot. Why should he? He was going the other way.

Linda Fischer and her husband drove from D section, after coffee and a sandwich, about nine fifty-five, she thought, out through A again and they saw Michele's car still there, jacked up. They supposed she had gone off with the friend who had been helping her because his car was gone.

"A friend?" asked the police.

How could Linda know that? She and her husband had seen this man there at nine thirty or thereabouts. No, they couldn't see him very well, he'd been tall and thin and had dark hair, she thought. He seemed to be fooling around with the jack, and his car—at least they assumed it was his car—had been parked next to Michele's so they supposed she had come out from the store, found a flat, and called him, a friend.

What kind of car? Linda was asked. She didn't know; light, probably white—at least a pale color.

Anyway, Michele waved to Linda, and she wouldn't wave if anything were wrong would she?

Linda did not add that her husband had wanted to stop. "Maybe I can help," he had said in his involved way. "Don't be silly," Linda had answered. "She's got help." Anyway, Michele was pretty, and it was Linda's mission in life to keep her husband away from pretty girls.

Just the same, ever since that Tuesday morning when the police had questioned her, Linda was nagged by the guilty suspicion that maybe it wasn't a happy hand greeting Michele had waved at nine thirty Monday night, but a frantic wig-wag of terror.

Well, she couldn't tell the police that, could she? And what would be the use now?

On Tuesday morning Sue Copeland, Michele's mother, prepared to leave her daughter Dorrie's home in Tremont immediately after breakfast.

"But Mom, why so early? It's only a couple of hours' drive and, anyway, by the time you get there, Dad'll be at work and Michele at school. Why not wait and leave this afternoon?"

Sue did not know why unless, being unaccustomed to the demands of three small children during a long weekend, she felt the abrupt need of the quiet of her home. "Oh, I don't know, Dorrie," she said. "I guess I just want to get the house straightened up. . . ."

A limp excuse since Michele was neat as a pin and Jim never got anything out of place.

Dorrie firmed her lips and spoke precisely. "Well," she said, "if you don't want to hear about the trip and the speech Hal gave at the convention," a snappish attempt to cover up and superimpose the selfish guilt of a married daughter who would call a mother out on the freeway two hours away to go through a three-day brat-race just because it was cheaper and more convenient than hiring a babysitter who would babysit only, and not clean and wash and cook and rock. "If you don't want to have a *visit* and just *enjoy*. I thought you'd stay a little while, at least, after we got home and Hal had gone off to work. So we could talk *alone*. I thought you wouldn't leave until afternoon. At least noon."

"I know, honey," said Sue vaguely, gathering her bags together and picking up her car keys. "I know," she said, feeling a compulsion to get home without knowing why.

She kissed the three grandchildren and Dorrie walked with her out to the car.

"I wanted to talk about the trip, Mom," said Dorrie, leaning inside the car, the guilt, now that her mother did not allow her to assuage it with hospitality, melting into tears. "I wanted to have a little while with you. I mean, after you'd taken care of the kids and all, it seems kind of awful that you should pick up and run without a visit with me."

Sue, starting the motor, said, "I know, honey, but another time," unable to explain her obsession that she must hit the freeway and hurry home.

She worked her way through the early morning traffic, away from the city, into the fast lane north through the coastside fog and the overhanging clouds of winter. She made the trip in less than two hours, leaving the freeway and turning onto Sargent, where she drove past the Plaza shopping center's morning-filled parking lot without noticing the little green car jacked up in the A section directly behind Harper's department store.

She crossed the back residential streets toward the old suburban area and turned onto Rio Mesa. From the end of the block, the moment she turned, Sue routinely observed that Michele's car was gone from the driveway, which was as it should be at ten o'clock on a Tuesday morning. She drove up the quiet street, made the sharp turn required to enter the open garage and braked with startled surprise.

What was Jim's car doing home at this hour of the day?

She eased her car in beside it, then hurried from the garage up the steps of the porch. She noticed the forgotten porch light glowing faintly in the gloom of a cloudy day.

Now alarmed, Sue turned the key and flung open the door.

There sat Jim, sunk in the big chair, his head in his hands.

Before she could speak, he lifted his head and said, "Michele is gone."

"Gone?" Sue's voice rose on the word and reached a shrill note. "What do you mean, gone?"

He told her then about dropping off to sleep, and awakening to discover that it was one o'clock in the morning, with Michele not in her bed and her car not in the driveway.

Sue backed against the door so that it closed with her weight. *Is this what she had been hurrying home to?*

Jim told her, in a dead voice Sue had never before heard, how he got out his car and raced through sleeping streets to the Plaza shopping center and found Michele's little green car there, the only car in the entire parking lot, jacked up, with the spare lying on the pavement; not Michele—only Michele's car.

He went on to explain, in this freshly dead voice, his hurried search for a phone booth in among the fog-wet planters and the darkened shops of the mall and how he finally found one and called the police.

The police had it all wrong from the beginning. At first, over the phone, they thought Jim Copeland had wanted them to fix a flat or get someone to fix a flat. Then they thought he was reporting a daughter's stolen car. Finally they got it straight. Well, not really straight because, even after meeting him out there at the lighted parking lot and seeing the jacked-up car and hearing his garbled account, the two patrol officers still confused Michele with the usual teenager encountered during the course of their varied, colorful night duty.

"You know who she might have run away with?" asked one.

The other mentioned drugs and possible pregnancy.

However, they did not press charges when Jim Copeland took a poke at one of the officers, even though they did tell him that was no way to find his daughter.

At headquarters, the man at the desk recorded the necessary descriptive information. Name, Michele Copeland. Age, 18. Height, 5'1". Weight, 98 pounds. Brown eyes. Blonde hair. Occupation, full-time college student, part-time department store employee. It was not a complete description since Michele's dependable character and her reserved personality had been left out, but the man at the desk said that information was unnecessary.

Because Michele was eighteen and legally an adult, the police could not get out an all-points bulletin on her disappearance for seventy-two hours, and by that time, through interviews with students and faculty members of the college as well as co-workers at the store, it had been well established that she was indeed a good, dependable, conscientious, and reserved girl; therefore not the type to take off willingly with some strange man.

This left the police with two theories. Either the tall, thin, darkhaired stranger, described by Mrs. Linda Fischer, had used physical violence to force Michele into his car, necessitating a search of the hillside arroyos and deserted rocky points of the beach for a body, or the tall, thin, darkhaired stranger was a friend with whom Michele had gone willingly and the highway patrol was alerted to cover the brushlands and cliffsides for a wrecked, probably white, car and possibly two bodies.

"Can't you describe the guy's car any better than that?" the police asked the Fischers. "You just say a light-colored car, probably white. How about make? Was it a late model? Sedan, convertible, station wagon, compact maybe?"

Linda said she didn't know one car from another, and anyway she hadn't looked at the car. She had just waved back at Michele as they drove on.

At that, her husband glared at her. He would never forgive her for talking him out of stopping on Monday night. He had wanted to stop. He had slowed down even, but know-it-all Linda, who acted like she owned even the breaths he took, hurried him on as she turned and waved and smiled as if butter wouldn't melt in her mouth at that poor girl who was God-knows-where now.

"I'm sorry, officer," said Linda Fischer's husband, "I didn't notice much about the car either, except that it was light—white, probably—and stuck out farther than her little green job in the diagonal parking space right in front of it. What I was noticing was that her trunk was open and it looked as if the guy was getting out the jack, so everything seemed to be under control, with him there and all . . ." He ended his excuse for noninvolvement with a sigh, feeling only partial absolution and none at all for his wife.

Again he glared at her. "Is it true the tire was slashed?" he asked.

Jim Copeland was sure the tire had been slashed. "The sidewall was punctured with a sharp instrument," he declared for the press. The crime-lab report offered the more conservative view that the tire could have been damaged accidentally and routinely by a sharp rock or a piece of glass.

Carrie Mason didn't know what to do.

She had seen Jim Copeland arrive home on Tuesday morning at seven o'clock, just about the time it was beginning to winter-light. Watching from her bedroom window with the blind slats carefully slanted, she had seen the car pull into the garage and Jim Copeland walk heavily up the porch steps.

The porch light remained on and the driveway remained empty, and she didn't know what to do. She should go over there, shouldn't she? After all, they were neighbors and she was a good friend of Sue's. But then, being a widow and with Sue gone, it might look . . . Well, it might look *funny*, like she was trying to . . . well, trying to promote something.

At eight thirty she saw the patrol car pull up to the curb, and two officers walk up to the Copeland front porch. They went inside the house.

What in the world?

At nine o'clock they left the house and drove the patrol car away, and Carrie Mason was again faced with the question of what to do? Offer her services, her condolence, her sympathy, whatever it was that she should offer? She felt a nagging anxiety that the offer might be coming too late, but she couldn't just stay here in her house with a neighbor in trouble. My goodness, daughter gone, up till all hours, out all night, and then the police. It was time, certainly, to throw caution to the winds. Even if she was an attractive forty-five-year-old widow—well, almost fifty—still, this was a duty; but first she must do something about her jumping nerves after seeing the patrol car and the policemen, so she tottered to the kitchen and swallowed a jigger of bourbon which calmed her, but also caused her to realize that she could not possibly, being a nice widow and all, visit a man alone with liquor on her breath.

An hour later she saw Sue Copeland's car turn into the garage.

With Jim's shocking announcement, Sue's reaction was immediate. She went into his comforting arms to comfort him. From that moment on, until he drove Michele's little green car home on Thursday, or perhaps it was with Dorrie's arrival which also occurred on Thursday, Sue leaned upon Jim and encouraged him. She was his hope as he was hers, with never a thought of recrimination for this accidental tragedy.

They were interviewed together by a young reporter that Tuesday noon, and together they described their daughter—a good, responsible girl, not the type to go off with a stranger, so it had to be foul play. They described the dress she wore, a brown wool with matching coat, and her quiet, orderly habits which would never allow her to act heedlessly. Her grades were excellent. She had no problems. Yes, she dated on occasion, but seldom, what with her studies and part-time clerking job, and no one steadily.

At the reporter's request, Sue offered him Michele's latest pictures—the year-old graduation photograph, careful to point out that her hair had been long then, but now was cut short, as shown in the more recent snapshots. She broke down and wept, feeling bereft and frightened as if, by relinquishing the pictures of Michele, she were giving up her daughter for lost.

Sue got through that first day by drinking coffee and keeping the pot ready for Jim when he arrived home from either an anxiety-filled trip to the police station or a fearful cruise along lonely roads. She paced the floor and phoned those of Michele's friends who were available and might know something. No one knew anything, or so they said.

She looked with aversion at the plate of cookies Carrie Mason brought apologetically over about two o'clock in the afternoon, smelled Mrs. Mason's mouthwash-spiked breath, and listened with an edge of surprise as Mrs. Mason groped through a perplexing maze of nonintervention excuses for not arriving earlier. Then Sue roused to realize that Mrs. Mason, widowed and somewhat humiliated by it, had probably been on target behind her venetian blind since last night when the pattern of the Cope-

ALFRED HITCHCOCK'S ANTHOLOGY

lands had been smashed, wanting to know, to be a part of it, wanting to help but unable to because she was a widow and envious of the non-widowed.

Sue told her all that she knew and they wept together.

The paper, with the front-page item and picture of Michele, was delivered at five, when the winter day began to be night. Sue read about her daughter and looked at the darkening sky, knowing that she was out there someplace.

Through the night, Sue made frequent trips to the front porch to test the black, cold dampness, ashamed of being warm and safe. She stood on the porch in terror of the night and what it might be doing to her child, until Jim urged her back into shamed warmth and safety.

It was during those times that Sue and Jim were close, with the compassion of mother for father and father for mother, not thinking of blame or self-blame, of guilt or self-guilt—not until Thursday, after the seventy-two hour lapse, when flyers would be distributed to 250 law-enforcement agencies within the state and extending into adjoining states, when the case would reach the television newscast and be released to the press through the AP and the UPI services, when the little green car would be returned to the driveway, and Dorrie would arrive.

Wednesday morning, Carrie Mason divided her time between the venetian blinds of her bedroom and the kitchen stove, cooking up food the Copelands could not possibly eat.

She anguished as she watched the television people haul out their equipment from the truck in front and drag it up the porch steps and into the Copeland house. She castigated herself for her Monday-night-eleven-o'clock-bourbon-breath when she identified the reporter returning to the Copeland house for a second interview. She cooked and watched, flagellating herself for her anxious-widow sins of omission, for had she awakened Jim Copeland from his sleep, his daughter might be home now.

The Wednesday evening article in the local newspaper covered the lower section of the front page, displaying another picture of Michele—one of the snapshots showing her hair cut short and with a smile on her face—that broke Sue's heart. The picture looked back at Sue now under the heading: HAVE YOU SEEN THIS GIRL?

It was then that Sue phoned her married daughter, knowing that she could put it off no longer in the hope it would not be necessary at all, because now, if she were not warned, Dorrie would have the shock of finding out from her own newspaper or through her television.

Dorrie became immediately emotional. "When did it happen?" she cried. "On Monday night? When you were *here?*" She was silent for a time, interrupting her mother at last with, "But if you had been home, it might not have happened," and quickly adding, "What was Daddy *doing* all that time? *Sleeping?*" and she had the hook upon which to hang her guilt. "You mean he didn't *do* anything? Mom, I'll be there," making the immediate decision to transfer her fault of needlessly needing her mother, to her father, so that he could be the sinner and not she. "Mom, I'll drive up tomorrow as soon as I can arrange about Hal and the kids."

"No, honey," protested Sue, knowing Dorrie's tendency to dominate, to push like a bulldozer and whack away like a pile driver. Sue did not want to be pushed or whacked at this point, but wanted only to wait and worry and hope so that she didn't go to pieces, with all the pieces flying out into limbo.

"Absolutely, Mom," said Dorrie. "This is awful! Why, it's awful! I'll be there. You don't have to do a thing. I'll take care of everything."

Just as Michele could not legally be presumed a missing person until seventy-two hours had passed, so could her car not be legally presumed to be abandoned for the same length of time, and it stood there in the parking lot just as she had left it. No fingerprints had been found and none had been expected, due to the heavy fog of Monday night and early Tuesday.

Thursday afternoon the sun came out with brief and pale promise as Jim Copeland changed the tire on his daughter's car.

The shoppers who had parked in A section, most of whom had read the front page of the local paper, and many having heard a number of the news spots from the local radio station, walked an arc of sympathetic self-consciousness around Jim Copeland and his daughter's car. All were hurried and embarrassed except for one, the man who drove into A section in a light gray compact and stepped out of it with an offer to help Jim Copeland change the tire.

The man, youngish, about thirty-five, Jim decided, squinting up at him, really wanted to help. He was slim, personable, conservatively dressed, of medium height and with medium brown hair—unless, of course, he might have been seen at night in the deceptive light of the floods with their elongated shadows, making any man tall, especially if standing next to a girl of five feet one inch, just as night light colors all brown hair dark, particularly when contrasted with blonde.

With the spare in place, the damaged tire, jack, and lug wrench back in the trunk, the young man leaned against his car to talk about Monday night.

Grateful for his interest, Jim Copeland listened to ideas that were neither as objective as those of the police nor as emotional as Jim's own, but a combination of emotional objectivity that could be trusted.

"I read about it in last night's paper," said the man, "and I've been hearing radio reports all day. I'm a salesman and in my car a lot and have the radio on. I wonder if the police are going about it in the right way."

"I wonder, too," said Jim Copeland. "They say they aren't even sure if the man with whom those people saw Michele had anything to do with it. They say it's possible he might have driven away and Michele walked off to find a phone, and whatever happened, happened then."

The man shook his head. "He had everything to do with it," he said with certainty. "I'd bet on it. The one with the white car."

"I think so, too," said Jim. "I think he slashed the tire and waited for her."

The man gave the damaged tire a token glance. "No. In the first place, how would he know the driver was a girl? Even if he looked in and saw the registration on the steering wheel post, how would he know the girl would be alone? Whoever it was didn't plan the thing. It just happened."

Jim closed the trunk and leaned against it. "You think the tire was flat and he saw it and just waited and when it turned out to be a girl, especially a pretty girl, he went through all the motions, and then as soon as there wasn't anyone around, he forced her into his car? She sure as hell wouldn't go with him willingly."

"What if he seemed like a nice sort of fellow? Clean-cut, pleasant, helpful, not a long-haired hoodlum kid or old enought to be a dirty old man, but somewhere in between, and he says he'd be glad to help and he gets out the jack and gets to work. What can happen under the lights? Then he hauls out the spare and bounces it up and down on the pavement and says it needs air—"

"But it had plenty of air," interrupted Jim, kicking the tire.

"Okay," said the man, "but would your girl have known any different if somebody'd told her it hadn't?"

No, thought Jim Copeland. All Michele had known about a car was how to drive it. It could have happened the way the man had said.

"So he says he guesses she'd better ride with him down to the filling station to get some air in the tire. The filling station's down on the corner. You can see it from here."

Obediently, Jim Copeland, who was a regular customer of that filling station, shaded his eyes toward the corner of Sargent and Oak where he could see the top of the station sign.

"What's she going to do? Even a girl like yours, who wouldn't willingly get into a car with a stranger, this time she's going to think nothing of it. After all, the guy's knocking himself out for her, and he's honest enough not to want to take off with her tire, leaving her to stand there all alone, scared he might steal it and not come back." The man smiled, curving the smile into a combination of arrogant pity for the father and pompous regret for the daughter.

"You mean you think she might have been tricked into this weirdo's car?" asked Jim Copeland.

"Not tricked, exactly," said the man, "and the guy wasn't necessarily a weirdo. He might have been sick."

"*Sick?*

"Look, I'm basing this hypothesis on the psychology I have learned. You see, I set out to be a consulting psychologist and then my wife got sick and I had to drop out of school and make money to take care of her. That was years ago. Haven't had any married life since and no career either. Just work at a sales job to give an invalid wife the things she needs and wants . . ." He shook his head with self-pity. "That's what I was doing here Monday night, getting her one of the things she's always after me to get—a prescription, ice cream, a heating pad or an ice bag, anything, something—"

"You mean you were here at the shopping center that night?" Jim Copeland leaned forth from the trunk of the little green car to grab the jacket lapels of the man. "You were here that night? Did you see something? Did you see any of that stuff you've been talking about?"

The man shook loose. "I told you," he said, "everything I told you is theoretical. I think about it. The police in a case like this want fingerprints or a hair or something before they're satisfied, and the relatives keep saying 'My daughter wouldn't,' and all I'm doing *is* showing how your daughter *might*, because I have studied those things and understand them. And I think he's sick, but a kind of a nice guy so your girl got into his car . . ."

Jim Copeland smoothed the man's lapels with apologetic pats. He was only trying to help and, God knows, this theory he'd come up with was a lot more believable than those of the police—talking about drugs and pregnancy and running away—none of which could apply to *Michele!*

"So we assume the guy was sick," explained the man. "Oh, not ordinarily, but just when the pressures build up. Let's say he's a nice guy. Your girl wouldn't go with anybody but a nice guy . . ."

Jim Copeland nodded.

"He doesn't plan anything. It gets planned for him."

"Gets planned?" asked Jim.

"That's the psychology of an impulse crime and I think it was a crime of impulse; nothing premeditated, but an extemporaneous impulse triggered by a series of circumstances. The guy's under a lot of pressure, he's at the exploding point. He drives into the parking lot late, just before closing time. He's in a hurry, probably doesn't even notice the little green car with its flat, at first. When he gets ready to leave, he notices but he doesn't think too much about it. The parking lot's thinned out, customers have taken off for their homes filled with loving, healthy, undemanding wives. He starts his motor. Then the girl comes, your girl, and she sees the flat and the guy turns off his motor and gets out."

Jim Copeland swallowed.

It could have been exactly like that.

"He's a nice guy," repeated the man. "He really wants to help, so he helps. He gets the jack out. Then the people drive by, those people who saw your girl and the guy. They slow down. They wave. And the guy wonders if your girl might be signaling, might be rejecting him and his help, signaling to her friends.

"But they go on and he jacks up the car and starts to reach for the lug wrench, still helping. Then the explosion comes, the pressures blow sky-high and he reaches for the spare, instead, and bounces it on the pavement. The whole thing's set up for him. He's sick and can't help what happens."

Jim Copeland looked away, feeling ill.

The pale sun hid behind the clouds that were rising on the horizon. It would rain again; sure enough, it would rain again tonight.

"He gives her the filling station pitch. She goes for it because there's not much else she can do. He helps her around his car and opens the door, then goes around to his side, leaving the spare on the pavement. He jumps in and they're off before she can even yell."

Jim Copeland felt as if he were swimming in the filtered light of the winter day. "You think," he said faintly, "that's the way it happened? That anyone could just—"

"That's the way it could have happened," said the man. "There were no signs of struggle. The police pointed that out. You said your girl wouldn't go off with a stranger willingly, so what other way could there be? It's a psychologically sound theory that a sick man, but a nice guy, found a setup just made for him to act on at a time that his pressures exploded . . ."

Jim Copeland looked away.

Then the man gave him hope. "A sick mind like that, though," he said, "knows he's sick and wants to be stopped."

Jim Copeland jerked his head back, and listened with intent.

"He'll cover—self-preservation, you know, being the first law—but at the same time, he'll drop clues, just hoping someone will find them and stop him from doing again what he has already done."

The man opened his car door and stepped inside. "I'm sorry, Mr. Copeland," he said, genuinely sorry.

He turned on his motor and the radio sounds came on immediately, faintly at first, to grow stronger into the on-the-hour news broadcast. . . . "Nothing yet on the Michele Copeland disappearance," came the voice of the announcer. "If you know of anything, or think you might know, or suspect . . ." The man turned down the volume to a whisper and started to back his car from its parking slot.

Jim Copeland straightened from the trunk of the little green car. "What do you think he did with her?" he asked the man.

"What do *you* think?"

Jim Copeland swallowed again.

The man turned the wheel, straightened out, and started down the A section of the parking lot.

"Hey," called Jim Copeland, "I didn't get your name."

The man shouted it out the window, but the sound was lost in the rising wind of the early evening and the growl of the motor as he turned to make the off-ramp onto Sargent.

The police didn't think much of Jim Copeland's theoretical story as told to him by the stranger in the parking lot when he immediately drove the little green car to headquarters and related it.

"A crackpot," they stated. "We get them all the time. A mother who's had it up to here with this rotten kid of hers thinks he did it and wants us to lock him up and throw away the key. Some dame says it's the kind of trick her ex-boyfriend would pull. You been in this work as long as we have, you expect all kinds of trumped-up-stories."

"But this was a theory," argued Jim. "This man seemed to know a lot about psychology, and he was basing this theory on his psychological knowledge."

"Every crackpot is a psychologist," said the officer. "They know everything about nothing and are eager to talk about it."

"But it sounded," said Jim with hesitation, "as if it could have really happened. It sounded right, somehow. If you could talk to him . . ."

"Sure," and the officer poised a pencil over a scratchpad. "Sure, we'll talk to him. We talk to all of 'em. Just give us his name and address."

Jim didn't know his name or where he lived. That bit of information had been snatched away in the wind, and maybe he *was* a crackpot, like the officer said. What had the man offered, after all? Just a theory.

Dorrie arrived late that Thursday afternoon, at the beginning of the storm that had been brewing and slacking off, allowing the sun to peek through, then closing in again. The storm broke, dark and vicious and Dorrie walked in about the same time her father drove the little green car home and parked it, once again, in the driveway.

From then on, every time Sue looked out the window she saw that little green car and shuddered, and every time she turned from the window Dorrie told her it was Jim's fault that Michele was gone, until she believed it.

"Your own daughter," she denounced him, "and you slept through it all."

"What could I have done?" he asked. "She was gone by ten. That's what those people at the parking lot said."

"With you home here, asleep," accused Sue, appalled at her own vindictiveness, but relieved to have a victim at last.

Jim was confused. "If I'd been awake, I wouldn't have gone after her by ten. Why would I? I'd have thought she'd stopped to have coffee with somebody."

"But not Mom," Dorrie broke in. "If Mom had been here, she'd have known Michele is never late. She'd have been out of here like a flash."

"But she wasn't here," said Jim, seeing his opportunity to fix blame, knowing that if the blame were to be circumvented it must be fixed upon someone else. "She was at your house, babysitting. That's why she wasn't here."

Ready for him, Dorrie answered in triumph, "Because she trusted you, that's why she wasn't here. She trusted you to take care of things and protect Michele so this awful thing wouldn't happen."

Thursday evening the story in the paper was more compact and without a photograph, headlined simply, HUNT CONTINUES, with a quick synopsis and the usual vague promise of an expected break.

The taped television interview had been cut to the bone to allow newscast pictures and commentary on the storm in progress, with accounts of sliding hillsides in the city to the north and stories of boiling rivers within the sprawling megalopolis to the south. The town in between lay ignored, as usual, except for the tape-cut interview with the parents of Michele Copeland.

However, it, too, was having its storm troubles with minor erosion of the hills and overflowing river banks, its greatest problem being the flooded streets and, more particularly, that corner at the intersection of Sexton and Sargent where the new tract of houses was under construction. There the water rose and flowed down the grade, bringing with it mud and debris, clogging the curbing outlets and flooding the Plaza shopping center parking area so that the water swirled into the mall and threatened the shops.

The storm lasted three days.

During that time, Sue could not sleep, her fearful nights being filled with terror-thoughts of her baby, out there someplace, out there alone or with a monster in the cold and the rain, out there dead or dying. Sue could not eat, her frightful days being consumed by horror-pictures of ravishment and death. She lived on coffee and the wakefulness it engendered. She lashed out at Jim as an object for her emotion. She worked him over, discovering after all their peaceful years together that she had a talent for it.

Dorrie, having shifted the weight of her own guilt, now carried a new burden. Her parents, always friends, were now enemies, and was that her fault?

"Mom," she cried, "I never heard you talk to Dad like that before."

"He never killed my daughter before," said Sue.

Periodically, Jim drove through the storm to the police station to find the officers engaged with traffic problems and slick-street accidents.

"About my daughter . . ." Jim Copeland asked anxiously, apologetic with this new deep guilt his wife had thrust upon him.

"We're working on it, Mr. Copeland," said the officer. "We've got those flyers out, you know. We wish we had more information, like a better description of the man and what kind of car he drove. We did the best we could with what we have. A picture of your daughter is on the flyer, and anything suspicious—well, we'll hear about it. I know how you feel, Mr. Copeland."

Jim Copeland looked at him blankly. This officer, too young yet for guilt, too young for teenage daughters, could not possibly know how he felt. Jim turned and left the police station, knowing that he would return shortly, to learn nothing again; but he had to come, a telephone call would not suffice. He had to come through storm-filled streets, and climb the stairs and open the heavy doors, and ask whichever officer was on the desk at the time, "Have you heard anything about my daughter?" He had to. There was nothing else he could do now.

The storm hampered the search, but it did not hamper Mrs. Carrie Mason. Daily, she made a tent of her late husband's raincoat and crouched under it, a platter of baked, fried, grilled, or broiled food covered and clutched, and scampered from her house to the Copelands'.

There she made her offering, always hoping it would be only Sue she might encounter in the kitchen. Even Sue, who had changed so drastically during the last of these few days from a soft and warm anxiety to being anxiously hard and cold, was better than her daughter Dorrie; Dorrie, who looked down her nose from the enviable heights of her youthful, husband-filled life, and caused within Carrie Mason great pangs of guilt for her own manless old age of almost fifty—no, actually fifty-two, almost fifty-three—and sometimes looked it.

So, guiltily, when it was Dorrie in the kitchen, she handed out the covered plate of whatever she had prepared and asked softly if there had been any news, any news at all.

Dorrie, taking the covered plate without even glancing under the cover, looked down from her pinnacle of security and said there was no news but, "We thank you for your kindness."

"No kindness!" protested Carrie. "It was Monday night when I should have been kind, the night I was sure something was wrong. At eleven o'clock I saw the porch light on and the driveway empty. I should have come then, and I didn't."

"Then it would have been too late," said Dorrie.

It might *not* have been too late, worried Carrie. On a Monday night this town was in bed by eleven and so, with the few cars on the streets at that time of night, they might have found Michele.

Carrie could not easily shift her burden of guilt, being neither young enough nor egotistical enough. Her guilt caused her to make a firm resolve: from now on she would be warmly friendly—instantly. She would not hesitate or vacillate, distrustful of her breath, apprenhensive as to appearances, but she would, so help her, aid, assist, succor, and befriend anyone who might need her, and she would be watchful for the need.

By Sunday, the storm was over.

On Monday, a week after Michele's disappearance, the street maintenance crews were out in full force and got to work to find out what was wrong in the area extending from the hills into the Plaza shopping center, which was a mess. The trouble was found to be at the intersection where the new tract of houses was under construction and now a sea of mud. The storm drain there seemed to be clogged, allowing an overflow of water and muck down Sargent, where it spread into the side streets and filled up the parking lot.

A work crew was called, and when they opened up the storm drain they found Michele's body doubled up and stuffed into it, plugging up the opening.

Linda Fischer heard it on the radio.

This was her late day at Harper's department store, starting at one and extending to nine o'clock closing time, so she was, that Monday morning, cleaning her apartment with the radio on when the newscast broke in to announce the discovery of Michele Copeland's body. She cringed, thinking what if, oh my goodness, what if she had allowed her husband to stop that night! He, too, might have been killed. Thus she absolved herself of any guilt, and turned her act of remission into one of nobility.

Her husband heard it during his lunch hour. "That girl," said the man on the stool next to him, "they found her. You know, the girl who disappeared a week ago."

Linda's husband swallowed the bite he had already taken from his sandwich and carefully laid the sandwich back on the plate.

"They found her in the storm drain up on Sargent and Sexton. Awful!" Mrs. Fischer's husband pushed back his plate, got off his stool, and walked woodenly from the drugstore. He walked down the street to the parking lot next to the business-machine office where he worked, got into his car, drove carefully down Main Street, past all the Caution signs to protect the street workers, entered the on-ramp to the freeway at the edge of town, and sped north.

He never wanted to see his wife, Linda, again. He would lose himself somewhere, in some city far away, and try to forget that if Linda had not stopped him a week ago, Michele would be alive now.

On that second Monday morning, Carrie Mason was busy preparing a hearty vegetable soup for the Copeland family. The radio in the kitchen, as always, was turned to the local station but she knew, even before the newscast told her so, that Michele had been found. She knew it when the police car drove up and the two police officers, their faces blankly reluctant, slowly climbed the steps to the Copeland front porch. So Carrie Mason knew, and as soon as the news was announced, remembering her always-be-friendly, help-in-time-of-need resolution, she knew that she would take the bowl of soup over even though, by the time the soup was ready, her breath would be redolent of bourbon, that she would look every minute of her almost fifty-three years, and that she wouldn't know what to say.

Jim Copeland took the news like a doomed man, dully aware of the fact that he was, indeed, doomed.

Sue turned on him with a final, "This is your fault," knowing that she would never speak to him again.

Dorrie, in the depths of her new guilt, wished that she could have the old one back, realizing at last that the guilt she had bequeathed herself would be lasting and difficult to endure.

By Monday night the body, having been properly identified, was properly resting in the funeral home.

Monday night, at nine ten, Linda Fischer emerged from Harper's department store into the parking lot of the Plaza shopping center. She walked out with a part-time co-worker, a college girl from the notions department in which Michele had worked the week before. The girl hadn't known Michele, but claimed acquaintanceship because they went to the same college and worked in the same store and it was all terribly exciting.

"We actually saw him that night," Linda said, and the girl hung on her words. "It was just a good thing my husband didn't stop. He might have been killed, too."

There were few cars left in Section A. The two walked carefully on the dry, caked mud. "Well, here's my car," said the girl. "Isn't your husband here? Do you want a lift?"

"No, thank you. You go ahead." Linda consulted her watch. "He'll be along," she said. "I'm out a little early. He'll be here by nine twenty for sure. He always is."

She didn't begin to worry until nine forty, and the last car was gone from Section A. Then she became frightened and ran past the now darkened shops to the coffee shop, still light, but empty of customers. The proprietor was just closing up.

"Would you drive me home?" Linda asked him breathlessly. "Would you please drive me home? I'm scared to wait for my husband out there all alone because of what happened . . ."

He would be glad to. He closed up the doughnut case, covered the cakes, turned off the lights, and locked the door. He was very kind and solicitous. He helped her into his car and headed toward the apartment section of town where Mrs. Linda Fischer said she lived.

It was not until they reached the turn-off into Sargent that Linda realized she was in exactly the same situation Michele Copeland had been at this very same time last Monday night.

She froze on her side of the seat and her voice, as she gave directions, emerged as a thin thread of sound, stitching together the man's earnest talk of the dangers that lurked for a woman alone in the night. She lived only a few blocks from the Plaza shopping center, and she was sure she would never arrive there, but the man drove her directly to her destination and she was startled when he stopped and she looked out at her very own apartment building. She leaned on the door and staggered from the car, too voiceless from her moments of terror to thank the man. Her strength returned with her relief as she ran toward the apartment door, banged it open, and stumbled up the stairs.

The moment she opened her own door upon darkness, she realized what an awful thing she had done when she prevented her husband from stopping to help Michele Copeland a week ago. It was the next moment that Mrs. Linda Fischer realized that her husband had left her and would not be back, because the awful thing she did to Michele she had also done to him.

Wednesday was the morning of the funeral. In the curtained-off mourners' section of the chapel, Dorrie sat between Michele's father and Michele's mother so that each parent wept alone through the ceremony.

Wednesday afternoon, Carrie Mason took over a pumpkin pie, and Dorrie had to push aside a mountain of dishes and a stack of pans to find room for it.

The kitchen looked as if a tornado had torn through, and there was Sue, dragging out linens and piling them up, making lists, dashing from one task to another. Carrie Mason wondered what in the world was going on and thought perhaps now that Jim and Sue Copeland were to be alone and with diminished needs, they had decided to reward Dorrie for all her self-sacrificing help by sending her home with extra household goods.

"You will probably be leaving now," Carrie said to Dorrie.

"Tomorrow," said Dorrie.

"I am going with her," said Sue without interrupting the even rhythm of her activity.

"Well," said Carrie, doubtfully supposing that maybe it was all right for a bereaved mother to go off and grieve with her daughter and grandchildren instead of staying home to grieve with the bereaved father, but she wasn't sure. "Well," she said, "that's nice. Now you go right ahead and have a wonderful vacation . . ." and halted mid-sentence, appalled at her poor choice of words, and unaware of the conversation going on around her until she heard the last part of Sue's amazing announcement, " . . . and I am not coming back. Not ever. I am going to live with Dorrie and her family."

"Yes," said Dorrie. "Mom will live with us."

The minute she said it, Sue knew that she didn't want to go. The minute she said she was never coming back she turned sick at the thought of leaving Jim. The minute she declared, "'I am going to live with Dorrie and her family,'" she wondered how she would be able to bear her daughter's domination and the tyranny of three spoiled grandchildren.

When Dorrie added, to make it stick, "Yes, Mom will live with us," she knew she had saddled herself with a live-in mother, Hal with an unwanted mother-in-law, and the children with a grandmother who would not be good for them and to whom they would not be good. She had done this to herself and hers, and now she would have to live with it.

The two loaded cars, Dorrie's and Sue's, departed on Thursday, leaving

Jim Copeland alone. Carrie Mason certainly wanted to take him some food, wanted to be warm and friendly as she had so firmly resolved, but she could not find him. He had gone back to work, of course, but he came home quietly and late. The porch light never went on any more, nor the light in the living room. Carrie Mason could not see even the flicker of the TV screen.

He was home only twice during the weekends; once when a long-haul moving van carted away certain pieces of furniture, and another time when a local van carted away the rest of it.

Three weeks after the funeral, Michele's little green car had been driven away and the house had been dismantled and a For Sale sign went up in the front yard.

Then Jim Copeland came over to see Mrs. Carrie Mason.

She offered him coffee, which he refused, explaining that he was busy and in a hurry. She noticed how thin he had become and she fluttered over him, not caring that she had bourbon on her breath, only wishing to be warm and friendly.

He told her he was living in a small apartment in town and was in the process of selling the house, which was why he was here; he wanted to leave one of the house keys with her, "Just in case," he said, and she wasn't sure whether he meant just in case Sue returned or just in case a prospective buyer wanted to take a look at the house.

The rest of the keys, he explained, were in the hands of the real estate agent who would be showing the house, but he wanted her to have one of them, "just in case."

Then he left and Mrs. Mason had nothing more to look at through the venetian blinds of her bedroom; nothing except the closed drapes of the living room next door, and a corner of the For Sale sign out in front.

Money being tight and interest rates up, not many people came to look at the house, but enough so that Carrie learned to recognize the real estate agent's car and to know it wasn't his when the light gray compact drew up to the curb in front of the Copeland house. It drove on again, but returned a few days later.

The third time she saw it, she was out in her front yard planting the last of her spring bulbs and hopeful that she could finish before the twilight turned to darkness. She rose from her knees when the car pulled up out in front, dropped her trowel, and walked from her yard to the next and down to the curbing.

"If you are interested in the house," she said to the young man in the car, "I have a key and I can take you through. But we'll have to hurry because the electricity has been turned off and it's getting dark. There won't be much time."

"Oh. Oh, yes," he said, momentarily startled, as if he were so fascinated by the house that he had been totally unaware of her approach. "Didn't the Copelands used to live here?"

"Yes. Such a tragedy." Mrs. Carrie Mason could not see the young man very well in the shadows of the car. He seemed nice, though, and personable. "Did you know them?" she asked.

"I met the girl just once," said the man.

"Michele? The one who was killed?"

"Yes. That one. And I talked to her father once." Abruptly, as if suddenly conscious of her existence, the man leaned across the car seat and looked directly at Carrie Mason in the now-purple twilight. "I have a wife, you see," he said, "who is an invalid . . ."

Carrie clucked with sympathy.

"We live in an apartment now, and I thought if we had a house, she could be outdoors more."

"Oh, she could, and that would be wonderful," said Carrie.

"I'm a salesman and out a lot and I would insist upon a good neighborhood, one I wouldn't have to worry about leaving her alone in. Nice and quiet. Decent."

Carrie started to describe the utter niceness, the restful quiet and the pure decency of the neighborhood when he broke in with, "I would like to see the house very much, but as you warned me, it is getting a little dark for that, but if I could look around the neighborhood, Mrs. . . . ?" his voice rising in inquiry.

"Mrs. Carrie Mason," she said.

"Mrs. Mason, I think this might be just the house I have been wanting. I can come back tomorrow, of course, to go through it, but I do want to get a look at the neighborhood first. It's still light enough for that. I wonder if you would show me . . ."

Carrie moved back a step.

"Just a short drive around the block. Only to point out the market and the nearest drugstore." He chuckled in a half-sorrowful, half-rueful fashion. "My wife needs and wants so many things at all hours—a prescription, ice cream, a heating pad or an ice bag, anything, something—"

Carrie remembered her firm resolve to aid and abet in a warm and friendly fashion.

"And if I had someone to show me around so I could describe the neighborhood to my wife tonight, perhaps rouse her interest, then tomorrow . . ."

Carrie gave one backward glance at her lawn, almost dark now, where the trowel and the remaining bulbs lay on the ground, and at her dark and unlocked house. "It will be only a few minutes?" she asked.

"Only a few minutes," he assured her.

She stepped inside the car, and the gray compact moved down the street.

ALFRED HITCHCOCK'S ANTHOLOGY

Big Tony

by Jack Ritchie

"**G**ot three daughters and it's about time they got married," Big Tony said. He turned away from the french windows. "O'Brien, it's up to you to see that it gets done."

I gave it about two seconds' thought. "You want me to go around and knock on doors and ask who wants to marry one of Big Tony's daughters?"

"No." He took a cigar out of the humidor. "Why do you think I moved out here to River Hills three years ago?"

"You wanted to be knee deep in the best people? But they won't talk to you and nobody will go out with your daughters?"

"Maybe I'll never get into the country club," Big Tony said, "but the girls don't have no trouble with the boys. How long since you saw them, O'Brien?"

"Four years. When you sent me out to the coast."

He nodded. "Well, they're better looking than ever."

"But still they can't get married?"

"It's like this, O'Brien. I'm their old man and my name still gets in the papers every once in a while, but not on the society pages." He paced back and forth on the deep rug. "I don't want to be one of them interfering parents, but I know what the score is, and it makes me sad."

He waved the cigar. "Like Angelina and Herbert Bradford. They're crazy about each other, but still he won't ask her."

"Why not?"

"Because Herbie's afraid of his old man. This Grover Bradford says that Herbie should wait for a girl whose ancestors used the Plymouth rock for a dock. And you know my own folks just missed getting steerage on the *Titanic*."

"What's the problem with Faustina?"

"Morley Wilson."

"What's he afraid of?"

"Fifteen million dollars. That's what he won't get from his grandma if he marries Faustina."

"And he's not ready to give up fifteen million dollars for Faustina?"

"Look, O'Brien," Big Tony said. "I don't blame the boy too much. A woman is a woman, but fifteen million is fifteen million."

"And I'm supposed to buck fifteen million dollars and come up with a happy ending?"

Big Tony grinned. "When I sent you to the coast, it looked like everything was crumbling out there. I really didn't expect nothing. But you put everything together and ticking. So I admire anybody who does a job like you do and hope you can make another miracle back here."

"What's Cecelia's trouble?"

"Philip Courtland. He played football for one of them eastern colleges. Real class and he's got maybe a million in his own name."

"What's making him timid?"

"I don't know. But find out and do something about it."

One of the side doors opened and Cecelia walked into the room. "Well, if it isn't O'Brien. I haven't seen you in a long, long time." Her gray eyes studied me. "What made you leave the coast? Business?"

"A friendly visit," Big Tony said. "He's staying here a while." He glanced at his watch. "I got a date with my golf pro. Why don't you show O'Brien around the place?"

Outside on the grounds, Cecelia said. "What's the real reason you're here?"

"You're not supposed to know."

She shrugged. "Have it your way."

She indicated some hedges. "Just ahead of us you will find Angelina and Herbert Bradford holding hands. Every Tuesday and Thursday between two and four Herbie sneaks away from the handball court at the country club and comes to look at Angelina."

We turned the hedge and found them sitting on a stone bench.

Angelina was dark and probably five foot two. "Hello, Mr. O'Brien," she said.

Cecelia smiled at them. "Here we have a repeat performance of the Montagues and the Capulets. Sometimes I think I ought to kidnap the two of them and drive to the nearest justice of the peace."

Angelina shook her head. "We don't do things that way in the twentieth century, Cecelia."

ALFRED HITCHCOCK'S ANTHOLOGY

Herbert nodded. "You see, Mr. O'Brien, despite the fact that my father doesn't care two beans about me, I still have a terrific need for his approval in everything I do. I am an extremely dependent personality."

A Jaguar turned into the driveway and pulled up in front of the house.

"My tennis date," Cecelia said. "But I can cancel it if you insist?"

"No. I have work to do."

The man behind the wheel got out and met us halfway.

"Philip Courtland," Cecelia said. "And this is Jim O'Brien."

Courtland was about my size and we looked each other over.

"O'Brien is one of my father's business associates," Cecelia said. "He has charge of disposing of bodies and things like that."

"I'll have to remember that," Courtland said.

I watched them go and then drove to town and looked up a drinking friend at the *Morning Chronicle*. After we got out of the bar, he led me back to his paper's morgue and let me do some research.

The next morning, when I left Big Tony's place, I bought a briefcase. At the Bradford Laboratories, I gave my name to Grover Bradford's secretary and sat down to wait.

The secretary came out of his office in one minute. "Mr. Bradford will see you now."

It was a very large office, deeply carpeted.

Grover Bradford rose from the desk to shake hands. He was a large man and probably spent his weekends on a boat.

He waited until I was seated and then said, "My secretary tells me that you're from the Food and Drug Administration."

"That's right."

He waited warily.

"Mr. Bradford," I said, "six months ago the Department ordered you to cease and desist your advertising claims concerning the merits of Sleep-So-Ezee. You were fined five hundred dollars."

His face became expressionless. "That's in the past. It's a closed book."

I smiled. "That's correct. You stopped manufacturing Sleep-So-Ezee and you paid the five hundred dollar fine. But that hardly made a dent in the million and a half that Sleep-So-Ezee brought you before the Department got around to acting."

He said nothing.

"The Department works slow," I said. "And some people take advantage of that fact to make their money. I believe we were testing Sleep-So-Ezee for eighteen months before we finally got around to doing something about it."

I paused a moment. "And now we come to your new product, Dream-8. Two little pills at bedtime and you sleep like a baby for eight hours. You began manufacturing and advertising Dream-8 two months ago. It should bring in another million dollars or so before the Department gets around to fining you another five hundred."

He reached for his cigar humidor and brought out a panatella. He didn't offer one to me.

I waited until he lit up and then said, "The Department can act slow. Or it can act fast. It can act a million dollars from now. Or tomorrow."

He studied me. "Are you telling me that you got something to say about how fast it moves?"

This time I was the one who said nothing. But I smiled.

He leaned forward. "All right. I recognize blackmail when I hear it. How much money do you want?"

"No money," I said. "I've already been bought. I want happiness. For me. For you. For everybody."

His eyes narrowed. "Be more specific."

"A couple of days ago a man came to me. He wanted to know if I could get the Department to move fast in the case of Dream-8. I looked at the money he carried and told him that it could be arranged. But it turned out that he really didn't want me to do anything at all unless . . ." I paused.

He stepped in. "Unless what?"

"It seems that the man has a daughter named Angelina and he wants to make her happy. And her idea of happiness is to marry somebody named Herbert Bradford."

Grover Bradford's fist came down on the desk. "I won't allow it!"

I rose. "It's up to you, Mr. Bradford. A million or Herbie."

"Wait a minute," Bradford said. "How long can you make the Department hold off?"

"Possibly two years," I said. "If I work at it real hard."

His eyes brightened and he seemed to be adding figures.

I paused at the door. "One more thing, Mr. Bradford. Big Tony would like to get into the country club. See what you can do about it."

That evening at Big Tony's house, I met Morley Wilson. He was thin

36

and balding and eventually he said, "It is most difficult to understand Grandmother. She absolutely forbids my marriage to Faustina and yet she does not object to my presence here. She even encourages it."

"Did you take your vitamin C tablets today?" Faustina asked.

Wilson nodded.

Faustina was naturally pallid and would probably remain that way until she died at the age of ninety-seven. "I don't think it will be too much longer before I can convince my doctor that I need thyroid pills, Morley."

"Look, Morley," Big Tony said. "I just bought a couple of canneries in Illinois. Corn, peas, and stuff like that in season. I'll give you the whole works as a wedding present."

Wilson considered that. "How much are they worth?"

"Three hundred thousand dollars."

Wilson shook his head. "No. I couldn't sleep nights. I'd still be thinking about the fifteen million I lost."

Herbie Bradford and Angelina walked into the room.

"My father's given me permission to marry Angelina," he announced proudly.

"And it's going to be a big wedding." Angelina said. "We'll have a lawn party when we make the announcement of our engagement."

The next morning after breakfast, I went to the garage for my car.

Cecelia followed me, "More business?"

"That's right."

"But you won't tell me what it is?"

"Why should I?"

"Because I am the boss's daughter and because I'm curious. Things seem to be moving around here, and I have the feeling that somehow you're responsible. Now why don't you tell me what you're up to?"

"Maybe some day."

"When?"

"After you're married."

It was less than half a mile to Morley Wilson's grandmother.

Hilda Wilson wore faded jodhpurs, moccasins, and a sweater.

"Hello, sonny," she said and continued on to the sideboard. "Care for a drink?"

"It's a little too early," I said.

"At my age," she said, "nothing's too early. Usually it's too late. Though I will say I haven't missed much." She downed a jigger of bourbon. "All right, sonny, what can I do for you?"

"Mrs. Wilson," I said. "I am an author. I specialize in writing the biographies of famous families. There are a few points which I would like to verify about the Wilson family before I go ahead."

"Keep talking, sonny."

"Well," I said. "Is it true that your husband founded the Wilson fortune in Colorado by jumping another man's claim?"

"Bill sure did. Rest his soul."

"And approximately one year later he shot a man in a drunken brawl?"

"Right between the eyes," Hilda said. "Bill would of got hung, but he bribed the jury."

I had the feeling that things weren't going exactly my way. "Mrs. Wilson," I said. "This biography doesn't have to be written."

"Is that right?" She went back to the sideboard, poured another drink, and brought it to me. "Swallow that, sonny. I think you'll need it."

I took the glass and waited.

"Sonny," she said, "so far six of you so-called authors have come to me with the story that they're going to write the biography of the Wilson family. And then they get around to telling me that they can restrain themselves from doing the job if I just slip them ten thousand dollars or so. Is that what you had in mind?"

I downed the drink and said nothing.

Hilda Wilson went on. "The Wilson family isn't so well known that anybody really gives a damn what it did. All my friends know about us anyway, and I don't care what my enemies or strangers know or think. How much were you going to ask for? Ten thousand? Fifteen?"

"I wasn't going to ask for money."

"But you were hoping to ask for something? What?"

"None of your business."

She laughed. "Would you care for another drink, sonny?"

"Bring the bottle," I said. "And damn it, don't call me sonny."

She brought the bottle and two glasses. "You remind me a lot of my husband. I'll call you Bill."

She pulled up a chair.

"Why the hell won't you let your grandson marry Faustina?" I demanded.

Her bright blue eyes sparkled. "So that's it? You were going to blackmail me into telling Morley to go ahead? Why do you think I let Morley go over to Big Tony's house all the time?"

"I pass."

"Morley is a fool," Hilda said. "He has eyes but he won't see. I want him to marry Cecelia."

I stared at my empty glass. "Cecelia?"

"Sure," she said. "Faustina is pretty enough, but Cecelia's the one with the brains and the spunk."

I thought about that. "Okay. Let's put it this way. If you were Cecelia, would you marry Morley?"

She reached for the bottle. "If he had fifteen million I would."

"Big Tony has a few million of his own," I said. "I don't think money would interest Cecelia."

We were silent through another drink.

Finally Hilda sighed. "All right, Bill. Morley's no prize and I guess I was hoping for too much, Maybe he and Faustina will be happy sharing each other's vitamin pills."

When I got back to Tony's place, he was putting his golf bag on the front seat of his car. "What do you know? Grover Bradford invited me to the country club. I got the feeling that from now on I'm in."

That evening Morley Wilson came to the house. "My grandmother's approved my marriage to Faustina," he announced.

"Did you take your salt tablets today?" Faustina asked.

Morley nodded.

Big Tony waited until he and I were alone.

"Damned if you didn't do it," he said. "And in less than forty-eight hours." He puffed his cigar. "And now I suppose you'll tackle Philip Courtland?"

"Sure."

I decided to see Courtland on Monday, but I didn't have to wait that long. He came to see me Saturday afternoon.

He studied me and then said. "You're Big Tony's right-hand man?"

"Something like that."

"You've done a lot of things for him?"

"A lot."

That seemed to satisfy him. "How would you like to make some money? Big money?"

"I wouldn't mind."

He decided to light a cigarette before he went on. "I've got some warehouses in town. If they should happen to burn down, I'd be grateful. Twenty thousand dollars' worth."

I grinned. "You want me to burn down some warehouses for the insurance money? I thought you had a million stashed away."

Some color came to his cheekbones. "Never mind what I have or haven't got. Do you want the job or don't you?"

I nodded. "All right. But I don't want money."

He stared at me suspiciously. "What the hell do you want?"

For a minute I thought I wasn't going to tell him, but then I said. "I want you to ask Cecelia to marry you."

His eyes flickered. "That's your price?"

"You heard me."

He took a few slow drags on his cigarette and eyed me carefully. "If that's the pay you want," he said, "I'll do it."

I went to the door and opened it. "Go ahead and ask."

He shook his head. "No. The warehouses go first."

When he was gone, I went to the liquor cabinet.

Big Tony came back from the country club about an hour later and I told him all about it.

He rubbed his neck. "So he wants us to burn down his warehouses? What the hell does he think we are?"

"The same thing everybody else does."

Big Tony shook his head. "I been legit for so long I don't know nobody who would burn down a warehouse. I'll have to give it some thought."

I reached for the bottle and poured another drink.

Cecelia came into the room and leaned over my chair. "What were you doing in California, O'Brien? Taking people for rides and kidnapping babies?"

"I've been taking the little drugstores Tony bought and knitting them into a chain," I said. "I haven't killed anybody since I was five, but I think I could start again now." I looked up at her. "What the hell makes Philip Courtland so special?"

She blinked. "Special? Who said he's special?"

"Then why do you want to marry him?"

"Who said I wanted to marry him?"

"Then you don't?"

"Of course not. He's asked me a dozen times. Isn't that right, Dad?"

I looked over at Tony, but he was busy looking for a cigar.

I took a deep breath and went to the phone. When I got Philip Courtland, I said, "Burn down your own damn warehouses."

I hung up and glared at Big Tony. "What's this all about?"

He lit the cigar. "When I sent for you, O'Brien, I didn't think you'd get Angelina married. Or Faustina. I didn't think anybody could and I didn't expect anything."

"So why did you send for me in the first place?"

Big Tony grinned. "Cecelia's twenty-six and I thought it was about time she got married. Even if I had to reach to the west coast to find somebody I liked."

He went to the door and turned. "I leave the rest up to you, O'Brien. You're the operator."

Martin for the Defense

by Jaime Sandaval

My bedside phone rang at ten minutes after midnight, waking me. I turned on my reading lamp and lifted the receiver from its cradle.

"Mr. Martin? It's me—Mickey Bananas," a bass voice said hurriedly. "I'm in trouble. They just booked me at headquarters. How soon can ya get down here?"

I dropped the receiver back in its cradle, clicked off the light, and rolled over. As far as I was concerned, whatever problem Michael "Mickey Bananas" Murdock was having with the police this time was destined to remain his alone. Lawyer I was, but fool I wasn't. The last time Mickey had crossed swords with the law, I had given him my all, but he had paid only half my fee. This is an unforgivable breach of the lawyer-client relationship.

There was no danger of his calling back again and once more disturbing my sleep. Prisoners are allowed only one phone call, and he'd made his. In the morning, however, a man being released carried a message to one of Mickey's friends, and a bondsman bailed Mickey out. By noon he was at my office, badgering my secretary and demanding to see me.

I waited until the noise from the outer office made it difficult for me to concentrate on my crossword puzzle, then pushed the button on the intercom and told my girl to show him in.

"What'd ya hang up on me for?" Mickey demanded as he charged into the room and came to a lumbering halt in front of my desk. He was a red-faced, soft-looking man in his mid-forties, standing six feet and weighing close to three hundred pounds, a combination of physical traits which in the past had made him susceptible to recognition and identification from the witness stand. "What'd ya hang up on me for?" he repeated, his initially belligerent tone fading to injured puzzlement. "Didn't I tell ya I was in trouble?"

"I'm a very busy man, Mr. Murdock," I said with great formality. "I have time for clients only."

"But *I'm* a client!" he protested.

"You *were* a client," I corrected him. "You ceased to be a client one burglary trial, three months, and five thousand dollars ago."

Mickey hates to part with money, but he knew when he was in a vise. With the police pushing him from one side and me squeezing him from the other, he had to come up with cash or resign himself to a few years in the pokey. Since he wasn't about to take the train to Sing Sing or Attica without giving the police a battle, he reluctantly produced a stack of fifty mint-fresh hundred dollar bills.

I made the currency disappear after verifying its validity, then leaned back in my chair and nodded approvingly. "That takes care of old business," I said. "Now, did you wish to place me on a retainer?"

I waited while an additional stack of bills was even more reluctantly produced. Mickey counted them three times before shoving them across the desk to me. "You'd better be worth it!" he growled.

"You know I'm always worth it," I said equably, "or you wouldn't be coming to me. You'd better let me have the gory details."

Criminal clients come in three categories: those who lie and whom no lawyer can successfully defend; those who claim neither innocence nor guilt but simply say, "Here's my story," and tell it; and those who relate everything down to the most minute detail, thereby keeping the prosecution from presenting the defense lawyer with unpleasant surprises.

Mickey was one of the last group, and he told it all, holding back nothing despite the damage it must have done to his pride. He had stolen an oil painting from a cathedral in the inner city, in full view of half a dozen witnesses, all nuns. He had been captured minutes later by a middle-aged priest, a former Fordham All-American, who'd tackled Mickey a few blocks away as he tried to hail a cab.

I drummed thoughtfully on the desk top with my fingertips. It was hardly a prepossessing set of circumstances. It looked as though Mickey's life of crime had finally caught up with him.

"What's the charge?" I asked him.

"Grand larceny. The painting's worth a couple hundred G's."

That made it just about perfect—for the prosecutor. Not only had Mickey been caught with the loot in his hands, but there were six witnesses to the theft whose word no jury would doubt.

"Do ya think ya can get me off?" Mickey asked. He smiled feebly and nodded his head in an unconscious effort to prod a favorable reply from me, but without conviction.

I refrained from replying. If I were ever going to collect an entire fee from Mickey, this seemed like an auspicious occasion. Once a client is lodged in the Walled-off Astoria, I've found he's noticeably dilatory in the payment of his legal fees. I told Mickey I wasn't working for him in the present case until I had the full fee, and I named a figure.

It was a measure of his current anxiety that he had the money for me in twenty-four hours. I used it to finance two weeks' fun and frolicking in Las Vegas. Mickey's case wasn't the kind a lawyer can prepare for in advance, so I wasn't cheating him of my time. All I could do was hope for a miracle, and I could do that in Las Vegas as well as in my office.

Over a year passed before Mickey's case came up on the court calendar. We had drawn Judge Charles Fitch on the bench. Fitch was an eccentric, but in a manner uniquely his own. I had observed in the past that defendants who had model trains in their basements, or who had coin or stamp collections, seldom received maximum sentences from him. I told Mickey to buy an old stamp album and carry it to and from court every day. If things turned out as badly as I suspected they might, providing him with that piece of advice was about all I'd be able to do to earn my fee.

The prosecutor was Bill Ogden, a courtroom veteran of twenty years. Bill didn't make many mistakes and his carefully coached witnesses didn't, either. We'd been adversaries a couple of dozen times before, and we were about tied for wins and losses. I could tell from the flare of Bill's nostrils that he was counting upon this case to put him into the lead.

The selection of the jury went quickly with neither of us bothering to use up a challenge. Then Bill Ogden called the six nuns to the stand, and one by one they described the theft and identified Mickey. After that, the arresting officers and the priest who had tackled Mickey came to the witness stand. They described Mickey's capture with the painting in hand. I listened carefully to what was said, but declined to cross-examine any of them, although I could see Mickey was getting nervous.

After that, Bill Ogden had the stolen painting entered into evidence as the state's Exhibit A. He then called to the stand Monsignor O'Malley, the cathedral's sixty-year-old administrator. As the painting's guardian, if not its owner, the monsignor had been the one who signed the criminal complaint that made my client's arrest legal. I couldn't contest that.

It's almost impossible to cross-examine a clergyman without making the jury angry at both you and your client, but this time I had no choice. When Ogden finished with his questions, I stood up and asked mine.

"Monsignor O'Malley, you are the one who reported the theft of the painting to the police?"

"Yes."

"Was it a full report you made?"

"I reported that it had been taken from the cathedral, if that's what you mean."

"Did you make a statement as to the value of the painting?"

Bill Ogden rose to his feet immediately. "I object to that, your Honor. I don't think it's relevant at this time."

Judge Fitch mulled it for a moment, then turned to me. "Mr. Martin, I don't know that Monsignor O'Malley is an expert on art, but if it's your intention to call upon him for a statement of value, I will allow it to be done now rather than have him returned to the stand later."

"Thank you, your Honor," I said. I turned back to the witness box. "Monsignor O'Malley, at the time you reported the theft, did you give the painting's valuation?"

"I told them that the painting was one of reportedly great value," he returned guardedly.

His answers were such that I could see that Ogden had been telling him some truths about me.

"Did you say what that reportedly great value was?" I asked.

"I did not. It was taken from newspaper accounts published at the time the painting was given to the cathedral."

"Newspaper accounts," I repeated. "When was the painting given to the cathedral?"

"I believe in 1955 or 1956. Somewhere in that period. I'm not sure of the date."

"Do you know what valuation was given at that time?"

Ogden was on his feet again. "I object to that, your Honor. It's hearsay."

"If he knows of his own knowledge, he may answer," Judge Fitch ruled.

But Ogden wasn't about to be put down so easily. "Your Honor, the question as phrased asks for the value given by someone else, and I would therefore be put in the position of being unable to cross-examine as to that value." Ogden gesticulated a lot when he talked. I can always tell when a prosecutor has watched a lot of Perry Mason re-runs on TV.

Judge Fitch looked at me. "Mr. Martin, the objection is sustained as to the form of the question."

I decided to try a different approach. "Monsignor O'Malley, do you know who donated the painting to the cathedral?"

"Yes."

"By whom was it donated?"

"By Mr. Nicholas Fisher."

"The same Nicholas Fisher who is an actor in the movies and on television?"

"Yes."

"Is Nicholas Fisher a member of your congregation?"

"No."

"Do you know why he gave the painting to the cathedral?"

"No."

"Who made the donation for him?"

"Mr. Sylvester Benton."

"Is Mr. Benton a local resident?"

"If Brooklyn is considered a local residence, yes." The monsignor permitted himself a small smile.

"Do you know Mr. Benton's occupation?"

"He is a professional art critic and appraiser."

I nodded knowingly. "When Mr. Benton made the donation in the name of Mr. Fisher, were there accompanying certificates or documents attesting to the authenticity of the painting?"

"I don't recall any."

With that we ended the first day of the trial.

I was feeling pleased with the outcome thus far, but Mickey Murdock didn't share my satisfaction. He didn't see that I'd made any progress. "You ain't tryin' to rip me off, are ya?" he glowered as we headed for the building exit.

"Mickey," I said reasonably, "you've been charged with grand larceny, but so far no one has proved the painting is worth ten cents. They can prove you took it from the cathedral, but that isn't good enough to justify a charge of grand larceny. They must also prove the value of the painting. Rather than go to the expense of bringing in an expert witness, I think the prosecutor may let you cop a plea to a lesser charge when we get back in court tomorrow."

But I was wrong.

Instead of offering the expected deal in chambers, Ogden called Sylvester Benton as the morning's first witness. Benton was a small man, well below average height. He was balding, a fringe of white hair framing a pink scalp. I noticed that his ankles seemed to be exceptionally high above his shoes, indicating he wore lifts to make himself taller. At his age, it was quite a proclamation of vanity, and I was interested to see it. In this case I was going to need any edge I could get.

Benton was sworn in and Bill Ogden began the questioning. "Will you state your name, please?"

"Sylvester Benton."

"What is your business or occupation, sir?"

"I'm an art critic for a newspaper and several magazines in the city. I'm also an art appraiser, specializing in the Italian masters."

"You live in New York City or thereabouts?"

"Yes. Brooklyn."

"Where did you attend undergraduate school?"

"Columbia University."

"And what did you study there?"

"Art and art history."

"Did you do graduate work?"

"Yes."

"Where was that, sir?"

"At the University of California in Los Angeles, and at the Akademie Der Bilden Kunsten in Munich, Germany."

"Did you receive a degree?"

"Yes. A master's."

"Have you studied anywhere else?"

"Yes. I studied at the Kunthis Torisches Institut in Florence, Italy. It has a German name because it's operated by the German government."

"How long did you study there?"

"About a year."

"How long have you been an art critic and appraiser?"

"Over twenty years," he replied.

Ogden nodded with satisfaction and addressed Judge Fitch. "Your Honor, at this time I would tender Mr. Benton as an expert not only on art, but an expert on the art of the Italian masters."

"Do you desire to cross-examine as to the witness's qualifications, Mr. Martin?" the judge asked me.

I stood up, said "No," and sat down again. Mickey scowled at me. I ignored him.

"Very well, you may proceed, Mr. Ogden," Judge Fitch said.

"Your Honor, I would like the easel to be placed closer to the jury so they may observe the painting more easily."

"You may move the easel," Judge Fitch said.

Until then the painting had been on an easel in front of the judge's bench. Ogden, with the help of a couple of bailiffs, placed the easel between the jury box and the witness chair, facing the courtroom, so that everyone could see the painting plainly.

When he was satisfied with the position of the painting, Ogden returned to the direct examination of his witness. "Mr. Benton, will you please step down for a moment for a closer look at this painting?"

Benton left the witness stand and took a position beside the painting. The picture was thirty inches wide by forty inches high. From its place on the easel, it towered over the little appraiser. I had a mental picture of Mickey Murdock trying to wrestle it into the back seat of a taxi. I glanced at him, and—reading my mind—my client had the grace to blush.

"Have you had a chance, sir, to examine this painting before today?" Nothing equals the studied respect a prosecutor shows his witnesses except, perhaps, the careful disdain he reserves for opposition witnesses.

"Yes," Benton answered. "I examined it carefully for an appraisal Mr. Nicholas Fisher asked me to make prior to his donating the painting to the cathedral."

"Did you reach an opinion as to the antiquity and the value of the painting?"

"I have no doubt at all that it's a work performed between 1500 and 1530, probably closer to 1530. I estimate its current value at approximately two hundred thousand dollars."

Ogden smiled broadly. "Would you please state to the ladies and gentlemen of the jury and to his Honor and to everyone present, including Mr. Martin, the basis of that opinion and how you arrived at it?"

Benton indicated the painting with a sweeping gesture. He was obviously enjoying the limelight. "There are quite a number of paintings very similar to this one which are known to be the work of Marco Delgardi and his students. Few, however, show the fine workmanship of this particular painting, and I therefore attribute it to the master himself."

Benton stood on tiptoe, preening himself. "Delgardi and his students turned out a hundred Madonnas similar to this. The same pattern was followed in each case. The Virgin is shown either seated or standing in front of a fabric backdrop. This curtain is usually green as it is in this instance. The Christ Child is held in the Virgin's arms or is seated or standing on her lap. There are hills and clouds in the background, and—"

"Who are the other two people in the foreground?" Prosecutor Ogden interrupted.

"The kneeling man who is being blessed by the Christ Child is a representation, a portrait if you will, of the person who commissioned the painting. The long hair, not unlike today's style, was common in the Veneto, the area around Venice. The fourth person is the patron saint of the kneeling man, shown presenting him to Virgin and Child. In this case, the patron saint is St. Nicholas of Bari, as indicated by the bishop's biretta and the three gold balls in his hand," he elaborated.

Benton was warming to his task. "St. Nicholas appears in many of these paintings because there were a great many men named Nicolo in Italy at that time. He is identified first by the bishop's hat, the biretta, although there are many bishop-saints, and by the gold balls which symbolize one of his good deeds. It seems a poor woman wanted to marry, but had no dowry to bring to the union. St. Nicholas came one night and left the three gold balls beside her while she slept. It's this story which led to the use of St. Nicholas as a giver of gifts at Christmas time, and in Europe his name-day is celebrated almost to the same extent as Christmas."

"Mr. Benton," Ogden asked, "can you tell us more about the technique of the artist?"

"Certainly. This painting was produced entirely in the Delgardi manner. The most difficult part of the painting, the Virgin, was rendered with transparent glazes over a white ground. This technique gives the color more intensity than is common with other schools of painting, and the style existed only until 1530 at the latest.

"Factors like the positions of the figures and the color of the Virgin's gown, in this case blue, often varied. The artists may have tired of doing everything exactly the same each time they painted a Madonna upon commission, and the choice of colors would have affected the cost of the painting, since some pigments were more expensive than others. But the typically Venetian colors and the expert brushwork make me certain this is a genuine Delgardi, painted when his artistic powers were at their fullest."

"I have just one more question, Mr. Benton," Ogden said suavely. "You have stated you believe this painting to be worth two hundred thousand dollars, is that correct?"

"It is."

"Will you kindly tell us how you established the figure?"

"A few months ago a Chicago museum purchased a similar work at an auction in Sotheby's London showroom. The price paid was seventy-five thousand British pounds, approximating two hundred thousand American dollars. I feel that this painting is in every way comparable to the work which was auctioned."

"Thank you, Mr. Benton. I have no more questions at this time," Ogden said.

"We will have a ten-minute recess," Judge Fitch announced, and then instructed the bailiff to take the jury to the jury room.

Mickey and I stepped outside into the corridor so he could smoke a cigarette. I abandoned the noxious weed some years ago. Mickey puffed hungrily and asked me how I thought things looked. I made confident-sounding though noncommittal noises while I continued to do what I had been doing all along—hoping for a miracle.

Not that I wasn't thinking furiously. A successful criminal must be able to imagine himself in the position of the police; a successful policeman must be able to put himself in the criminal's place; and a lawyer has to be able to outguess both or he'll lose more cases than he wins.

Unfortunately, I wasn't able to put myself in the art expert's place. Since I hadn't expected to have to cross-examine him, I wasn't prepared to do so. I hadn't anticipated that the value of the painting would be established by expert testimony, rather than sales receipts or other documentation. Now I was going to be forced to ask questions whose answers I didn't already know, the most dangerous thing a trial lawyer can do.

'Mickey dropped his cigarette stub into an urn at the door to the courtroom, and we returned to our seats. The judge went back to the bench, the clerk called the court to order, and the jury filed back into its box. Benton resumed his seat in the witness chair, and I began my questions.

"Mr. Benton, are you the person who donated this painting to the cathedral?"

"Acting as Mr. Fisher's representative, yes."

"Monsignor O'Malley testified earlier there were no documents attesting to the painting's antiquity at the time you presented it to the cathedral. Is that correct?"

"Yes."

"You have testified you made an appraisal of the painting's value prior to its being given to the cathedral. Would you tell the jury what value you placed upon the painting at that time and how you arrived at it?"

"I appraised the painting at one hundred and fifty thousand dollars, after satisfying myself that it was indeed a genuine Delgardi. The valuation was based upon the then current demand, the prices being asked and received for Delgardis and Delgardiesque Madonnas."

"Don't you feel that the absence of documentation certifying the painting's history may indicate the work is a forgery?"

"On the contrary, I seldom pay much attention to a painting's certification. Such papers are far more easily counterfeited than a painting itself. I trust my own judgment more than any documents."

Mr. Benton's cocksureness wasn't making a favorable impression with the jury, but his words were. I groped for a lever with which to pry him from his pedestal. "Mr. Benton, as an expert on Italian art, is there any reference work you would recommend to someone wishing to learn more about Delgardi and his paintings?"

"*Delgardi E I Delgardiani*, which means Delgardi and the Delgardi-like painters, is a fairly complete work on the subject. The book is in Italian, however, and has never been published in English."

"You read Italian?"

Benton smiled. "Of course."

"Why do you say—" a blinding revelation struck me too late, "—of course?" I stumbled to a conclusion.

"Because I wrote the book."

Prosecutor Ogden half-hid a smile behind his hand. Judge Fitch was almost visibly embarrassed for me. I had started out attempting to impeach a witness's credibility and had ended by establishing his expertise to an even greater extent than the prosecutor had.

"Mr. Martin," Judge Fitch said charitably as I stood there like a fish out of water, "do you have many more questions for this witness?"

I glanced at the wall clock and saw it was a few minutes past noon. I couldn't think of a single thing to ask Sylvester Benton right then, but I grasped at the offered straw. "Yes, sir," I lied. "I have quite a few more questions."

"In that case it would appear to be an excellent place to stop for lunch," Judge Fitch announced. "Court will recess until two o'clock this afternoon."

Mickey and I left the courtroom together, but we separated outside. He crossed the street to have lunch, while I grimly took a cab to the 42nd Street Public Library. Mickey returned to the courthouse with a stomach full of lasagna, and I returned with a head stuffed with facts. I had a feeling Mickey was going to see me earn my fee. Of all the charges that could have been proved against Mickey, I was hopeful that the prosecutor might have selected the one he couldn't prove.

I waited until art expert Benton had settled down in the witness chair again, then began. "It's true, isn't it, Mr. Benton, that various pigments were used at different times to produce the colors employed by artists, and that the types of pigment used can indicate the age of a painting?"

"Yes, that's true."

"Did you make any tests to determine exactly which pigments were used in the painting of this alleged Delgardi Madonna?"

"It's not alleged!" he bristled. I had reached him for the first time. "You're attempting—"

"You will please answer the question, Mr. Benton," Judge Fitch instructed him.

"No," he said reluctantly.

"Can you tell us what material the Madonna was painted upon?"

"The wood, you mean?"

"You're the expert, Mr. Benton. Is it wood?"

"Yes," he replied sullenly. I wasn't playing by the rules and salaaming to his expertise.

"When was it that artists first began painting on canvas?"

"About the middle of the 16th century. After the middle of that century, about 1550, it became so prevalent that wood was hardly used any more." He was gaining confidence again from the sound of his own voice.

"Can you tell us what kind of wood was used in this case?"

"Well . . ." he stumbled. "Since it's an Italian painting, it would be on some kind of Italian wood."

"But you don't know what it is?"

"No," he said defensively. "The back of the painting is covered by a cradle."

"A cradle?"

"Yes. Old paintings on wood are often fitted with what is known as a cradle to keep the wood from buckling."

"So you can't say with any certainty what type of wood is beneath this painting?"

"No, not with any certainty."

"It might possibly be modern plywood?"

"Of course not! Why, I—"

"But you've testified you didn't examine the wood, therefore it could be *any* kind of wood, isn't that so?"

"Well, yes."

"Can you tell us why you didn't make a more careful examination of this reputedly valuable painting, Mr. Benton?"

"I didn't believe it was necessary," he said stiffly.

"Have any so-called old masters been forged successfully?"

"How do you mean, 'successfully'?" he asked suspiciously.

I pretended an air of great patience. "Has anyone been able to create a painting which, without detailed examination, has appeared to be the work of a famous artist of an earlier era?"

"Well, there have been some instances—but a scholar who knows his business should be able to detect a forgery."

"Are you familiar with the name Hans von Meegeren?"

Benton looked as though he had bitten into a sour apple. "I've heard of him."

"He was an art forger, was he not? A professional art forger?"

"Yes." Benton's lips were compressed tightly.

"He sold millions of dollars' worth of paintings which experts had sworn were genuine Vermeers, is this not so?"

"Yes."

"And this forger produced paintings which were completely different from one another, but all of which were still in the style, subject matter, and execution to be expected of a genuine Vermeer?"

"Ah . . . yes, I believe that is so."

"Then wasn't the feat which Hans von Meegeren accomplished far more difficult than merely following a format established in several dozen paintings of similar subject and design? By comparison, wouldn't it be far less difficult for a skilled forger to produce a fake Delgardi?"

There was a silence. Judge Fitch stared at Benton. "Yes," the witness replied.

I paused to allow the jury to digest the full significance of my questions and Benton's answers before I took off in another direction.

"Mr. Benton, you've testified that Mr. Nicholas Fisher hired you to make an appraisal of this painting, and that you also acted as his representative when it was given to the cathedral."

It wasn't a question but Benton answered, "Yes."

"Have you made other appraisals for Mr. Fisher?" I then asked.

"Yes."

"Of paintings?"

"Yes."

"And were these—" I made a face more sour-looking than Benton's previously, "—*works of art* subsequently given away?"

"Yes."

"Will you tell us why Mr. Fisher was so concerned with establishing the value of items he didn't plan to sell or keep?"

Bill Ogden was on his feet instantly.

"Your Honor, the witness is an art expert, not a mind reader." Ogden glared at me. "He can't be expected to know what motives, if any, his employer might have had."

I couldn't afford to have the objection sustained. "Your Honor," I protested, "I'm sure Mr. Benton's answer will show that Mr. Fisher's action was not unusual and that Mr. Benton was well aware of the reason for it."

Judge Fitch nodded. "If the witness can answer from his own personal knowledge, he must do so."

I turned back to Benton. "Well, Mr. Benton, why did Mr. Fisher want an appraisal of the painting, this one and the others you mentioned?"

Benton hesitated, then spoke slowly. "It's a standard practice for people who plan to give an art work to a charity or other non-profit organization to have the item appraised first."

"Why is that, Mr. Benton?"

"For tax purposes. The appraisal establishes the current value of the work of art."

"In other words, your appraisal sets the amount of tax deduction a man can claim legally when he donates a work of art?"

"That's correct."

"You are paid a fee for your appraisals?"

"Yes."

"You are paid well?"

"Moderately well."

"Then it wouldn't be in your best interests to be too critical of paintings brought to you for appraisal?"

"What do you mean?"

"I mean," I said, advancing upon the witness stand and shaking a finger in front of Benton's suddenly pasty-looking face, "it's to your advantage to have large numbers of paintings brought to you for appraisal, and by giving high appraisals to doubtful paintings, you insure there will be future high fees."

Bill Ogden was erect, baying at the moon. "Your Honor, I must protest defense counsel's behavior! He's badgering the witness!"

"Objection sustained," Judge Fitch pronounced, but with no fire in his voice. "Kindly confine yourself to relevant questions, Mr. Martin, and refrain from attacking the witness in your interrogation."

"I apologize, your Honor." I turned back to Benton with a ferocious gleam in my eye that Judge Fitch couldn't see. "Mr. Benton, if this painting were a forgery, what would its value be?"

Bill Ogden jumped up again. "Your Honor, Mr. Benton isn't—"

"If a witness is qualified to set a value on a genuine painting," I broke in, "I submit he should know what a proved forgery would be worth."

"The witness may answer," Judge Fitch decreed.

"If it were a forgery," Benton conceded, "I don't know that it would have any value, except as a curiosity."

"Thank you, Mr. Benton. Now, are you familiar with the methods of art forgers, men like Hans von Meegeren?"

"Yes, in a general way. They try to do everything exactly as it was done in the past by the artist they are impersonating."

"You mean they use the same type of materials, wood or canvas, pigments, brushes, and so on?"

"Yes. They also try to duplicate the artist's technique."

"In other words, a forger tries to use materials which are identical to the ones the original artist used, and he tries to do everything the original artist would have done? He copies methods and materials as exactly as he can?"

"Yes."

"Mr. Benton, did it ever strike you as strange that the artist, whoever he was, gave us Nicholas as the name of the person who commissioned the painting?"

Benton stared at me with renewed suspicion at this new tangent. "No, why should it? I mentioned that Nicolo was a very common name in Italy during that period."

"Mr. Fisher's first name is also Nicholas."

"Coincidental, surely," Benton answered.

I went to the defense table and opened my briefcase. I removed a movie fan magazine and held it up. "I purchased this magazine during the noon recess," I said.

"Your Honor, I hardly see where Mr. Martin's choice of reading matter has any bearing on this case!" Prosecutor Ogden snapped.

I approached the bench. "If you will allow me to continue, your Honor, I'll soon make everything clear."

Judge Fitch considered for a moment. "Proceed, Mr. Martin," he said at last. Ogden sat down with an exasperated look on his face.

I opened the magazine to a page I had marked while I was in the taxi returning to court. It carried a profile photo of a tall, middle-aged man whose head was completely bald. The effect was similar to that achieved by Yul Brynner, but the photo suggested self-indulgence rather than Brynner's lean masculinity.

I handed the opened magazine to Benton. "Is this a photo of your employer, Nicholas Fisher?" Since the photo's caption identified the actor as Nicholas Fisher, I had no doubt of Benton's answer.

"Yes, this is a picture of Mr. Fisher."

"May I call your attention to the painting of the Madonna? You stated earlier, during direct examination by Mr. Ogden, that the kneeling figure is a representation, a portrait, of the person who commissioned the painting. Is that right?"

"Yes."

"Examine that figure's head and face, Mr. Benton, and then tell me if you see a resemblance to your client, Mr. Fisher."

"Why, no," Benton replied in a voice intended to indicate I was putting him on. "I see no resemblance at all."

I took the magazine photo from his hand and drew thick sideburns and longish hair on the actor's profile. Nicholas now wore the same classic hair style as the painting. "Take another look," I told Benton, holding the altered photo for him to see.

Benton was even more suggestible than I'd hoped. His mouth dropped open, and his head swiveled back and forth from photo to painting. He looked like a spectator at a tennis match. "Why, it's Mr. Fisher!" he exclaimed.

"Thank you, Mr. Benton. No more questions, your Honor."

Prosecutor Ogden tried desperately to repair the weaknesses I'd revealed in his case, but he was flustered. During redirect examination he made the mistake of concentrating on the implication of tax fraud, while overhanging the courtroom was the subtle thought of an actor so vain he commissioned an art forger to paint the actor into the forgery. Ogden didn't recall Benton to the stand to have him reaffirm his appraisal of the painting's value.

When the prosecution rested its case, I quickly rested mine. Then I made a motion for a directed verdict of acquittal on the ground that the value of the painting had not been established sufficiently to justify a charge of grand larceny.

Mickey Murdock left court a free man, and I felt rather pleased. I felt even better when I read in the paper ten days later that the Delgardi Madonna had been examined by several experts who had subjected it to various tests to determine its age and authenticity, and it was their unanimous opinion that it was actually a clever forgery, possibly no more than fifteen years old.

The night the article appeared in the paper, my bedside phone rang at ten minutes after midnight, waking me. I turned on my reading lamp and lifted the receiver from its cradle.

"Hey, Martin!" A voice I recognized as Mickey Murdock's boomed over the wire in alcoholic belligerence. "Didja see that piece inna paper? You owe me that fee back. I really *was* innocent of grand larceny, an' I'da never hired ya if I'd known that. Ever'body knows heaven pertecks th' innocent."

I hung up on the blithering idiot, then on second thought left my phone off the hook.

Can you imagine the nerve of that crook?

The Waiting Room

by Charles W. Runyon

Pawley watched the rain streak the dirty glass. He liked the way the droplets started out small at the top, hung there for a moment, raced downward until they met a companion, hung for a shorter time, and then began the long swift plunge to the bottom of the pane, taking everything with them. Life is like that. Nobody likes to go down alone.

The air inside the station was warm, diffused with dampness and the smell of road dust and old rubber. New rubber was better, rich and pungent. When he was a kid, he always liked to smell new rubber. He always liked to watch rain on a window, too. Funny, he'd had to run like hell for thirty-two years just to get back where he started. Not in a geographic sense, of course. The southern California plain was a lot different from the piney slopes of Arkansas. Flat as a table, like you weren't on the earth at all, but on some kind of mirror.

Pawley was a tall man, rather gaunt. His prominent nose hooked slightly, and his blue eyes sat steady inside deep sockets. He wore a gabardine jacket and gray trousers, a white shirt and a maroon tie. He dressed as people do who are not aware of clothes; they didn't exactly fit, and he made no attempt to adapt his bony frame to them. There were wrinkles at the collar, and though the tie was pulled up tight below the thrusting larynx, the top button of his shirt was undone. The hat was a chocolate brown felt, crushed on one side, somehow failing to adapt its shape to Pawley's narrow skull. The coarse hair above his ears was threaded with gray.

Pawley placed his palm flat against his face and with his fingers tipped the hat onto the back of his head. He put his forehead to the glass, not surprised that it was the same temperature as the room. Glancing out to the right, he saw rows of cabbages stretching to infinity, pale green, with sheets of water in between. He saw a movement of pale blue. Finding a broken pane, he lifted the heavy .45 from his pocket and thrust it through the window, bending his elbow at a right angle. The gun bucked in his hand. A geyser of muddy water shot up and the patch of blue dropped out of sight.

Pawley withdrew his hand. At least he was dry. The cops were all wet. He laughed.

John looked up, his broad face drawn in a puzzled frown. He was stocky, stooped in the shoulders where his brown suit jacket pinched. He always looked as though he didn't quite understand what he was seeing.

"How many you got left?" he asked.

Pawley flicked on the safety and withdrew the magazine, counting the coppery eyes which glinted through the slot. "Four."

"I'm all out." John spun the chamber of his .38 and let it drop from his fingers. Thunk! on the concrete. Pawley heard the sound echoing inside his head. Thunk. Sound of clean-shot squirrel falling out of high pine tree. Thunk. Sound of bat against ball, grandslam homer in the last of the ninth. Thunk. Fist against jaw. Thunk, thunk, thunk. Well, I've had all those things.

He watched John tie his shoelaces. "Think you'll walk out?"

John stretched his legs in front of him, heels on the floor, toes pointed outward. He cupped his broad, blackhaired hands over his groin and shook his head.

"Wouldn't get far. They dragged back two dead ones. There's another one out in that car. 'Spect they're pretty mad at us."

Pawley looked out the window. The asphalt ribbon dwindled almost to a point before it climbed into the mountains. Fifty yards away sat the patrol car with two sunbursts in the windshield. The front wheels were cramped hard and part way in the grader ditch, the rear wheels were in the road, back end lifted high. Something funny about those wounded cars; Pawley could never see them all shiny and neat in a showroom without imagining how they'd look this way, too. He always thought of dead grasshoppers.

He saw his own car pulled up beside the dry pumps. They'd done all right until they met the patrol car. Must have had a description from the bank guard, because the car did a switch-itch and took after them. One hundred miles an hour, and a lucky shot holed their gas tank. Just made it to here and found the station closed, empty. Pawley had realized, with a certain relief, that it was the end of the road.

He could see the roadblock a quarter mile away, cars beginning to pile up behind it. Word must have gotten out. Spectators, reporters coming in for the kill. Make him famous for a day. Hell, he didn't care about being famous. Just tried to get in a few licks, it was only a game. He always shot to kill, that was part of the game. Always ate till he was full. Always got a woman when he felt like a woman.

A clot of blue reared up among the green. He aimed the gun and felt it buck in his hand. The man fell. He aimed the gun and felt it buck in his hand. The man fell. He aimed the gun and felt it . . .

Take him down behind the shed and shoot him. Acting nonchalant, you snapped your fingers and old Brindle, shaggy old brown mongrel, worth nothing to anybody, followed you down behind the shed and you stood him up there among the round black pellets of sheep droppings. He cocked his head while you raised the old single-shot, octagon barrel .22 with the magic sight. He looked at you, wondering what the game was, and you tried to force the hatred you were supposed to feel. Dirty sheep-killer. He ran and licked your hand and you slapped him and cursed him, you dirty sheepkiller, but only sickness came and Brindle stretched out his long jaw on the two paws, looked up, and you let him have it right between the quizzical brown eyes. Though you didn't know it then, there were two deaths that afternoon, the boy and the dog. You remember the weather, too, hot July day, acrid smell of sheep droppings, the sun had set, but heat still radiated from the old pine building. There are moments like these slicing right through the layers of your life, Pawley, cutting right through and connected, back to back, like a pair of aces and everything in between is just so much filler, like insulation, because if you lived your whole life at that level, man, you'd *burn. . . .*

Dirty sheepkiller. The man in the blue uniform humped along the watery ditch, raising his rear in the air like an inchworm. He wants to be a hero. Pawley raised the gun and it was a clear shot, but the mist in his eyes clouded his aim, and he decided to save the bullet for the creation of another hero. He pulled out his handkerchief and wiped the sweat from his face, wiping his eyes at the same time. "Three left," he said.

"How long do you figure?"

"Half hour, just as a guess. They'll get rifles and stay out of our range. Keep us pinned down while the others make a rush."

The building was built of cinder block, waist high. From there to the tile roof were ten-inch panes of glass set in a steel frame, painted red. It shared the same level as the highway, about five feet above the sur-

ALFRED HITCHCOCK'S ANTHOLOGY

rounding fields. The only interruption of view came from the washroom, which was cinder block to the ceiling, and occupied a six-foot square in the northwest corner. Pawley gazed a long time at the closed door. Shirley had been inside a long time. He called out, asked what she was doing.

"Changing my underwear."

He looked at John, who raised his shoulders in a shrug. Then Pawley understood. She knew this was the end and she wanted to die with clean underwear. It struck him as funny, and he started laughing.

She came out a moment later, her eyes naked and defenseless. Strange, the way her high cheekbones pushed up her eyes into narrow slits. They were knife-points that stuck into him and made him tingle. She always did it to him; stripped him clean of pretense. Her red-brown hair was brushed into a soft wave, which curled out beyond her ears, then curled back to lie against her collarbone. The bony structure of her chest showed above the low line of her jersey. Some kind of sleazy material, shot full of gold. He didn't like that kind of material, he wondered why she wore things he didn't like, particularly at this time. No makeup, her mouth wide, upper lip long. Nose a straight shiny line, high forehead. A scent about her that no perfume had ever hidden, like hay molding, like butterscotch and cracked walnuts, a sense of richness which made his nerve-ends stretch until they touched emptiness.

He watched her sit down in the swivel chair behind the desk and light a cigarette. A piece of paper clung to her lower lip, she caught it between long, unpolished nails and peeled it off. Every movement did something for him. The bend in her elbow was more important to him than the articulation of his own muscles. He'd met her when she was sixteen and now she was twenty-four. He didn't know if he liked her or not; just that when she wasn't around, everything was flat and dead and lifeless, and the wine and the other women had nothing for him. Twenty-four. That was too young.

"You could go out," he said. "I don't think they'd shoot you, you could live."

"What for?"

Casual and final. You made your own choice, he thought.

Then he wondered if she'd had any choice. From the time they'd met, they'd fit together like dovetails. He'd never talked about his feelings, never even felt the emotions that raced inside him. She found them and brought them out. She didn't dig. She just knew they were there, and she didn't give a damn for his feelings or his pride, or anything like that—just him.

He watched her open a magazine and start thumbing through it. One of the pages caught his eye and he read a paragraph. The words were like gruel, like food chewed up and swallowed by some Eskimo woman, then regurgitated, absent of all spice, flavor, and sauce. She had her legs crossed, the short skirt off her knees. She had bony knees. He loved her bones. She could have been waiting for a dentist.

He thought of her flesh and the death of her flesh—her teeth shattered, organs ripped and skull blown apart in the smash of lead. He felt a longing for her that was not sexual, a desire to enclose her in his arms and take all the bullets into his own flesh.

He went to a wall calendar. It was eight years old and had obviously hung in the station long after its primary purpose had been exhausted. It was adorned by a picture of a girl whose body was impossibly perfect and unblemished, whose breasts were so impossibly round that they were a—what was the word? Cliché. When he said something that Shirley didn't like, she said he was using clichés. Well, baby, how do you like this for a cliché? We're going to die. Everybody does *that*.

Notes on the side of the calendar. *Call Mrs. Cardoza about grease job.* Probably the car was junk by now, and the woman could be dead. Somebody had written *Thelma* and drawn an arrow to the calendar girl. He wondered where Thelma was in the outside world. Here she was lovely, young as ever, desired and desirable. And Mrs Cardoza was still waiting for her grease job. Here had nothing to do with anywhere else.

"I wonder if they had kids? Wives and kids?"

Shirley was looking out the window, talking about the cops, and thinking about herself. Eight years of love and violence, now ended.

"It doesn't matter," Pawley said.

"How can you say it doesn't matter?"

"With my lips and tongue and throat. Like this." He leaned over her and spoke with exaggerated lip movements. "It doesn't matter."

She raised her face and gave him a flat, blank stare. The light fell on the planes of her face and revealed the fine white hairs on her cheekbones. For a moment he saw violence lying in her eyes like a coiled viper. Then it melted away and she asked in a tone of sincere curiosity, "Are you crazy?"

He thought about it. "That doesn't matter either."

John scraped his feet on the concrete. "We're all crazy, I think."

Pawley turned to look at him. John sat indolently with his back against the wall, the valise between his knees. With a lopsided smile, he opened the bag, took out a deck of currency, pulled out a bill and wadded it up, then snapped off the rubber band and gave the sheaf a backhanded flip toward him. The neat pile disintegrated and fluttered down like feathers. "There. That's what it was about. Now, what the hell good is it?"

Pawley saw the desolation in his eyes. He leaned over, picked up a fifty-dollar bill, struck a match and lit it. Then he shook a cigarette out of his pack and held it to the flame. He held the cigarette out to John and looked into his eyes.

"Everything is good for something."

For a minute, they looked into each other's eyes. Slowly the fear disappeared, and was replaced by puzzlement.

"Pawley, why is it always . . . ?"

Pawley waited, but the puzzlement deepened.

"What?"

John shook his head. "I don't know. For a minute it seemed like I was somebody else . . . waiting for Indians."

"We used to play Indians, back in Arkansas. You ever play Indians, Shirley?"

"I used to get tied up a lot—and tortured."

He looked at her. They had clawed each other's flesh until the blood had mingled. Life was a melting process. A milking process. Life was . . .

He shook his head. Life was.

John was retying his shoes. "I never liked to play Indians. That was you. I never got to be myself. You wanted to make the team. Okay, I made the team. Quit school and go to the coast, ship out and see the world. I went along. When I met a girl I wanted to marry, you said she was a slob, so I dropped her."

Pawley looked out the window. Quiet too long. *Soon* . . . "She was a slob."

"Okay. I could have discovered that myself."

"Why didn't you?"

"I don't think she was. You turned her into one. You'd look at her and make her feel stupid. You turned her into one."

"Well, no matter how she got that way, she was—that way." Pawley turned. "John, you left her and came with us. Maybe you ought to find out why you came with us."

"*Why?* Why anything? Why are we here? I mean . . ." He slapped his palm on the concrete floor, then waved at the wide expanse of the world. "Here. You know."

"We're here to find out why we're here," said Shirley. She was looking out the window. There was no expression on her face. Pawley wished he were she, having thoughts, nice thoughts. When he considered what was about to happen, his brain turned into an ivory doorknob, all white and shiny and nothing on it at all.

"Why are we *here* then?" asked John. "Sitting in a lousy station. Dad raised us, why did he do that?"

"Because we were there," said Pawley.

"But why were we—"

"Shirley told you. To find out why we're here."

John rose and walked stiff-legged to the center of the room. His shoes crumpled the bright green currency. His eyes were wide. "You mean, there's no reason? None of it makes any difference?"

"None of it."

John looked at Shirley. "You agree with that?"

"I agree."

For a moment longer he looked at her, then his face seemed to settle. "I've wanted to do something for eight years."

She looked at him. "Do it."

He stepped forward and caught the shoulders of her jersey, jerking it downward. Her small breasts thrust into the light.

"Does that made a difference?"

She moved her shoulders slightly. "Does it?"

"Hell!" He jerked himself away fast, strode across the room and turned. "Okay, it doesn't make any difference. So why don't we just walk out that door now?"

"Because I want a cigarette," said Pawley. He lit two, and held one out to John. John took it and slumped down with his back against the wall, looking at the floor between his feet. His wrists hung limply from his knees, his cigarette smoked between his fingers.

After a minute, Shirley pulled up her blouse, walked over to John and sat down beside him. She took the cigarette from his fingers and drew slowly, looking at Pawley. Something glittered in her eyes. Pawley knelt down, facing her. John looked up, and for a moment they were all enclosed in a single sweaty hand, breathing with one breath, seeing with a single eye . . .

A bullet came through one of the upper glasses. Ping! Then another. They had rifles now, but they were shooting high. It wouldn't be long. Pawley reached out and squeezed Shirley's shoulder, and felt the bones give beneath his hand. Then he squeezed John's knee, and stood up, not for any reason, but because he wanted to make one last gesture of free will.

Shirley rose and stood beside him. John rose on the other side. Pawley thought of telling him, *You could have had her any time, boy, but I couldn't stand for that because then I'd have lost both of you,* but there was no need to say anything.

"This is the way it is, John."

"Yeah, but I don't have to like it."

"No, you don't have to like it."

Then the bullets came in.

Scream All the Way

by Michael Collins

If I have a nightmare, it always concerns my falling from some great height, screaming helplessly into the abyss all the way down. I wake up in a shivering sweat, my missing arm aching where there is no arm to ache. I light a cigarette. I don't go back to sleep for some time. I am afraid of the vision of falling to my death.

That is why I remember so well what Captain Gazzo called The Sussex Tower Case.

It walked into my office on a hot Monday in August in the person of a small, dapper man wearing a gray tropical suit and a brisk manner. The heat that oozed through my one window must have made him think he was in a swamp, because he stepped as if his feet were in mud to the ankles.

He saw that my arm was missing. "You're Daniel Fortune?" The tone of his voice, and the look in his quick eyes, denoted silently, *You? A cripple?*

I was tempted to tell him that he would get his money's worth because I had two heads to compensate for the arm but, no matter what they show in the movies, humility gets more work than wit.

"Yes, sir," I said humbly. "What can I do for you?"

"You're a licensed private detective?"

"They'll give anyone a license these days," I said, and so much for humility and good business manners. Luckily, he had other matters on his mind. He sat down without even a thin smile at my wit.

"My name is Wallace Kuhns. I'm an attorney. I have a job: two men to guard $250,000 in cash, five P.M. to nine A.M. for five days. Fifty a day for each man."

"Fifty isn't much," I said, ready to bargain.

"Oh, damn," Kuhns said, and he transformed before my eyes. The starch went out of him, he slumped in the chair, stretched out his legs,

ALFRED HITCHCOCK'S ANTHOLOGY

reached for a cigarette, and looked ten years younger.

"This whole thing is a pain. Listen, Fortune, I know that fifty is peanuts. If Ajemian weren't a big client, I wouldn't be here at all."

"Who's Ajemian?"

"Ivan Ajemian, president of Tiflis Rug and Textile Company. Factories in New Jersey, North Carolina, and Connecticut. Offices on East 26th Street. Real headquarters in apartment 16A, The Sussex Towers. That's his apartment."

"He has the $250,000 in cash there?"

"He does. He's a modern businessman, with some quirks. One of the quirks is that once a year, during the annual sales meeting in August, he hands out bonuses personally to the best salesmen. They come to his apartment one at a time. He gives them one drink, a pep talk, and the cash bonus."

"The insurance company doesn't like it?"

"You guessed it," Kuhns said. "Two weeks ago the apartment was broken into. The insurance boys are howling. They want two guards. Ajemian says okay, but no more than fifty a day per man."

"What was stolen two weeks ago?"

"Nothing. The police think Ajemian came home and scared the thieves off. The insurance people think the thieves were after the bonus money, and made a two-week mistake."

"Why guards only at night?"

"Ajemian says two company men can guard during the day and save money. At night they'd get overtime."

"When do I start?"

"Tonight. Can you get the other man?"

"Yeh. Pay fifty in advance for each of us."

That's how it began. After Kuhns had gone, I called Ed Green. I'd worked with Green before, and he'd take the fifty.

We arrived at apartment 16A, The Sussex Towers, at five thirty P.M. Green was grumbling about the heat and the lousy fifty bucks.

"I hope it's at least air-conditioned," he said.

It was. It was cool, and big, and bizarre. Ivan Ajemian went in for ornate furniture from a shah's palace, heavy decoration, velvet drapes, Oriental hangings and Persian rugs—all in one of those old "depression" apartments for the really-rich that had rooms they couldn't even find.

"The detectives?" Ajemian said when we were ushered in by an Oriental houseboy. "With one arm? What was Kuhns thinking of?"

"I'm sneaky," I said.

"Spare me the humor," Ajemian said. "I need protection, not comedy. I've got a lot of cash, I'm not especially brave, and my nose tells me that the last so-called burglary might have been an inside job."

"What tells your nose that?" I asked.

"Follow me."

We followed him to the back door that opened into the kitchen from a service stairway. He was not what I had expected, from what Kuhns had said. Kuhns had made Ajemian sound old, but he wasn't a day over fifty. A big, calm-looking type, no matter what he said about his bravery, he moved with power, had sharp eyes, and looked like he could take care of himself.

"There," he said, "look at the lock."

I looked. So did Green.

"It's scratched," Green said, "but it could be a fake. What about it, Dan?"

I studied those scratches. They might have been made by a picklock; they were certainly intended to look like the work of a picklock, but they could have been fake scratches, too.

"I'm not sure. Somebody could be trying to make it look like entry from outside without a key."

"That's what I think," Ajemian said. "I want the doors watched carefully, you hear? Now, people come and go here, and I don't want them bothered. Keep out of the way. The money is in my study safe. Stay in the study, or at the doors. Nowhere else. Is that clear?"

I turned for the door. "Let's go, Ed."

Green nodded and started after me. Ajemian watched us.

"All right," he said, "I'm impressed. What do you want?"

I turned back. "We decide what we do, and how we do it. Take it or leave it. I can always sleep."

Ajemian laughed. "Touchy, eh? I always said a handicap makes a man tougher. Very well, but try to keep out of my way. I happen to have a friend who comes here often. Understand?"

Ajemian winked at me. I understood.

"We'll check the money now," I said.

"Check the money? Why?"

"I've been hired before to guard what turned out to be an empty safe from the start."

I thought he was going to turn purple, but he checked himself and started for the study. Green followed him.

"I'll count," Green said. "You check the layout."

I checked the layout. It was simple, a lot of rooms but only two doors. The front door opened into the main corridor with the elevators. The back door opened from the kitchen onto a landing of the service stairs. The study where the money was had two doors, one from the living room and one from the kitchen. Nothing but a fly could get in through the windows, even though there was a ledge outside the study windows.

"Money checks," Green reported.

"The only entry is through the two doors, and there are two of us," I said. "It's a vacation with pay if we stay awake."

Green agreed with me. I took the living room door, and he parked at the kitchen door. Ajemian worked in his study with the cash. It looked like a quiet week ahead.

It wasn't.

About ten o'clock I heard a key turn in the outer door. Ajemian had already gone to the living room. I jumped to the wall on the far side of the front door, my ancient revolver in my hand. The door opened, and one of the trimmest shapes I ever saw came into the room from the corridor.

"Ivan, honey!"

She was small and wore a blue summer suit she filled beautifully. She saw me behind her, and my jaw must have been hanging. She smiled, preened for me, and then saw my empty sleeve.

"Goodness! What happened to your arm?"

"Do you have a couple of days to listen?"

She giggled. "I bet you were a soldier."

"Who are you, miss?"

"Mary Kane. Isn't Ivan here?"

This, then, was the reason for Ajemian's wink. She had no handbag, and she couldn't have hidden a razor blade under the suit without its showing clear against her curves.

"He's back in his bedroom."

She tripped off toward the bedrooms, calling, "Ivan! Honey!"

I went back to my chair. Mary Kane had a key. I wondered who else had a key to the apartment? It was a nervous thought. The next visitor didn't have a key. At least, he didn't use it. He knocked, lightly.

Since there was a doorbell, I approached the door with care. The knock had the sound of someone checking to see if anyone were in the apartment. I opened the door quickly, my pistol in my solitary hand.

A tall, thin man stared at my gun.

"In!" I snapped. "Back away. Fast."

He came in, backed away, and I leaned out and checked the corridor. It was empty. I closed the door and faced him.

"Who are you?"

"Max Alvis." He was thin and nervous. "Executive VP of Tiflis Rug Company. Are you one of the detectives?"

"Yeh. Dan Fortune."

"You're alone?"

"My partner's around."

"You always remain separate?"

"We don't do anything always. We mix it up."

"I see, yes. Quite clever."

"No, standard routine," I said.

Alvis nodded. "Kuhns seems to have hired good men. It's an annoying situation all around. I wish the insurance company had never found out about the earlier burglary attempt. We've gone along without guards for years. That stupid attempt was probably of no importance anyway." He glanced around. "Isn't Mr. Ajemian here?"

"In the bedrooms."

"Alone?"

"No."

"Ah," Alvis said. "Well, I suppose it can wait."

The executive VP wheeled around, strode to the door, and went out. Green appeared behind me.

"What was that all about?" he asked.

"I don't know. I guess he decided to change his mind, if he had any real reason to come here at all."

"Yeh," Green said dubiously. "At least he didn't have a key. Let's change posts, you're having all the company."

"Ajemian's not working any more tonight," I said. "I'll sit in the study."

I went into the study. All was quiet. I opened the door into the kitchen and sat where I could see the rear door. I thought about Max Alvis. What had he really wanted? There was something about my conversation with him that bothered me, but I couldn't place what it was.

I thought about it, and must have dozed lightly, but jerked alert when I heard voices in the living room, a man's, a woman's, and Green's. The man was Ajemian, and he burst into the study with his arm around a tall woman in black. He was all smiles. She wasn't.

"My dear wife needs her blood money," Ajemian said. "I'm opening the safe. You men want to draw your guns?"

"Ivan has such a sense of humor," the woman said. "That's why I left him. He made me laugh too much."

"Two years, Beth, and no divorce," Ajemian said. "Admit that you miss me."

Mrs. Beth Ajemian wasn't a strudel like little Mary Kane, but a fine figure of a woman. Redhaired and full-bodied, she walked with grace and just enough sway. She was a woman, she knew it and liked it.

"I miss you, Ivan, exactly as you miss me," she said. "Do you perhaps want a divorce to marry your latest little friend?"

"I never claimed to be a saint, Beth."

"I didn't want a saint. I wanted a husband who was sometimes at home with his wife."

Ajemian shrugged. "I guess that's water under our bridge."

He opened the wall safe and took out an envelope. I saw the big bundle of $250,000 still intact. Ajemian handed the envelope to his estranged wife.

"A little extra, Beth. Don't tell my lawyer."

"Thank you, Ivan."

She looked around the study slowly, as if remembering better days. Or studying the layout? Then she left the study, crossed the living room, and went out without looking back.

"We just didn't work out," Ajemian said.

"How come she came for her money at this hour?" I asked.

Ajemian looked at me. "I don't know. She called, said she needed it. Why?"

"Nothing special," I said.

Ajemian went back to Mary Kane in the bedroom. Green resumed his post in the living room. I remained in the study, but I didn't like the feel of it. I went into the kitchen and looked at that lock again. The marks were still there, and they still could be the work of a jimmy, or the work of someone who wanted to make them look like a jimmy.

I went back to the study and settled in. I didn't doze, but nothing more happened that night.

We were relieved at nine the next morning. On our way to the elevators we met the first salesman. He had the gleam of bonus in his eyes.

Green headed for home and some sleep. I didn't. I went across the street and sat on a bench just inside the park, from where I could see both the front and service entrances to The Sussex Towers. Last night had been too busy, too much traffic in that apartment. I sensed it. Ajemian was nervous. So was Max Alvis, and what was it about Alvis' talk with me that rang wrong?

There are only two ways to plan a crime and get away with it: hide it, or disguise it.

Amateurs tend to disguise a crime. They plan it to look like something else, or look like the work of someone else, to prevent anyone's looking in the right place for the obvious motive. They have to resort to illusion.

Most professionals hide their crime, but they don't disguise it. They don't care if the crime is known for what it is, as long as they're not caught doing it, or have it proved against them later that they did this particular job.

Both methods have their problems, and both require some planning, so I sat in the park and watched The Sussex Towers. For a few hours I saw nothing more interesting than what looked like more hungry salesmen hurrying into the building; nothing suspicious, no one who looked like pro or amateur casing the place.

Then Max Alvis appeared in a taxi. He didn't get out at the front entrance, but at the rear, then walked into the alley that led to the service entrance. I could see him all the way. He stopped at the service entrance and seemed to study it. Then he went inside. I waited, but he didn't come out.

A half hour later he did come out—the front—and hailed a cab. Making a quick decision, I sprinted for another taxi. Luckily, The Sussex Towers attracted cabs.

"No wisecracks," I said, "but follow that cab."

The driver muttered, but he followed. We ended up at an office building in the East Thirties. Alvis went inside. I tailed him to the elevators. There was no way I could follow him any farther without being spotted, so I checked the building directory. Wallace Kuhns, Attorney, had an office in room 310.

Fifteen minutes later Alvis appeared again in the lobby. Kuhns was with him—and Mrs. Beth Ajemian.

They hurried out into the heat and split up. Alvis took another taxi, while Kuhns and Beth Ajemian walked toward Third Avenue. I had no choice, there were no other empty cabs, so I followed Kuhns and Mrs. Ajemian. I would have followed them, anyway. Kuhns was holding Beth Ajemian's hand—tight.

On Third Avenue they went into a cocktail bar. I followed. Inside there were booths, dim light, and a small bar. Kuhns and Beth Ajemian slid into a middle booth. I sat at the bar and watched them. They had all the aura of lovers, and not new lovers.

Kuhns held her hand as he talked, hard and fast. I watched through three beers, then I saw Kuhns dig for his wallet, and I left first. I picked them up as they came out. They went straight back to Kuhns' office.

I headed for home. There was nothing in itself suspicious about Kuhns' being close to Beth Ajemian. The wife and Ajemian seemed to have gone their separate ways, and Kuhns would have known the woman for a time. I remembered that Ajemian had said, "Don't tell my lawyer," when he had given Beth Ajemian some extra money last night, so Ajemian knew that his wife and Kuhns were close.

Too, Kuhns had hired me—or was that part of some scheme? I felt more than a little uneasy. At the very least, Kuhns might have been forced to hire detectives against his will. It was something to think about. So I thought about it, and I didn't get much of the sleep I needed.

I got back to The Sussex Towers at four fifty P.M. to find Green already there, the company men on their way out, and Ajemian in a lousy mood.

"I've got two hours of work," Ajemian growled. "Stay out of the damned study, and keep quiet. If anyone comes, tell him I've gone to China."

It looked like the start of a long night. I filled Green in on what I'd seen that day, while we waited for the last of the Tiflis Rug Company men to leave.

"We'd better keep a close eye on people with keys," Green said.

"I hear you loud."

When the last man had gone, and Ajemian was closed up in the study, I double-locked the front door, then went to check all the bedrooms to make sure no one was lurking around. Green took the rear and the kitchen to check.

I found no one in the bedrooms—not in the rooms, the closets, or under the beds. I had one more room to check when I heard the shot—a single shot that echoed through me like an atomic bomb.

From the rear—the study!

I ran with my old revolver in my lone hand. I reached the door into the study from the living room, but didn't barrel on through. That way lay suicide. I flattened beside the door, and kicked it open, then jumped through, crouched low, with the old cannon out ahead of me.

Ajemian lay on the floor, bleeding. No one else was in the study. I ran to Ajemian, who struggled up.

"One man. Masked! Tried to stop him," Ajemian croaked. "Waiting for me in here. He got it all!"

"Let's see the—"

"No! Flesh wound. Back door! Get him."

I hesitated a second. No amount of money is worth a life, no matter what the victim thinks, but the wound didn't look bad. I ran out into the kitchen.

Green lay on the kitchen floor, out cold. An ugly lump on his left temple showed what had happened to him.

The back door was open. I went out onto the service landing. The only way out of The Sussex Towers was down. Even if the thief had gone up, he would have to come down sooner or later. I ran down those sixteen flights as fast as I could, listening all the way. There was no sound like that of a running man.

In the basement I listened. I heard nothing. I went out into the alley at the rear. In the hot sunlight there wasn't even a cat. I ran out into the street that bordered the park. At this hour traffic was thick, and if he'd made it this far there was no way to catch him, not if he was a pro.

A woman's high, shrill scream shattered the hot evening.

I looked up toward the windows of Ajemian's apartment sixteen floors above.

For one brief instant the whole evening seemed to hold its breath in frozen silence, no sound at all. Sixteen floors above, I saw the man seem to hang in space, his face masked, his arms spread, his feet and legs twisted, a black bag floating beside him. All seemed motionless for the one split second.

Then I stood there and watched the man fall the whole long, endless sixteen stories in slow silence, like a grotesque sequence from some old silent movie.

He hit on the roof of a parked car, and bounced off into the street. Two cars ran over him before they could stop. The black bag hit some twenty feet away, split open, and spilled bundles of money across the street. A small pistol hit near the bag.

I ran to the fallen man through screams and squealing brakes. Blood spread all around him. Two patrolmen were running up, and a cruise car was in sight. I bent over the man. He was still masked. I took off the mask.

It was Wallace Kuhns. He didn't have much face left, but it was Kuhns. I stared at him for a long count of ten, then looked up at the tall building isolated from all the other buildings around it.

I grabbed the police sergeant from the cruise car.

"Put a man on the back and front doors!" I said. "Now!"

"Who the hell are you? What do you know about—"

I showed him my license. "Dan Fortune. Call Captain Gazzo at Homicide. Ask about me, and get him up here fast. But put men on the doors now. No one in or out. No one! You've got to do that!"

I was in luck. The sergeant was a good cop who would take no chances. Maybe I was crazy, but he'd find that out later. Meanwhile, maybe I knew what I was doing.

He sent one patrolman to the back door, and one to the front doors; no one in or out until further orders. The windows on the first two floors of the building were barred. It would do. A minute had barely passed since Kuhns had taken his fall.

I went back up to the apartment.

I revived Green and checked Ajemian's bleeding, and by then the doctor had arrived.

So had Captain Gazzo. The captain looked at me, at Green, at Ajemian, and got down to business.

"Okay, what's the story?"

Ajemian's wound was minor—a deep flesh wound that had bled but wasn't serious. Green had a nasty lump and a headache.

Ajemian said, "He was hiding in here in the study when I came in tonight. He was masked. He held the gun on me, and made me open the safe. He heard Fortune lock the front door, and go off to search the bedrooms. He heard Green in the kitchen."

Green nodded. "I was checking the lock on the back door when I heard him behind me. He slugged me good and that's all I know."

"After he hit Green," Ajemian went on shakily, "I tried to jump him and he shot me. He ran out the back way. Fortune came into the study. You know the rest."

I said, "Didn't you know Kuhns hadn't left tonight?"

"He did leave," Ajemian said, "An hour before you arrived. He must have come back in through the rear and hid in the study."

Gazzo gave me an odd look, and went out. I sat while the doctor worked some more on Ajemian and Green. I lighted a cigarette. Gazzo came back after about fifteen minutes.

"M.E. says Kuhns died from the fall, no doubt," the captain said. "We found a money wrapper under the window on the service landing outside the back door. There's a ledge out that window. Looks like he tried to hide there while Fortune was chasing down the stairs, only he slipped."

I said, "Nuts."

Gazzo glared at me. "There are fresh picklock marks on the back door, but we think they're fake. Kuhns had keys to the apartment in his pocket. He knew the routine of Green and Fortune, timed it for when they would be separated. If Ajemian hadn't made him shoot he'd have gotten away. He had bad luck."

"Bad luck, hell," I said. "Kuhns was murdered, captain."

Gazzo nodded wearily. "I figured that's why you called in Homicide and had the doors sealed off. What've you dreamed up this time, Dan?"

"Kuhns didn't fall, he was tossed over. Whoever tossed him didn't have time to get out of the building. There's no way off the roof, so the killer's still inside. Keep the building sealed tight, no one in or out without identification."

"You're saying Kuhns wasn't alone? You want to tell me how you figure all this?"

"No, you wouldn't believe me."

"I'll bet," Gaxxo said drily. "Any idea who?"

"Someone who knows Kuhns, this apartment, and where the money was," I said. I turned to Ajemian. "Is there anyone besides your ex-wife Beth, Max Alvis, Mary Kane, and the insurance people who fit that bill?"

"Myself," Ajemian said, "and the company guards we have in the day. The insurance people don't know the apartment."

"Okay," I said to Gazzo, "those are who you look for."

"I'll check them out," Gazzo said, "and a few other things, if that's okay with you? Like Kuhns' actions?"

"Why don't you just do what I'm going to do now, captain?" I said.

"What's that?"

"Wait," I said, and that's what I did, I waited.

Green was carted off to the hospital for observation, and Ajemian and I waited alone in the apartment. Ajemian watched me watching television for two hours before he blew up.

"Are you just going to sit here, Fortune? Do you expect me to pay you for that?"

"What do you want me to do?"

"Work! If you think Kuhns was murdered, go and solve it!"

"It's being solved, Ajemian," I said.

"By the police? Couldn't you help them, for what I'm paying?"

"Not the police," I said. "It's being solved by time. Time will solve it, and I've done my part. The killer is still in the building, for sure. No one gets out now, and sooner or later we have our killer."

"Just like that? It's not very imaginative," Ajemian said.

"Most police work isn't," I said. "Follow routine, set up your conditions, and wait. That's the way it plays most of the time. Why don't you just go to bed if waiting gets you?"

"With a killer loose in the building?"

"There's a police guard on both doors," I said.

He went to bed. I sat and waited alone. It was a long night. I began to jump at every noise, and from time to time in my mind I saw Kuhns falling those long, silent sixteen stories to his death.

Gazzo came back at eight o'clock the next morning. I was groggy from lack of sleep. Ajemian had slept fine and was bright as a pin. Gazzo hadn't slept any more than I had, but he was as bright as Ajemian.

"Here it is, Dan," Gazzo said. "Kuhns needed money. He'd lost a few clients, and had a big stock option. Beth Ajemian admits Kuhns wanted to marry her, but she wasn't about to divorce Ajemian until Kuhns had cash. She also admits Kuhns could have copied her set of keys to this place.

"The bag with the money in it was bought by Kuhns yesterday. The pistol is a Tiflis Rug office gun that vanished two months ago. He probably didn't want to hire detectives, but his hand was forced, so he hired two of the cheapest he could get. He probably figured you and Green were dumb. Maybe he was right."

I shrugged. "All circumstantial, and all a setup. Someone wanted it to look like Kuhns was only out to rob the place, or maybe force him to rob the place. No one tried to get out of the building yet?"

"No," Gazzo said. "I'm waiting for a call to finish off your little hunch."

"What call, captain?" Ajemian asked.

"Fortune will find out," Gazzo answered.

I said, "You know, that first robbery attempt really stinks. If it was unknown thieves, it's too much coincidence. If it was Kuhns, it was crazy; it just drew attention when the money wasn't here. I figure it was a fake, to make everyone think about robbery. All part of a big illusion, only there was a flaw in the illusion that made me think."

Ajemian said, "What kind of flaw, Fortune? Are you sure you're not just dreaming, as the captain says?"

Before I could answer, which I didn't intend to then anyway, the telephone rang. Gazzo answered. He listened for a time, nodded a few times, and hung up with a big grin at me.

"That's it, Dan. Everyone is accounted for. Beth Ajemian's been home all night, Max Alvis is in his office, Mary Kane is at her modeling school, the two company guards are at work, and even the insurance men are where they should be. None of them are in this building."

"Right," I said. "Then Ajemian's the killer."

The big rug company executive was on his feet, red as fire instead of pale, and spluttering at me.

"Is this a joke, Fortune? I'll have you—"

"No joke," I said. "Simple elimination. I told you time would solve it. No one got out of this building. You're the only one still in the building. So you're it."

Ajemian was so red I thought he would choke to death then and there. He whirled on Gazzo. "Are you going to let him sit there and accuse me? I'll ruin both of you!"

Gazzo said nothing. He was watching Ajemian and me and waiting for my story. I gave it:

"Kuhns never left the apartment. You, Ajemian, knocked him out and hid him in the study. He wouldn't stay quiet long, so you pulled it off as soon as Green and I were alone. You hit Green, opened the rear doors, and shot yourself. When I chased after the supposed thief, you hauled Kuhns up on the window sill and heaved him out with the money and the gun.

"It was just luck I'd gone all the way down. You saw me down there,

ALFRED HITCHCOCK'S ANTHOLOGY

and figured it was the perfect touch—I'd *see* Kuhns fall—but that was a mistake. It broke a good illusion."

Ajemian tried a laugh. "You expect anyone to believe all that? An intricate scheme like that?"

"Not so intricate. It almost worked. The groundwork was harder than the killing trick. You had to fix it so Kuhns needed money. You got clients to leave him, and he was your lawyer so you had him take a big stock option for you, but in his name. We'll find he's done that before. The gun was easy, and he'd have bought the bag for you if you told him to. I'll bet we find he had other bags he could have used safer."

"He did," Gazzo said quietly. "Two attache cases we found."

I nodded. "I guess you were really jealous, wanted your wife back. That'll be easy to prove, the motive, or you wouldn't have tried for such a big illusion of robbery. Gazzo should be able to trace those keys eventually. Anyway, a paraffin test will show you shot a gun last night, and with—"

Ajemian waited for no more. He had a gun. He'd been ready. He took a shot at me, missed, and went out the door. Gazzo picked himself up and went after him. I sat down. I had a cigarette. A one-armed man isn't much help in a fight, and I value my skin. Catching him wasn't my job.

After a time I heard shots on the roof. I went to the window. Then I heard the scream, and I leaned out the window to look up. I was just in time to see him fall, his gun still in his hand. He screamed all the way down.

I was still at the window when Gazzo came back.

"We didn't have much," Gazzo said. "You know we don't use a paraffin test any more, it's useless. No court will take it."

"He didn't know that," I said. "It's not the truth that counts, Gazzo, it's what people think is true. He knew he did it, and he had to be a little crazy."

"All right, tell me. I'll believe how you figured it, now."

"There was one thing Max Alvis said. He didn't know how the insurance people learned about that first supposed robbery attempt. Only three people could have told them. Alvis didn't. Kuhns didn't. That left Ajemian himself. He wanted the insurance men to know, so they would insist on guards. He needed witnesses for his fake robbery illusion."

"That had to come later, Dan. How did you start to think it was murder in the first place?"

I said, "What happened on the roof just now?"

"He tried to shoot it out, slipped, and went over the edge."

"He fell," I said, "and he screamed all the way down."

"So?"

"They always scream, Gazzo. Or almost always."

"Okay, so they scream. So what, Dan?"

"Kuhns didn't scream," I said. "Kuhns fell sixteen floors without making a sound. Even when they jump they usually scream, it's a reflex I guess. Kuhns fell, by accident, and he didn't make a sound. The only way that could have happened was that Kuhns had been unconscious. He'd been tossed out—murdered."

Gazzo stared at me. "Damn it, Dan, who can prove everyone screams when he falls? Maybe Kuhns was a man who just didn't scream!"

"It doesn't matter," I said. "It was the little flaw that made me wonder. It made me think."

Gazzo groaned. "Dan, you've got dumb luck."

"Like I said, it's not what's true that counts, but what a man thinks is true. If you build an illusion, it has to hold all the way. I didn't believe a man would fall sixteen floors without a scream. So I just couldn't believe the illusion."

Gazzo had no more to say. He was a cop, and he'd sweat for days about my shaky reasoning that could have been dead wrong. I won't sweat. Maybe someday I'll find a man who falls sixteen floors in silence, and then I'll be wrong. This time I'd been right, and that's what counts in detective work.

ALFRED HITCHCOCK'S ANTHOLOGY

Thieves' Bazaar

by W. L. Heath

I am not an abnormally suspicious man, but there are some people I mistrust almost on sight. In my work I travel around considerably, and without paying myself any excessive compliments I think I can say that I have developed a pretty good eye for a "shady."

There are lots of them in the Middle East and the Orient, where I have had to do most of my traveling. Shadies come in all colors, shapes, and sizes, of course, but they are birds of a feather and easy enough to recognize, once you have seen them go into their act. They all peddle the same commodity—namely a deal, a skin game of one kind or another. In less time than it takes to buy them four scotch and sodas they will tell you, in confidential undertones, how to make a killing overnight—provided, of course, you have the sporting blood to lay a couple of American Express checks on the line. They flourish in second-rate bars all the way from Casablanca to Hong Kong, and while most of them are nothing more than small time confidence men, some are dangerous. If you think I'm talking melodramatic nonsense you simply haven't traveled in that part of the world.

Thompson was a shady, and I was sure of it from the start. He was one of those derelict white men you run across out there from time to time. They are always alone, these men, and shabbily dressed, and if you ask about their business they tell you they are in "export-import." That is the standard reply. Thompson's appearance alone was enough to make me suspicious, but the circumstances of our meeting him and his over-eager courtesy to Jan were what really put me on guard.

We met Thompson in a bar across the street from the Paradise Theater, in Karachi. Jan and I had been shopping since noon in the bazaar and had stopped there to cool off before going back to the hotel. It was a fairly typical bar of the Great Eastern variety, more like an old fashioned American drugstore than a cocktail parlor.

We took a seat under a fan, ordered a drink, and Jan spread out her purchases to admire them.

"I'm still not satisfied," she said.

"Why not? You've got all the standard items—the ivory comb, the *sari*, the brass elephant bell. What more could the folks back in Philadelphia expect?"

She looked at me with a twinkle in her brown eyes. "A star sapphire, Dave. I simply can't leave India without a star sapphire."

I was tired. "Well, maybe tomorrow," I said.

"We won't have time tomorrow. Go with me this afternoon—please?" She put her hand on mine and gave me the little pleading look I'd seen her use on her father. Jan was a handsome girl with long dark eyelashes and the sort of figure you expected of a wealthy American debutante.

"The ship won't sail till four," I said.

"I know, but there's so much to do—packing and all that. I'm just positive we won't have time for any more shopping tomorrow."

"But, honey, my feet are dead. They've quit. They've surrendered."

She smiled at me and I thought she was about to give in, but just then this man who called himself Thompson made his gambit. He materialized suddenly at Jan's elbow, cleared his throat and bowed. He was a big, pallid, puffy-eyed man wearing a bush jacket and holding a soiled topee in his hands.

"If you'll pardon the intrusion. I couldn't help overhearing what madam said."

The rest happened very fast, too fast for me to stop it. The next thing I knew, Thompson had introduced himself and pulled up a chair, and I was paying for another gin and lime.

"The important thing in buying gems is recognizing a valuable one when you see it," he said. "I presume you do know gems?"

"No, I don't," Jan said. "That's just the trouble."

Thompson frowned slightly and drummed his fingers on the crown of his sun helmet. "Then I'm afraid you do have a problem," he said. "Of course, I'm not suggesting that you'd be in any great danger of getting swindled—many of the merchants are scrupulously honest—but on the other hand we are in a foreign country and these Orientals . . ." He let his voice trail off on a note of regret, then looked up at me and smiled. "What we'd like to do is eliminate the element of doubt, wouldn't we?"

"What I'd like to do is go soak my feet," I said.

He evaded me with a laugh. "Shopping in this heat does tire one." He turned back to Jan and sipped his drink thoughtfully. I was trying to place his nationality. British, I thought, but possibly an American with a British accent.

"Maybe you could recommend a place where we'd be sure we were safe," Jan said.

"As a matter of fact, I was just about to suggest that," Thompson said. Things were going nicely. "There's a little shop down on—but no, you'd never find it alone." His face lit up suddenly and he looked at his watch. "Tell you what. I'm going that way and I'd be delighted to drop you off."

"Swell," Jan said.

"No," I said.

"Why not?"

"We couldn't impose on the gentleman that way."

"That's nonsense," Thompson exclaimed. "It's no imposition. I'd consider it a privilege. I say, we Anglos have to stick together out here, you know. We have to look out for one another."

"No," I said, "we appreciate your courtesy, but . . ."

"Oh, let's do go, Dave. It may be the last chance I'll have."

Thompson pressed his advantage carefully, and I argued, but it was no use. Jan had swallowed the bait, and though I didn't know her very well, I knew she was the sort of girl who's accustomed to having her way. Finally, out of fear that she might try it alone, I consented to go. The worst that could happen wasn't likely to be very bad, I thought, and if she wanted to throw away a hundred bucks or so on a back alley bargain that was her business, not mine. Her father could probably foot the bill without any discomfort and maybe the lesson would be good for her.

As we were about to leave the bar, Thompson excused himself and went to the rear of the room to make a phone call. I had expected that, too. We waited at the door. And when he joined us again, I asked him what his business was in Karachi.

"I'm in export-import," he said.

We hailed a cab—a horse-drawn victoria—and Thompson gave the driver instructions in Urdu, which he seemed to speak quite well. As we rode across town and through the bazaar, he sat facing us on the little jump seat behind the driver, chatting pleasantly and inquiring politely into our reasons for being in Pakistan. I explained that I was a photographer for *Geographics Illustrated,* now on my way home from an assignment in Ceylon.

"Then you two aren't married?"

"Oh no," Jan said. "We've only known each other for two weeks. We met on board ship after leaving Calcutta."

"Are you traveling alone?"

"No, my father is with me," she said. "He stayed at the hotel this afternoon to take a nap." She explained that her father was a steel manufacturer from Philadelphia, and that they were making a trip around the world. Her mother had died in February the year before, and she had pressed her father into making the trip, hoping it would take his mind off her death.

Thompson, apparently satisfied, was silent after that, and we clopped across Elephant Stone Street and down a wide avenue bordered on both sides by tall thirsty looking trees. I had never seen that section of the city before, and it still isn't clear to me exactly where we went. We passed through a park at one place, and then turned into a narrow, crowded street where half-naked children trotted beside the carriage crying for *baksheesh*—a handout.

Finally, we stopped in front of a shop with a corrugated tin awning, and I got out with considerable misgivings. It was a bad part of town, and I was beginning to be uneasy about letting Jan come here. The facade of the building was very ornate and above the street floor there was a sort of turret, a crown-shaped hexagonal chamber with shuttered windows on each side and several small minarets carved like the posts of a spool bed. In front of the shop a blind beggar sat on a filthy pallet.

We went up a flight of stone steps and into the arched doorway, where we were greeted by a little man wearing a black alpaca suit and a fez.

"Good afternoon," he said, indicating that we would be able to speak in English. He bowed and smiled and ushered us into a sort of anteroom to the right of the entrance. It appeared to be clean enough in there, but the odors of the street had followed us in. Thompson introduced us, explaining to the proprietor that we were interested in gems. We were given chairs then, and when we were seated the man in the fez began to bring out the stones. Thompson sat quietly at one side.

I suppose we stayed in the shop for half an hour, and though I watched everything as carefully as I could, I saw nothing wrong. The little man in the fez was patient and polite, and Thompson kept aloof from all the bargaining.

Jan was disappointed in the prices, and that surprised me, because I thought they were reasonable enough. She looked at sapphires first, then at rubies, and finally asked to see diamonds. I hoped that she wouldn't decide to buy a diamond because they are the most difficult stone of all to be sure about.

In the end, and partly due to my insistence, she bought a small sapphire for ninety rupees. We thanked the proprietor and prepared to leave.

"Will you ride back with us?" Jan asked Thompson.

"No, thank you," he said. "I'm going the other direction."

He went out with us to call a carriage, and then said goodbye. The whole episode left me completely baffled. I had seen nothing wrong, and yet I had the feeling that something was very wrong.

As we were riding back to the hotel, I asked Jan to let me see the sapphire again. She opened her purse and gave it to me, and I examined it carefully, rolling it around in my palm. It had a good star, and though it was small, the color was deep and blue and it was almost perfectly shaped. I felt certain it was worth every cent she had paid for it, maybe even more.

"Count your money again," I said. "See if he gave you the correct change."

"It's all here," she said, thumbing through her bills. "What makes you so suspicious?"

"I don't know. I honestly don't. I had a strange feeling back there in that shop. Something fishy was going on, but I can't figure out what it was. It was like watching a shell game or a crooked poker hand. Know what I mean?"

"Yes," she said, "I think I do. I had that feeling myself."

When I looked at her I thought she had gone a little pale.

Back in my room at the hotel, I poured a drink and went out on the balcony to cool off. A moment later there was a knock at the door and Jan came in. "Dad's still asleep," she said. "I thought I'd come down and have a drink with you."

"Fine. I can give you scotch, but there's no ice."

"Mother India. Well, make it without ice and make it stiff. That jewel shop gave me the creeps."

She sat on the bed while I made the drink, and when I brought it to her, she asked for a cigarette to go with it. She had on a white linen skirt, but she had taken off the jacket she'd worn while shopping, and her blouse was open several inches down from the neck. I couldn't help noticing that she was not wearing a brassiere, but I put it down to the heat and took a chair by the window where the view was not quite so distracting.

"You know," she said, "we've been together almost constantly for two weeks now, and you haven't even tried to kiss me."

"I'm a married man, I told you that. I've got a wife and kids at home, young lady.

She pursed her lips and gave me a reproachful look. "I didn't say I'd *let* you, but it's not very flattering when you don't even try."

"The trouble with you," I said, "is too much sun."

She laughed and got up. "I believe you're right. Mind if I go in and wash my face? I've felt positively dirty ever since that shop. I wish we hadn't gone." When she came out of the bathroom again, I noticed that the blouse was buttoned and I was relieved.

"What about dinner?" I said.

"We'll meet you in the bar at six. That is, if I can wake Dad. He was sleeping soundly a while ago."

When she was gone, I took a bath and shaved, and at six I went down to the bar to wait. I was still wondering about Thompson, but I couldn't find a flaw in it anywhere: Jan had got her money's worth in the stone; she had not been short-changed; the ever-obliging Thompson had departed without even hinting at a tip for his services. It was a bit thick, as the British would say. It didn't make sense, not in terms of what I knew about men like Thompson. But where was the catch?

I had a second drink as I mulled it over, and then all at once I realized I had been waiting for quite a long time. It was six thirty now, and Jan and her father still hadn't showed up. I distinctly remembered hearing her say she would meet me in the bar at six. They were not the most punctual people in the world, but half an hour was a long time to be late and I felt sure they would have called down to tell me if something was delaying them. I began to be worried. So after a few minutes more, I decided to go back up to my room and give them a ring.

As I left the bar, I took a look around the lobby to make sure they were not waiting there by mistake, but there was no sign of them anywhere. I consequently went up the wide, red-carpeted stairs two at a time, feeling more worried with every step. The business with Thompson had set my mind in a high state of suspicion.

At the second landing, I turned left along the corridor and immediately saw that someone was in my room. The light was on and the door was open. When I reached the door, the first thing that caught my eye was my suitcase. It was lying open on the bed, and one of my cameras was lying beside it with the leather case taken off. The bed covers had been stripped from the bed and were piled in a heap on the floor, and several drawers of the dresser were hanging open. The next thing I saw was a little man in a black alpaca suit and a fez—the man from the jewel shop. He was standing in the bathroom door, looking over his shoulder at me in a rather surprised manner, and there was a pistol in his hand.

As he turned to face me, I took a step backward and dodged out of the door. I collided with a big man dressed in khakis and wearing a turban. The big fellow made a grab for me and caught my arm. When I tried to pull away, he gave my arm a twist. I swung around as far as I could in the other direction and hit him solidly in the mouth with my left fist. He let go and covered his mouth with his hands, and I hit him again, driving him back against the wall. But now another one had come up out of nowhere like the first—another big man dressed in what appeared to be a soldier's khakis. As I tried to go around him, he swung a short club at me. The blow missed my head, but hit my shoulder, and I went down to my knees, holding him around the waist. He swung again, and that's all I remember for quite a long time.

When I came to again, I was lying on my own bed looking up at the mosquito net, and the little man in the fez was bending over me with a wet towel. "We're sorry about this," he said.

"So am I." It was all I could think of at the moment.

He crossed the room and came back with my passport in his hand.

"We've checked all your papers and established your identity," he said. "We realize now that it was a mistake."

"I can agree with that. But what kind of a mistake?"

"We thought you were implicated with the girl. Now we have it straight."

"Jan?" I said. "Where is she?"

"They've both been arrested."

"Arrested? For what?"

"For the theft of several thousand dollars' worth of gems." He took a manila envelope from his pocket and emptied it into his hand. There were half a dozen rubies and pearls, an emerald and one large yellow looking diamond. "We found them in your bathroom," he explained. "Evidently she became suspicious after leaving the shop, and she brought them down here to hide."

"Wait a minute," I said, "I haven't kept up with you. Are you telling me you're a police officer?"

"That is correct, sahib," he said. "We were warned by the Bombay authorities to watch for these people; so when they arrived here, we prepared a trap for them. They've been working this system all the way from Hong Kong."

"What kind of system was it?"

"You see, they have synthetic gems. The girl substitutes a synthetic stone for a real one of similar shape and size wherever she finds it. Today, while you were with her, she obtained a ruby and this six carat diamond. She palmed off two synthetics, as you Americans would say."

I pulled myself up and let my feet down over the edge of the bed. My ears were ringing, and there was a terrific pain above my left ear. The big fellow with the turban was standing by the door with a swollen lip. He was a policeman all right.

"We're sorry about what happened in the hall," the man with the fez went on, "but there was much confusion and we still weren't sure who you were."

"What about Jan's father?"

The little man shook his head sadly. "I'm afraid the man wasn't her father, sahib. A most regrettable situation."

We were silent for a minute. My head was beginning to clear a little.

"Now about Thompson," I said. "He was your decoy, right?"

"I beg pardon?"

"He led us to the shop."

"Oh yes, Thompson." He smiled. "Thompson has been helpful to us on a number of occasions."

"But he's not a police officer?"

"Oh no. Thompson is—what would you call him? He does anything for a little money."

"A shady," I said. "I knew it all the time. Those people can't fool me for a minute."

The Keeper

by Clark Howard

Charles Lawson, the new warden, took over the prison at noon on a gray, rainy Monday. He held his first staff meeting one hour later.

"Gentlemen," he said from behind a desk vacated by his predecessor just that morning, "you all know who I am and why I'm here. I've been appointed by the governor to succeed the former head of this institution, and I've been given full authority to act in whatever manner I feel will be in the best interests of the state."

Lawson rose and turned to the window behind his chair. He looked out at the big yard, still scorched and blackened from the riot that had been contained barely forty-eight hours earlier.

"Two inmates dead," Lawson said quietly. "Sixteen men injured; five of them guards. And," he turned back to his chair, "many thousands of dollars in damage done to the prison itself."

He sat back down and fingered a worn pipe from his coat pocket. The men seated in front of him—a deputy warden, the guard captain, and three guard lieutenants—watched as he carefully filled the pipe from a leather tobacco pouch. When the bowl was packed to suit him, he clamped the stem between his teeth and dug one thumbnail into the head of a stick match, snapping it to flame. He put the match to the bowl and lighted the tobacco, puffing pungent, gray whirls of smoke into the room.

"My instructions from the governor are threefold," he said, shaking the match out and tossing it into the former warden's ashtray. "First, and most important, I am to restore complete order throughout the prison. Second, I am to tighten and maintain strict internal security. And third, I am to conduct an in-depth investigation to determine the factual causes of the riot, to place formal blame on any guilty parties, and to rectify, if possible, the conditions that sparked the trouble in the first place. Now then," he leaned back in the unfamiliar chair, "I would like to hear recommendations for a procedure to accomplish the first objective: restoring complete order throughout the prison."

"I can answer that for you," said Fred Hull, the prison's guard captain. "In fact, I can tell you how to accomplish *all* of your objectives. Lock Ralph Starzak in the hole and throw away the key."

"Ralph Starzak," Lawson reflected. He drummed his fingers silently on the arm of the chair. "That's Ralph Starzak, the big-time fence from the early 1950's? Been up here fourteen or fifteen years?"

"Sixteen," said Hull. "Doing twenty, and he'll be with us the max, too. The parole board turned him down for the last time three months ago; they gave him a four-year set, so he'll have to do the full twenty."

"Are you saying that Starzak is the *entire* problem, captain? That he's the cause of *all* the prison's problems?"

"I am," said Hull flatly. "I'm saying exactly that."

"Well," Lawson said.

He puffed at his pipe and nodded slowly. "What about you other men? Do all of you agree with Captain Hull?"

For a moment there was silence in the room. The three guard lieutenants glanced at one another but said nothing. Finally Roger Stiles, the young deputy warden, spoke up.

"Sir," he said to Lawson, "with all due respect to Captain Hull's position and experience, I'm afraid I'll have to disagree with him. I'm sure I'll be a minority of one, but I think the captain is exaggerating Starzak's importance among the prisoners. I don't think he has anywhere near the influence that Captain Hull credits him with—"

"Influence!" Hull roared. "He's behind every racket in the whole joint! He controls every con in every responsible position in the place."

"That's not entirely true," Stiles said mildly. "He doesn't control the inmate teachers in the school—"

"The inmate teachers!" Hull spat the words out scornfully. "Who'd *want* to control them? They're nobodies to the rest of the cons! I'm talking about control over cons who *matter*—the ones in the inmate commissary, the dining room, the laundry. I'm talking about the ones a con has to pay off if he wants clean denims twice a week and a thicker slice of meat on his tray at supper, and a full tobacco allowance instead of a three-quarter measure."

"Are you insinuating that Starzak controls all of that?" Lawson asked.

"That and more," Hull said, "and I'm not insinuating; I'm stating a *fact*. There is no doubt about it."

"An unsubstantiated opinion isn't a fact," Stiles said quietly.

"I'm afraid he has a valid point there," the new warden said to Hull. "Do you have any proof, captain? Any definite infraction of an inmate regulation that you could charge him with?"

Hull glared briefly at the young deputy warden sitting beside him. "No," he said in a near sullen tone.

"Are there any inmates who might be willing to cooperate with us in an investigation of Starzak?" Lawson asked.

Hull shook his head.

"You must have an informant or two on the yard," Lawson said. "I've never seen a prison that didn't."

"Sure," Hull admitted, "we've got stoolies. They'll stool on any con in the joint—except Starzak."

"Then we really have no basis for disciplinary action, do we?"

"Not unless you want to accept my personal recommendation and put him in solitary," Hull said rather stiffly.

Lawson drummed his fingers on the desk again.

"Let me give the matter some thought," he said neutrally. "Let me get a better feel of the place. I'll discuss it with you in greater detail before I make a final decision. In the meantime, I think we'd all better get busy with the primary objective of restoring order in all areas. What is our situation at the present?"

"We're in good shape securitywise," Hull answered. "A and B Blocks are completely under control, and Tiers One through Five in C Block have been secured. Tier Six in C Block is locked in; they're on a hunger strike, haven't eaten since breakfast Saturday."

"How long do you think they'll hold out?"

Hull rubbed his chin reflectively. "Tuesday noon at the latest."

"All right. What else?"

"Eight of the rioters are still holed up in the shoe shop. They're unarmed—" he looked pointedly at the deputy warden, Stiles, "but we've been instructed not to take them out by force."

Lawson turned to Stiles and raised his eyebrows inquiringly.

"We have more than twenty thousand dollars' worth of shoe manufacturing machinery in that shop," the deputy warden explained. "The men will destroy it if we try to force them out. I'm negotiating with them through Father Cahill, the prison chaplain; I think they'll come out voluntarily—" now he looked pointedly at Hull, "*without* costing the state a new shoe shop."

"All right," Lawson said. He directed his attention back to Hull. "What else?"

The guard captain shrugged. "That's about the extent of it. Isolation is more than half full; so is the dispensary, nearly. All three blocks are on early lockup; privileges have been suspended."

"Very well," Lawson said. "Now here's what I want you to do: continue the early lockup, but restore radio and reading privileges in all cells except the tier on hunger strike. At supper tonight have a couple of steam carts sent over and offer a tray of hot food to each man participating in the strike; whoever eats can be restored to dining-hall status. As far as the men in the shoe shop are concerned, let the chaplain continue to try talking them out." He glanced fleetingly at Hull's three guard lieutenants. "By tomorrow noon I want a written appraisal from each of these officers of the situation in each cellblock, along with summary recommendations from you on further general steps to be taken. You can exclude any suggestions regarding Starzak; we'll talk that over between ourselves later." He paused, then said, "Any questions?"

"No questions," Hull answered. He rose from the chair, his three lieutenants doing likewise. The four of them, with Hull in the lead, filed out of the room.

When Stiles and Lawson were alone, the young deputy warden cleared his throat and said, "I'm sorry for the dissension, sir. I'd hoped your first staff meeting would go a little more smoothly."

"Don't give it a thought," Lawson said, smiling. "Frankly, in light of the present situation, I didn't expect it to go nearly as well as it did." He stood up and stuck his pipe in the corner of his mouth. "Let's walk down to the dining hall and get better acquainted over a cup of coffee."

In the huge inmate dining hall, deserted now except for the convicts who worked there, Lawson and Stiles took metal cups and helped themselves to coffee from a large urn behind the steam table. They walked to a nearby aluminum table with self-attached seats, their footsteps resounding hollowly in the great expanse of room. Lawson sipped his coffee in silence for a moment, then looked squarely at the young deputy.

"I hate to put you on the proverbial spot this early in our association," he said flatly, "but as you well know, I myself am also on one. Needless to say, I want to get off of it as quickly as possible. So—what's your evaluation of Captain Hull as a correctional officer?"

Stiles grinned uncomfortably. "You certainly don't beat around the bush about matters, do you?"

"Normally I'd be subtle about it, but in this case I don't have the time. For the present, we'll keep it off the record if you like."

Stiles shrugged. "It's immaterial to me; I'd say the same thing off the record as I would on the record."

"Good," said Charles Lawson. "I like that. Let's have it."

"All right." Stiles swallowed dryly and took a quick sip of coffee. "Fred Hull is probably one of the ablest, most efficient security officers any prison could ask for. He put down a riot in two days that would have lasted a week anywhere else. When it comes to keeping inmates behind walls, there's not a better man in the business than Hull. A perfect example of his ability is the fact that he's been here sixteen years and in that time there hasn't been a single escape.

"But—" Stiles lowered his voice considerably, knowing how it would carry in the big room, "in the areas of rehabilitation, inmate education, vocational training—all the modern aspects of penology—Captain Hull is a total failure. He's completely out of his element; a throwback to sweatbox days. His thinking, as far as motivating inmates toward self-improvement, is as archaic as a chain gang. In short, he feels that the function of a penitentiary is simply and solely to punish, which I think is all wrong."

Lawson pursed his lips briefly. "Do you like Captain Hull personally?" he asked bluntly, quickly.

"No," said Stiles, "I'm afraid I don't. I don't *dis*like him, mind you. It's just that we have nothing in common; there's no basis for a friendship."

"I see," Lawson nodded. "Well, I appreciate your honesty." He drummed his fingers, as he seemed to have a habit of doing, on the gleaming metal tabletop. Stiles noticed that where they touched, faint fingerprints were left on the shiny surface. "What about Starzak?" Lawson said. "Is he top con in here or isn't he?"

Stiles shrugged. "Hull thinks so. I don't."

"Hull doesn't just *think* so," Lawson corrected him. "Hull is flatly and firmly convinced of it. Why?"

"Warden, I don't know," the younger man said. "I'll be the first to admit that Starzak has probably been mixed up in a shady deal or two; I mean, he's been here like a decade and a half, and any old con in any prison is going to cut a touch now and then to make life a little easier.

But I don't believe that he controls the entire inmate population."

"Do you think that Captain Hull might have a personal grudge against Starzak for some reason or other?"

Stiles rubbed his chin thoughtfully. "It's possible, I suppose. They've both been here a long time; they could have had some kind of run-in a long time ago."

Lawson thought about it for a moment and then said, "Well, I'll have an opportunity to explore that possibility; tomorrow, as a matter of fact, when I ask Starzak his views on how the prison can be improved."

Stiles frowned deeply. "You're going to ask *Starzak* how to improve the prison?"

"Yes. Starzak and every other old-timer in the place. I tried that tack once before, when I went in as warden of Danville. You'd be surprised at the insight that can be gained from interviews of that sort; not to mention the constructive criticism that comes out of them." He noticed that Stiles had quickly replaced his frown with a smile. "I take it you approve," he said.

"Very much," the young deputy replied at once. "It's just the sort of enlightened thinking that the institution needs."

"Well, I just hope some successful results come of it," Lawson said. "I'd like you to schedule the interviews for me, beginning at nine tomorrow morning. Let's make it every inmate with fifteen or more years' time. Give me a quarter hour with each of them. I'd like all their files on my desk by six this evening, too, so I can look them over tonight."

"Yes, sir. I'll take care of it."

"Good." Lawson finished his coffee. "Well, shall we get back?"

The two men rose and walked toward the nearest door, their footsteps again echoing sharply in the vast expanse of the room.

At nine the next morning, Warden Charles Lawson began interviewing privately his new prison's long-time inmates. He went through the routine efficiently, professionally, probing the minds and thoughts of the men much as a skilled surgeon would probe their bodies for a tumor; except that Lawson used not his fingers but rather an alert mind and quick, leading words to encourage the men as individuals to express themselves candidly to him. Having read their records the previous night, he was familiar with them as criminals of society and as prisoners of the institution. Now, in seeking to tap their prison-developed wisdom, he took care to approach them on the basis of one mature man to another.

Lawson was pleased to find that his plan worked in the new prison even better than it had at Danville. Most of the old cons were not only willing, but eager, to help. From the surviving member of a notorious pair of young thrill-killers, for instance, who was now well past middle age after thirty-one years behind the walls, Lawson learned of some serious shortcomings in the operation of the Diagnostic Depot, the separate section of the prison where new arrivals were isolated until let into the general prison population. Then, from a former surgeon serving life for the murder of his wife, came information on laxity in the prison dispensary. From an infamous midwestern gangster, now working as a prison butcher, Lawson found out about a low grade of meat being sold to the prison by a local supplier. From the oldest of the oldtimers, the leader of a kidnap gang which had snatched a wealthy bootlegger in the late twenties, and who had been a convict there for forty-two years, the new warden learned that the general consensus of inmates was that the riot had been the result of a lot of little discontentments built up over an extended period of time, rather than any one incident which could be directly linked to its cause.

After Lawson had spoken with half a dozen long-termers, it came Ralph Starzak's turn. Lawson was surprised at the appearance of the convict as he entered and sat down. Contrary to the flamboyant multi-million-dollar fence who in the early 1950's had been sent to prison for twenty years, the man before Lawson now was a slightly stoop-shouldered, balding, watery-eyed individual who, with his gray, unhealthy complexion, hardly looked capable of influencing even a single inmate, much less inspiring an entire prison population to violence.

"Starzak," the warden said, after he got over his initial surprise at how the man looked, "I am calling in all of the long-termers in the institution in an effort to determine what, if anything, in the minds of the inmates, needs to be done to improve conditions in the prison. Do you have any suggestions which might be helpful along those lines?"

Starzak, sitting on the very edge of the chair, holding his prison cap in both hands almost apprehensively, shrugged noncommittally. "I . . . I don't know anything about . . . conditions, warden."

"Starzak, you don't have to be afraid to say anything that's on your mind," Lawson pointed out. "Before the day is out, I will interview every inmate who has served fifteen or more years. There is absolutely no way for anyone in here to know who told me what. Now, please be frank with me. Surely you have some ideas on improving prison conditions."

Again the shrug. "Well, sure, warden—I mean, you know, there are lots of ways to make things better. The food could stand improvement, too much boiled stuff on the menu; and the movies we've been getting on Sundays are so old some of them still have Dean Martin with his old nose—"

"Those are general complaints," Lawson told him. "Some of the inmates are always going to be displeased with the food; just as some of them will always be unhappy with the movies shown every Sunday. What I'm looking for are *specifics*, Starzak; particularly causes of discontent that might spark trouble. For instance," he casually opened Starzak's thick prison record, "it isn't unusual for guards—or even guard *officers*, for that matter—to favor certain inmates, while at the same time perhaps being too harsh with others. Would you say situations like that exist in this institution?"

Starzak twisted his cap in his hands and avoided Lawson's eyes. "Maybe, maybe not," he said. "I don't know anything about any situations."

Lawson quietly drummed his fingers. "Would you report such an officer if you felt he were being unduly harsh with *you*, Starzak?"

"Sure," Starzak's shoulders raised and dropped, "Why not? I mean, I've been here a long time, warden. I've done my time clean," he bobbed his head at the desk, "you can see for yourself right there in the record. I've hardly gotten a discipline ticket in sixteen years. I'd have been paroled a long time ago if I'd had a job to go to and a family to take me in—"

"So you *would* report a guard—even an officer—who was carrying a grudge against you and was out to get you?"

"Yes, sir, I would," Starzak said unequivocally, "and because of my clean record in here, I'd expect to get fair treatment in the matter, too."

"I see," Lawson nodded. "Well, that's a very realistic attitude, Starzak." He pretended to study very thoughtfully a page in the convict's record. Forcing a frown, he then said, "Do you get along all right with Captain Hull?"

Starzak shook his head. "The captain doesn't like me very much," he admitted.

"Why? Did you have some kind of run-in with him?"

"Well, yes, sir, once—but it wasn't anything really serious."

"Let me be the judge of that. What was it about and when did it

ALFRED HITCHCOCK'S ANTHOLOGY

happen?"

Starzak pulled on one ear. "Let's see, it was about five years ago, maybe a little longer. I was working as a checker in the laundry—same job I've got now.

"What I do is make sure that the sheets are collected from certain tiers in certain blocks on certain days. The cons strip them off their bunks, fold them up, and leave them on the gunwalk outside the cells. Then laundry runners go along and pick them up and bring them to the laundry. They get scalded and bleached, blower-dried, then run through a folding machine, and returned to the cells before lockup the same day—"

"I am familiar with prison laundry routine," Lawson said patiently. "Just tell me what happened between you and Captain Hull."

"Yes, sir. Captain Hull came to me on the second Tuesday of a particular month and said my runners hadn't picked up the sheets on B-Five and B-Six. I told him we didn't do those two tiers until the next Tuesday. The captain said I was crazy, there were sheets outside of every cell door on B-Five and B-Six. I said maybe so, but that second Tuesday wasn't their laundry day. Then he said I obviously didn't know what I was doing and that I shouldn't be in a position of any responsibility; so he relieved me of the job."

Lawson nodded. "And?"

"Well, I didn't think it was fair so I went to the deputy warden—that was Mr. Grimes, before Mr. Stiles came. Well, Mr. Grimes looked into the matter and found out I was right and Captain Hull was wrong. Laundry day for B-Five and B-Six *was* the next Tuesday. What happened was, some con on B-Five got mixed up on the days and put his sheet out by mistake. Another con saw him and without thinking did the same thing. Pretty soon it set off a kind of chain reaction and every guy on both tiers had his sheet out on the gunwalk. When Captain Hull saw it, he naturally figured there was some foul-up at the laundry—"

"Do you blame him for thinking that?" Lawson interjected.

"Not a bit," Starzak said emphatically. "I'd have thought the same way myself if I'd been in his place. I mean, you wouldn't expect two tiers of guys to all make the same mistake at the same time."

"What was the outcome of your complaint to the deputy warden?"

"Mr. Grimes restored me to my job," Starzak answered with a hint of self-righteousness. "It was the only fair thing to do."

"And you don't think it was a serious enough matter to cause Captain

Hull to build up a grudge against you?"

"No, sir. It was just a minor thing, and it was all straightened out that same day. I don't think anybody even knew about it except Mr. Grimes, Captain Hull, and me."

Lawson smiled. "You mean you didn't brag to the other inmates about getting the best of the guard captain?"

"No, sir!" Starzak said quickly. "Not me, warden. I've got more sense than to *look* for trouble "

Lawson sat thoughtfully for a moment, staring intently at the slight, balding, altogether insignificant convict who sat before him. So, he thought, it was no more than a petty incident; a case of Hull's being in the wrong and an inmate's being in the right. A thing which in itself was nothing at all, but which to Hull was probably of paramount importance. Hull knew that he had been wrong, and he knew that *Starzak* knew. That, Lawson concluded, was probably the whole rub. Hull was as much an old-timer as Starzak; he had been carrying a club as long as Starzak had been wearing a number. He was, as young Stiles pointed out, a throwback to the sweatbox days; the days when a guard was *always* right, a convict *always* wrong—the old days, when convict riots were put down by shotguns and blackjacks.

Lawson sighed quietly and closed the manila folder on his desk. "Well, Starzak, I think that will be all. I appreciate your frankness and I'm certain what you've told me will be of value in getting our institution back in proper order. Thank you."

Lawson pressed a button on his desk to let the reception guard know that Starzak was leaving.

The warden had his second staff meeting at the end of the day on Wednesday. Once again Captain Hull, the three guard lieutenants, and Deputy Warden Roger Stiles sat in an arc of chairs facing his desk.

"I won't keep you gentlemen long," Lawson said for the benefit of the two lieutenants who were off shift. He laid his pipe aside and shuffled through the reports which had been submitted to him the previous day. "I've gone over the situation summaries on the cellblocks," he said, "and I think they are very well done. The suggestions they contain for general security improvement and protection against future riot incidents are particularly good. After some additional study I'm certain we'll want to implement most if not all of the recommendations." He laid the reports aside and referred to a note pad. "What's the status of the eight men barricaded in the shoe shop?"

"They're out, warden," said Stiles. He could not resist a glance at Hull. "They came out voluntarily, and there was no damage to the shop machinery."

"Where are the eight men?"

"Isolation."

"All right."

He made a checkmark on the note pad and turned to Hull. "I understand that the hunger strike in C-Six has been resolved."

"Yes, sir," said Hull. "Your idea of using steam carts worked just fine. At the morning meal today there were only three men on the tier still refusing to eat. We've removed them to Isolation, so we now have all of C Block on the same routine as the other two cellblocks."

"How's the atmosphere in the blocks?" Lawson asked. "How does it *feel* to you?"

"Quiet," Hull said with the confidence of his years. "I'd say the spark is gone."

"You don't think it could flare up again?"

"I think it would take something big to do it."

"What kind of something big?"

Hull shrugged. "Guard killing a con; something on that order."

"I'm sure nothing *that* serious is likely to happen," Roger Stiles said dryly.

"I wouldn't be *too* sure," Hull replied, looking at him coldly. "It's happened four times in four different prisons in the past year. A con is sent for by an officer, or maybe asks permission to see the officer; he's alone with the officer in a block room or guard office; out of the blue he comes unglued and jumps the officer; the officer guns him." He leaned slightly toward Stiles. "It could happen any time, deputy warden. Any time at all."

"Well," Lawson cut in, "let's assume that nothing of that magnitude will occur. Barring any such serious incident, you are of the opinion that our riot *is* over."

"Yes, sir," Hull admitted quietly.

"Very well." Lawson made another checkmark on the pad and turned to the guard lieutenants. "If all goes well tonight and tomorrow, suspend the early lockup tomorrow night and restore full recreational privileges, including the gymnasium and the tier television sets. Restrict all cellblock movement to the tiers, however, and instruct all tier guards to stay inside the tier control rooms; I want no guards on the gunwalk until after lockup. Understood?"

"Yes, sir," the three lieutenants said in broken unison.

"Good." Lawson's fingers commenced drumming. "As for the men in Isolation, keep them there until we can review their offenses individually. We'll begin that tomorrow." He glanced at his watch. "That's all for now, I think. Captain Hull, would you mind staying a moment longer?"

Roger Stiles and the lieutenants rose and left the office. Hull, his jaw tightening defensively, remained behind.

"Hull," Lawson began when they were along, "I've done some checking into your theory regarding Ralph Starzak's connection with the riot, and very frankly I can't find any basis for it—"

"You aren't likely to, either," Hull said. "Starzak's a smart cookie."

"He could be the smartest cookie in the whole jar and still not get away with *everything*," Lawson said pointedly. "Isn't there anyone in the entire institution who can support your claim?"

"My lieutenants—" Hull began, but Lawson shook his head firmly.

"You know better than that, Hull. Your lieutenants would simply be giving lip service to your position. Surely there must be someone else, in some other department of the prison. How about the hospital personnel, the civilian shop foremen, the volunteer teachers—?"

"They don't know anything," Hull grumbled. "All they do is work here; they don't have to *run* the place."

"What you're saying then is that you can't produce an independent opinion to corroborate your own. You can't *prove* that Ralph Starzak is anything worse than a long-term con who occasionally stretches a regulation like any other long-term con."

"Are you saying I need proof? Proof to throw a con like Starzak in the hole?"

"That's exactly what I'm saying—not only regarding Starzak but every other inmate in here. We can't teach honesty unless we practice it."

Hull sat back and pursed his lips thoughtfully. "I thought you were here to *tighten* security," he said. "You talk like you're planning to pamper these hoodlums."

"I don't intend to pamper anyone," Lawson said coolly, "inmates or guards." He stood up behind the desk and began to pack his briefcase. "I think we've discussed this particular matter as much as we need to, captain. If you can develop any evidence to support your opinion of Starzak, I'll be happy to review it; if not, please see to it that he is accorded the same treatment as any other inmate. And while we're on the subject of treatment, you may as well advise your lieutenants, and pass it on down through the guard ranks, that I will not tolerate harassment or maltreatment in any form as long as I am in charge of this institution. Any breach of that rule will result in immediate suspension and charges before the civil service board. Is that understood?"

"Yes, sir." Hull had risen now also. He watched quietly as Lawson closed and snapped the catch on his briefcase.

"You know, Hull," the warden said, coming around the desk, "you only have four more years before you're eligible for an early pension. In light of the continuing changes in prison policies and administration, you might do well to consider taking it and finding another line of work." He paused and put a not unfriendly hand on Hull's shoulder. "I don't mean to sound harsh, Hull, it's just that some men don't adjust to change as well as others. You're a . . . well, a *keeper* of men; Stiles and I, on the other hand, look upon ourselves as rehabilitators, remakers of men. You were valuable in your day, Hull, but I'm afraid your day is nearly over." He gripped Hull's shoulder once and removed his hand. "I hope you won't take any of this personally."

"No," Hull said quietly. "No, I won't." He followed Lawson out of the office, through the reception room, and into the hall. They passed out of the administration building and down half a dozen concrete steps to the warden's private parking space. Lawson put his briefcase in the car and got behind the wheel.

"You play it smart, Hull," he advised. "Stop trying to break guys like Starzak. If they become problems, leave them to Stiles and me. You just ride out those four years and collect that early pension."

Lawson backed the car out and swung it in a slow arc toward the personnel gate. Hull stood next to the empty parking space and watched him go. After a moment, one of his lieutenants, Finer, who was on night duty, came out of the building and stood beside him.

"Captain?" he said. His voice carried a hint of nervousness.

"Yeah?" Hull answered without looking at him.

"Do you think the new warden's right? Do you think the riot *is* all over?"

"Probably," Hull replied. "Unless something happens like I said inside.

Unless a con gets killed or something like that."

Finer nodded. He was visibly relieved. "Well, like the deputy warden said, that's not likely to happen."

"No," Hull said tonelessly. "No, that's not likely to happen." He looked at Finer. "Made your rounds yet?"

"Just on my way now."

"What order are they in tonight?"

Finer took a card from his shirt pocket. "B Block, then A, and C last."

Hull glanced at his watch. "I'll meet you over in the dining hall when you're finished. We'll have a cup."

"Sure thing, captain," Finer said.

Hull turned back to the concrete steps as Finer started across the yard. He climbed the steps slowly and reentered the administration building. Walking along the hall, he glanced to his right and to his left to see if any of the clerical offices were still occupied; he found they were not. He ignored the warden's office, knowing no one was left there, and came to the closed door of the deputy warden's office. He paused and knocked briefly, then opened the door. Sticking his head in, he saw that Stiles too had gone for the day. The administration building—except for himself—was deserted.

Hull walked farther down the hall to his own office. Entering, he sat at his desk. He waited exactly fifteen minutes, until he was sure Lieutenant Finer had completed his inspection of B Block; then he called the B Block guard sergeant.

"This is Captain Hull," he said. "Have Ralph Starzak, Number 1172307, brought to my office."

The guard who escorted Ralph Starzak to Hull's office was one of the new probationary men whom the captain barely knew. He and Starzak entered and stood before Hull's desk. Presently Hull looked up. He gave Starzak a cursory glance, then reached for the inmate receival slip the young guard was holding.

"No need to wait," he said as he signed the slip. "I'm going over that way in a few minutes; I'll take him back myself."

"Yes, sir," the young guard said. He took the slip back and touched the brim of his cap in an informal salute.

"Close the door as you leave, please."

"Yes, sir." The young guard left and closed the door behind him.

In the quiet that remained in the office, Ralph Starzak and Hull locked eyes for a brief moment across the desk. Then, very casually, Hull opened the bottom drawer and took out a bottle of whisky and a glass tumbler. He poured a double shot into the tumbler and pushed it across the desk. Starzak grabbed it eagerly and bolted it down. Then he sighed heavily and slumped into a chair.

"I *needed* that," he said.

"I figured." Hull grunted, then capped the bottle and put it back into the drawer.

Starzak leaned forward and put the glass on the desk. "Okay," he said tensely, "let's have it."

"You can relax," Hull said. "Our new warden is a reformer. He's going to be too busy rehabilitating people to pay any attention to prison rackets."

"You're sure?" Starzak asked. "I mean, we've got a nice thing going for us in here—"

"Of course I'm sure," Hull said easily. He rose and walked to the window, from which he could see the lighted cellblocks, the guard towers, the yard, the wall. He looked out on it, knowing that it was his domain. "You don't have to tell me we've got a good thing going for us, Ralph; I *know* we've got a good thing going for us." He put an expensive cigar between his lips and lighted it. He took a deep, expansive drag. "We've got two thousand cons in here," he said reflectively, "and every day of every week at least half of them kick in fifteen cents to a quarter for one thing or another. The little luxuries of life—pressed dungarees; a commissary pass; a book reserved in the library; an extra outgoing letter; a second scoop of ice cream at Sunday dinner; a full tobacco ration instead of sweepings from the floor. Just the little things that make life in here at least bearable."

Hull turned his back to the window and faced Starzak. He smiled around the cigar. "Fifteen cents to a quarter a day, Ralph. Sounds like chicken feed, doesn't it. But how much does it come to? From all sources, how much?"

Starzak shrugged. "We make a hundred and eighty, two hundred a day, on the average."

"Right. And you and I split a hundred a day, and use what's left to pay off the inmate librarian and the inmate dining hall workers and the inmate commissary clerks and whoever else needs paying off. But first," he reached over and hit the desk solidly with his open palm, "first, my friend, you and I, we take our hundred, right?"

"Sure. Right," said Starzak. He shrugged again. "I mean, why shouldn't we? After all, we engineered this scheme, we set it up—"

"Exactly," said Hull. "It's our baby and we get the cream. Fourteen years we've been working this joint; fourteen long years." He smiled again. "Do you know how much money we've got in our Swiss bank account now, Ralph? Better than *three hundred thousand dollars!* Why, we make a thousand dollars a month in interest alone." He removed the cigar from his mouth. "In four years, Ralph, when you finish your time and I apply for my stinking early pension, we'll have close to half a million dollars."

"If this new warden doesn't start getting wise," Starzak said, "like the old one did."

"If he does," Hull's smile faded, "we'll get rid of him just like we did the last one. We'll pull another riot; and anyone who's cooperated with him, given him information, will get what's coming to him during the rioting—just like the two big-mouths we got rid of during the riot we just had." Viciously Hull crushed out the cigar in his ashtray. "*We* are running this joint, Ralph; you and me! And nobody is going to interfere. I haven't devoted fourteen years of my life to this setup for nothing." He snatched up Starzak's glass and put it in the drawer with the whiskey. "No do-good warden or anybody else is going to undo what I've spent fourteen years building," he said self-righteously. He closed the drawer and reached for his hat. "Come on, I'll take you back to the block."

The two men left the office and walked side by side down the long corridor. They went outside and down the concrete steps and started across the yard. Hull took a deep breath and looked up at the sky.

"Pleasant night," he said casually.

"Yeah," Starzak agreed, also looking up. "Lots of stars. When you're a con, it's nice to have nights with lots of stars. Gives you something to look at after the cell lights go out."

"I never thought of that," Hull said. "That's interesting, Ralph."

They continued walking together across the broad prison yard until finally they were just two darkly shadowed figures and it was impossible to tell them apart.

Nice Guy

by Richard Deming

We got the case instead of the Robbery Squad, because when somebody gets hurt or killed during a holdup, it's Homicide's baby. The place was a small jewelry store in the eight hundred block of Franklin Avenue. All the shops in that area are small, mostly one- or two-man businesses. The jewelry store was bracketed by a pawnshop on one side of it and a one-man barber shop on the other.

Gilt lettering on the plate-glass window read "Bruer and Benjamin, Jewelers." A squad car was parked in front and a muscular young cop in uniform stood on the sidewalk before the shop door. A few bystanders were clustered before the pawnshop and barber shop, but the area in front of the jewelry store had been cleared.

I didn't recognize the cop, but he knew me. He touched his cap, said, "Hi, sergeant," and moved aside to let me pass.

Inside, the store was long and narrow, with display cases on either side and with only about a six-foot-wide aisle between them. There was another short display case at the rear of the room, with an open door beyond it.

Another uniformed cop, this one of about my vintage, was inside the store. I knew him. He was a twenty-year veteran named Phil Ritter, and also a sergeant.

I said, "Morning, Phil."

He said, "How are you, Sod?" then jerked his thumb toward the rear display case. "Victim's lying back there."

I nodded, then looked at the other occupant of the place, a mousy little man of about sixty who stood near by with an expression of numbed shock on his face.

"Witness," Ritter said briefly.

I nodded again and continued on back to the rear of the place. There was a space on either side of the rear counter. I walked behind it to look down at the still figure on the floor. The man lay on his left side with his knees drawn up in a fetal position. He was lean and thin-faced, with long sideburns and a hairline mustache which made him resemble the villain of some mid-Victorian melodrama. I guessed he had been in his late forties.

His right arm blocked the view of his chest, but a thin trickle of blood running from beneath the arm indicated that he had a hole in it. There wasn't much blood, suggesting he had died almost instantly.

I came back around the counter and asked Sergeant Ritter, "Doctor look at him?"

"Just enough to verify he was dead. A Dr. Vaughan in the next block. Mr. Bruer here called him." He nodded toward the little man. "He had to go back to his office, but he said you could contact him there if you want. He also said to tell you he didn't move the body."

"Good."

I looked at the little man. He was only about five feet six and weighed possibly a hundred and twenty-five pounds. He had thinning gray hair, wore steel-rimmed glasses and the expression of a frightened rabbit.

I've been accused of intimidating witnesses with my sour manner. This one looked so easily intimidated that I deliberately made my voice as pleasant as possible when I said, "I'm Sergeant Sod Harris of the Homicide Squad. Your name is Bruer?"

"Yes, sir," he said in a shaky voice. "Fred Bruer. I'm one of the partners in the jewelry store."

"He was the other one?" I asked, nodding toward the rear.

"Yes, sir. Andrew Benjamin. This is awful. We've been business partners for ten years."

"Uh-huh," I said. "I know this has been a shock to you, Mr. Bruer, but we'll do the best we can to get the person who killed your partner. You were here when it happened?"

"Yes, sir. It was me he held up. I was out front here and Andy was back in the workshop. I had just made up our weekly bank deposit—I always go to the bank on Friday morning—and was just drawing the strings of the leather bag I carry the deposit in, when this fellow came in and pulled a gun on me. I guess he must have been watching us for some time and knew our routine. Casing, they call it, don't they?"

"Uh-huh," I said. "What makes you think he had cased you?"

"He seemed to know what was in the bag, because he said, 'I'll take that, mister.' I gave it to him without argument. Then he came behind

     ALFRED HITCHCOCK'S ANTHOLOGY

the counter where I was, emptied the register there into the bag, then went behind the other counter and did the same with that register."

I glanced both ways and saw identical cash registers centered against the walls behind each counter. "Which counter were you behind?" I asked.

He pointed to the one to the right as you faced the door. "I can tell you exactly how much he got, sergeant."

"Oh?" I said. "How?"

"I have a duplicate deposit slip for the cash and checks that were in the bag, and there was exactly fifty dollars in each register in addition to that. That's the change we start off with in each register, and we hadn't yet had a customer. We'd only been open for business about thirty seconds when the bandit walked in. I always make up the deposit before we unlock the door Friday mornings."

"I see. Well, you can hold the figure for the moment. First, get on with what happened. How'd he happen to shoot your partner?"

"I think he just got rattled. He was backing toward the door with the deposit bag in his hand when Andy suddenly appeared from the back room. Andy didn't even know a holdup was in progress. I imagine he came out to take over the front because he knew I would be leaving for the bank at any minute. But he opened the workshop door and stepped out so abruptly, he startled the bandit. The man shot him and fled."

Typical, I thought sourly. It's that kind of skittishness that makes cops regard armed robbers as the most dangerous of all criminals. They're all potential murderers.

I asked, "What did this jerk look like?"

"He was about forty years old and kind of long and lanky. I would guess about six feet tall and a hundred and seventy-five pounds. He had a thin white scar running from the left corner of his mouth clear to the lobe of his left ear, and he had a large, hairy mole here." He touched the center of his right cheek. "His complexion was dark, like a gypsy's, he had straight, black, rather greasy hair and a rather large hooked nose. I would know him again anywhere."

"I guess you would," I said, surprised by the detail of the description. Witnesses are seldom so observant. "How was he dressed?"

"In tan slacks, a tan leather jacket, and a tan felt hat with the brim turned down in front and up in back. And oh, yes, on the back of the hand he held the gun in—" he paused to consider, then said with an air of surprised recollection, "his left hand, now that I think of it—there was the tattoo of a blue snake coiled around a red heart."

"You *are* observant," I said, then gave Phil Ritter an inquiring glance.

"We put the description on the air soon as we got here," Ritter said. "Mr. Bruer didn't mention the tattoo or that the bandit was left-handed before, though."

"Better go radio in a supplementary report," I suggested. "Maybe this one will be easier than the run-of-the-mill. The guy certainly ought to be easy to identify."

I was beginning to feel a lot more enthusiastic about this case than I had when the lieutenant sent me out on it. Generally you find almost nothing to work on, but here we had Fred Bruer's excellent description of the bandit.

According to figures compiled by the FBI, eighty percent of the homicides in the United States are committed by relatives, friends or acquaintances of the victims, which gives you something to work on, but in a typical stickup kill, some trigger-happy punk puts a bullet in a store clerk or customer he never saw before in his life. Most times your only clue is a physical description, usually vague and, if there is more than one witness, maybe contradictory. Too, you can almost bank on it that the killer was smart enough to drop the gun off some bridge into deep water.

While Phil Ritter was outside radioing in the additions to the bandit's description, I asked Bruer if he had noticed what kind of gun the robber used. He said it was a blue steel revolver, but he couldn't judge what caliber because he wasn't very familiar with guns.

I asked him if the bandit had touched anything which might have left fingerprints.

"The two cash registers," Bruer said. "He punched the no-sale button on each."

Ritter came back in, trailed by Art Ward of the crime lab, who was carrying his field kit and a camera.

"Morning, Sod," Ward greeted me. "What sort of gruesome chore do you have for me this time?"

"Behind the rear counter," I said, jerking a thumb that way. "Then dust the two cash registers for prints, with particular attention to the no-sale buttons."

"Sure," Art said.

He set down his field lab kit and carried his camera to the rear of the store. While he was taking pictures of the corpse from various angles, I checked the back room. It was a small workshop for watch and jewelry repairing. Beyond it was a bolted and locked rear door with a key in the inside lock. I unbolted it, unlocked it, pushed open the door, and peered out into an alley lined with trash cans behind the various small businesses facing Franklin Avenue.

I wasn't really looking for anything in particular. Over the years I had just gotten in the habit of being thoroughly nosy. I closed the door again and relocked and rebolted it.

Back in the main room I asked Sergeant Ritter if he had turned up any other witnesses from among nearby merchants or clerks before I got there.

"The barber just west of here and the pawnbroker on the other side both think they heard the shot," Ritter said. "As usual, they thought it was just a backfire, and didn't even look outdoors. Nobody came to investigate until our squad car got here, but that brought out a curious crowd. Nobody we talked to but the two I mentioned heard or saw anything, but we didn't go door-to-door. We just talked to people who gathered around."

I said, "While I'm checking out this barber and pawnbroker, how about you hitting all the places on both sides of the street in this block to see if anyone spotted the bandit either arriving or leaving here?"

Ritter shrugged. "Sure, Sod."

I called to Art Ward that I would be back shortly and walked out with Sergeant Ritter. Ritter paused to talk to his young partner for a moment, and I went to the pawnshop next door.

The proprietor, who was alone, was a benign looking man of about seventy named Max Jacobs. He couldn't add anything to what he had already told Phil Ritter except that he placed the time he had heard what he took to be a truck backfire at exactly a minute after nine. He explained that his twenty-year-old nephew, who worked for him, hadn't showed up for work, and the old man kept checking the clock to see how late he was. It was now nearly ten, and the boy still had neither appeared nor phoned in, and his home phone didn't answer.

"What's your nephew's name?" I asked.

"Herman. Herman Jacobs. He's my brother's boy."

"Mr. Bruer next door know him?"

Jacobs looked puzzled.

"Of course. Herman's worked for me ever since he got out of high school."

That was a silly tack to take anyway, I realized. The jeweler had described the bandit as around forty, and Jacobs' nephew was half that age.

"Following the shot, you didn't see or hear anything at all?" I asked. "Like somebody running past your front window, for instance?"

The elderly pawnbroker shook his head. "I wasn't looking that way. When I wasn't watching the clock, I was trying to phone Herman, that good-for-nothing bum."

There didn't seem to be any more I could get out of him. I thanked him and headed for the door.

"How's poor Fred taking it?" he asked to my back.

Pausing, I turned. "Mr. Bruer, you mean? He's still a bit shaken up."

Jacobs sighed. "Such a nice man. Always doing good for people. Ask anybody in the neighborhood, nobody will tell you a thing against Fred Bruer. A man with a real heart."

"That so?" I said.

"Only thing is, he's such an easy touch. Gives credit to anybody. Now, Mr. Benjamin was another proposition entirely. I don't like to speak ill of the dead, but there was a cold fish."

It intrigued me that he was on a first-name basis with the surviving jewelry-store proprietor, but referred to the deceased younger partner as *Mr. Benjamin*. Perhaps he hadn't known the younger man as long. I decided to ask.

"Have you known Mr. Bruer longer than Mr. Benjamin?"

He looked surprised. "No, of course not. They opened for business together next door about ten years back. I met them both the same day."

"But you were on friendlier terms with Mr. Bruer, was that it?"

"Now how did you know that?" he inquired with rather flattering admiration for my deductive ability. "Yes, as a matter of fact. But everybody's a friend of Fred. Nobody liked Mr. Benjamin very much."

"What was the matter with him?" I asked.

"He was a vindictive man. When he had a little spat with somebody, he was never satisfied just to forget it afterward. He had to have his revenge—like his trouble with Amelio Lapaglia, the barber on the other side of the jewelry shop. Last time haircut prices went up, Mr. Benjamin refused to pay, they had an argument, and Amelio threatened to have him arrested. Mr. Benjamin finally paid, but he wasn't content just to

ALFRED HITCHCOCK'S ANTHOLOGY

stop going there for haircuts after that. He did things like phoning the police that Amelio was overparked, and the health department to complain that he had no lid on his garbage can out back. Actually I think Mr. Benjamin stole the lid, but Amelio got fined for violating the health laws."

I made a face. "One of those. I've had that kind of neighbor."

"I don't think even Fred really liked him, although he was always making excuses for him. I doubt their partnership would have lasted so long if they hadn't been brothers-in-law," he added matter-of-factly.

I gave him a surprised look. "They were brothers-in-law?"

"Sure. Mr. Benjamin is—was married to Fred's baby sister. She's not a baby now, of course. She's about forty, but she's twenty-one years younger than Fred. She was just an infant when their parents died, and he raised her. She's more like a daughter to him than a sister. He never married himself, so Paula and her two kids are all the family he has. He's absolutely crazy about the baby."

"The baby?"

"Paula had another baby just a couple of years ago. She also has a boy around twenty in the army."

The phone at the rear of the pawnshop rang. As Mr. Jacobs went to answer it, I wondered if anyone had bothered to phone the widow that she was a widow.

The pawnbroker lifted the phone and said, "Jacobs' Small Loans." After a pause his voice raised in pitch and he said, "Where are you, and what's your excuse this time?" There was another pause, then, "That's supposed to be an excuse? You get here fast as you can! You hear?"

He slammed down the phone and came back to where I stood near the door. "My nephew," he said in an indignant tone. "He stayed overnight with a friend and overslept, he says. More likely he was in an all-night poker game and just got home. Good for nothing, he'll be, all day."

I made a sympathetic noise, thanked him again, and left.

The young cop was still guarding the entrance to the jewelry store when I went by, but the crowd of curious onlookers had thinned considerably. It wouldn't disperse completely until the body was carried away, though, I knew. There are always a few morbid people in every crowd who will hang around forever on the chance of seeing a corpse.

Near the end of the block on this side of the street I spotted Phil Ritter coming from one shop and entering another. At his apparent rate of progress it looked as though it wouldn't take him long to finish both sides.

Amelio Lapaglia was cutting a man's hair all the time I talked to him. He had been cutting hair when he heard what he assumed was a backfire, too, he said. He hadn't noticed the time, but it had to be just after nine, because he had just opened for business and had just started on his first customer.

His customer must have heard the shot, too, he said in answer to my question, but neither of them had mentioned it.

"Aroun' here trucks go by all day long," he said. "You hear *bang* like a gun maybe two, three times a day."

He hadn't noticed anyone pass his window immediately after the shot, he said, but then he had been concentrating on cutting hair.

I didn't bother to ask him about his feud with the dead man, because it had no bearing on the case. He certainly hadn't been the bandit.

When I got back to the jewelry store, Art Ward had finished both his picture taking and his dusting of the cash registers. He reported there were no fingerprints on either register good enough to lift, which didn't surprise me.

I told the lab technician he could go, then went back to give the corpse a more detailed examination than I had before. Aside from discovering that the bullet hole was squarely in the center of his chest, I didn't learn anything new from my examination.

Then I asked Bruer for the duplicate of his bank deposit slip. After adding the hundred dollars which had been in the registers to the amount shown on the slip, the sum stolen came to seven hundred and forty dollars in cash and two hundred and thirty-three in checks. The jeweler said this represented a full week's gross receipts.

From Fred Bruer I got the phone number of the doctor who had examined the body and phoned to ask him to mail a report to Dr. Swartz, the coroner's physician. After that I had nothing to do but wait for someone to come for the body and for Phil Ritter to finish.

While waiting I asked Bruer if he had phoned his sister.

He looked startled.

"I—I never even thought of it."

"Probably just as well," I said. "The phone isn't a very satisfactory way to break news like this. She should be told personally. I'll handle it for you, if you want. I have to see her anyway."

"You do?" he asked in surprise.

"It's routine in homicide cases to contact the next of kin, even when it's open-and-shut like this one. What's her address?"

He hesitated for a moment before saying, "She lives down on the south side, but she's staying with me in my apartment on North Twentieth at the moment. This is going to hit her awful hard, sergeant, because she and Andy were having a little squabble. It's terrible to have somebody close to you die when things aren't quite right. You have trouble forgiving yourself for having a fight at that particular time."

"Uh-huh," I said. "I understand." I asked for his address and wrote it in my notebook.

A couple of morgue attendants came for the body before Phil Ritter completed his survey, but he returned only minutes later.

"Nothing," he reported. "Nobody saw the bandit come in here, leave here, or walking or running along the street. If anyone aside from the two next-door neighbors heard the shot, he paid no attention to it and can't remember it."

There was nothing more to be done at the scene of the crime. I dismissed Sergeant Ritter and his partner, and took off myself.

The apartment on North Twentieth was on the first floor of a neat, modern brick building. A slim, attractive brunette of about forty answered the door.

I took off my hat. "Mrs. Benjamin?"

"Yes."

I showed my badge. "Sergeant Sod Harris of the police, ma'am. May I come in?"

She looked startled. "Police? What—" Then she stepped aside and said, "Certainly. Please do."

I moved into a comfortably furnished front room and she closed the door behind me. A plump, pretty little girl about two years old sat in the center of the floor playing with a doll. A redhaired man in his mid-forties, with wide shoulders and a homely but cheerful face, sat on a sofa making himself at home. He had his shoes off, his suit coat was draped over the back of the sofa, his tie was loosened, and his collar was open. A glass with some beer in it and a half-empty bottle of beer sat on the cocktail table before the sofa.

The man rose to his feet. The little girl gave me a sunny smile and said, "Hi, man."

I smiled back. "Hi, honey."

The woman said, "Robert Craig, Sergeant—"

"Harris," I said. "Sod Harris."

Robert Craig held out his hand. He had a firm grip.

"And this is my daughter, Cindy," Mrs. Benjamin said proudly, looking at the child almost with adoration.

I smiled at the little girl again and got a big return smile. I could understand how her uncle would be crazy about her. I was a little crazy about her myself, and I had just met her.

Mrs. Benjamin said, "What can I do for you, sergeant?"

"I'm afraid I have some bad news, ma'am." I glanced at the child. "Maybe she'd better not hear it."

Paula Benjamin paled. The redhaired man said, "Let's go see if your other dolls are asleep yet, Cindy." He scooped up the little girl and carried her from the room.

Mrs. Benjamin said, "My—it isn't my brother, is it?"

"No," I replied. "Your husband."

Her color returned and I got the curious impression that she was relieved. "Oh. What happened?"

Her reaction was hardly what Fred Bruer had led me to expect. She sounded as though she didn't particularly care what had happened. I saw no point in trying to break it gently, so I let her have it in a lump.

I said, "The jewelry store was held up this morning. Your brother is unharmed, but the bandit shot your husband. He's dead."

She blinked, but she didn't turn pale again. She merely said, "Oh," then lapsed into silence.

Robert Craig came back into the room alone. The woman looked at him and said, "Andy's dead."

A startled expression crossed the redhead's face, then he actually smiled.

"Well, well," he said. "That solves the Cindy problem."

Paula Benjamin stared at him. "How can you think of that now?"

"You expect me to burst into tears?" he asked. He looked at me. "Sorry if I seem callous, sergeant, but Andy Benjamin was hardly a friend of mine. He had me named co-respondent in a divorce suit. What did he die of?"

"A holdup man shot him," I said and glanced at the woman.

Her face had turned fire red. "Did you have to announce that?" she said to Craig. "Sergeant Harris isn't interested in our personal affairs."

Craig shrugged. "You and your brother! Never let the neighbors see your dirty linen. Everybody was going to know after it broke in the papers anyway."

"It won't break in the papers now!" she snapped at him.

Then her attention was distracted by little Cindy toddling back into the room, carrying two dolls. Her mother swept her up into her arms.

"Oh, honey!" she said, kissing her. "You're going to get to stay with Mommie forever and ever!" I thought it was a good time to excuse myself. I told both Craig and Mrs. Benjamin it was nice to have met them, traded a final smile with Cindy, and left.

By now it was noon. I stopped for lunch, then afterward, instead of checking in at headquarters, I went to the courthouse and looked up the divorce case of *Benjamin vs Benjamin*.

Andrew Benjamin's complaint was on file, but as yet an answer hadn't been filed by Paula Benjamin. The disagreement between the two was more than the "little squabble" Fred Bruer had mentioned, and Andrew Benjamin's reaction had been characteristically vindictive.

The dead man's affidavit was in the usual legal jargon, but what it boiled down to was that he and a private detective had surprised his wife and Robert Craig together in a motel room and had gotten camera evidence. Divorce was asked on the ground of adultery, with no alimony to be paid the defendant, and with a request for sole custody of little Cindy to be granted the father. Benjamin's vindictiveness showed in his further request that the mother be barred from even having visitation rights on the ground that she was of unfit moral character to be trusted in her daughter's presence. As evidence, he alleged previous adulteries with a whole series of unnamed men and charged that Paula was an incurable nymphomaniac.

When I left the courthouse, I sat in my car and brooded for some time. Fred Bruer's remarkable powers of observation took on a different significance in the light of what I had just learned. Maybe his detailed description of the bandit hadn't been from observation after all, but merely from imagination.

I drove back to the ten hundred block of Franklin Avenue. The jewelry store was locked and there was a "Closed" sign on the front door.

I went into the pawnshop. A pale, fat boy of about twenty who looked as though he were suffering from a hangover was waiting on a customer. Mr. Jacobs glanced out from the back room as I entered, then moved forward to meet me. I waited for him just inside the front door, so that we would be far enough from the other two to avoid being overheard.

I said, "Mr. Jacobs, do you happen to know if the partners next door ever kept a gun around the place?"

He first looked surprised by the question, then his expression became merely thoughtful. "Hmm," he said after ruminating. "Mr. Benjamin it was. Yes, it was a long time ago, but I'm sure it was Mr. Benjamin, not Fred. Right after they opened for business Mr. Benjamin bought a gun from me. To keep in the store in case of robbery, he said. Yes, it was Mr. Benjamin, I'm sure."

"Wouldn't you still have a record?" I asked.

"Of course," he said in a tone of mild exasperation at himself. "It won't even be very far back in the gun book. We don't sell more than a dozen guns a year."

He went behind the counter and took a ledger from beneath it. I moved over to the other side of the counter as he leafed through it. The fat young man, whom I took to be nephew Herman, was examining a diamond ring through a jeweler's loupe for the customer.

Max Jacobs kept running his index finger down a column of names on each page, flipping to the next page and repeating the process. Finally the finger came to a halt.

"Here it is," he said. "September 10th, ten years ago. Andrew J. Benjamin, 1726 Eichelberger Street. A .38 caliber Colt revolver, serial number 231840."

I took out my notebook and copied this information down.

"Why did you want to know?" the old man asked curiously.

I gave my standard vague answer. "Just routine."

I thanked him and left before he could ask any more questions. The customer was counting bills as I walked out, and nephew Herman was sealing the ring in a small envelope.

Amateur murderers usually don't know enough to dispose of murder weapons, but just in case, when I got back to headquarters I arranged for a detail to go sift all the trash in the cans in the alley behind the jewelry store.

They didn't find anything.

There was nothing more I could do until I got the report on what caliber bullet had killed Andrew Benjamin. I tabled the case until the next day.

The following morning I found on my desk the photographs Art Ward had taken, a preliminary postmortem report and a memo from the lab that the bullet recovered from the victim's body was a .38 caliber lead slug and was in good enough shape for comparison purposes if I could turn up the gun from which it was fired. There was also a leather bag with a drawstring and an attached note from the local postmaster explaining that it had turned up in a mailbox two blocks from the jewelry store. The bag contained the original of the deposit slip of which I already had the duplicate, two hundred and thirty-three dollars in checks, and no cash.

I had a conference with the lieutenant, then together we went across the street to the third floor of the Municipal Courts Building and had another conference with the circuit attorney. As a result of this conference, all three of us went to see the judge of the Circuit Court for Criminal Causes.

When we left there, I had three search warrants in my pocket.

Back in the squad room I tried to phone the Bruer and Benjamin jewelry store, but got no answer. I tried Fred Bruer's apartment number and caught him there. He said he didn't plan to open for business again until after his partner's funeral.

"I want to take another look at your store," I told him. "Can you meet me there?"

"Of course," he said. "Right now?"

"Uh-huh."

He said he would leave at once. As Police Headquarters was closer to the store than his apartment, I arrived first, though. He kept me waiting about five minutes.

After he had unlocked the door and led me inside, I got right to the point. I said, "I want to see the .38 revolver you keep here."

Fred Bruer looked at me with what I suspected was simulated puzzlement. "There's no gun here, sergeant."

"Your brother-in-law bought one next door right after you opened for business, Mr. Bruer. He told Mr. Jacobs it was for protection against robbers."

"Oh, that," Bruer said with an air of enlightenment. "He took that home with him years ago. I objected to its being around. Guns make me nervous."

I gave him the fishy eye. "Mind if I look?"

"I don't see why it's necessary," he said haughtily. "I told you there's no gun here."

Regretfully I produced the search warrant. He didn't like it, but there was nothing he could do about it. I went over the place thoroughly. There was no gun there.

"I told you he took the gun home," Bruer said in a miffed voice.

"We'll look there if we don't find it at your apartment," I assured him. "We'll try your place first."

"Do you have a search warrant for there, too?" he challenged.

I showed it to him.

I followed his car back to his place. Paula Benjamin and Cindy were no longer there. Bruer said they had returned home last night. I searched the apartment thoroughly, too. There was no gun there.

"Let's take a ride down to your sister's," I suggested. "You can leave your car here and we'll go in mine."

"I suppose you have a warrant for there, too," he said sourly.

"Uh-huh," I admitted.

Paula Benjamin still lived at the same address recorded in the pawnshop gun log, 1726 Eichelberger Street, which is far down in South St. Louis. It was a small frame house of five rooms.

Mrs. Benjamin claimed she knew nothing of any gun her husband had ever owned, and if he had ever brought a revolver home, she had never seen it.

I didn't have to produce my third warrant, because she made no objection to a search. I did just as thorough a job as I had at the other two places. Little Cindy followed me around and helped me look, but neither of us found the gun. It wasn't there.

Paula Benjamin naturally wanted to know what it was all about. Until then, her brother had shown no such curiosity, which led me to believe he already knew. Belatedly, he now added his demand for enlightenment. I suggested that Cindy be excluded from the discussion.

By now it was pushing noon, so Mrs. Benjamin solved that by taking Cindy to the kitchen for her lunch. When she returned to the front room alone, I bluntly explained things to both her and her brother.

After carefully giving Fred Bruer the standard spiel about his constitutional rights, I said, "I reconstruct it this way, Mr. Bruer. You got down to the store early yesterday morning and made out the weekly bank deposit. Only you didn't put any cash in that leather bag; just the deposit slip and the checks. And you didn't put any money in the cash registers. You simply pocketed it. Then you drove two blocks away, dropped the bag into a mailbox, and got back to the store before your brother-in-law arrived for work. I rather suspect you didn't unlock the front door until after you shot him and had hidden the gun, because you wouldn't want to risk having a customer walk in on you. Then you unlocked the door and phoned the police."

Paula Benjamin was staring at me with her mouth open. "You must be crazy," she whispered. "Fred couldn't kill anyone. He's the most soft-hearted man in the world."

"Particularly about you and Cindy," I agreed. "You would be surprised what tigers softhearted men can turn into when their loved ones are threatened. None of your brother's fellow merchants on Franklin, and probably none of your neighbors around here knew what your husband was trying to do to you, because both of you believe in keeping your troubles secret. But I've read your deceased husband's divorce affidavit, Mrs. Benjamin."

Paula Benjamin blinked. She gazed at her brother for reassurance and he managed a smile.

"You know I wouldn't do anything like that, Sis," he said. "The sergeant has simply made a terribly wrong guess." He looked at me challengingly. "Where's the gun I used, sergeant?"

"Probably in the Mississippi River now," I said. "Unfortunately I didn't tumble soon enough to search for it before you had a chance to get rid of it. We can establish by Max Jacobs' gun log that your brother-in-law purchased such a gun, though."

"And took it home years ago, sergeant. Or took it somewhere, Maybe he sold it to another pawnshop."

"I doubt that," I said.

"Prove he didn't."

That was the rub. I couldn't. I took him downtown and a team of three of us questioned him for the rest of the day, but we couldn't shake his story. We had him repeat his detailed description of the imaginary bandit a dozen times, and he never varied it by a single detail.

Finally we had to release him. I drove him home, but the next morning I picked him up again and we started the inquisition all over. About noon, he decided he wanted to call a lawyer, and under the new rules stemming from recent Supreme Court decisions, we either had to let him or release him again.

I knew what would happen in the former event. The lawyer would accuse us of harassing his client and would insist we either file a formal charge or leave him alone. We didn't have sufficient evidence to file a formal charge, and if we refused to leave him alone, his lawyer undoubtedly would get a court injunction to make us.

With all the current talk about police brutality, we didn't need any publicity about harassing a sixty-year-old, undersized, widely esteemed small businessman. We let him go.

I'm in the habit of talking over cases which particularly disturb me with my wife. That evening I unloaded all my frustrations about the Andrew Benjamin case on Maggie.

After listening to the whole story, she said, "I don't see why you're so upset, Sod. Why do you want to see the man convicted of murder anyway?"

I stared at her. "Because he's a murderer."

"But according to your own testimony, the dead man was a thoroughgoing beast," Maggie said reasonably. "What he was attempting to do to that innocent little girl just to obtain vengeance on his wife was criminally vindictive. This Fred Bruer, on the othe hand, you characterize as a thoroughly nice guy who, in general, devotes his life to helping people, and never before harmed a soul."

"You would make a lousy cop," I said disgustedly. "We don't happen to have two sets of laws, one for nice guys and the other for beasts. Sure, Fred Bruer's a nice guy, but do you suggest we give all nice guys a license to kill?"

After thinking this over, she said reluctantly, "I guess not." She sat musing for a time, then finally said, "If he's really as nice a guy as you say, there's one technique you might try. Why don't you shame him into a confession?"

I started to frown at her, then something suddenly clicked in my mind and the frown came out a grin instead. Getting up from my easy chair, I went over and gave her a solid kiss.

"I take back what I said about you being a lousy cop," I told her. "You're a better cop than I am."

At ten the next morning I phoned Fred Bruer. "I have an apology to make, Mr. Bruer," I said. "We've caught the bandit who killed your brother-in-law."

"You what?"

"He hasn't confessed yet, but we're sure he's the man. Can you come down here to make an identification?"

There was a long silence before he said, "I'll be right there, sergeant."

As soon as the little jeweler arrived at headquarters, I took him to the showup room. It was already darkened and the stage lights were on. Lieutenant Wilkins was waiting at the microphone at the rear of the room. I led Bruer close to the stage, where we could see the suspects who would come out at close range. When we were situated, Wilkins called for the lineup to be sent in.

Five men, all of similar lanky build, walked out on the stage. All were dressed in tan slacks and tan leather jackets. When they lined up in a row, you could see by the height markers behind them that they were all within an inch, one way or the other, of six feet.

The first one to walk out on stage was exactly six feet tall. He had straight black, greasy-looking hair, a dark complexion, and a prominent hooked nose. A thin white scar ran from the left corner of his mouth to his left ear and there was a hairy mole in the center of his right cheek. He stood with hands at his sides, the backs facing us. On the back of the left hand was the tattoo of a blue snake wound around a red heart.

I glanced at Fred Bruer. His eyes were literally bugging out.

"Don't try to pick anyone yet," I said in a low voice. "Wait until you hear all the voices." Then I called back to Wilkins, "Okay, lieutenant, and let's hear them."

Lieutenant Wilkins said over the microphone, "Number one step forward."

The dark man with the hooked nose stepped to the edge of the stage.

Wilkins said, "What is your name?"

"Manuel Flores," the man said sullenly.

"Your age?"

"Forty."

There is a standard set of questions asked all suspects at a showup, designed more to let witnesses hear their voices than for gathering information.

But now Lieutenant Wilkins departed from the usual routine.

He said, "Where do you work, Manuel?"

"The Frick Construction Company."

"As what?"

"Just a laborer."

"Are you married, Manuel?"

"Yes."

NICE GUY   121

"Any children?"

"Five."

"Their ages?"

"Maria is thirteen, Manuel, Jr., is ten, Jose is nine, Miguel is six, and Consuelo is two."

"Have you ever been arrested before, Manuel?"

"No."

"Ever been in any kind of trouble?"

"No."

"Okay," Lieutenant Wilkins said. "Step back. Number two step forward."

He went through the same routine with the other four men, but I don't think Fred Bruer was even listening. He kept staring at number one.

When the last of the five had performed, and all of them had been led off the stage, Fred Bruer and I left the showup room and went down one flight to Homicide. He sank into a chair and stared up at me. I remained standing.

"Well?" I said.

The jeweler licked his lips. "I can understand why you picked up that first man, sergeant. He certainly fits the description of the bandit. But he isn't the man, I'm sorry to say."

After gazing at him expressionlessly for a few moments, I gave my head a disbelieving shake. "Your friends along Franklin Avenue and your sister all warned me you were softhearted, Mr. Bruer, but don't be softheaded, too. It's beyond belief that two different men could have such similar appearances, even to that scar, the mole, and the tattoo. On top of that, Manuel Flores is left handed, just like your bandit."

"But he's not the man," he said with a quaver in his voice. "It's just an incredible coincidence."

"Yeah," I said. "So incredible, I don't believe it. You're letting his formerly clean record and his five kids throw you. He has no alibi for the time of the robbery. He told his wife he was going to work that day, but he never showed up. The day after the robbery he paid off a whole flock of bills." I let my voice become sarcastic. "Claims he hit a long-shot horse."

Fred Bruer's voice raised in pitch. "I tell you he really isn't the man!"

"Oh, come off it," I said grumpily. "Are you going to protect a killer just because he has five kids?"

The little jeweler slowly rose to his feet. Drawing himself to his full five feet six, he said with dignity, "Sergeant, I told you that is not the man who shot Andy. If you insist on bringing him to trial, I will swear on the stand that he is not the man."

After studying him moodily, I shrugged. "I think we can make it stick anyway, Mr. Bruer. Once we net the actual culprit in a case like this, we usually manage to get a confession."

He frowned. "What do you mean by that?"

"Manuel Flores isn't as influential a citizen as you are, Mr. Bruer. He's just a poor, uneducated slob and not even a United States citizen yet. He's a Mexican immigrant who only has his first papers. He doesn't know any lawyers to call. We don't have to handle him with kid gloves, like we did you."

"You mean you intend to beat a confession out of him!" Bruer said, outraged.

"Now, who said anything about that?" I inquired. "We never use the third degree around here. We merely use scientific interrogation techniques."

I took his elbow and steered him to the door. "If you decide to cooperate after all, you can let me know, Mr. Bruer. But I don't think your testimony is essential. I would thank you for coming down, but under the circumstances, I don't think you deserve it."

I ushered him out into the hall, said, "See you around, Mr. Bruer," and walked off and left him.

He was still staring after me when I mounted the stairs leading up from third to fourth.

I found lanky Sam Wiggens in the men's room on fourth. He had removed the wig and false nose and was washing off his makeup, including the snake and heart tattoo.

Sam let out the stained water in the bowl and started to draw more. "How'd it go?" he asked.

I shrugged. "I don't think he suspected anything, but it's too early to guess. We should find out just how softhearted he is when I increase the pressure tomorrow."

I let Fred Bruer stew for twenty-four hours and phoned him about eleven the next morning.

"We're not going to need your testimony after all, Mr. Bruer," I said. "Manuel Flores has confessed."

"He didn't do it!" Bruer almost yelled. "You can't do that to an innocent man with five kids!"

"Oh, stop being so softhearted," I told him. "The man's a killer." I hung up on him.

Bruer came into the squad room twenty minutes later. His face was pale but his thin shoulders were proudly squared.

"I want to make a statement, sergeant," he said in a steady voice. "I wish to confess the murder of my brother-in-law."

I pointed to a chair and he seated himself with his back stiffly erect. After phoning for a stenographer, I waited for the familiar glow of triumph I usually feel when a case is finally in the bag.

It didn't come. Over the years, I have trapped suspects into confessions by playing on their greed, their fear, their vindictiveness, and every other base emotion you can think of, but this was the first time I had trapped a murderer through his compassion for others. I could only wonder why I was in this business.

ALFRED HITCHCOCK'S ANTHOLOGY

A Funny Place to Park

by James Holding

I didn't believe the kid at first. Janie, who took care of telephone and reception for us, had brought him in from out front and left him standing in my doorway.

"I want to see the sheriff," he said in a high voice. He had spiky red hair and big freckles on his face and crooked front teeth. I guess he was about ten years old.

I said, "I'm the sheriff, son, what can I do for you?"

He looked me over with serious brown eyes and said, "You ain't the sheriff. The sheriff's fat, I seen his picture in the paper."

Smart kid. I explained that I was the sheriff's deputy, and the sheriff wasn't there, and what could I do for him. Or *must* he see the sheriff in person?

He considered this, then shook his head. "I guess you'll do. I wanted to tell the sheriff about these two men I seen just now."

"What two men?"

"I don't know who they are. They're tied up. With wire around their hands."

I sat up and gave him a really sharp look for the first time. "Wire around their hands?" I said. The kid watched too much TV.

"Yeah. Well, maybe not right around their hands. Around their wrists, kind of. I couldn't exactly tell when I passed them."

"Anyway, they were tied up, is that it?"

He nodded, and his eyes went blank, the way kids' do when they're remembering something. "And they had stuff like adhesive tape across their mouths, too."

"Where was this, son?"

"Out by Donaldson's Crossroads."

That was two or three miles out of town in the middle of flat truck-farming acreage, where State Highway 26 runs into County Line Road.

It was outside the jurisdiction of the town police, all right. Our territory. So I said to the kid, "There's nothing at Donaldson's Crossroads, not even a gas station. You sure that's the place?"

"I live out there, don't I? I pass Donaldson's Crossroads every time I ride into town."

We seemed to be wandering from the subject, but it was a slow day and I had nothing better to do than jaw with the kid. "So you passed it today, is that right?"

"I been telling you. On my bike. And I saw these men all tied up."

"Where were they?"

"In the ditch. By that big pipe that goes under the road."

Some imagination. I nodded as though I believed him. "And you rode past on your bike?"

"Yep."

"Why didn't you stop? Maybe you could have helped them."

He shook his head solemnly. "Oh, no. I ain't supposed to get mixed up with any strange men, my mom says. Any time I'm alone and I see something that looks funny or scares me any, Mom says I should tell the sheriff." He paused, troubled.

"But you ain't the sheriff. He's fatter'n you."

"You already said that, son. How come nobody but you saw these two men, you suppose? Lots of cars go by there."

He shrugged. "I don't know." Then, after a second's thought, "I ride right next to the edge of the road on my bike. I could see down into the ditch."

"The ditch is pretty deep there, is that right? Under the culvert?"

"What's that?"

"The pipe that runs under the road."

"Yeah." He moved his head up and down.

"That's where the men were. In the ditch. All tied up. With stuff over their mouths. Laying down."

He spoke with such earnestess that I almost believed him. But I said sternly, "You kids get a big charge out of playing jokes on the police, don't you? Makes you feel smart. Like on TV when the cops are all so dumb."

He said, "I ain't playing a joke. I'm only doing what Mom told me." There was scorn in his high voice. "Well, I guess that's all. I'll go now." He turned around and started out without a backward glance.

126   ALFRED HITCHCOCK'S ANTHOLOGY

I called after him, "Wait a minute! You want to go out there with me and show me where you saw the men?"

He stopped. "Nope. Can't. I gotta go to the dentist by ten o'clock, my mom says."

"Who's your dentist?"

"Dr. Charles. He's going to fix these teeth." The kid bared his front teeth at me like a tiger yawning. They were crooked, all right.

"What's your name?" I said.

"Donald Start."

"Come back and sit down a minute, will you, Don?" He came back and sat down near my desk, giving our wall clock a worried look. It showed ten minutes to ten.

I picked up my phone and asked Janie to get me Dr. Charles's office on the line. When his nurse answered, I asked her if a Donald Start had an appointment at ten o'clock. She said yes, why, was he canceling? And I said no, he'll be there, and hung up.

Donald's serious and now slightly accusing eyes stayed pinned on me the whole time. When I hung up, he said, "I shoulda told the sheriff. You don't believe me."

I cleared my throat. "Sure I believe you. But you got to admit it sounds crazy. I'll go out there right now and check out your report." I stood up and so did Don. As we started for the door, a train rumbled by on the railroad embankment twenty yards south of our office. It sounded, as usual, like it was going to come busting right through the walls of my room. The ashtray on my desk did a little dance from the vibration.

When we could hear ourselves talk again, I said to Don, "Were these two men you saw still alive when you passed them? Could you tell that?" I *was* taking him seriously now. As far as I was concerned, that call to Dr. Charles's office had turned Don from a practical joker into a dutiful citizen of the county cooperating with the law.

"They were laying pretty still."

"I guess they wouldn't have tapes over their mouths if they were dead," I said. I patted him on the shoulder, man to man. "You can go ahead and go to your dentist now. And thanks for telling me about the men, Don. You did just right. I'll take care of them, don't worry."

"Okay." Now that I believed his story and was taking action, Don sounded more than a little disappointed that he couldn't go back to Donaldson's Crossroads with me. Kids hate to miss any excitement, especially if they're responsible for it, I guess. But Don's mom was obviously the boss. When she said go to the dentist, Don went to the dentist, no matter how many tied-up men he saw lying in the ditch.

I told Janie where I was going and went outside. Don Start was just disappearing on his bike through the arch that carries Front Street under the railroad tracks. I figured if they straightened out those front teeth, the redhead would be a goodlooking kid someday—provided he didn't let his hair grow down to his waist or something.

I was on the early trick that day, been in the office since six that morning, so it was good to get out and stretch my legs for a change. It was a bright cool Saturday in October, and I knew the foliage out in the country was real pretty by then, all splashed with autumn colors. You couldn't tell it in Circleville, though, especially on Front Street where the County Building was, because there wasn't a tree or a bush in sight, and the stores and buildings formed solid ranks on both sides of the street, leading traffic like a funnel down to the railroad embankment and through the underpass.

I walked up Front Street a ways toward where I'd parked my cruiser when I came on duty. We normally use the County Building parking lot, of course, but it doesn't open for business until seven each morning, and has a big steel gate locked across the entrance at night to keep out romantic couples and discourage car thieves who might try to borrow one of the county cars that are left in there at night. Whoever has the early trick in the sheriff's office usually leaves his car on the street.

Mine was hidden behind the big tractor-trailer that had parked right in front of me. The nose of the truck wasn't quite the required twenty feet from our parking lot entrance, I noticed, and I would have mentioned it to the driver, but there was nobody in the cab. Getting morning coffee at the Greek's across the street, probably.

I got in my car, pulled out around the truck, nosed into the parking lot entrance to turn around, and then headed north on Front Street for Donaldson's Crossroads.

The Crossroads looked as deserted as a nagging wife when I got there. It's a T-intersection: Highway 26, an old-fashioned two lane road coming from the Tri-Cities over west of Circleville, dead-ends at our County Line Road there. If you turn south on County Line Road at the intersection, you come to Circleville. If you turn north, you run into the big east-west turnpike to Chicago and New York.

ALFRED HITCHCOCK'S ANTHOLOGY

I turned left onto Highway 26 and drove a hundred yards to the only culvert in sight, where I parked on the shoulder and started to get out. Before I got one foot on the ground, even, I heard a voice yelling from across the road. I crossed over—there wasn't a car in sight—and looked down into the ditch over the edge of the culvert bulkhead.

And there they were, just like the kid said.

Two guys with their wrists tied behind them, lying on their sides, tethered by their wrist wires at ground level to the concrete piers that supported the culvert so they couldn't stand up. They had adhesive tape over their mouths, too, except one of them had managed to scrape one end of his gag loose by rubbing it on the ground, and he was the one who was yelling.

When I stuck my head over the edge of the culvert and he saw me, he said, "Brother, are we glad to see you!" He put a lot of heart into it, but his voice was hoarse like he'd been shouting a lot. I guess he had, come to think of it.

I waved a reassuring hand over the ditch and said. "Be right with you. I'll get the pliers out of my car." I got the pliers and slid down the steep bank into the culvert ditch. First thing I did was pull the tape off the second one's mouth. He worked his jaws around some, and spit, and then said, "Thanks. That kid on the bicycle send you?"

"Yeah. I'm from the sheriff's office. The kid reported to us." I was busy trying to unhitch them from the concrete piers.

"I about died when the kid went by without stopping," the first one said. "I knew he saw us. But he didn't stop, and I didn't have my gag loose then, so I couldn't yell to him."

"Wouldn't have done you any good anyway," I said, working on their wrist wires with my pliers. "The kid's mom don't want him getting mixed up with any strange men." I turned the first one's wrists loose. "You're gonna hurt for a spell," I warned him. "The wires were on there pretty tight."

The fellow just nodded, but stood up and stretched. He was dressed in blue jeans and a leather jacket and had a shock of black hair. I turned the second guy loose and he stood up, too. They both started rubbing some circulation back into their hands.

"Now then," I said, "what's the story, boys?"

The second fellow had hair about the color of creamery butter, crew cut, and was dressed just like the first one. His name was Pete. The dark one was Joe. Pete said, "We were hijacked."

I helped them climb up out of the ditch onto the road. "Truck drivers?"

"We were," Joe said, "until those fellows took our truck away from us this morning." He didn't actually say "fellows," but that's what he meant.

"Come on over and sit down in my car for a while," I said. "You been lying in that ditch very long?"

"Since quarter of six this morning is all," Pete said sarcastically.

They climbed into the back seat of my cruiser and sat back, still rubbing their hands together and doing some fancy cursing as the circulation began to return. I said, "How come nobody saw you except the kid?"

"Everybody driving east on the highway is slowing down for the stop sign at the intersection," Joe said, "and looking straight ahead, I guess. And everybody driving west is on the wrong side of the road to be able to see into the ditch. Even after I got my tape off, I couldn't make anybody hear me."

There were plenty of cars going by now, some of them slowing up out of curiosity like they do every time they see a police car.

I said, "Well, I'm sorry this happened to you in our county. Want to tell me about it now?"

"We had a load of Universal TV color sets consigned to a distributor in Chicago," Pete said. "We're slowing for the stop sign at the intersection back there, just before daylight this morning, going to take a left for the turnpike, when this Chevy blazes past us and pulls up dead, right in the middle of the road, right here on this culvert. This road is narrow enough over the culvert so we can't squeeze by, so I pull up behind the Chevy, just barely managed to do it, too, without clobbering the damn fool good. The second I get the rig stopped, a guy in a silk stocking mask hops up onto the step of the cab and pokes a double-barrel shotgun in the window and says get down. And at the same time, another guy in a mask jerks open the door on Joe's side."

"He shows me an automatic pistol as big as a cannon and tells me to get down too." Joe ran a hand through his crewcut, scrubbing at his scalp.

"Then what?"

"Then we both get down," Joe said. "What else? You don't argue with that kind of firepower, at least we don't."

"While all this was going on, no other car passed or approached?"

"Nary a car," Joe said. "Was there, Pete?"

Pete shook his head. "Just before daylight there's never much traffic on these back-country secondaries," he said. "One guy held the shotgun on us. The other two wired us up, pushed us down into the ditch, made us lay down, and hitched us to those concrete pillar things."

"Wait a minute," I said. "There were three of them?"

"Sure. One waiting in the ditch on each side of the road when we stopped, and one driving the car that blocked us. He came back and helped tie us up. Then he went back to his car and drove off, and the two others got into our truck and followed him."

"Which way did they turn on County Line Road?" I asked. I was beginning to get a kind of creepy feeling in my bones.

"Couldn't see them," Pete said, "but the rig noise faded off south."

My feeling was getting stronger. "Universal TV sets. Was the truck marked that way?"

"No. The trailer says 'Royal' on the sides. Royal Trucking in Chicago. We're just haulers for Universal, see."

I said, "Stainless steel trailer body?"

"Aluminum," Pete said sourly. "And brand new, too. The boss will play hell about this."

I gave them the clincher. "What license number?"

"Illinois T24-783," Pete said. "She's got Indiana, Ohio, and Pennsylvania plates, too, but I can't remember them."

"Illinois is enough," I said. "How you feeling by now, boys? Back in driving condition yet?"

They looked at me kind of funny, and didn't say anything.

"If so," I said, "we might as well go and pick up your stolen truck."

"You know where it is?"

"When I left town fifteen minutes ago, it was parked right in front of the sheriff's office," I said.

While we were driving back to Circleville, I quizzed them some more about the hijacking. "What color was the Chevy that blocked you off?"

"Black or dark blue with a white vinyl top. New model four-door," Pete answered promptly.

"Remember the license number?"

"Never saw it. Too busy stopping the rig. Wish I had, now."

"Joe?"

"Me neither," Joe said. "Probably covered up with mud or stolen, anyway. In the back window of the car was one of these stupid little dogs with a head that weaves around. I remember that."

"And with only one headrest," Pete added. "On the driver's side."

"How about the men? Anything you remember about them that might help us to identify them?"

"Silk stocking masks. All about the same size as Pete and me. Couldn't see much in the dark."

"Dark?"

"Sure. They reached in and turned off our lights soon as they stopped us. The car lights, too."

"I saw one thing," Pete remarked. "The guy who held the shotgun on us had a finger missing. Had his second finger through the trigger guard because his first finger was just a stump."

"Which hand?"

He thought for a moment. "Right hand."

"What about the shotgun?"

"Sixteen gauge, over-and-under," Pete said, "like I use for birds."

"Anything about their voices you'd remember?"

Pete shook his head, but Joe said, "Fellow who told me to climb down stuttered a little bit. Said 'G-g-get down,' like that. Course he may just have been scared or excited."

"What would he be scared for?" Joe wanted to know. "We was the ones who was scared."

We were still a block away from the County Building, coming south on Front Street, when Pete leaned over the back of my seat and looked ahead and said to Joe, "There she is, Joe, sure as hell. That's our rig." He said in my ear, "You've got to be some kind of a terrific cop, mister, I'll say that."

I said, "I just have an extra good memory, is all—for figures and stuff like that. I noticed the truck when I came out of the building to go rescue you boys, and I took in the license numbers and so on without even knowing it, I guess. That's the way my memory works."

I pulled into the County Building parking lot, saying, "First thing to do is see whether the TV sets are still there."

"Couldn't be," Joe said positively. "Else why leave the truck here? The load is either already stashed somewhere or transferred to another truck by now and long gone."

We got out of my cruiser and walked back to the truck. Pete unlocked the side door of the big trailer and stuck his head inside and said, "Well, I be damned! The TV's are still here!"

Joe couldn't believe it. Neither could I. I said, "The hijackers must've run out of gas."

Pete shook his head. "There was still forty gallons in the tank."

"Well," I said, "then you got to admit that this is a funny place to park a truckload of stolen TV sets."

"Wherever they parked them, we're damn glad to get them back!" Joe said.

"Come on into the office," I said, "and let me get down the details on this thing for my report. Then you can take off for Chicago."

We went inside. Twenty minutes later we came out again, and I held up traffic on Front Street for them while Pete jockeyed the big trailer backwards into our parking lot entrance far enough to turn the rig around and head it north for the turnpike and Chicago. It was a tight squeeze to get turned, but Pete finally got her straightened away. I got up on the cab step on his side and said, "Now don't stop for any Chevys between here and Chicago, you hear?"

"Don't worry!" Pete said. "And thanks, Bill." They were calling me Bill by now.

"So long, boys." I jumped down and the rig pulled away.

Johnny Martin, the police reporter for Circleville's only newspaper, was standing on the steps of the County Building when I started back into my office. He'd apparently been watching the whole thing, me holding up traffic while the truck turned around and so on. He said curiously, "What was that all about, Bill?"

I told him about the hijacking and the quick recovery of the stolen TV sets with a certain amount of pride, because I figured it was probably the fastest recovery of stolen goods on record, and that the sheriff's office could use a little good publicity with an election coming up. The Circleville *Chronicle,* Johnny's paper, had already declared for the opposition candidate and was always printing a lot of jazz about how inefficient the incumbent sheriff and his staff were, meaning me and my boss, Sheriff Blore.

I typed up a report of the hijacking and put it on the sheriff's desk for when he showed up, and all the time I felt kind of proud of myself, because, face it, the main reason the hijacked truck was found so quick was me and my good memory.

Yeah, I felt pretty proud—but only for a while. About twenty-four hours, as a matter of fact. Until Sheriff Blore came storming into my office the next day and put his sagging paunch up against the edge of my desk and said with unaccustomed venom even for him, "Bill, you're fired!" I could tell by the squint in his eye that he meant it, too.

I say eye, singular, because the sheriff only has one good eye. The other one's covered by a black eyepatch. But that one good eye can look mean enough for two. He's actually a pretty easygoing fellow for a sheriff; a lot of his meanness is put on for the benefit of the citizens who might be tempted to break the law in our county. This time, though, he wasn't putting anything on.

He had the morning *Chronicle* in one hand and his reading glasses in the other. I was afraid he'd break his glasses, he was squeezing them so tight.

He caught me by surprise. I said, "Me? What am I fired for?"

"You're fired for making the sheriff's office the laughing stock of this county," he barked at me. "That's what you're fired for!" He put the newspaper down on my desk and pointed a finger as round and fat as a dollar cigar at a headline on page two. I hadn't had time to look at the paper yet. I read the headline: SHERIFF'S EFFICIENCY IMPROVES AS ELECTION NEARS.

"That's a compliment," I said, "That's good publicity for a change. What are you so steamed up about? Did you read my report about the hijacking?"

"Of course," he answered. "But read that article."

I read it. It told about how we had recovered the stolen TV sets almost as soon as they were reported missing. And where. Far from complimenting our office, the article suggested baldly that the sheriff was rigging a few little incidents as election time approached to make his office look good—instances of heads-up law enforcement calculated to give the lie to the opposition's accusations about the inefficiency of the sheriff's office. The recovery of the stolen television sets was broadly hinted to be one of these rigged incidents.

The sheriff glared at me. "They might as well say we *stole* the damn truck ourselves, just so we could impress the voters with how fast we found it!" He stuck his thumb under his eyepatch, pulled it out half an inch, and let it snap back against his eye socket—a sure sign of almost unbearable irritation.

"Wow!" I said. "They're playing pretty rough."

"You gave them the story, didn't you?"

"Sure. To Johnny Martin yesterday. I figured it for good publicity. I never thought Johnny would twist the thing like this. . . ."

The sheriff simmered down a little. "I suppose you didn't. But he has. And the radio station picked it up this morning on the eleven o'clock news. Same insinuations. As a result, we both look like crooked politicians trying to win an election." He snapped his eyepatch again. Then he said, "To give the *Chronicle* its due, it *is* a damn funny place for a stolen truck to be found by a sheriff's deputy . . . right outside his own office."

"Yeah." I couldn't think of anything else to say.

"Why?" said the sheriff. "*Why* did they abandon the truck there? That's what we've got to know if we want to prove this article is wrong, Bill. Since you were so smart at locating the truck in a hurry, how about figuring out *why* it was left there? With its load intact?"

I looked up at him, five foot four and two hundred pounds topped by a black eyepatch, and said, "Pete and Joe said whoever drove the truck away from Donaldson's Crossroads was a lousy driver. He sounded like gangbusters going through the gears, they said. So maybe they just figured the rig was too much for them to handle."

This brought a snort from him. "Even if that's the reason, it isn't worth a belch in a wind tunnel to us. I gotta have a *good* reason why the truck was left there, Bill. You're so damn observant," he sneered at me, pulling up his fat lip at one end, "maybe you can come up with an explanation people will believe!" He turned around and waddled into his own office.

I put my feet up on my desk and shut my eyes. Like I told the two truck drivers yesterday, I've got a pretty good memory. So I turned the switch on it, got my memories of the hijacking all in a row, and started to look them over one by one. Nothing turned up that gave me a clue to the big question—till I'd got almost to the end of the line.

Then, all of a sudden, it hit me. Breathing a big sigh of relief—because I didn't really want to get fired—I went over to the window in my office and raised the venetian blind far enough so I could look south a ways. Then I went into the sheriff's office and sat down on his old leather sofa with a solution.

He was surprised to see me so quick. "You haven't thought of something, Bill?"

"No," I kidded him, "I came in to resign so you can't fire me."

His one eye glared at me for a second. "Don't clown. This is serious."

"Well," I said, "I've figured it, Clint. The hijackers didn't run out of guts, and the truck didn't run out of gas. What happened was it ran out of room." I grinned at him. "Right in front of our office."

"Room? I don't get it."

"I stepped up on the cab's step before they rolled away yesterday and what do you think was painted on the trailer's body, right behind the driver's door?"

I was dragging it out a little, to pay him back for firing me.

"What?"

"A warning."

He snapped his eyepatch. "What kind of warning, damn it?"

"It said, 'Caution. This is a high truck. Clearance thirteen feet.' "

"So?"

"So do you know the clearance of the Front Street underpass out there?" I jerked a thumb toward the railroad embankment.

"Hey!" He jumped. "The truck was too high to go through the underpass?"

"That's it. The clearance is only twelve foot ten under there. I just looked at the sign out my window."

"Well, well, well!" His mind started ticking over smooth and easy. "So when the hijackers get the truck this far, they suddenly realize it won't go under the arch. They've got to turn around to get clear. But they can't turn that big rig around. The street's too narrow and our parking lot entrance is closed off for the night. So what's left? Back up to Worley's gas station where they might be able to turn? But they were lousy drivers and didn't dare try to back the rig. Backing up for any distance in one of those things is too tricky for anybody but a professional truck driver. So what's the only thing left to do? Park the truck right there and scram. How's that sound?"

"Sounds pretty," I said. "How's it sound to you?"

"I think you just got me reelected, Bill. Now we've got something to work with. I'll show the *Chronicle* who's inefficient around here!"

He was as good as his word. He may be fat around the middle, but there's no fat between his ears. For two days he was busier than a one-armed paperhanger, bustling in and out of the office, making phone calls, applying for warrants and I don't know what-all. On the third morning, he told me to call him a press conference.

That was a laugh. In Circleville we only have one newspaper and one radio station, so a press conference usually consists of two guys at the most: Johnny Martin from the *Chronicle* and Abe Calhoun from the radio station's news staff. Anyway, they both showed up at two o'clock as requested and I took them into the sheriff's office. He was behind his desk with a fresh eyepatch on. The rest of us sat down on his scruffy leather sofa.

He didn't waste any time. He said, "Howdy, boys, you both been giving me a hard time over that truck hijacking a few days ago, haven't you? Implying that this office has been rigging crimes in order to gain political advantage by solving them. You been making out that we're not only inefficient as hell, but crooked as well."

"Oh, now, wait a minute, sheriff," Johnny began.

"Shut up," the sheriff said. "I want to tell you a few facts about that hijacking right now. Facts, I said. Not a lot of loose opinions like you boys throw around. First off, I want to say that if I wanted to, I could air a few loose opinions myself about that stolen truck being found in front of my office. For instance, that the setup was arranged deliberately, not by this office to make us look good, but by our political opponents to make us look bad—just what you boys have been urging them to think. But I don't deal in groundless accusations. Facts only. Okay. First fact: that hijacked truck wasn't parked in front of this office because somebody wanted to needle the sheriff's office. It was parked there because it *had* to be parked there."

"How come?" Abe Calhoun asked without much interest. So far, the sheriff's spiel sounded like a pretty bad political speech.

Sheriff Blore told them about the clearance under the railroad on Front Street, just twenty yards from our office. They showed a little more interest at that.

"Now," he went on, "the sheriff of this county is supposed to do more than merely recover any property that's stolen. He's supposed to catch the thieves, right? In the case of the stolen TV sets, I've done that, too."

Now they really began to pay attention. Johnny Martin even got out some copy paper and a pencil.

The sheriff went on talking. "Before I tell you who hijacked that truck, I'm going to describe how I tracked down the criminals and what my reasoning was, so you'll see how an *efficient* police officer works." He snapped his eyepatch a couple of times for emphasis. "Okay? All right, one thing about the hijacking kind of stuck out like a sore thumb: that it was the work of amateurs, not professional hijackers. Leaving the drivers in the ditch, practically in plain view; bad timing in blocking the truck on the culvert so that they almost got their Chevy clobbered; silk stocking masks like a bunch of Halloween kids; the lousy driving of the one who handled the rig; these were all marks of an amateur operation. But the most striking of all was the fact that the hijackers didn't realize until too late that the truck wouldn't go under the railroad arch here on Front Street."

"How come they realized it at all?" Johnny Martin asked. "Why didn't they try to drive through?"

"Listen, it stands to reason that even if they were amateurs, they must have cased this job *some* beforehand, right? Because they seemed to know that Universal TV sets were trucked down Highway 26 in Royal trucks twice a week from Tri-Cities to Chicago. And they seemed to know when the Royal trucks reached Donaldson's Crossroads. They'd cased the Crossroads, obviously, to plan where they'd block the truck and where they'd leave the drivers. And they'd certainly cased their getaway route beforehand, including the clearance of the railroad underpass. Get it?"

Abe Calhoun said, "You aren't answering Johnny's question, sheriff."

The sheriff gave him a mean grin. "I answered it, only you aren't efficient enough to see it, I guess. Look. The guys were expecting to hijack a load of TV sets in a truck just like all the other trucks that they'd seen hauling Universal sets down Highway 26 to Donaldson's Crossroads. But because they were amateurs, and consequently very flustered and nervous when they pulled the actual hijacking, they didn't realize the truck they hijacked was brand new and *bigger* than the ones they'd based their planning on. Not until they saw the railroad underpass ahead of them, with its big sign saying, 'Clearance twelve feet ten inches,' did the driver suddenly recall the big words, 'High Truck,' painted right behind his shoulder when he got into the hijacked truck. *Then* they realized they were sunk. And they abandoned the truck, load and all."

"Been me, I'd have brought up another truck small enough to fit under the railroad embankment, unloaded the big one, and taken off again," Johnny said.

"The hijackers might have done just that," the sheriff said, smiling, "except for the time element."

Abe Calhoun caught on quick this time.

"You mean it was daylight by the time they got this far, and they couldn't transfer the load right in front of the sheriff's office? Without somebody getting suspicious?" He snickered.

"Yeah," the sheriff said, "or recognizing them."

Johnny Martin gave in. "Who was it, sheriff?" he asked. "Who did the hijacking? We'll admit you're efficient as all hell, so come on, tell us who the hijackers were."

"Shut up," the sheriff said. "You're going to hear this whole thing for the good of your souls, boys. Where was I?"

"Time element," Abe reminded him.

"Yeah. Well, the time element tipped me off to something else, too. The fact that this was a *local* crime. That is, committed by somebody in or around Circleville, or with accomplices here, at least."

"How did you figure that?" This was Johnny, taking notes now.

"When it got to be daylight, those two truck drivers in the ditch were going to be found before long," the sheriff said. "That was a cinch. And once they were found, an alarm would be out for the stolen truck almost at once. From that I figured the hijackers expected to get the truck off the roads and under cover by daylight, see? Only the underpass fouled things up for them, stopped them from reaching their hideout with the truck before daylight. All right. Now, the very fact that they were using Front Street as a getaway route showed that they were local, too. Because Front Street runs onto Highway 67 a quarter of a mile through the underpass, and Highway 67 won't take you anywhere where you can get rid of fifty thousand dollars' worth of TV sets in a hurry. For that, you need Chicago or some big city where you got a big black market going. And Highway 67 only leads to Dempsey City and a bunch of farms all over the southern part of the state. Are you with me so far?"

Abe and Johnny were nodding their heads. "We're with you," Abe said.

"Okay, I start wondering about this point; where would a hijacked truck be heading if it was going through the Front Street railroad arch? Obviously, for some place big enough to hide the truck while they're repainting it to disguise it, or transferring its load to other transport, or hiding the TV sets for later disposal. Right? So what do you think I found, four miles out Highway 67? A big old barn of a building that would be just the ticket. And it's the only place between here and Dempsey City big enough to hide that truck in and for them to reach by daylight."

Abe and Johnny were frowning, trying to think of the place the sheriff meant.

He saved them the trouble. "Another funny thing was, this big old place was actually being used as an automobile body shop, with spray-painting equipment and such laying around all over the place."

"Weldon's Garage!" Johnny and Abe said together.

"That's exactly right. And auto painting equipment wasn't the only thing kicking around at Weldon's, either. I got me a search warrant and I personally gave the place the fine-tooth treatment. And I found the following items of interest. . . ."

The sheriff paused while Johnny turned over his copy paper to get a clean side, and then he went on.

"Item: one Chevrolet four-door, dark blue, with white vinyl top, loose-necked toy dog hanging in back window, only one headrest in place, and registered to Arthur Weldon. Item: one double-barreled, shotgun, sixteen-gauge, over-and-under. Item: one .45 automatic pistol, empty but well-oiled, a war souvenir. Item: one man missing his right index finger, name of Arthur Weldon, Junior. And item: a slow-witted grease-monkey and boy-of-all-work named Goose Hervey who stutters when he talks."

"Art Weldon and his boy!" Calhoun exclaimed. "And Goose Hervey! Where are they now, sheriff?"

"In the county jail, that's where," said the sheriff, meaning our two barred rooms at the back of the County Building which are generally as empty as a teenager's belly. "Before they could stop him, Goose Hervey admitted the whole thing. He thought it was a great lark, the entire hijacking adventure."

"What'd they use poor Goose for?" Johnny said. "He's only half there."

"They needed somebody to drive the car. And Goose promised not to talk, of course. But he couldn't help boasting a little."

Johnny started to say, "Escobedo . . ." but the sheriff grinned a wolfish grin at him and said, "He had been informed of his rights and there was a lawyer present. Anything else?"

Abe said, "Why would the Weldons try to hijack a truckload of TV sets? They've got a pretty good business of their own going out there."

"Not good enough to pay off the twenty G's that Art is into the bookies for," the sheriff said. "Art, Junior, told us about that." He paused. "*Now* if you still think the sheriff of this county is crooked and inefficient, go ahead and say so in the paper and on the air. But if not, we think the only fair thing to do is to tell the story like it happened. Okay?"

Johnny and Abe got up. "We will," Johnny promised. "And say, sheriff,

ALFRED HITCHCOCK'S ANTHOLOGY

I'm sorry about those innuendos before. But you can't blame us too much for thinking that was a funny place to park a stolen truck."

They left. I gave it as my loose opinion to the sheriff that the press boys would make good on their promises.

They did, too. But do you know whose picture they used in the paper? Not the sheriff's, much to his disappointment, and not mine, even though I was the one who came up with the really tough answer.

No. They used the picture of that redheaded kid with the crooked teeth. Don Start.

The Jade Figurine

by Bill Pronzini

La Croix had not changed much in the two years since I had last seen him. He still wore the same ingratiating smile. We sat together in a booth in the rear section of the Seaman's Bar, near the Singapore River. It was eleven thirty in the morning.

La Croix brushed at an imaginary speck on the sleeve of his white tropical suit. "You will do it, *mon ami?*"

"No," I said.

His smile went away. "But I have offered you a great deal of money."

"That has nothing to do with it."

"I do not understand."

"I'm not in the business any more."

The smile came back. "You are joking, of course."

"Do you see me laughing?"

Again, the smile vanished. "But you *must* help me," he said. "Perhaps if I were to tell you of—"

"I don't want to hear about it. There are others in Singapore. Why don't you try one of them?"

"You and I, we have done much business together," La Croix said. "You are the only one whom I can trust. I will double my offer. I will triple it."

"I told you, the money has nothing to do with it."

"*Mon ami,* I beg of you!" His gray-green eyes were pleading with me now; sweat had broken out on his forehead.

We had done business before, that was true enough, but I did not owe him anything. I would not have helped him, even if I had.

I stood abruptly. "I just can't do it, La Croix," I said quietly. "I'm sorry, but that's the way it is. I hope you find somebody else."

I turned away from him, walked through the beaded curtains into the bar proper, and ordered beer, on ice.

La Croix hurried through the curtain and pushed in beside me. "I beg of you to reconsider, *M'sieu* Connell," he whispered. "I will be in most grave danger if I remain in Singapore."

"La Croix, how many times do I have to say it? There's nothing I can do for you."

"But I have already—" He broke off, his eyes staring into mine, reading them accurately, and then he turned and was gone.

I finished my beer and went out into what the Malays call the *roote hond*, the oppressive, prickly heat that was Singapore at midday. There were a few European tourists about—talking animatedly, taking pictures the way they do—but the natives had sense enough to stay in where it was cool.

I walked down to the river. The water was a dark, oily bluish-green. Its narrow expanse, as always, was crowded with sampans, *prahus*, small bamboo-awninged Chinese junks, and the heavily-laden, almost flat-decked *tongkangs*, or lighters. There was the perennial smell of rotting garbage, intermingled with that of salt water, spices, rubber, gasoline, and the sweet, cloying odor of frangipani. The rust-colored tile roofs that cap most of Singapore's buildings shone dully through the thick heat haze on both sides of the river.

I followed the line of the waterfront for a short way until I came upon one of the smaller *godowns*—storage warehouses. I found Harry Rutledge, a large, florid-faced Englishman, without any trouble; he was supervising the unloading of a shipment of copra from one of the lighters.

"Can you use me today, Harry?" I asked him.

"Sorry, ducks. Plenty of coolies on this one."

"Tomorrow?"

He rubbed his peeling red nose. "Got a cargo of palm oil coming in," he said musingly. "Holdover, awaiting transshipment. Could use you, at that."

"What time is it due?"

"Eleven, likely."

"I'll be here."

"Right-o, ducks."

I retraced my steps along the river. I had never really been able to get used to the heat, even after fifteen years in the South China Seas. I wanted another iced beer, but I thought it would be a better idea if I had something to eat first. I had not eaten all day.

Here and there along the waterfront are small eating stalls. I stopped at the first one I saw and sat on one of the foot-high wooden stools, under a white canvas awning. I ordered shashlick and rice and a fresh mangosteen. I had gotten down to the mangosteen—a thick, pulpy fruit—when the three men walked up.

The two on either side were copper-skinned, stoic-featured and flat-eyed. They were both dressed in white linen jackets and matching slacks.

The man in the middle was about fifty, short and very plump, and his skin had the odd look of kneaded pink dough. He was probably Dutch or Belgian. He wore white also, but there any similarity between his dress and that of the other two ended. The suit was impeccably tailored, the shirt was silk; the leather shoes were handmade and polished to a fine gloss. On the little finger of his left hand he wore a huge gold ring with a jade stone in the shape of a lion's head—symbolic, I supposed, of the Lion City.

He sat down carefully on the stool next to me. The other two remained standing.

The plump man smiled as if he had just found a missing relative. "You are Mr. Connell, are you not?" he asked. His English was flawless.

"That's right."

"I am Jorge Van Rijk."

I went on eating the mangosteen. "Good for you."

H thought that was amusing. Gold fillings sparkled. His laugh had a burr in it that made my neck cold. "You were observed at the Seaman's Bar a short while ago," he said. "You were conversing with an acquaintance of mine."

"Is that right?"

"Yes. *M'sieu* La Croix."

"Interesting."

"Isn't it?" Van Rijk said. "May I inquire as to the nature of your conversation?"

I met his eyes. "I don't suppose that's any of your business."

"Ah, but it is, Mr. Connell. It is, indeed, my business."

"Then why don't you ask La Croix?"

"An excellent suggestion, of course," Van Rijk said. "However, it seems that *M'sieu* La Croix is, ah, nowhere to be found at the present time."

"That's too bad."

"Necessarily, then," Van Rijk said, "I must ask you."

"Sorry. It was a private discussion."

"I see." Van Rijk smiled, studying me with his mild blue eyes. "I am given to understand, Mr. Connell, that you are an aeroplane pilot."

"You've been misinformed, then."

"I think not," he said. "This is, of course, the reason La Croix spoke with you."

"Is it?"

"He wished you to transport him from Singapore."

"Did he, now?"

"And did you agree to this proposal?"

"What proposal?"

"I desire to know his destination, Mr. Connell."

I shrugged. "I couldn't tell you."

"His destination, Mr. Connell."

"Well, he did mention something about Antarctica," I said. "They say it's very nice there this time of year."

He stiffened slightly, and said in a cold voice, "I have become rather bored with this game of verbal chess, Mr. Connell. You would be most wise to tell me what I wish to know. Most wise."

"I don't have to tell you a damned thing," I said, keeping my own voice equable. "I don't know who you are, and I really don't much care. I do know that I don't like you or your manner or your implications. Do I make myself clear?"

I watched his eyes change. They were no longer mild. "I am not a patient man, sir," he said. "When I have lost what little forbearance I possess, I am also not a very pleasant man. Ordinarily, I abhor violence in any form, but there are instances when I find it to be the only alternative."

"I see." I put my hands flat on the table, leaning toward him slightly. "All right, Van Rijk," I said. "You've made your point. Now I'll make mine. I'm not going anywhere with you, if that's what you had in mind. I'm sure your two bodyguards, or whatever they are, are armed to the teeth, but I doubt if you'd have them shoot anybody in a crowded bazaar like this. In fact, I doubt if you'd want to make any trouble at all. Your boys would get into it, too, and I think you know what that would mean. Would you care to spend some time in a city *penjara* for street brawling, Van Rijk?"

Anger blotched his pink cheeks. The other two were poised on the balls of their feet, watching me. They were waiting for Van Rijk to let them know which way it was going to be.

Abruptly, he stood. "There will be another time, Mr. Connell," he said softly, acidly. "When the streets are not so crowded, and when the sunlight is not so bright." Then he pivoted and stalked off, threading his way between the closely-set tables, the other two at his heels. The three of them disappeared into the waterfront confusion.

I sat there for a time, thinking. I was a little bothered by Van Rijk's threats, but they could have been a bluff; I decided I had handled the situation well enough. I was also a little curious about his relationship with La Croix, but not enough to get myself involved in it. It had an odor about it with which I was all too familiar.

I got to my feet and put it out of my mind, decided it was time for that iced beer now.

On Jalan Barat, there is a bar which is called The Malaysian Gardens. The appellation is a gross misnomer. If any flower, shrub, or plant has ever been cultivated within a radius of one hundred yards of the place, I am not aware of it. With a facade reminiscent of nothing so much as a Chinatown tenement, its barn-like interior does little to dispel this image, both in decor—or rather, lack of decor—and in the distinctive smells of human close-quarter living and the perfumed incense called joss.

In short, The Malaysian Gardens is a dive which I first discovered many years ago, and I cannot explain why I continue to frequent it on the somewhat regular basis that I do. Perhaps it is because their price for beer is unparalleled in moderation anywhere on the island, or perhaps it is because they cater to those individuals like myself who desire a minimum of conversation and a maximum of solitude in which to do their varying degrees of drinking.

I had my iced beer there that afternoon, and then, after a nap in my flat and supper at a small, inexpensive restaurant, I had decided to return to the Gardens for a generous portion of both their solitude and their beer; there was not much else to do.

I had been there for perhaps three hours, sitting alone at a rear table and thinking a lot of old and useless thoughts, when I noticed the girl for the first time.

She stood just inside the arched entranceway, and she seemed to be staring at me, or at least in my direction. Her bearing appeared uncertain, as if she were prepared to bolt at the slightest disturbance.

ALFRED HITCHCOCK'S ANTHOLOGY

I watched her over the rim of my glass, and after a moment our eyes met. Her mouth made a small, round circle and she half-turned toward the street; then her body stiffened, perhaps with a resolution of sorts, and she walked toward me quickly.

As she approached, I saw that she was very tall, finely-proportioned; her face was heart-shaped and perfectly symmetrical, suggesting European—or at least Western—ancestry. She wore her dark hair long and sweeping. In the smoky dimness of the Gardens it was difficult to determine her age, though I thought she could not have been much more than twenty-one.

She stopped in front of my table, appearing very nervous or very embarrassed, or perhaps it was a combination of both, and said, "You're . . . Daniel Connell, aren't you?" Her voice reflected the uncertainty in her manner.

I nodded. "Yes."

"I wonder if I could speak with you. It's . . . it's very important."

I indicated an empty chair and invited her to sit down.

"I don't know quite how to say this," she said. "I'm . . . not very well-versed in this sort of thing."

"What sort of thing is that?"

She hesitated. "Well, *intrigue,* I guess you would call it."

I smiled. "That's a very melodramatic word."

Her voice dropped to a furtive whisper. "Mr. Connell, I've been told you sometimes . . . do favors for people."

"Favors? I don't think I understand."

She chewed at her lower lip. Then, in a rush, as if she needed to relieve herself of the pressure of the words: "I've been told you're a pilot, a pilot-for-hire, and that you would fly persons anywhere they wanted to go no matter why they wanted to go there, just as long as they could get enough money to pay you."

I was silent for a moment, then asked, "Who told you this?"

"Some . . . some people I talked with."

"What people?"

"I don't know their names. There were several. I tried to be very discreet about it, but I'm just not very good at such things. I asked along the waterfront and in Raffles Square if there was anybody in Singapore who would be able to fly me home without asking a lot of questions and some of the people said that Daniel Connell was the man I wanted to see and they said I could find him here most likely at night, and so I . . ." Her voice trailed off, and she looked down at her hands.

I drank from my glass, and then I said, "Just where is it that you want to go?"

"The Philippine Islands," she answered. "Luzon."

"Those people of yours were wrong about my not asking any questions," I told her. "Why do you have to get to Luzon in such a hurry? And why so secretively?"

She paused, as if debating confiding in me. Then, in a hushed voice, she said. "It's . . . my father."

"Your father?"

"There was a telegram this afternoon, when I returned to my hotel. It was from the . . . the police in Luzon. It said my father had been arrested. There have been a rash of terrorist attacks there lately, and they think he's involved with some kind of Communist guerrilla organization responsible for them." She took a deep, shuddering breath; she had, I decided, desperately needed someone to confide in. "It's not true! It can't be true! I know my father. He's a very patriotic and individualistic man, and he would never get mixed up with such people."

I did not say anything for a time. Then, slowly, I said, "I think it would be better if you began at the beginning. Suppose you start with your name."

Again, she gnawed at her lower lip. "Tina Kellogg."

"You're on a holiday in Singapore?"

"Yes, sort of. I just graduated from the University of Manila, and I thought I would take a tour of the Orient before I settled down to a position I've been offered at home."

"Your home is Luzon?"

"Yes."

"And your father—who is he?"

"He's an import-export dealer, just a small businessman, really, with a few American and European clients. That's why it's so ridiculous for anyone to believe that he would be involved with Communist guerrillas. What would he have to gain?"

Her question was rhetorical. I said slowly, "I can understand your wanting to get home so quickly. But why can't you simply take one of the scheduled flights to the Philippines?"

"I haven't any money, and no means of obtaining credit with any of the airlines. My father was supposed to send me a check to cover my expenses for the next month, but he . . . he didn't, he just didn't."

I said, "Can't you wire home for the money? To your mother, someone in your family?"

"My mother died when I was eleven," Tina answered. "My father is the only family I have."

"His business associates then? Personal friends?"

She shook her head convulsively. "There's no one. I suppose I could arrange something with his bank, but that might take days, weeks. And we have no close friends in Luzon; we were sort of self-sustaining, do you know? But even if we had, they wouldn't agree to send me money for fear of being implicated with the Communists."

I asked, "Have you tried the Philippine Consulate?"

"Yes," Tina said. "I went there immediately after I received the telegram, but they refused to help me. They said that if my father was involved with guerrillas there was nothing they could do. I tried to tell them it was all a mistake, but they just wouldn't listen."

"I see." I rotated my glass slowly on the scarred surface of the table. Even in the half-light, I could see the pleading in Tina's eyes. I ignored it; there was no other way. I said, "Tina, I'm sorry. I wish I could help you, but there's nothing I can do. I don't fly any more; what those people told you is false rumor. I haven't flown a plane in two years now."

"But I can pay you, really I can," Tina said with a note of desperation in her voice. "After we arrive, I can arrange with my father's bank—"

"I don't mean to be harsh, but don't make it any harder than it is to say no. I can't help you. That's all there is to it."

"Then . . . then what am I going to do?" She seemed on the verge of tears.

I felt like a heel at that moment, but I had enough burdens of my own. "Come on," I said gently. "I'll get you a taxi back to your hotel. Maybe something will turn up tomorrow."

"No, no . . ."

"Tina, this way is no good for you. If I agreed to do what you want, or if you found somebody else to do it, you would be breaking the law. You don't need that kind of grief, too. Listen to what I'm saying; it's good advice." I paused. "Now if I were you, I'd go back to the Philippine Consulate in the morning and camp in front of the ambassador's door. He'll see to it that you get back home, I'm sure of it."

I thought for a moment that she was going to protest, to beg, but she gave a resigned little sigh and then stood. I took her arm and led her out to the street.

It was very dark—street lamps on Jalan Barat are few and far between—and the night air held the same overt mugginess of the afternoon. There were few automobiles on the street. On the next block, I knew, was a taxi stand and I steered Tina in that direction. She looked up at me once as if to say something, but she apparently thought better of it and remained silent.

We had taken a few steps into the next block when I heard the car coming down Jalan Barat behind us, traveling very fast. Curious, I turned to look, and the car, a small English car, was just coming through the intersection. There was the pig squeal of hurriedly applied brakes then, and the driver pulled the wheel hard, skidding the car in at an angle to the curb ten yards in front of where Tina and I stood.

Both front doors opened simultaneously, and two men came out in a hurry. In the pale yellowish glare of the tropical moon, I could see their faces clearly. They were the two flat-eyed men who had been with Van Rijk that afternoon.

I had time for the quick thought that he was carrying out his threat after all. I pushed Tina out of the way just as the driver reached me. His right arm was raised across his body, and he brought it down in a back-hand, chopping motion, karate-style. I got my left arm up and blocked his descending forearm with my own. The force of his rush threw him off balance, and he was vulnerable; I jabbed the stiffened fingers of my right hand into his stomach, just below the breastbone. All the air went out of him. He stumbled backward, retching, and sat down hard on the sidewalk.

The other one had got there by then but when he saw the driver fall, he came up short, and I saw him fumble beneath his white linen jacket. I took three rapid steps and laid the hard edge of my hand across his wrist. He made a pained noise deep in his throat, and there was a metallic clatter as the gun or knife dropped to the pavement. I hit him twice in the face with quick jabs, turning him, and then drove the point of my elbow into his kidneys. The blow sent him staggering blindly forward, and he collided with the side of the car, slid down along it, and lay still.

I looked at the driver again, but he was still sitting on the sidewalk, holding his stomach with both hands. I let my body relax, breathing

ALFRED HITCHCOCK'S ANTHOLOGY

jaggedly. There was no sign of Tina. The whole thing must have scared the hell out of her, and I was sorry for that. She seemed to have enough troubles.

I heard shouts from the direction of The Malaysian Gardens, and when I looked up there, several people began to run down toward us. I thought briefly about waiting for the *polis* and telling them about it, but I decided against that. The less I had to do with them, the better it would be for me. Even though it had been two years since the trouble, memories are long in the South China Seas.

I could decide later what to do, if anything, about Van Rijk, so I began to walk toward the running group from the Gardens.

A tall, grayhaired man was in the lead, and when he reached me he asked breathlessly, "What happened here?"

"An accident," I said. "Happened right in front of me."

He looked past me. "Are they all right?"

"I think so."

I started to push past him. "Where are you going?" he asked.

"To call the constabulary."

He seemed satisfied with that, and the group left me to see about the two men from the English car. I angled across the street and walked west. I did not look back.

Somebody was at the door.

I rolled over on the perspiration-slick sheets and opened my eyes. It was morning; the sun lay outside the bedroom window of my Chinatown flat like a red-orange ball, suspended on glowing wires. I closed my eyes again and lay there, listening to the now impatient knocking. I listened for several minutes, not moving, but whoever it was did not go away.

"All right," I called finally. "All right."

I drew back the mosquito netting covering the bed and swung my feet down. Then I stood and crossed to the rattan chair near the bed. The fan on the bureau had quit operating sometime during the night, which accounted for the stagnant air. I put on my khaki trousers and went to the door and opened it.

Standing there was a little, wiry, dark-skinned man beneath a white, pith-type helmet, dressed in white shorts, knee-high white socks, black shoes, and a short-sleeved bush jacket. He wore his uniform proudly, the way only a native Malayan in an official capacity can.

He said, "You are Mr. Daniel Connell?"

"Yes?"

"I am Inspector Kok Chin Tiong of the Singapore *polis*. I would like to speak with you, please."

"What about?"

"May I come in?"

"If you don't make any comments about my housekeeping," I said, and stood aside.

He came in past me and stood in the middle of the room, looking about him. He turned to face me as I shut the door, his eyes expressionless. "Do you know a man by the name of La Croix, Mr. Connell, a French national?"

I went to the bureau and shook a cigarette from the pack there. "Why?"

"Do you?"

"Maybe."

"We have reliable information that you spoke at length with him yesterday."

I decided I would be wise in leveling with him. "All right, then," I said, shrugging. "I know him."

"So? And how well, please?"

"We've met a few times."

"You have been acquainted how long?"

"Two or three years."

"How did this meeting yesterday occur?"

"He looked me up."

"For what purpose?"

"He wanted to hire me."

"To do what?"

"Fly him out of Singapore."

"To what destination?"

"He didn't tell me."

"Singapore has excellent airline service to all major cities," Tiong said pointedly.

"Maybe he couldn't get immediate passage."

"This was his reason?"

"He didn't give me one."

"Did you agree to his wishes?"

"No."

"Why not?"

"I don't fly any more," I said.

"Ah, yes," Tiong said. "There was an accident two years ago, was there not? Involving an aircraft belonging to you."

"Yeah," I said shortly. "There was an accident."

"You were co-owner of an air cargo company at that time, Connell and Falco Transport. The aircraft, piloted by you, I believe, crashed under rather strange circumstances one night in a remote jungle sector on Penang. You escaped without serious injury, but your partner, Lawrence Falco, was killed in the crash."

I pressed my lips tightly together, not speaking.

"What were you and Mr. Falco doing in that particular area on Penang, Mr. Connell? And at that hour? No flight plan had been filed for such a journey."

"There was a full investigation at the time," I told him. "I gave a statement. Look up the records."

He smiled slightly. "I have already done so. There was strong speculation that you and Mr. Falco were involved in the smuggling of contraband. Among other things."

"Nothing was proved," I said slowly.

"Yes, the plane's cargo was burned beyond recognition," Tiong said. "But your commercial license was nonetheless revoked."

I'd had enough of this. "Listen," I said, "I don't know why you're here, inspector, but what I was or wasn't doing two years ago is a dead issue, just like Larry Falco. I haven't been up in a plane since then, and I don't intend to go up in one. Now, if you don't mind, I'd like to wash up and get dressed."

His black eyes searched my face for a moment, and then he put his hands behind his back and walked to the window. He looked down at Punyang Street, and the palpitating ebb and flow of Chinese there. After a time he said, "I would like to know your whereabouts last evening, Mr. Connell."

I told him. He asked what time I had arrived at the Malaysian Gardens and what time I had left, and I told him that, too. He rubbed at his upper lip with the tip of one forefinger. "Are you familiar, Mr. Connell, with the East Coast Road, near Bedok?"

"A little."

"The French national was found there shortly past midnight," Tiong said. "He had been dead for some three hours at that time. He was quite badly used, and then shot through the temple with a .25 caliber weapon."

Very carefully I stubbed out my cigarette in the glass ashtray on the bureau. "How do you mean, badly used?"

"Tortured," Tiong said. "Quite methodically, it would seem, and quite without compunction."

The back of my neck felt very cold. I said, "And you think I had something to do with it, is that it?"

He turned away from the window and looked at me squarely again. "Did you, Mr. Connell?"

"I told you where I was."

"Yes," he said. "Do you own a gun, please?"

"No."

"Would you object to a search of your quarters?"

"Be my guest," I said. "But I'll tell you something. You're wasting your time coming around to me. I didn't kill La Croix, I didn't have any reason to kill him. But I've got a very good idea who did. Look up a guy named Van Rijk, Jorge Van Rijk, and ask him the questions you've asked me."

Tiong's eyes narrowed. "What do you know of Van Rijk?"

I still did not want to get involved in this thing, but La Croix's death, and the way Tiong had said he died, seemed to make it necessary. "We had a little chat yesterday," I told him. "He wanted to know what La Croix and I discussed, too. I wouldn't give him the time of day, and he made a few very plain threats. Last night, when I left The Malaysian Gardens, the two men he'd had with him earlier jumped me. They didn't have any better luck."

"I see," Tiong said slowly.

"I take it you're familiar with Van Rijk?"

"Most familiar."

"Who is he?"

Tiong hesitated for a moment. Then he shrugged lightly and said, "Ostensibly, Jorge Van Rijk is a tobacco merchant in Johore Bahru. But we have reason to believe he has some other, more profitable—and more illegal—interests. He is also quite an avid collector of rare jade."

Tiong had made that last statement as if I should have attached some significance to it. I said, "Rare jade?"

"Quite so. You are aware, of course, of the recent theft from the Museum of Oriental Art?"

"No," I said.

"It has been prominent in the newspapers."

"I make it a point never to read the newspapers."

"Early last week," Tiong explained, "a priceless white jade figurine, the Burong Chabak, was taken from an exhibit at the museum. The robbery was quite cleverly accomplished, suggesting most careful premeditation."

"You think Van Rijk was involved in it?"

"We are quite certain he was. And we are also quite certain the Frenchman was involved as well."

I was beginning to get an idea what it was all about. La Croix, I knew, had once put in time in a French prison for burglary; he was accomplished at that sort of thing. And he had never heard, from what I knew of him, of that old saw about honor among thieves. It looked like a nice little doublecross on La Croix's part, a doublecross that had backfired. I said so to Tiong, but it didn't stun him.

He made a noncommittal gesture. "Possibly."

"Have you picked up Van Rijk?"

"We have been unable to locate him as yet."

I had a sudden thought. "Listen, Tiong," I said, "if you've got all this information, then why did you come around to me at all? Unless you've got some foolish idea that I was in on the doublecross with La Croix."

"The possibility entered our minds," Tiong said mildly. "You are, after all, known to us as a dealer in contraband. And you were seen with the French national the very day of his murder. We are naturally most curious about this."

I felt a slow anger begin to burn at my neck. Once you acquire a reputation in the South China Seas, it clings to you like a satellite; any time there is any trouble, and the *polis* can put you within fifty miles of it, they come around badgering the way this Tiong had done. I said coldly, "Are you satisfied now?"

"Possibly yes, and possibly no," he said. "Have you anything else you would care to tell me?"

"No."

He stood there for a moment, trying to read something in my eyes, and when he couldn't, he said. "Very well. I will take up no more of your time. But may I suggest that you do not attempt to leave Singapore until this matter is disposed of?"

"I hadn't planned on it."

He went to the door and opened it, nodding curtly as he turned to me again.

"Then, *selamat jalan*, Mr. Connell."

"Yeah," I said, and shut the door in his face.

The sun bore down with a merciless fire on the bared upper half of my body. My khakis were soaked through with a viscid sweat, and the back of my neck was blotched and raw from the *roote hond*.

I rolled another barrel of palm oil from the deck of the *tongkang* across the wide plank and onto the dock. One of the Chinese coolies took it there and put it onto a wooden skid. An ancient forklift waited nearby.

I rubbed the back of my forearm across my eyes and thought about what an iced beer would taste like when we were through for the day. It was a fine thought, and I was dwelling on it when Harry Rutledge came walking over to me.

"How's it going?"

"Another hour or so should do it."

"Well, you've got a visitor, ducks. An impatient one, at that."

"Visitor?"

"Bit of a pip, too," Harry said. "You bloody Americans have all the luck."

"A woman?"

He nodded. "Fetch Mr. Dan Connell, she tells me. Urgent. Now I don't like the birds coming round here bothering my lads when they're on the job. But like I said, she's quite a looker. Young, too. Never could say no to them."

"Did she give you a name, Harry?"

"Tina, she says. Tina Kellogg."

I frowned. I had thought I had seen the last of her after my gentle but firm refusal of last night—and after the incident on Jalan Barat. "Okay," I said to Harry. "Where is she?"

"My office," he told me. "You know where it is."

"Thanks, Harry."

He gave me a grin. "My pleasure, ducks."

I picked up my shirt and put it on, then went inside the huge, high-raftered *godown* and threaded my way through the stacked barrels and crates and skids to Harry's small office.

Tina was sitting in the bamboo armchair near the window. She wore a tailored white suit today; the skirt was very short, revealing fine legs. In the light of day, she looked somewhat older than I had first thought.

She stood as I entered, smiling hesitantly; I saw that her eyes were green, and that they had a kind of frantic pleading in them. She said, "Mr. Connell, I . . . I'm sorry to bother you like this, but I was, well, worried about you. Those men last night . . ."

I tried a reassuring smile. "Street muggers," I lied. "They're a native hazard in Singapore."

"Yes," she said. "Well, I guess I shouldn't have run away like I did. But I was very frightened."

"You did the right thing."

"Yes." She sat down in the armchair again, and began twisting her hands nervously in her lap.

I sighed softly. "Your concern over my well-being is very flattering, Tina," I said, "but I don't think it's the only reason you looked me up again today. Am I right?"

Her cheeks flushed. "I . . . I went back to the Philippine Consulate this morning, as you advised, but the ambassador is in Manila attending some sort of conference and won't be back for a week, and the man there told me the same thing he had yesterday. They just won't help me. I . . ."

Abruptly, she began to cry. Her shoulders trembled, and large, glistening silver tears spilled down over her cheeks. I stood there uncomfortably, not speaking. What was there for me to say?

Silence began to build, a strained silence, for we both knew what was coming next; I became aware of how damnably hot it was in there. Finally, Tina said in a tiny voice, "Mr. Connell, please, please help me. I know what you said last night, but I don't know anyone else in Singapore. I don't know where to turn, and if I can't get home to help my father . . ."

"Tina," I said as quietly, as gently, as I could, "there are reasons I can't help you, several reasons. For one thing, it's strictly illegal. I'm treading on very thin ice with the government here; they've made it plain that if there's one more mark against me, I'll be declared *persona non grata*. For another, when I said last night that I don't fly any more, I meant it. I don't have access to a plane any longer. I couldn't fly you to Luzon for just that reason alone."

"But . . . one of those people I talked with said that you used to keep a DC-3 in a hangar at an abandoned airstrip on the island." She brushed at the wetness beneath her eyes. "Isn't it still there?"

I studied her for a long moment, and then I went over to Harry's paper-littered desk. I sat on one corner and took a cigarette from my pocket. "Yes, it's still there."

"Then . . . ?"

I did some thinking, some very careful, methodical thinking. I weighed things in my mind. It's not up to me, I thought. It's none of my concern. I don't have to get into it.

Then I said, "All right, Tina."

"You'll help me?"

"I'll help you."

"Oh, Mr. Connell, thank you, thank you!" She came up out of the bamboo chair and threw her arms around my neck. "I'll never forget you for this!"

I pushed her away gently. "I'm probably a damned fool, but if your father is falsely accused, as you think he is, then I guess it's worth the risk."

Her eyes held a mixture of eagerness and relief now. "When can we leave?"

"It will have to be tonight," I said. "Late, around eleven. It would be idiocy to try it in the daylight."

"Where shall I meet you?"

I thought about that. "Are you familiar with the Esplanade on Cecil Street?"

"I think so, yes."

"There, then, at ten thirty."

"Whatever you say." She stood looking at me, and then quickly, lightly, daughter to father, she kissed me. "Thank you, Mr. Connell," she said again, and seconds later she had stepped into the storage area and was gone through one of the side entrances into the bright, sunlit afternoon.

It rained the early part of that evening, a torrential tropical downpour that lasted for perhaps two hours and left the air, as the daily rains always did, smelling clean and sharp and sweet; but by ten, when I left my flat, it had grown oppressively hot again.

Tina was waiting in the shadows near the Esplanade when I arrived at Cecil Street. She had shed the white suit of the afternoon for men's khakis and a gray bush jacket.

After exchanging soft hellos, I said, "No luggage, Tina?"

"No," she answered. "I didn't want to bother with it. I can send for it later."

I nodded. "All right. Then we'd best get started."

I hailed one of the yellow taxis that roam the streets of Singapore in droves. The driver, a bearded Sikh, did not ask any questions when I told him where we wanted to go. I did not imagine he got many fares to the remote Jurong sector of the Island that I named—there was nothing much there but mangrove swamps and a few native fishing *kampongs*—but like all competent drivers in the South China Seas he kept his thoughts to himself. We rode in silence.

It was ten fifty when he turned onto Kelang Bahru Road, leading toward the abandoned airstrip, Mikko Field. The moon was orange brilliantine in the black sky; the road was illuminated enough so that you could have driven it without headlights.

When we neared the access road that led to the strip, the Sikh began to slow down. "Do you wish me to drive you directly to the Mikko Field, sahib? The road is very bad."

"Go in as far as you can," I told him. "We'll walk the rest of it."

"As you wish, sahib."

He made the turn onto the access road. It was badly scarred with chuckholes and heavily grown over with tall grass and tangled vegetation. We crawled along for about a quarter mile. Finally, in the bright moonlight, I could see the long, pitted concrete runway, raised some ten feet on steep earth mounds from the mangrove jungle on both sides. At its upper end, to our left, were the rotting wooden outbuildings, and farther behind them the huge domed hangar. The airstrip had been deserted since the Japanese were driven from Singapore at the tag end of the Second World War. Few people remembered, or cared, that it was still there.

The Sikh braked the taxi to a stop. The road was impassable here; the marsh grass was very tall and thick, and parasitic vines and creepers and thornbushes braided together to form a barrier that was more effective than any man-made obstruction. The Sikh turned to look at me. "We can go no farther, sahib."

"This is fine."

Tina and I stepped out into the night. The air was alive with the buzzing hum of mosquitoes and midges, and with the throaty music of Malayan cicadas. There was the smell of decaying vegetation, and of dampness from the rain.

I paid the Sikh and thanked him and stood there watching while he made a U-turn, and started back along the access road. I watched his taillights fade, disappear, and then I turned to look again at the airstrip.

Tina had not spoken during the ride out. Now she said, in a voice that was almost breathless, "Where do we go?"

I wet my lips. "Suppose—"

I broke off, listening. There was the high, unmistakable whine of a four-cylinder automobile engine being held in low gear, and it was approaching, not retreating. I pivoted to look along the access road. I could see nothing, even in the moonshine, and it was very close now. They were coming without headlights.

A coldness crept over me. "Somebody's coming," I said.

"But who—?"

"I don't know yet. But I've got a good idea."

I caught her arm and we ran for the protective cover of the mangroves, but they must have seen us outlined against the moonlit sky. Headlights stabbed on, and I heard a familiar pig squeal of brakes. Without halting stride, I veered to the left, into the tall marsh grass at the edge of the road. There was a hoarse shout behind us. I pulled Tina deeper into the swamp jungle, parallel to the airstrip. Thorns ripped at my bare arms; unseen creepers tugged at my clothing; something brushed my face, whispering, cold.

We had traveled perhaps fifty or sixty yards when the grass began to thin out, leaving us without protection. I could hear two men, possibly three, moving through the morass behind us. I looked about wildly. To the left was the access road, relatively free of growth here and bathed in moonlight, where it curved around to the outbuildings. I discarded that direction immediately. The only other way was up onto the airstrip. The outbuildings were only a distance of a hundred yards down the runway, and I knew that if we could make them, find a hiding place, we would have a chance.

I pushed Tina to the right, through a clump of wild shrubs, and up to the base of the embankment. The mounded earth was a quagmire from the evening rain, but we managed to fight our way up onto the strip. "Run!" I hissed to Tina.

We ran. Our muddied boots slapped wetly on the concrete. There was

ALFRED HITCHCOCK'S ANTHOLOGY

another shout from behind us, and I heard the roar of a large-caliber pistol. I glanced back over my shoulder. There were two of them at the base of the embankment; I could not see their faces. A third stood in the twin headlamp beams of an English car where we had been on the access road. He was doing the shouting, and even though I could not see his face, I knew, of course, who he was—Van Rijk.

I turned my head. We were almost to the outbuildings now. I heard another roar from the pistol behind us, but they were not going to hit much at the range from which they were firing.

The closest building was a long, rectangular, low-roofed affair that had been used to quarter duty personnel. All the glass had been broken out of its windows, a long time ago, and some of the wooden side boarding had rotted or pulled away, leaving shadowed gaps like missing teeth. Off to one side was a much smaller, ramshackle substructure, a shed of some kind.

I steered Tina toward it, and we went around the corner of the rectangular building and along the side of the shed. At the rear, a semicircular, jagged-edged hole in the wood yawned black, like a small cave opening.

I came to a stop, fighting breath into my lungs. "Through there!"

She obeyed instantly. She dropped onto her knees and scrambled through the hole, inside the shed. I followed close behind her.

Thin shafts of moonlight made a pale, irregular pattern on the debris-ridden floor inside. The shed was empty, and it was close, humid in there—a pervasive heat like that in an orchid hothouse.

Tina's breath came in thick gasps. She crouched on her knees with her head bowed. I left her and crawled across the damp wooden floor to the front of the shed. I peered through one of the smaller gaps there. I had a full view of the airstrip.

I saw the headlights then—two sets of them—coming down the access road, coming very fast. I felt some of the tension in my body ease. I could not see the portion of the road where the English car and Van Rijk were, but the other two, up on the runway now, fifty yards away, could see it clearly. They pulled up, looking back, uncertain.

The sound of jamming brakes, of doors slamming, of men shouting, carried faintly to me on the night air. They had not used their sirens. Part of the strip was illuminated from the automobile headlamps.

"What is it?" Tina asked, coming beside me to look out. She had got her breath now. "What's happening?"

"The *polis* are here, Tina," I said.

"The *polis?*"

I watched the two men on the airstrip. One of them extended his arm, crouching, and I saw the gun in his hand, but before he could use it, there was a short, sharp burst from an automatic weapon. The man fell, sprawling headlong. The other one veered off to the right, running in a low zigzag. The automatic weapon sounded again. He went off the side of the embankment, feet first, like an Olympic broadjumper. Pistol shots rang out, three of them, and then another burst from the automatic weapon. After that, there was only silence.

I turned away from the opening. "It's all over now," I said.

Tina's fingers dug into my arm. "The plane!" she breathed. "Maybe there's still time to reach the plane, Mr. Connell . . ."

I straightened, placing my hands flat on my knees, looking at her. "There isn't any plane, Tina."

Her face was shadowed, and I could not see her eyes. "I . . . I don't understand."

"There's no plane here," I repeated slowly. "There hasn't been one here for two years now."

She stared at me for a full minute, and then, suddenly, her hand flashed to the belt of her khakis, under the bush jacket. She was very quick, and I did not have time to react before she had the gun pointed levelly at my stomach. It was plainly visible in one of the shafts of pale moonlight, and I saw that it was of Belgian manufacture, a .25 caliber automatic. I said quietly. "Is that the gun you shot La Croix with? After you tortured him?"

She leaned forward slightly, and I could see her face then. The frightened little girl no longer existed; in her place was a cold, hard, and very deadly woman. "All right," she said. "So you know."

"I've known since this afternoon, Tina," I said. "Oh, it was a very nice act you put on, a clever little farce. I'll admit you had me fooled last night at The Malaysian Gardens, and that you had me fooled for a while this afternoon. But you made a mistake, then, and it didn't take long before I saw the whole thing for exactly what it was."

I watched the automatic; it did not waver. I went on.

"You said that one of those fictitious people you talked with mentioned an abandoned airstrip where I used to keep a DC-3. But you didn't know, couldn't have known, that there were only three people besides my-

162

self—and eventually the *polis*—who ever knew I once kept a plane in a hangar here. One of those men was my partner in an air cargo business, and he's been dead for two years. Another is a German named Heinrich; he's serving ten years in a Djakarta prison for hijacking. And the third man, the only man you could have gotten the information from, was a French national named La Croix. But La Croix was on the run, trying to get out of Singapore. He sure as hell wouldn't have been wandering around Raffles Square; he couldn't possibly have been one of the people you claimed you'd talked to.

"That started me thinking, Tina, about a lot of things, and the way they added up. But just to make certain, I went down to the Philippine Consulate after you left the *godown* this afternoon, and asked a few pertinent questions. They had never heard of any Tina Kellogg, much less a Luzon import-export dealer being arrested for Communist conspiracy. So I went to see an Inspector Tiong at the government precinct building and told him about it, and he did some very efficient checking. He uncovered a bit of interesting information. Like the fact that your real name is Tina Jeunet, and that you're a Canadian by birth. The fact that, although nothing was ever proved, you were implicated in the theft of several valuable uncut diamonds in England two years ago. And the fact that you were in Brussels last July when an original Gauguin was stolen from a private collector there. Again, nothing proved. But there was no doubt in police minds.

"When we had all this, the inspector and I devoted a long and careful discussion to the theft of the Burong Chabak, the jade figurine, from the Museum of Oriental Art. I suggested this little trap tonight and paved the way by agreeing to fly you to Luzon. We didn't expect Van Rijk to fall into it, too, but I guess it worked out all right that way. I would have had you picked up right away at the Esplanade tonight, if I'd thought you were carrying the figurine—the inspector was waiting there for my signal. It had me a little puzzled when I saw you didn't have it, and later when you didn't make some excuse so we would stop and you could pick it up. But then I remembered something La Croix had started to tell me, that I hadn't let him finish, when he talked to me two days ago. I'm sure what he had started to say was that the figurine was here at Mikko Field. You never had it at all. And that's the reason you came to me: to find out the name of this strip, and because I would know where the Burong Chabak was hidden."

She smiled, an ugly curving of her mouth. "You're going to take me to it," she said. "Right now."

"Don't be a fool, Tina. This whole area is alive with *polis*. You can't get past them."

"*We'll* get past them," she said pointedly.

I smiled in the darkness. "If you're thinking about using me as some kind of hostage, you can forget it. They don't give a damn about me."

"We'll see about that."

"No," I said, "we won't see about it at all."

She moved the automatic again, and that was exactly what I had been waiting for. I brought my left hand off my knee, swinging it out and up, palm open. My closed fingers hit the barrel of the automatic, driving it upward. There was a roar as she squeezed the trigger reflexively, and I felt a searing heat along my forearm, but the bullet thudded somewhere into the shed's roof. I caught Tina's wrist with my right hand and pressured it heavily. She cried out in pain; the automatic fell to the floor.

I picked it up, sliding back away from her. Then I got to my feet and put the gun in my belt. My arm was blistered from the discharged bullet, and stung badly, but I thought that it would be all right. I looked out through one of the gaps in the boarding. Four men were on the airstrip now, running. One of them had a machine gun and the others drawn pistols. Inspector Kok Chin Tiong was in the lead. I turned, looking down at Tina Jeunet; she was crouched there on the floor, hating me with her eyes. "Let's go," I said.

She did not move. I shrugged. I felt very tired, and it did not make any difference now anyway. I went to the rear of the shed and crawled through the hole and came around onto the strip. The running men slowed when they saw me. Tiong approached. He was out of breath. "You are all right, Mr. Connell?"

"Yeah," I said. "I'm just fine."

"The woman?"

"In the shed there. She's not hurt, but I don't think she's going anywhere."

Tiong said something in Malay to one of his men. The officer nodded and hurried off toward the shed.

I asked, "What about Van Rijk?"

"We have him in custody."

"And the other two?"

"They are both dead."

"You could have been saying the same thing about me," I told him. "You took your sweet time getting here."

He smiled. "When your taxicab drove away from the Esplanade, we saw an automobile following closely behind it. An automobile with its headlamps dark and containing three men."

"And you figured it was Van Rijk," I said.

"Yes."

"Why didn't you just pick him up instead of letting him come out here?"

"We wished to—how is it you Americans say—give him further rope with which to hang himself?"

"Yeah," I said. I lifted the automatic from my belt and handed it to him, butt first. He accepted it with a polite gesture, then turned it over to one of his men.

There was a sound from the direction of the shed. The officer Tiong had dispatched was bringing Tina Jeunet out, her hands shackled in front of her. The officer led her toward the access road and the waiting *polis* cars.

I watched them for a moment and then I told Tiong what I had said to Tina Jeunet about the Burong Chabak. He nodded silently. I said, "I think we'll find the figurine at a drop point La Croix and I used when we did business together. He would leave payment there for whatever I was carrying if everything went all right."

I led Tiong to the rear of the huge domed hangar, near two large and heavily corroded tanks that had once been used for the storage of airplane fuel. There, set into the ground beneath a layer of foliage, was a wooden box housing regulating valves for the airstrip's water supply.

The Burong Chabak was there.

I learned the full story the following morning, in Tiong's neat little office at the government precinct building; it was just about as we had speculated when I saw him the previous afternoon, after Tina Jeunet's visit to the *godown*.

La Croix and Tina had done the actual stealing of the figurine from the museum, but it had been Van Rijk's idea originally. But instead of delivering the Burong Chabak to Van Rijk afterward, the two of them had decided to pull a doublecross. It would have worked out all right for them, too, if La Croix had not attempted to make a triplecross out of it by taking the figurine for himself, and leaving Tina in virtually the same position as Van Rijk.

Then La Croix came to me. Someone who knew that Van Rijk was looking for both Tina and La Croix had seen La Croix talking to me, and called Van Rijk. He knew, of course, that he had been doublecrossed, but he still thought both La Croix *and* Tina were in it together. His idea was that I would lead him to La Croix, and Tina, and eventually to the figurine.

Tiong had told me La Croix was killed somewhere around nine; assuming it was Van Rijk who had done it, then he would have had no reason for having me followed at eleven. He would have got the information he wanted from La Croix.

Tiong and I had reasoned earlier that this meant Van Rijk had not killed La Croix; that left only one person who could have—Tina Jeunet. She found out where he was hiding, and she tortured him. He told her then that he had hidden the figurine at an abandoned airstrip, at a place known only to him—and to me—but he had died before he could name the strip, and the cache point. Tina Jeunet had shot him in the head in blind anger, and then she had come looking for me.

That was all of it.

I saw the jade figurine for the first time there in Tiong's office. Intricately, painstakingly carved, it depicted a nightbird—a *burong chabak*—in full flight, wings spread, head extended as if into a great wind. The bird itself was of white jade, the purest, most valuable of all jade; the squarish pedestal upon which it rested was of a dark green jade.

"Is it not beautiful?" Tiong asked when I had examined it.

I said nothing; it had felt cold, a faintly repulsive coldness, in my hands. "How much is it worth on the black market?" I asked him. "To an underground collector, say?"

"Perhaps four hundred thousand Straits dollars," he said. "I would not know the exact figure, of course."

"A hundred and fifty thousand or so, American," I said. "That's why Tina Jeunet wanted to get to Luzon. She had a buyer there."

"Yes," Tiong said. He gave me a thoughtful look across his desk, as if something were puzzling him. "That is a great deal of money. Enough to tempt any man."

I said that it was.

"And yet you chose to notify the *polis* when you suspected the woman of possessing the figurine. Your past record indicates no hint of such civic-mindedness. Why, Mr. Connell?"

"All right," I said. "The main reason is Larry Falco."

"Your former partner?"

"My *dead* former partner," I said. "A nice guy, with a lot of fine ideas about how to make a comfortable living from an air cargo transport company, who is dead because I had other ideas—running contraband, for instance, to a small airport in disrepair. Larry tried to talk me out of it, but I wouldn't listen. I could take the plane in, I said. Well, I was wrong, and Larry died because of it. It should have been me."

Tiong was silent for the longest time. Then, finally, he said quietly, "I see."

I do not think he really saw at all.

A Small Down Payment

by Stephen Wasylyk

As Lazarus Neap finished spreading the photos of the dead girl out on his desk, a gust of wind from the open window spun several of them to the floor.

Neap sighed. Even the little things weren't working out this week.

It had begun on Monday. Arbosh, a rookie detective, had been assigned to Neap, and he and Arbosh had been sent to pick up a burglary suspect who had not taken kindly to being arrested. Arbosh's lack of experience had cost Neap a smashing fist high on his right cheek that left a jagged tear that throbbed occasionally and had swelled his eye half shut. Hardly the best-looking detective sergeant on the force ordinarily, the stitches and swollen cheek gave him a leering Satanic look.

Then on Tuesday, a young woman named Ann Cheyney had been found strangled in her apartment. After twenty-four hours, Neap still didn't have an inkling of a lead. The girl, only twenty-two, had lived alone, had few friends, and worked as a secretary for a small law firm. No one in the garden-type apartment where she had lived had seen or heard anything.

Now, on Wednesday, there was another strangled girl. The lieutenant, working shorthanded, had given that one to Neap, too, because he had once worked on the park detail and the body had been found alongside one of the park roads where it had evidently been thrown from a passing car. The road through the park was little used, deserted late at night, and the gravel on the shoulder showed no tire marks. Again Neap had nothing with which to work.

Neap slid the window down, closing out the warmth of the early afternoon spring day, and rearranged his photos. This one is worse than the other, he mused. We don't even know her name.

He studied the photos, struck by the superficial resemblance of his unknown Jane Doe to Ann Cheyney. Both had been young, with straight long blonde hair, and both had been rather plain, even in death. Neap

ALFRED HITCHCOCK'S ANTHOLOGY

wondered if there could be some connection between the two killings. The preliminary report on Jane Doe indicated she had been strangled in much the same manner as Ann Cheyney.

Arbosh, a smile on his round face, came in swinging a woman's handbag by its long strap. He deposited it carefully on the photos. "Look what they found in the park."

Neap almost smiled. "Near the body?"

"About a half mile away in a field, as if it had been tossed from a car."

Neap looked at him suspiciously. "You handle it at all?"

"Nobody did. We thought there might be prints on that smooth leather. You want to take it to the lab?"

"Right now," growled Neap. "I don't even want to open it here."

It took Short, the lab technician, only a few minutes to find one print that wasn't smeared. "Even that isn't good," he said. "You'll never use it in court."

"I'm not surprised," said Neap. "Let's find out who it belongs to."

Short slipped on a pair of cotton gloves and emptied the bag on the table. Among the usual contents was a plastic identification badge for a Center City department store and a wallet with a change purse.

Short picked up the identification badge carefully. "If this belonged to your Jane Doe, her name was Needa Stone." He checked the contents of the wallet. "No robbery, and it couldn't have been a purse-snatching. The money's still here."

"That wallet have an ID card?" asked Arbosh.

Short nodded. "Needa Stone, 127 South Twelfth."

"I know the place," said Neap. "A couple of apartments above a delicatessen."

"You think this belonged to our Jane Doe?" asked Arbosh.

"I'd bet on it. Let's take a picture over there and see."

"I'll tag all this stuff and check it for prints," said Short.

"Give it the full treatment. We need all the help we can get."

Neap was right about the address in the wallet. The building was old, the delicatessen squeezed between a multilevel garage and a hotel. The name "Stone" above a mailbox in a foyer indicated the girl had occupied the second floor rear.

They found the delicatessen owner arranging cold cuts in the meat case. "How are you, Mr. Satinsky?" Neap said, waving a hand.

Satinsky, a stooped old man, smiled. "Welcome, Lazarus. We don't see you around here since you became a detective. Who hit you in the face?"

"It's a long story." Neap introduced Arbosh and handed Satinsky the photo. "This one of your tenants?"

"That's Miss Stone." Satinsky peered at the picture closely, understanding washing over his wrinkled face. "She's dead?"

"She's dead. Maybe you could go down to the morgue and identify her."

"No," said Satinsky. "I would like to help but I cannot leave. You understand. How did she die?"

Neap told him.

The old man shook his head. "You catch the killer, Lazarus. She was a nice girl."

"She have any friends or relatives?"

"Friends, a few. Young girls like herself. No men. Relatives, I do not know."

"Did you see her last night?"

"No. I do not think she came home. She would have stopped in to pick up some things. She did not last night."

"We'd like to see her apartment," said Arbosh.

Neap considered. He had no choice but to let Arbosh loose and see what he could do. "I'll check the apartment," he said. "You take the car to where she worked, see what their personnel records show, and see if you can find any friends. We still need someone to identify the body. If you can find a volunteer, bring him back to the office."

Arbosh nodded. "I'll do what I can."

The apartment was small; a living room, bedroom, bathroom and kitchenette. The furniture could have been purchased used and had seen many years of wear since.

Needa Stone had made some attempt to imprint her personality on the apartment, but failed. The curtains on the windows and the prints on the walls did nothing for the room except point up its shabbiness.

Curious, reflected Neap. There really wasn't much difference between this apartment and Ann Cheyney's. Lonely young women must have the same life-style, and drab apartments were part of it.

He moved into the bedroom. The bed was neatly made, undisturbed. Neap opened the closet, fingering through the meager collection of dresses. The bedroom yielded nothing.

The bathroom rated no more than a minute; neither did the kitchenette. Needa Stone had been a neat person.

Back in the living room, he thoughtlessly fingered the bruise on his cheek and winced. If there was anything in the apartment of use to him, it had to be here.

There was a battered sofa along one wall, a small TV facing an easy chair, a hi-fi set along another wall and a small desk in the corner. A bookshelf alongside the desk was overflowing with paperbacks and magazines. Another similarity, thought Neap. Ann Cheyney's apartment had plenty of reading material.

Neap moved to the desk. It had two drawers. The upper one held an unlocked metal cash box with nothing inside except a personal checkbook and a bankbook. Neap fanned through the check stubs. The checks written for her apartment and utilities were easy to spot along with a few made out to the department store and a few made out to cash. One puzzled Neap. For twenty-five dollars, it was made out simply to "Date." He put the checkbook aside.

The bankbook indicated Needa Stone had faithfully saved ten dollars a week.

Neap bit his lip gently. Other than the amounts, he had found the same setup in the other apartment; the personal checkbook with a small balance, a bankbook showing regular deposits. The similar pattern disturbed him. There was little difference, if any, between the two young women who had been strangled. It was almost as if they knew each other and had mutually decided to follow a certain routine.

He closed the bankbook and opened the lower drawer, pulling out an expandable, accordion-pleated file. It yielded canceled checks that told him nothing new except that the check made out to "Date" hadn't been returned. Neap made a note of the number and the bank. He closed the desk, hoping he would have better luck with the neighbors.

It didn't take long. The tenant in the front apartment turned out to be a hard-of-hearing old woman who knew Needa Stone only enough to nod to, and had seen or heard nothing the previous evening. Neap glanced at his watch. He'd have to send Arbosh back to canvass the neighborhood thoroughly if nothing else turned up.

The afternoon had turned colder, the sun gone behind a heavy cloud cover, and the cold wind stung the laceration on his cheek.

Neap decided to walk back to headquarters. He was passing the bank

Needa Stone used for her checking account when he remembered the stub marked "Date." He turned in and was directed to a vice-president named Dial who couldn't have been more cooperative. It took Dial only one phone call to locate the check somewhere in the bank's records office.

"It is made out to Date, Incorporated," he said.

Neap frowned. "Never heard of it."

Dial smiled. "It is my understanding that Date, Incorporated, is a computer dating service. Men and women send in their applications and for a fee, the company will match them with a compatible member of the opposite sex. I really don't know too much about it, other than it is very popular at the moment. There are several firms in town advertising such a service."

Neap wrote the name in his notebook.

"The check has been cashed?"

"At least three weeks ago."

Neap thanked him, thinking that Needa Stone must have been very lonely and desperate for male company to pay twenty-five dollars to a firm that promised her a date.

He had reached the door of the squad room when he stopped, mentally cursing himself as an idiot.

Arbosh was at his desk, talking to a pretty young woman. "This is Terry Hutton," he said. "A friend of Miss Stone's. She has identified the body at the morgue."

Neap smiled at Terry Hutton, who looked as if she had been crying and was ready to start again. "How well did you know Needa Stone?"

"Quite well. We worked together."

"Any idea where she went last night?"

"She said something about a date, but she didn't mention the man's name. She was very excited about it because she didn't go out much."

"Did she say anything at all about the man?"

"There wasn't much she could say, I guess. I gathered that it was a blind date."

"He was to pick her up at her apartment?"

"No. She was to meet him after work at the eagle."

Arbosh grunted and Neap knew why. In the center of the ground floor of the department store where Needa Stone had worked, a large bronze eagle dominated the wide center aisle. It was a natural meeting place and had been used by thousands of people through the years. With the shop-

172   ALFRED HITCHCOCK'S ANTHOLOGY

ping crowds milling around, it was unlikely that a man and a young woman would attract attention.

"You have any idea who arranged the date or how it was arranged?"

"She didn't say," she replied.

"Did she ever mention Date, Incorporated?"

"I never heard of it."

She could contribute nothing else and Neap had the feeling he was looking at another blank wall, but this one had a little chink in it labeled Date, Inc.

He watched her walk out, male heads in the room pivoting with her passage. She at least would require no assistance in meeting a man.

"You find anything else at the department store?" he asked Arbosh.

"Next of kin on the personnel record shows an aunt living upstate. I've already arranged for her to be notified. How about you?"

Neap told him about Date, Inc.

"You think she got this date through them?"

"It's worth checking. Look up their address and let's go over there."

Date, Inc., was on the fifteenth floor of one of the newer office buildings in Center City.

Arbosh raised his eyebrows when they left the elevator. "I never would have thought loneliness would pay this well."

Neap grinned. "It's a big city with a lot of people who ignore each other." He held his badge out to the mini-skirted young receptionist. "I'd like to see someone in charge."

"What is it in reference to?" she asked brightly.

Somewhere Neap had acquired a headache to go with his throbbing cheek. He leaned over the desk. "Just get someone out here," he said softly.

The girl's smile faded, she picked up the phone and spoke briefly. "Mr. Owen will be out shortly," she said primly.

The only word Neap could think of for Owen was dapper. From the top of his carefully barbered head to the tips of his gleaming shoes, Owen looked like he had just stepped out of a men's store window. He looked at Neap's swollen cheek with distaste.

"Can I help you?" Even the voice was carefully polished.

No one should be so perfect, thought Neap, annoyed. He explained. "You have a Needa Stone among your clients?"

Owen beckoned them into his office. "I'll have it looked up." He pressed a buzzer on his desk, another young girl came in, he told her what he wanted, and she disappeared.

"How does your service work?" asked Arbosh.

Owen smiled. "Very simply. People who subscribe fill out an application. We code the information and feed it into a computer where it is stored. If you, for instance, also subscribe, we will code the information on your application and request the computer to print out the names and addresses of young women with similar personality characteristics. That's all there is to it."

"How about screening people?" asked Neap. "You could get applications from unstable personalities."

"Our questionnaire is scientifically designed to weed out people like that," said Owen.

"I'm sure it is," said Neap dryly as the young woman came in and handed Owen a card.

"Miss Stone was given the name of a Carleton Hoopes," said Owen.

"Was Hoopes given her name?" asked Neap.

"Yes, indeed. That is how our particular system works. We provide the names to each of the subscribers. From then on it is their responsibility to get together."

"I'd like you to pull Hoopes's card," said Neap carefully.

Owen looked at him steadily. "You have a reason?"

"I have a reason."

Owen nodded to the girl, who left. "We like to consider our file as confidential," he said.

"I could easily get a court order," said Neap. "This way saves a great deal of time for all, however."

"I hope you find what you want."

Neap shrugged. "We'll see."

The girl came back with another card.

Owen glanced at it. "Mr. Hoopes was given three names. An Ann Cheyney, a Miss Stone, and a Donna Whitford."

Arbosh whistled softly as Neap leaned back, no longer feeling like an idiot.

"You've found something interesting?" asked Owen.

"Two of those young women have been found strangled," said Neap. "It has to be a little more than coincidence."

Owen leaned back. "It is rather odd."

"We need the addresses of Hoopes and the third girl," said Neap.

"I suppose I have no choice," said Owen.

"None," said Neap grimly.

"Mr. Hoopes's address is listed as the Crescent Hotel at Seventh and South. Miss Whitford is at 1417 Monrovia."

Arbosh wrote them in his notebook. "I'm curious," he said. "Why would Hoopes receive three names and the Stone girl only one?"

"The fee, naturally," said Owen stiffly. "Mr. Hoopes paid more. The young lady paid only a small down payment under a special program."

"Would any other man have been given the names of these three young women?"

Owen spoke reluctantly. "Not in that combination. You see, the computer responses are arranged—"

He was wasting his polished voice on an empty chair. Neap was halfway out the door.

Arbosh had trouble keeping up with Neap's long strides. "You sure ended that in a hurry."

"Couldn't take him any longer," said Neap quietly. "Too smooth, trying too hard to sell us that it is all very scientific and legitimate, but I'll take the old village matchmaker every time. At least he knew who he was dealing with, and he didn't ask for down payments or money in advance. Something about this setup doesn't feel right. These services may be completely clean, but remind me to check with Davis in Bunco about this one."

"Where do we go first?"

"The hotel. If Hoopes does have a date with the Whitford girl tonight, and I think he does, it's too early yet. She probably works until five."

"One thing we know about Hoopes," said Arbosh. "If he lives at the Crescent, he can't have much money."

"Don't leap to conclusions. Maybe his address isn't important to him."

The clerk at the desk of the Crescent was small, narrow-shouldered, with closely cropped black hair and thick glasses. He was reading a paperback book that featured a nude man and woman on the cover. A sign on the desk said his name was E. G. Bauer.

Neap asked for Hoopes.

Bauer dropped the book, hesitated, took off his glasses, and polished them slowly. "Mr. Hoopes is no longer with us. He checked out today."

"Just our luck," muttered Arbosh.

"Did he leave a forwarding address?" Neap asked.

Bauer smiled. "People who stay here never do."

Arbosh pulled out his notebook. "What did he look like?"

Bauer hooked his glasses over his ears. "That's hard to say."

"You saw him, didn't you?"

"Only a few times. What I meant was, there was nothing distinctive about Hoopes. He looked like many other men."

"We can do without the editorial comment," growled Neap.

"Average height," said Bauer hastily. "Long brown hair. Maybe twenty-five. Big shoulders, looks like an athlete."

"What color eyes?"

Bauer smiled. "I don't pay attention to the color of men's eyes."

Neap chuckled. "Anything unusual about him that you can remember?"

"Nothing. I told you. He looked like a million other men."

"He either owned a car or rented one," said Neap. "You ever notice?"

Bauer shook his head. "I'm afraid I like to read too much. If it can't come up to the front desk, I don't see it." He indicated his glasses. "And even then I can't see too well."

"I may want to talk to you again," said Neap. "When do you go off duty?"

"Five o'clock. I stay here at the hotel. I'll be glad to help in any way I can."

"You can help now," said Neap, kneading the back of his neck. "Do you have any aspirin?"

Outside, Arbosh looked at him closely. "You should have listened to the doc and taken a day or two off."

"You explain how and I'll be glad to do it. Right now, we have to get to this Whitford girl and see if she has a date tonight with Hoopes."

Arbosh expertly wheeled the car through traffic. "Maybe he called her first and she's already had a date with him," he thought aloud.

"In that case, she'll be able to give us a good description but I doubt that it has happened yet or she would be dead. He went after the other two on successive nights and I'm betting he's seeing her tonight. Maybe he checked out because he's thinking of moving on. It would be the smart thing."

"If he's the man who did the killings, he's planned it well. You think it's the first time?"

"Who knows? He seems to have a big hate for a certain type of young woman. These dating services can serve them up to him on a silver platter."

Arbosh glanced at his watch. "It's a little too early for the Whitford girl to be home if she works until five."

"The way things have been going, she probably has moved," muttered Neap.

Monrovia Street was cobblestoned and hardly wide enough for the car. Once a fashionable address, time had changed it to an inexpensive, convenient place for young people to live, the two-story houses converted to first and second floor apartments. Donna Whitford was listed for the second floor.

Neap punched the bell, heard it ring somewhere upstairs, and waited, not really expecting an answer. He tried again, thinking that all they could do would be to wait until the girl showed up. Then the thought came that she might not come home.

He held his finger on the bell for the first floor.

The door was opened slightly by a slim blonde teenager who peered cautiously out at them. Neap held the badge for her to see clearly in the twilight. "We're looking for Donna Whitford."

"I heard you ringing. She won't be home until late."

Neap felt his nerves tighten. "Do you know where I can find her?"

"She's meeting a date somewhere."

Arbosh said something under his breath.

Neap glanced at his watch. It was almost five. "You know where she works?"

The teenager nodded.

"Can you get her on the phone for us?"

"I don't know," she said doubtfully. "I'm not supposed to let anyone in the building."

"You may be doing Miss Whitford a big service."

"Wait here," she said, closing the door.

"Great confidence in her police force," said Arbosh.

"We're not in uniform," Neap pointed out, "and the tin could be faked. Besides, would you trust anyone who looks the way I do now?"

The door opened again. "She's already gone," said the girl.

"You sure you don't know where we could find her?" asked Neap. "Think. Did she mention anything at all about where she was meeting her date?"

The girl shook her head. "I told you I don't know."

"Tell us what she looks like," said Arbosh.

"She's a little taller than I. She wears her hair in a ponytail."

"Blonde, brunette, red hair?"

"Blonde hair and brown eyes."

Neap grunted. He should have known. "What did she wear today?"

"I didn't see her go out."

Neap thanked her, motioned Arbosh into the car, then sat tenderly fingering his cheek. It still throbbed a little but the aspirin had driven away the headache.

"What now?" asked Arbosh. "And before you say it, I'll bet two to one we don't get very far with it."

"If you were Hoopes, where would you meet her?"

"It's a big city. Besides, we don't know if it is Hoopes she's meeting."

"You want to take a chance that it isn't?"

"No," admitted Arbosh. "I guess we'll have to find her. The question is, how? He could have reserved a table at some restaurant and is meeting her there."

"I don't think he wants to be noticed that much," Neap said slowly. "He'd want to meet her someplace where people wouldn't notice him. He might also want to size her up first if it's a blind date."

Arbosh was silent. Neap hoped that he would pick up the lead he had tossed him.

"The eagle again," Arbosh said finally.

Neap smiled. "I think so. He's used it before and it fits the pattern."

The department store was big, taking up an entire city block. The eagle, bronzed and benign, was situated in the center of the first floor, surrounded by a court that was filled with people; some passing through, others waiting.

Neap looked around. The first floor above them was a low balcony, one part of which was a paperback book department. He beckoned Arbosh. They mounted the stairs and walked through the book racks to the rail overlooking the court. From here they could watch without being noticed, yet they were not so far away that they couldn't run down the stairs to intercept someone in the court below. They studied the people waiting.

"I think we hit it," said Arbosh, pointing. "The one in the purple coat."

Neap peered closely at the girl. She could have been the sister of Needa Stone. "I think so."

"We could go down and ask her."

"No point. We just might scare him away if he's watching."

"This is ridiculous," said Arbosh. "We're watching a girl we *think* is Donna Whitford, while waiting for a man we've never seen to show up."

Neap grunted. "We can't be wrong all the time."

"If we are wrong, a girl might die tonight."

"I know that as well as you," snapped Neap. "If you have any other suggestions, I'll be glad to listen."

Arbosh moved away from the expression on Neap's battered face. He glanced around the book department, reached out and touched Neap's elbow. "Look who is here."

Neap turned. Almost hidden behind the head-high bookshelves was Bauer, the clerk from the Crescent Hotel, studying book titles.

Neap looked down into the court, then studied Bauer for a moment before reaching him with quick strides. "What are you doing here?"

Bauer almost dropped the book he was holding. "Looking for something to read. This place has the best selection in town."

Neap grasped his arm firmly. "We're looking for Carleton Hoopes. You can help. You've seen him, we haven't."

Bauer tried to pull away. "I don't want to get involved in anything."

"You're already involved." Neap pulled him to the railing and pointed. "All you have to do is tell us if you see him down there."

Bauer straightened his glasses and peered downward. "I can't see too well."

"Strain your eyes," said Neap harshly.

The girl with the ponytail and wearing the purple coat had moved impatiently from one side of the eagle to the other.

Neap held out his watch. They had been here for a half hour and no one had approached her.

A broadshouldered young man wearing a tan coat had taken up a position on the opposite side of the eagle, eyeing the girl occasionally.

Neap stiffened, pointing him out to Bauer.

"Is that Hoopes?"

"Too far for me to see well," complained Bauer.

Neap took his arm again. "Then we'll take a closer look."

He led Bauer down the stairs to the main floor and positioned him in an aisle close to the broadshouldered man. "Can you see now?"

Bauer squinted. "It might be him. The light isn't too good."

The broadshouldered man moved, slowly approaching the girl.

"The light is great!" whispered Neap fiercely. "Take a good look!"

"He's wearing a hat," said Bauer doubtfully. "I never saw him wearing a hat."

Neap stood indecisively. The young man was talking to the girl.

"What shall we do?" asked Arbosh. "If they move out, we could lose them in this crowd."

Neap made a decision. "It's time Hoopes showed up, and who else would approach her?" He and Arbosh moved in on the couple.

Neap held out his badge. "Miss Whitford?"

Puzzled, the girl nodded.

Neap breathed a sigh of relief and spun on the young man. "Your name Hoopes?"

The young man looked bewildered. He shook his head. "What's the matter?"

Neap turned back to the girl. "You were to meet a man named Hoopes here?"

Surprised, she nodded.

"You ever meet him before?"

She shook her head.

"Then you don't know if this is Hoopes or not?"

Her eyes widened. "He could be."

The man tried to pull away from Arbosh. "Take your hands off me!"

"Take it easy," snapped Neap. "You're in trouble."

"What for? All I did was try to pick her up."

"For more than that, Hoopes."

"Ny name isn't Hoopes. It's Foster."

"Look," said Neap wearily, "she had a blind date with a man named Hoopes. You show up and begin talking to her and then say you're not Hoopes. Can you explain that?"

"There's nothing to explain. I saw her standing there and figured I had nothing to lose. What's wrong with that?"

"Nothing, if true. You're just going to have to prove it."

"Even if he is Hoopes," said Donna Whitford, "what difference does it make? We have a date."

"No, we don't!" yelled Foster. "I never saw you before!"

Her mouth worked. She tearfully spun on Neap. "See what you've done?"

Neap looked at the curious crowd and sighed. "We're not going to settle it here. We'll talk about it at headquarters." He turned to Arbosh. "Get Bauer. We'll take him along."

Arbosh scanned the crowd. "He's gone."

Neap had the horrible feeling that it was all wrong again, that the bad luck which had haunted him all week was still working full time. He glared at Arbosh.

"As soon as we get back, put out an all points on him."

Two hours later, the young man was still insisting he wasn't Hoopes and he wanted a lawyer. All he knew about Ann Cheyney and Needa Stone was what he'd read in the paper, he'd never subscribed to Date, Inc., and he had alibis for Monday and Tuesday nights which Arbosh was checking.

Donna Whitford went home after Neap had explained his interest in Hoopes, leaving Neap with the feeling that she blamed him for ruining her evening and that if Hoopes were to show up, she'd be only too happy to go out with him. She had given Neap a statement saying that Hoopes had called her and his voice was deep and pleasant.

"He talked like an educated man," she said, sighing. "He was very smooth."

That certainly didn't sound like Foster to Neap, so he wasn't surprised when Arbosh arrived with Foster's brother.

"Foster is legit," he said. "No chance of being Hoopes. His alibis for both of those nights are tight."

The brother spent ten minutes telling Neap what he thought of the police force in general and Neap in particular.

After they had gone, Neap sat glumly staring out the window. His headache was back again and his cheek hurt.

Arbosh offered him a cup of coffee. "We haven't eaten all day."

"I'm not hungry. I've lost my appetite."

"At least we saved Donna Whitford," Arbosh said comfortingly. "We still have a chance to pick up Hoopes. I put out an APB on him. He'll turn up somewhere."

"We should have had him," said Neap. "He should have been in our hands."

"He probably never showed up."

Neap shook his head. "If I read him right, he showed up. He must have seen all the excitement and taken off. We moved too soon. If we had waited, the Whitford girl would have turned Foster away once she found out he wasn't Hoopes."

"We couldn't take that chance," said Arbosh. "Bauer should have been of more help. Too bad he can't see well."

"The more I think of it, the more I wonder. With all the reading he seems to do, his eyes can't be that bad," said Neap grimly. "But you haven't found him yet?"

"He's not at the hotel. I have everybody looking for him."

"He's a funny one," said Neap.

He and Arbosh looked at each other.

"You thinking what I'm thinking?" asked Arbosh.

"He could have used the name Hoopes and the hotel as his address, knowing he could intercept the mail," said Neap slowly.

"And it was a very convenient coincidence that he happened to be in the store at the time Hoopes was supposed to be there."

"That little guy just *might* be Hoopes," said Neap. "The way things have been going lately nothing would surprise me."

Arbosh stood up. "The question is, where is he now? Where would a guy like that go? Do you think he left town?"

"No reason for that. As far as he knows, we don't suspect him of being Hoopes. He'll take his time about leaving."

"He's probably sitting somewhere laughing at us."

"Not him. A guy like that has no sense of humor. Right now, he's feeling frustrated because we kept him from the Whitford girl. That would be uppermost in his mind. To him it's unfinished business."

"I remember one like that before," said Arbosh. "Didn't have a ghost of a chance of pulling it off but with that one-track mind of his, he had to try."

"Maybe this one will have to try, too," said Neap, kicking his chair back. "I just hope that Whitford girl believed me when I told her about Hoopes. She seemed to act as if I didn't know what I was talking about."

Monrovia Street by day was quiet and charming. At night it was too quiet and deserted, lit only by a couple of widely spaced, old fashioned, feeble street lights. Neap noted that all the first-floor windows were either barred or shuttered. A lot could happen on this street without anyone's noticing.

Neap hit the bell to Donna Whitford's apartment, received no answer although a dim light outlined the window. He probed gently at the door and it swung open. A flight of stairs stretched upward, lit by an inefficient wall fixture. Neap went up two at a time. At the head of the stairs was a landing and another door. To hell with protocol, he decided. He turned the knob and pushed. It was unlocked.

Then he saw the two figures in the semidarkness of the room.

Donna Whitford's eyes were wide and staring, fixed on him with a desperate pleading above a broad hand clamped over her mouth. The man's other arm was wrapped around her waist, his face half hidden by her head, and then she kicked out in an effort to break loose and knocked over the single lamp on the low table. The room went dark.

Neap sensed, rather than heard, the swift rush coming out of the black room and ducked too late. A fist smashed against his swollen cheek and Neap gasped. Behind him, still on the stairway, Arbosh yelled.

Neap's right fist smashed out, catching the man in the stomach. He followed with a left hook that carried all his weight and the frustrations of the past three days. He felt a shooting pain from his fist as it landed on something hard, and the man pitched past him into the hall.

Neap leaned against the wall, holding his numbed left hand, looking down at Owen, the man from Date, Inc.

A shaky Donna Whitford came to the door. "He said he wanted to talk to me about a refund. I had no way of knowing . . ."

"Neither did the other girls," said Neap.

Arbosh looked up at him. "We weren't so smart either."

Neap's appetite came back after everything had been wrapped up and he and Arbosh sat down to the first meal they'd had that day. His left hand splinted and bandaged, his right cheek more swollen than ever, and his right eye closed, Neap sat staring at the steak the waitress had brought.

"What's wrong?" asked Arbosh.

"I thought my luck had changed. I asked for rare. I got medium."

"Send it back."

"No chance. With my losing streak, they'd probably burn it."

"We didn't do so badly," argued Arbosh. "We did catch up with a guy who killed two women and almost killed a third."

"We're the world's greatest detectives," said Neap sarcastically. "I never even considered Owen, yet sitting in that office he had access to every girl who subscribed to the dating service. He could pick and choose the ones he wanted."

"I still don't get it," said Arbosh. "A man like that . . ."

"Forget it," advised Neap. "Just catch them. Don't try to analyze them or you'll go out of your mind. Some shrink may find out what he had against lonely young blondes. Then again he may not. We're out of it."

"Funny he picked the three that were sent to Hoopes."

"Not so funny. He figured to use Hoopes as a cover, and we bought it. The one thing he didn't know was that there was no Hoopes. It was Bauer using the name because of some fool notion that Carleton Hoopes sounded more romantic than his own. Of course he never received any names. Owen saw to it they were never sent."

"Owen had a lot of nerve. He knew we were looking for Hoopes and the Whitford girl, yet he showed up at the eagle anyway to see what would happen. If we hadn't been there, he'd have kept the date and the Whitford girl would be dead."

"I told you these people don't think the way we do. He had to try to prove something by killing her. That's why he went to her apartment. You can save yourself a lot of effort if you don't try to figure them out." He sliced at his steak. "I was too busy to follow it up, but where did they find Bauer?"

Arbosh chuckled. "A couple of the boys picked him up as he left the public library, of all places. One of the other guys took his statement. He said he almost fainted when we came looking for Hoopes so he gave us that description of Hoopes from a book he was reading. Then when we collared him in the department store to identify a guy who never existed, all he could do was claim he couldn't see him well and disappear the first chance he had."

Neap chewed painfully. "I guess the Whitford girl has had enough of dating services. She'll probably be content to die an old maid."

"Don't count on it. Maybe that computer works. The last I saw of her, she and Bauer were holding hands and discussing books. I've seen worse-looking couples."

Neap sighed and pushed his plate away. His bandaged left hand made it difficult to cut the steak and his right cheek made it too painful to chew. Even if Arbosh had worked out pretty well, it had not been the best three days of his life.

"It doesn't happen very often," he said.

"What's that?" asked Arbosh.

"Donna Whitford made a small down payment for some excitement and romance. She's one of the few to get her money's worth."

Coffee Break

by Arthur Porges

"**I** always thought that locked room cases occurred only in detective novels." Sergeant Black's tone was plaintive, as if he accused the universe of unfairness to the police.

Ulysses Price Middlebie, object of the remark, and former professor of the history and philosophy of science, but now a sometime crime consultant, looked thoughtful.

"Undoubtedly they began with mystery fiction," he said evenly. "But life does imitate art. To put it otherwise, I'm sure that many bright and imaginative crimes have been suggested—even guided step by step—by ingenious stories."

"Which means in addition to outguessing dumb apes with lengths of pipe, we now have to keep two jumps ahead of the best mystery story writers!" the sergeant grumbled. "I don't suppose *you* ever read such stuff," he added.

"To the contrary," Middlebie said. "I've always enjoyed a good crime story, especially of the puzzle variety. And now even more so." He glanced down at his heavily taped ankle, which was propped up on a hassock.

"As much my bad luck as yours," Black said. "It's the kind of case where you'd come in very handy. But you can't get around, even to watch birds, and anything that stops you from galloping over hill and dale with binoculars is pretty bad."

"Tell me about it, anyhow," Middlebie suggested. "I may still be of some help." Then he added dryly: "My head isn't taped."

Black had the grace to redden slightly.

"You're right, of course," he said. "It's your brains I've picked, mostly. But you must admit," he persisted, "that often I just miss seeing things that are significant to you because of your scientific background."

"True, but I'll try to pry out of you even the things you saw without noticing them. So go ahead, and give me all the facts."

The sergeant paused to organize his thoughts for a moment, and then began the recital.

"The dead man is Cyrus Denning, a bachelor of sixty-two. He's supposed to have poisoned himself with cyanide. His prints, and only his, are on the cup. He was found dead in a locked room. Nobody had been near him for at least half an hour before his death. From here on in," Black suggested, "we'd better change to that method—Socratic, wasn't it?—you liked so much in college, because I don't really know what to tell you or in what order."

"All right," the professor said amiably. "That's as good an approach as any. You say the door was locked. How?"

"Bolted on the inside; a heavy brass bolt."

"That's not such an impossibility. Such a door can often be locked by attaching a string or wire to the bolt, and shooting it home from the outside."

"Not this time," Black said grimly. "The door is recessed, and fits too tightly. Besides, no such string was found, and my suspect had no chance to remove it."

"Very well. What about a window?"

"One, at the back. It's been nailed shut for years, and undisturbed; that I'll guarantee. I went over every inch with a good magnifying glass."

"Could the glass have been cut out and re-puttied in?" There was a twinkle in the old man's grey eyes. "That's one from a mystery story I read some months ago."

"Not a prayer. It was old, crumbly putty; dry and hard, but still holding tight."

"Why nailed down?"

"Denning didn't care much about fresh air, and he was very secretive. Fancied himself a scientist and inventor. The place was a one room cabin by Lake Bradley, converted into a workroom and lab. The front door—the only one—he used to padlock on the outside when he left. When he was working there, he usually bolted it from the inside."

Middlebie frowned slightly. "Perhaps I should ask why, in the face of all this, you doubt he killed himself."

Black's lips narrowed. "Instinct—plus the fact that he left no note. In my experience, a suicide almost always leaves some explanation. Then there's the fact that Denning was filthy rich. When there's enough money as bait, the greedy rats can be inferred."

"Do you have a particular rodent in mind?"

"You bet. The old man's nephew. He was right there when they found him, and he's the lad to inherit two hundred thousand bucks, and who knows how to spend it fast."

"So he was at the cabin. Let's have the details."

"The boy—his name's Jerry Doss—admits seeing his uncle in the lab at noon. Sometimes he helped Denning, and managed to borrow a few bucks each time; not much because the old boy was tighter than a new girdle.

"Anyhow, he left Denning at one thirty, alive, he claims. The old man promptly bolted the door behind him. Then Doss went across the lake—that's about a hundred yards—to chat for a bit with the man at the dock, who rents boats in season. Things are quiet there now, of course.

"Well, he stayed there for half an hour, then left. But he asked the boatman to keep an eye on Denning's front door, which to me is one sign of a plot. The boy was obviously setting up an alibi."

"What reason did he give for such an odd request?"

"He told the fellow that Denning had been bothered by some of the kids—that they hammered at the door and ragged him. Doss said that if the boatman could catch them at it, and identify them, his uncle would be glad to slip him ten bucks."

"Very plausible," Middlebie said, with a wry grin. "The boy has imagination—*if* he invented the story."

"I'm betting he did. Anyhow, at this point all is clear. Doss left Denning half an hour before, and didn't go near the door, as the boatman can testify. He never took his eyes off the area, watching for the kids, and hoping to earn ten bucks the easy way.

"Then, about fifteen minutes after the boy left the dock, the man sees him at the front door, hammering away and yelling. Finally, he turns and motions to the boatman to join him. When the guy gets there, Doss tell him that he looked in the window, and saw that his uncle was either dead or unconscious. The window's in back, remember, so nobody could have seen the boy look in.

"Well, they break down the door—it takes both of them, because of the heavy brass bolt—and find Denning dead, with a cup of poison at his hand. He's slumped over the table near the window."

"Couldn't he have been killed when Doss first left? Before going across the lake to the boatman?"

"That's what bugs me," Black groaned. "There was a cup of coffee on the table, boiling hot. It must have been recently poured—and that's where the cyanide was. Cold water wasn't good enough for this suicide. He had to have his poison in fresh, hot coffee!

"And that isn't all," the detective almost shrieked. "A cigarette was burning on the edge of an ashtray. It couldn't have been lit more than a few minutes earlier." He looked at the professor, his whole face one agonized question mark.

"Hmm," Middlebie murmured. "I begin to see what you're upset about."

"So it has to be suicide, and I'm an idiot," Black said, more quietly, "only I don't like the smirk of that nephew, or the little spark in his beady eyes. He engineered this deal some way, and I want to nail him!"

The professor was lost in thought for the moment. Then he said absently: "You must have read about Sherlock Holmes."

Black gaped at him.

"I'm thinking of his brother, Mycroft," Middlebie said, smiling.

"Mycroft?"

"Like me, he was immobilized. In his case, sheer laziness and bulk. But he solved some very puzzling cases from his armchair, with brother Sherlock doing the leg work." He gave Black a quizzical stare. "Why don't we try that, eh?"

"I'll try anything," the sergeant said. "I'm good at leg work. Sometimes I think that's all I'm good at."

"Nonsense. You have brains and imagination," the professor assured him in a gruff voice. "Now, here's what I'd like you to do. Get me large, clear photos of the lab, inside and out, all four sides. And of the view from the place in all directions." His eyes clouded briefly, and he said: "Are you sure the bolt is brass, and not just painted that color?"

"Painted? No, but why—" He bit the question off short. "I'll certainly find out," he promised, his voice hard.

"You do that, and let me know. Is there a phone in the lab?"

"Yes."

"Then call me from there. And bring the pictures as soon as they're available."

"I'll phone you in three hours. We should have pictures by tomorrow afternoon."

"Good." Middlebie watched the sergeant stride to the door. When

Black had left, the old man opened a drawer in his desk, took out a fifth of bourbon, and after some painful limping about, made his favorite tipple of whisky, beer, and brown sugar. He sipped it appreciatively, his brow knitting with thought every few moments.

Two hours and forty-eight minutes later, Black phoned.

"The bolt seems to be brass," he said. "At least, it's not iron, steel, aluminum, or lead."

"Hmph," Middlebie said, his voice indicating some disappointment. "That's a pity." After a moment's silence, he spoke again, his tone sharper. "I want you to scrape that bolt all over, and study it with that magnifying glass you were bragging about. Call me back if you spot anything interesting."

"What am I looking for?" the sergeant demanded irritably.

"Just make a careful examination and see what develops," the professor said. And he hung up.

Half an hour later, Black called back; there was a hum of excitement in his voice.

"I don't know how you knew," he said, "but somebody's been at the bolt, all right. Looks as if he drilled a hole, and put in a plug of some kind."

"Ahh," Middlebie purred. "Soft iron, I'll bet anything. First hypothesis verified."

"What's it all about?" Black queried eagerly.

"Tell you when we get those pictures," the professor said. "Bring 'em over tomorrow, will you?"

"Damn right, I will. But tell me—"

"Tomorrow," was the firm reply. "It's not all clear yet. Not at all." Again he hung up.

The next day, early in the afternoon, the sergeant appeared with a stack of glossy eight-by-tens. Middlebie took them, and shuffled through the pile in an impatient way, finally fishing out a shot of the interior. He peered at it, and groaned.

"S'matter?" Black demanded.

"The table," Middlebie's voice was full of disgust. "It's too far from the window. If only it had been right next to it . . . I don't suppose," he said wistfully. "there was any way to introduce the coffee and cigarette after the door was bolted."

"None," the sergeant declared. "Oh, there is a chimney from the fireplace, but I'd like to see the man dexterous enough to get a nearly full cup of hot coffee and a lighted cigarette down that. And with the chimney in plain sight of Wilson—he's the boatman."

"Another good theory gone to pot," the professor said. Then he asked: "By the way, was the coffee pot also hot?"

"Had to be," Black said. "It was still on a tiny gas fire."

Middlebie shook his head in admiration.

"That killer, whoever he was—and *if* he was—has brains. Pity he's warped. The lad even avoided anybody's finding a discrepancy between boiling hot coffee in a cup, and a pot only lukewarm. He just left the coffee on the flame—damned foresighted."

A bit dubious now, he studied the pictures. Suddenly his gaze grew sharp.

"What's that behind the cabin—this thing on the pillar? It looks like an astronomical telescope."

"That's just what it is," the sergeant said. "Denning dabbled in astronomy, too. They say he even found a new comet."

"This seems to be a refractor."

"Could be. I didn't pay much attention."

"You'd better pay more. I want the name of the manufacturer. But don't touch it; there may be prints."

"Whose prints? And what difference? I wish I knew what was going on in your head these last few days." The sergeant was obviously exasperated.

"I'll tell you when I'm sure myself," the old man soothed him. "Wouldn't want you to think I'm senile. Be a good lad, and check that scope. Get the maker's name, and if that isn't on it, measure the diameter of the objective—the big lens at the end. But hands off. Got it?"

"All right," Black said. Then he smiled briefly. " . . . Mycroft!"

Middlebie blinked. That was the first time the sergeant had ever dared come back at him. Good! It was time they had a less formal relationship.

"Before I go," Black said, gazing directly into the grey eyes. "Please explain that bit about the bolt. Certainly you're sure of that part."

"Oh, yes. I didn't mean to conceal anything," the professor said. "Open that right hand cabinet, and take out what's on the second shelf up."

The sergeant obeyed him, and was amazed at his own former incomprehension.

"Right," Middlebie said. "That's a magnet; a big one. It weighs five pounds, and has a two thousand gauss rating. Which means, I would guess, that even through a thick wooden door it has enough pull on a bit of iron imbedded in a brass bolt to slide the thing into its socket. Did you notice if the assembly was smooth-working—oiled, perhaps?"

"You bet it was!" Black exclaimed. "So that's it. What a chump I've been. All Doss had to do was step out, shut the door on his dead uncle, and move this kind of magnet from left to right at the proper height against the door." He flipped the piece of heavy metal from hand to hand in his enthusiasm. Then his face darkened. "But we're still up the creek on that coffee and cigarette bit. We know he was away from the cabin for over half an hour. The coffee would have cooled by then, and the smoke gone out."

"I'm aware of the difficulty," the professor said. "That's why I hoped the table would be nearer the window. By the way," he asked, "what kind of a day was it—the weather, I mean?"

"Nice one; cool, clear, sunny. Anybody but an old idiot would have been outside, or at least had a window open to enjoy the fresh air."

"It takes all kinds," Middlebie said. "Go check on that telescope like a good lad."

Black seemed about to ask more questions, but the old man's face was forbiddingly wooden. With a sigh, the detective left.

When he returned that evening, Middlebie was working with a binocular microscope, and seemed almost reluctant to shift his line of thought. He shoved his chair back, gave a grunt of resignation, and raised one eyebrow questioningly.

"Well?" he demanded.

"No maker's name that I could find. But the objective was five inches across."

"Good. A five incher could have a focal length of from sixty to ninety inches."

"What does that mean?" Black's voice was querulous. He was tired of driving up and back, and almost sorry he hadn't certified the case as suicide. Only sheer persistence—plus the nature of a good cop—made him stay with it.

"Here's how it must have happened," Middlebie said, sounding the least bit smug. "Doss visits his uncle; maybe works with him a bit in the lab. Then they have coffee, either as normal routine, or at the boy's suggestion. There are cases of standard chemicals against the south wall; your pictures show them plainly. It's easy for Doss to put cyanide in the old man's cup. The moment his uncle collapsed, the boy wiped his own prints off the cup, pressed Denning's on, and left, closing the door behind him. But first he put an unlighted cigarette on the edge of the ashtray.

"Once outside, he unobtrusively—in case somebody was watching—stood facing the door, and with a magnet taken probably from his uncle's lab, shot the bolt. I assume that at some earlier visit, when left alone by the old man, he drilled out some of the brass and inserted an iron plug so the magnet would work.

"Now, then. He went to the dock and established that half hour alibi. After that, Doss approached the cabin from the rear, where neither the boatman nor anybody else could see him, took the objective glass—already loosened, I imagine, the boy being so thorough—and stood a foot or two from the window. There, he focused the bright sunlight—"

"By God!" Black exclaimed, almost in a whisper, and Middlebie frowned at the interruption.

"An ordinary magnifier wouldn't work unless the table was only inches from the glass, but this thing focuses at from sixty to ninety inches. The window glass would cut a lot of the heat, but there would be plenty to bring the coffee cup to boiling, and to light the cigarette.

"Then, very quickly, to the front door, there to pound and finally hail the boatman. Very neat!"

"You've got it," Black said. "No doubt of that." He shook his head gloomily. "But how to prove anything in court."

"Well," the old man said. "The drilled bolt has some evidential value."

"Not enough, I'm afraid."

"Prints on the telescope?"

"Weak," the sergeant said crisply. "After all, the boy helped out in the scientific stuff."

"Ah," Middlebie said. "But if you're lucky, there'll be some on the *inside* of the objective. They would be harder to explain; much harder, since few astronomers ever dismount the objective. There are realignment problems, and dust—all sorts of reasons to leave it alone. But frankly, I think if you go at it right, the boy may crack. He doesn't dream we're onto him. Feeling plenty smug, I imagine."

Black looked at the lean face and seemed to see cats' whiskers twitching.

He's not the only one who feels that way, the sergeant reflected with amusement. But aloud he said only, "In any case, you've done your share. No Mycroft could have done better."

192   ALFRED HITCHCOCK'S ANTHOLOGY

The Volunteers

by Reynold Junker

Somewhere he could hear a bell ringing. It was a faraway sound, lost in a dark attic under a heap of broken old toys or hidden in the bottom of a barrel that smelled of dark, sour wine. There was a child, a boy, in a white First Communion suit searching frantically. He could feel the warm sting of the starched collar against his freshly scrubbed neck. It had been his brother's suit. And before his brother? And since?

Then the ringing was right there inside his head, pushing against the warm numbness of sleep. The child was crying.

Santro Ristelli shifted his bulk into a half-sitting position and ran a hand over his black, day-old beard. The bed creaked someplace in its joints. He leaned back against his elbows and listened. The only sound was the hoarse, strained breathing of the child sleeping on the couch in the front room.

The phone rang. Santro didn't move. He wondered sleepily how many times it had already rung. He had been awake only seconds. Maria, his wife, jerked awake at the sound. She, like her husband, was a dark, heavy person but had learned to move quickly. With five children, she had to. "What's wrong? What is it?" Her voice was thick with sleep.

In a few seconds, Santro thought, she will be wide awake, but now her voice is like that, as though she was afraid to say all of the things that are bottled up inside her. In the old days she sang and cried and laughed, but now there is nothing to laugh and sing about, and what's the use of crying? There is only the slow, heavy voice always asking, "Is anything wrong?"

Without answering, Santro slipped from the bed onto the bare wooden floor. He picked his way through the darkness past the front room and out onto the landing. Outlined against the dirty grey light from the open roof, his squat hairy body looked like a circus bear. He lifted the phone from the wall before it stopped ringing. "Hallo?"

"Santro?"

Even in his sleep he would have known the voice. It was like a loud hissing in his ears, someone telling another a great secret, but very anxious that everyone should overhear. "Johnny— What the hell do you want?"

"Santro, my old friend, is that any way to talk to a buddy?"

"*Buddy*. It's the middle of the night. I need sleep, not smart talk. I'm the one who works for a living, remember?"

"Sure, Santro, sure. How could I possibly forget? Work all day, sleep all night. Someday you'll be the patron saint of the working class."

"Don't make fun, Johnny. Don't make fun." Santro could feel all of the sleep seeping out of him.

"Then listen, friend, and listen good. This is no smart talk. There's been a train wreck just outside of Fairfield. One of the specials coming up from Miami jumped the track or missed a stop. I didn't get it all exactly."

"So?" Santro heard the child groaning awake in the front room.

Johnny breathed sharply into the phone. "Is that all you can say? Think, Santro. Use something besides your belly for once. The special is loaded with a bunch of rich so-and-sos who have nothing to do but ride back and forth between New York and Miami looking for someplace to throw their money around."

Johnny paused, then continued slowly. He was saying each word carefully as though he were driving nails. "Fairfield is a small town. They're calling for volunteers to help with the bodies. The police can't handle it. They need help—with the bodies."

"I don't know," Santro said, more to himself than into the phone.

Johnny's voice became an angry hiss. Santro remembered the time the younger man had spoken at a local union rally. He remembered the voice and eyes and the arms rising and falling wildly.

"Santro, listen, do I have to go down there myself and bring back the stuff to show it to you? All you have to do is pick it up off the ground—at most empty a few pockets or fingers. They're dead! It's no good to them any more. They're dead! What do you say?"

"Shut up. Shut up for a second, will you? I've got to think about it. There are other things—" He shut his eyes and tried to ask himself what they were, these other things. The old words and answers he had learned as a child floated back across the years, but he could never be the child in the white communion suit again. How easy the answers had been then.

He had learned all of the answers, but nobody had ever really explained the questions. They had never told him that he'd have to choose and that no matter what the choice, someone had to get hurt. He had had to learn that for himself. Someone is always getting hurt. Every door you open leads to another door.

Johnny's voice was a whisper. "What about your old lady? And the kids? Is young Santro still having that trouble? It's a terrible cough. Sometimes, it's almost as though his chest were breaking in—"

"Liar," he whispered, but there wasn't any anger in his voice. Santro ran a hand across his face. He was wet with perspiration. Johnny was whistling softly under his breath. Santro tried to swallow. His mouth tasted of something stale and brown. "How soon will you be here?"

"Just as soon as I can."

"I've got to get dressed."

"Better get something to eat."

"I'm not hungry. I'll only need time to dress."

"Just as well. Tonight we'll be eating steak. Your old lady—"

"Don't come to the house. I'll meet you at the corner."

"Okay. I'll be driving my cousin Guido's truck. We'll need a couple of picks and a shovel and maybe some—"

"Bring them. Whatever you think." Santro hung up the phone without waiting for an answer and stood listening to the silence around him. He felt a little sick. He tried to think, but he could only remember.

Maria was sitting up on the edge of the bed. "Is anything wrong?" she asked dully. "Who was that?"

Santro picked up his clothes from the chair on which he had laid them the night before and began pulling them on.

"Where are you going? What's wrong?"

"That was Carlo," he lied quickly. "There's been a train wreck over near Fairfield and he wants us to go over and help with the—hurt. The police can't handle it. I guess it's pretty bad."

"Why you? What about the others? The younger ones?" The sound of her voice made him want to scream, to strike out at her.

"A bunch of us are going. It's pretty bad." He could feel the words catching at the bottom of his throat. It was hard to keep from shouting.

"Will you lose any time on the job? Will they pay you?"

He turned to face her. She looked far away, like a ghost or part of a dream. "Money!" he answered angrily. The words were coming loose now. "Always money. Isn't there ever anything else? Why can't there ever be something besides money?" He looked at her and found himself hoping that she'd be able to tell him something he hadn't been able to find for himself. There was still a chance. Somewhere, someplace maybe he had missed something.

"How can there ever be anything else for us?" Her voice neither fell nor rose. The words tumbled across her lips simply because the muscles expanded and contracted.

"I'm sorry," he said softly. "The company wants us to go. It will look good for them. We'll be paid. Maybe even a bonus."

He finished dressing in silence. When he looked back at the bed, Maria had rolled over on her side and lay facing the wall. He couldn't tell whether or not she had fallen back to sleep. He picked up his jacket, turned off the light, and started out through the front room.

Santro walked slowly through the soft grey morning. The streets smelled sweet and damp and a kind of freshness ran through them like something lost. His mind was flooded through with thoughts of Maria and of the children. They came into his mind, not separately and distinctly, but fused together, a jumble of names and faces without any real name or face: Maria's voice, the boy's eyes, a cough, a cry. They tumbled together crazily. It was like looking into a toy kaleidoscope or even more like being inside one. Everything was lost in the shifting patterns of colored glass. Everything he once thought was sure seemed to become tangled and changed each time he moved. He couldn't be certain of anything except that he seemed to be moving all the time; not going anywhere, just moving.

He turned quickly at the sound of the truck pulling up at the curb beside him. It rattled to a stop and the door swung open. Santro climbed up into the pickup and pulled the door closed behind him. He leaned back against the worn seat and tugged the collar of his jacket up around his chin. Johnny laughed lightly, shrugged his shoulders, and gunned the engine. The truck groaned around the corner and jerked heavily toward the highway.

"Don't be so gloomy, Santro. It's not the end of the world."

"Maybe it is. For some." He avoided looking at Johnny.

"The weak must die so that the strong may live, eh, Santro?"

"And vultures. What about the vultures?"

Johnny laughed softly. He reached across the seat and slapped Santro sharply across the thigh. "You and me, vulture and friend. The vultures going to loot the vultures. They loot from us when they are alive and we, like any self-respecting vultures, return the favor. Ha-ha."

They drove in silence to the highway where they turned north toward Fairfield. Johnny whistled the same tune over and over until it became like a faucet dripping someplace in the middle of the night. Santro shut his eyes against it and tried to relax.

"You know what's wrong with you, Santro? You're an Italian—" He said "Eyetalian" as though it were a word he'd never heard before except in street jokes. Santro opened his eyes and stared out along the narrow white ribbon of highway. It had already begun to grow quite light. "And you know what's wrong with *Eye*talians? They're a whole race of nothing but stomachs. Stomachs. The women are always pregnant and the men are always eating. I don't think there's been an *Eye*talian with an idea since—since Da Vinci."

"And you, Giovanni *mio,* of course we mustn't forget you," Santro said wearily.

"Not me. Not the kid." Johnny grinned at him and tapped his head just in front of his ear. "Up here, plenty of ideas, American ideas."

"Johnny, Johnny the American. Excuse me."

They approached Fairfield from the south along the highway that paralleled the railroad and then turned onto a dirt road that ran along the tracks on either side. The wreck wasn't visible until they had made a jogging turn to the right and drove up over the top of a softly sloping hill. The pickup jerked down the incline slowly. Santro had never seen a train wreck before. The only trains he could remember seeing were the shining blue and silver limiteds that screamed past the gangs working near the tracks and the faded red-brown locals that labored up and down the coast between the small resort towns. What he saw before him now looked like something he might have seen in a newsreel somewhere, something quick and alive and violent that had broken and snapped into silent deathlike pieces. Beams and splinters of wood and metal stuck out at crazy angles from the tangle of the wreckage. At places up and down the line he could see small puffs of smoke rising and settling. The narrow shoulder beside the tracks was dotted at places with dark blankets. He felt the same stale brown taste come up into his mouth. A couple of the bodies hadn't been covered over yet. Maybe they had run out of dark blankets.

THE VOLUNTEERS

Johnny drove down the sloping road to a small canvas tent that had been set up about halfway down the line. A dark, squat man came out and motioned for them to stop. Johnny waved back at him and pulled up beside the tent.

"Just in time." He grinned at Santro.

"There's hardly anyone here."

"That's what I mean. Just in time."

Santro reached over to open the door at his side. Johnny grabbed at his sleeve. "In case they ask us for our names, I'm Johnny Williams and you're Santro Candoli. Get it?"

"Got it, Johnny Williams." Santro nodded.

They dropped down from the truck and Johnny came around quickly, past Santro, to where the fat man was standing. "I'm Johnny Williams and this here's my friend, Santro Candoli. We came over to help. They said over the radio that the police couldn't handle it and you were sending out a call for volunteers."

The fat man spat into the dust at his feet and shrugged at Johnny. "Leave it to the radio."

"What do you mean?"

"I mean leave it to the radio to figure out a way to exaggerate the thing—anything."

"You mean this—" Johnny motioned with his arm at the wrecked train "—isn't the special from Miami?" He had stopped grinning.

"Kid, this ain't even the special from Hoboken." He spat again.

Santro looked closely at the faded red cars. He smiled weakly.

"But I guess since you're here, we can use you to help finish cleaning up this mess. We're short of tools. Did you bring any?"

"A pick and a couple of shovels," Santro answered. He felt sort of giddy, as though he were listening to someone telling a very funny joke. He could still get breakfast and make it to work on time, but there was something he wanted to watch: the American; the idea man. After all, they had come to help, he and Johnny Williams.

"You may as well grab them and start on down the line. We figure we already got all or mostly all of the bodies. There couldn't have been too many passengers. If you find one, call for one of the guys and he'll tag it and cover it up. Maybe you'd better check and see if they want you to start any place in particular." He spat again and went back into the tent.

Johnny stared down the line at the small group of men bending over their shovels. Santro walked back to the truck and pulled out the two shovels and the pick. He shouldered the shovels and tossed Johnny the pick.

"Let's go, volunteer."

"Of all the luck! Of all the rotten luck! It makes my blood boil!"

Santro laughed softly. He wanted to laugh out loud and clap Johnny across the back. Here they were, volunteers, clearing the track so that the Miami Special wouldn't be delayed. All of the rich devils who have nothing to do but ride back and forth between New York and Miami looking for someplace to throw their money around would be back in New York for dinner—thanks to the volunteers.

They started down the line toward the small cluster of men. Johnny walked behind Santro, kicking up the dirt with his feet. He didn't look at the older man. Santro didn't figure that he would, not for a while anyway.

"Son of a—of all the rotten, stinking luck!"

"Oh, well, it was an idea." Santro spoke evenly. He wasn't about to give Johnny the chance to explode. That would get it out of his system too soon, and Santro wanted him to live with it for a little while longer.

They made their way to a man who was standing over a shovel watching a couple of others. A small pack of yellow tags showed from inside his jacket pocket. "Volunteers," Santro said when the man looked up at them.

His eyes were like those of the man in the tent, and Santro half expected him to spit. Instead he straightened up and looked down the line to the rear of the train. "We already finished up most of it on this side. I don't know why he sent you down here. How about going around to the other side and checking with the boys around there? They started after we did."

Santro nodded and motioned to Johnny. They started slowly down the line toward the last car. Santro glanced at his watch. He should have been leaving for work. Neither of them spoke. Johnny picked up a rock and heaved it ahead of them at one of the beams that lay across the track. It hit something soft and kicked up a small puff of dust. Something yellow caught the light and flickered through the dirt. Something groaned.

Santro caught at Johnny's shoulder. "Listen!"

The groan came again. Santro caught his breath. He looked quickly back toward the others. One of the cars jutted out between them. They wouldn't be able to see him and Johnny. Something yellow flickered again in the dust.

Johnny dropped to his knees and began pawing at the dirt with his hands. He dropped back against his haunches and held a woman's gold bracelet in the sun for Santro to see. Santro dropped the shovels and shoved him aside, away from the woman. The younger man fell back heavily into the dust and glared up at Santro. He grabbed for the pick.

"You fool, she's alive! Didn't you hear it?"

"You're nuts. You're hearing things." Johnny pulled his hands away from the pick. It had been only a gesture. Santro knew that he wouldn't use it.

"Help me get her out of here."

Each of them grabbed at one end of the beam and lifted it from the woman's body. They cleared away the dirt and dragged her out from under the wreckage. She had been pinned there on her stomach.

"Turn her over gently."

They laid her out on her back. Santro dropped to his knees beside her and pressed his ear against her chest. He could hear her heart beating faintly. There were other sounds. Sounds of something breaking or broken inside her. He pulled himself up to his knees. "She's alive."

Johnny had moved off to one side behind him. Santro looked back at him. The younger man's eyes were like those of a frightened child. He tried to say something, but the words caught inside him and all that came out was a small whining sound. He pulled the bracelet out of his pocket and let it fall into the dirt. "Her face—her poor face," he muttered weakly.

Santro looked down at the face for the first time. It was broken and blue with bruises, and the eyes were open.

Santro heard Johnny drop to his knees. He was retching. Santro placed his hand against the woman's chest. He could feel the soft tapping cadence of the heartbeats. He looked down into the woman's face again. The colored glass dropped away. All of the faces in his mind became one final, distinct face—

He placed the flat of his hand against her chest and forced down against it. One final spurt of blood ran purple from the twisted mouth before the eyes rolled up into the lifeless head.

Santro reached down and removed a pin from the dead woman's dress. He took two rings, one a diamond engagement ring, from her fingers. "She was all but dead," he said to the stillness around him. "The children deserve a chance to live. I'm sorry, but that's the way it is—for us, anyway."

He stood up beside the body. Johnny was gone. The pick was still where he had dropped it. Santro reached down and picked up the bracelet. He turned and started back to the truck. The jewelry was heavy in his jacket pocket.

Death at Stonehenge

by Norma Schier

He found them disturbing, those great hulking shapes. The brilliance of the moon etched them sharply. He had been so pleased, it had gone so smoothly—but those stones! In daylight Stonehenge struck him as fusty, a few crumbling relics of a bygone age, but the moonlight breathed a terrifying life into the great forms, and in spite of himself his mind conjured up primeval watchers lurking in silent disapproval.

The stones threw giant shadows in thick black bars across his path. He staggered slightly under his burden as he walked—through the Sarsen Circle, the Bluestone Circle, between a monolith and a trilithon, on through the Bluestone Horseshoe, and so to the Altar Stone. The flattish boulder came about to his waist, and none too gently he laid her on its uneven surface. The winds swept howling across the Salisbury Plain, stirring her long yellow hair. He wiped wet palms on his trouser legs. Only the wind would stir it ever again.

Her hair was blowing next morning, too, when Chief Inspector Harlan Faulkner stood over the corpse. His long, agile hands were thrust into his pockets, and his tall, lean body was braced to resist the chilly, screeching wind that gusted in and out of the titanic trilithons. He felt at home in this odd place, having forsaken a career in archaeology only when he realized that he could not afford a doctorate. He had turned to detection of the criminal present as a substitute for the historic past, and seldom regretted it, for he found in police work unexpected human satisfactions.

With Stonehenge empty of reminders of the mundane present—the sightseers with their everlasting cameras had been turned away and his men were still in the car park collecting their gear—time here seemed to have slipped its moorings, and one could imagine that the ancient stones, looming as high as twenty feet over him, were imbued with the primitive spirits to which this woman had been sacrificed.

"Which is as great a nonsense as you'll ever think of," he grumbled to himself. "There never were sacrifices here, and this is the work of a more than somewhat cracked brain. Or," he amended, "someone who wants me to think so."

He felt profoundly sorry for the woman, baldly abandoned to the winds of the ancient place. Her coat was open and an unusual-looking dagger protruded starkly from her blue silk dress. She looked about thirty, with delicate, pretty features and, even in death, a wistful look. What, he wondered, had led her to this bizarre end?

On impulse, he brushed the hair back from her face, and started. It moved oddly under his hand. He shook his head to clear it of primitive vapors and returned to the twentieth century. She was wearing what he knew was called a fall, and he pulled it off. She looked quite different, somehow more interesting and at the same time less pretty, her face now framed with short, wispy locks.

The others came straggling up and set to work, following their usual routines. Faulkner, too, became businesslike. He picked up the purse that was lying on the ground and went swiftly through it. The only noteworthy item was a telegram addressed to Mrs. Alexander Carmichael at 21 Upper King Street, Salisbury. It read, "Meet me nine tonight car park Stonehenge. Urgent." It was unsigned.

"So that's it!" He whistled to himself. "*Cherchez l'homme*, after all." It fit with the silk dress and fancy hairpiece.

"Hugh," he said to his sergeant, a chunky, fresh-faced man who looked younger than he was, "take this stuff back to the station and we'll look it over later."

He handed him the purse and the fall. "But have the weapon checked out now. I want it."

While he waited, the police doctor made a quick examination and report. The dagger had apparently killed her, probably instantly, between nine and twelve the previous evening, at a rough estimate.

The sergeant returned with the dagger.

"No fingerprints, sir."

He nodded, slipping it into his coat pocket. "I'm going to pay a call. Check out this telegram and see what you can find out about the Carmichaels—and what she did yesterday. See you later at the station." He headed briskly across the ground, through the circles of stones—or what was left of them after nearly four thousand years—and on to the road, swinging along in an easy stride.

Dr. Alexander Carmichael was a quiet, shaggy-haired professor of mathematics, retired, with sad, nervous eyes. His face became tragic when Faulkner broke the news to him. They were in the small living room of the Carmichael home. Books and papers were lying around in casual disorder, many overlaid with a fine coating of dust. Some nondescript plants drooped on the windowsill, and badly fitting slipcovers sagged on two or three pieces of furniture. Whatever the dead woman had been, she hadn't been a zealous housekeeper.

Dr. Carmichael spent most of his time pursuing esoteric researches and writing them up for learned journals. Of medium height, he had to crane his neck to meet the eyes of the lanky inspector. He looked considerably older than his wife.

"Felicity dead?" he said dazedly in a high, thin voice. "*Murdered?* You're sure there's no mistake?"

"I'm afraid you'll have to identify her, sir," Faulkner said, "and then we'll know for sure." There was no mistake, and when he saw the woman lying on the impersonal morgue slab, he wept. Faulkner took him back home and gave him brandy. "Have you any idea, doctor," he asked quietly, "who might have done this?"

"Oh, yes," Carmichael said dully. "How could he do this to me? It was bad enough before, but now—now I'll never get her back."

He struggled for control, and then it came out. His cherished, adored Felicity—a sweet and gentle soul, according to him—was having an affair with an archaeologist in London. The man had come down to study Stonehenge the year before, and Mrs. Carmichael, a knowledgeable astronomer, had worked with him.

"At first I couldn't believe it, inspector. Not Felicity. She insisted she had just met him and their association was professional, and I tried to accept that. But they were *so* close. I often thought that they previously knew each other and cooked up the 'professional investigation' for my benefit. I suppose she couldn't help herself," he added wistfully. "But there's no doubt what developed afterward. She's been going up to London every week to see him. It's been horrible."

"How do you know?"

"She'd go out and lie about where she was going. Only yesterday she did that. Many times—you may think this strange behavior for a professor,

Faulkner, but I *had* to know—I followed her. On three occasions I saw her go into his house."

"But why would he kill her?"

"Why indeed?" Carmichael echoed hollowly. "Perhaps he'd found someone else and she was in his way. He's an evil man, inspector."

Faulkner reached into his pocket and brought out the dagger.

"Is that what did it?" Carmichael's voice was harsh. "It's his—Donat's! He showed it to us not long ago. That proves it, doesn't it?"

"We'll soon find out," Faulkner promised grimly.

On the eighty-mile drive to London, Faulkner went over the case with Hugh Preddie, his sergeant. The other man's enthusiasm entertained him, for Preddie still managed to find in crime investigation a fulfillment of boyhood dreams that had been nurtured by the detective magazines. This did not, however, prevent him from being an able investigator.

"Let's not forget, Hugh," Faulkner said now, "there are two Stonehenges—the scientific one of archaeologists and astronomers and the superstitious, romantic one of Druid temples and blood sacrifices. Pure nonsense, of course. No evidence the Druids had anything to do with the place, which was about fifteen centuries before their time. The scientific makes much more sense, naturally, and besides we're dealing with scientists. But still, you do hear of queer cults from time to time and I've always thought scientists are more credulous than they like to admit—as if a secret yearning to believe in the mystic attracts a lot of 'em to science in the first place. Not hope of finding disproofs, but an unconscious hope they won't. I noticed a sizeable collection of books on ancient cultism at the Carmichaels'. I don't know if they're his or hers, but there again the interest may or may not be purely scientific."

"Yes, sir," Preddie agreed dutifully. He himself leaned toward the Druid-temple-and-blood-sacrifice Stonehenge, and not unconsciously either, but he would have died rather than admit it to his chief.

"So we don't know," Faulkner said, "whether we can rule out some kind of cultist nonsense behind the murder, though the simplest explanation is that they used Stonehenge as a meeting place. They may have done so often, this time having a lovers' quarrel, or he having planned to murder her, maybe for some such reason as the husband suggests. Having the dagger with him looks like premeditation."

Preddie cleared his throat self-consciously. "It strikes me, sir, that the dagger points to this Donat *very* clearly. For a learned and, I should think, intelligent man, he's left a pretty obvious trail. Do you suppose he's being framed?"

Faulkner laughed. "You know very well that crimes are usually more obvious than your fiction writers make them out to be. Still, it could be. We're a long way yet from knowing all about it. I'll give you odds Donat will tell us the dagger was stolen. It might have been, Hugh, it might have been. But the rendezvous—and Stonehenge at that—sounds like another man.

"By the way, what did you find out about the telegram?"

"Came from London," replied Preddie. "They phoned it and got no answer, so they delivered it. It turns out she was at her hairdresser's in Salisbury—getting that fall thing, in fact. That's the only time she did go out, far as I could learn. No visitors, either, that anyone saw. And no one saw her go out last night."

"Which we know she did," Faulkner observed. "Her own car, too. It was still in the car park."

"It was the husband," Preddie doggedly pursued his original thought, "that put you onto Donat, wasn't it?"

"I see what you mean, but I'll swear he was really broken up. You can tell, you know. And crushed about the affair."

"Of which we have his word for its existence."

"He went up to London yesterday morning and got back by the early-morning train today—he says. We'll check after we see Donat. What did you find out about them?"

"Lived quietly. No one seems to have thought she was playing around. A devoted couple, I'm told. Him worshiping the ground she walked on and her very solicitous of him. No close friends, though, or anyone that really knew them well. Kept to themselves."

"What if it wasn't an assignation," Faulkner mused, "but a meeting to check out an astronomical position at firsthand?"

"How would that lead to murder?" Preddie was skeptical. "I've never understood," he added irrelevantly, "all the recent excitement over Stonehenge. Astronomers have said for years that the stones were aligned to show the position of the sun at the—uh—solstices, isn't it? To celebrate the sun god," he added in a welter of uncertainty.

"Ah, but a chap named Hawkins made quite an addition." Faulkner galloped happily away on his hobbyhorse. "The stones *do* show positions, like the sun rising right over the heelstone on Midsummer Day, and setting, if you're looking from the right place, within the framework of one of the trilithons at the Winter Solstice. Someone—Sir Arthur Evans, I think—pointed out it would look like the sun going into a tomb, which fits with a primitive religion, but Hawkins found more astronomical alignments than the earlier fellows dreamed of—sun *and* moon. However, the big thing he proved was that these supposedly primitive ancients could *predict* important astronomical events—especially eclipses, which terrified them—for all the years to come, with a little resetting of their computer every three centuries."

"Sounds fantastic." Preddie was impressed in spite of himself. "How did they do it?"

"You know the Aubrey holes around the stones. The scientists hadn't really been able to explain them, and Hawkins worked out that they were a digital computing machine, that all eclipses could be predicted in a fifty-six-year cycle, and there are fifty-six Aubrey holes! They could have been used to track the years. If six rocks are placed at certain intervals and moved one hole per year, when certain rocks are at certain holes eclipses occur. He proved it in one minute on a modern computer by feeding his data into it. They used to think the Aubrey holes were intended for more stones, or some ritual purpose. There were cremations in them, but that must have been secondary."

Preddie felt a twinge for the ritual cremations, but arrival at an impressive Georgian house in Mayfair bearing Donat's address forestalled further archaeological discussion. They parked and alighted, coattails flapping, though the winds were distinctly tamer in London than on the Salisbury Plain.

When they got inside, they learned that the house had been made into flats. They had no trouble locating Donat's and he himself opened the door to them. He was a dark, handsome man with an athletic build and the weathered face to be expected in a working archaeologist—or a big game hunter, Faulkner thought. He professed a courteous willingness to be helpful, combined with polite doubt that he could.

"The Carmichaels? Oh, yes, they were here recently," he said, ushering them into a living room in which the odors of leather and antiquity mingled. "Brilliant couple. She was invaluable on the Stonehenge thing. We were working on one of Hawkins' unanswered questions, the Bluestone Circle of Stonehenge II. It's been written up, if you'd like to see."

"I would, later," Faulkner said sincerely. "At present we're investigating Mrs. Carmichael's murder."

"Good Lord! I knew she was unstable, but—murder!"

"How do you mean, unstable?"

"Well, overemotional. Fearful. And terribly hipped on cultism. Unnerved me at times. She was seeing a psychiatrist, you know. Friend of mine, actually. Felicity met her here. Shall I call her?"

"In good time," Faulkner said, crossing his long legs. "I'd like to ask *you* some questions first."

"Of course," Donat said easily, leaning back in his black leather easy chair. "Background and so on, I suppose. I don't think I can shed much light, however."

Faulkner hesitated. Donat was putting on a good act—if it *was* an act. "She was attractive, wasn't she?" he began tentatively.

"Yes, if you like the type. Rather too much the perennial sweet young thing for my taste," Donat answered coolly.

"You weren't interested in her—personally?"

"Whatever gave you that idea?" he asked sardonically. "Don't tell me old Alex Carmichael had some such notion!" He chuckled. "No, inspector, forget that tack. Not my style at all."

He's acting, Faulkner thought. He asked, "Where were you last night?"

"You sound serious." Donat was still amused. "With a lady friend, as a matter of fact. She'll vouch for it."

"They usually do." Faulkner's tone was dry. "Have you seen this before?" Once again he displayed the distinctive dagger.

Donat was silent for a time, and the tension increased. "Faulkner," he said at last, "my apologies. I underestimated you. I thought this was plain silly, but I see I was mistaken. You won't believe me but that was stolen from me, and I can prove it. You really should talk to my lady friend. She happens to be the psychiatrist I mentioned, and she lives just across the hall."

As if on cue there was a tap at the door and, without waiting, a tall, beautiful woman with sleek, dark blonde hair came in.

"Gary, I—oh, I'm sorry. I didn't know you were busy." Her voice was soft and faintly accented. Vienna, thought Faulkner. He wondered if she'd been listening.

"As a matter of fact, I was just going to get you," Donat said quickly. "Inspector Faulkner and Sergeant Preddie are from the Wiltshire police and they're looking into Felicity Carmichael's murder. Gentlemen, Dr. Amalie Angel."

What a lot of doctors in this case, thought Preddie, and not one that could cure a hangnail. (In which he was mistaken, for Dr. Angel had a medical degree.)

Meantime, she was saying to Faulkner, "But this is terrible! Yes, she *was* my patient, but I cannot tell you anything about her without violating professional confidence."

"Since she is dead—murdered—don't you think you could best help her by letting us know what was the matter with her?" Faulkner wondered just how ethical a psychiatrist in love would be.

"Perhaps, but I would have to think about it. I do have an idea where you should look."

"That's a help," Faulkner said coldly. "Did her husband know she was seeing you?"

"Yes, though he didn't approve."

Since there was little more that either doctor was willing to say, Faulkner requested that they remain available till further notice, and he left with Preddie.

"One for you, Hugh," Faulkner conceded on the way back to Salisbury, shifting his long legs with difficulty in the small English car. "Carmichael was certainly in London all afternoon, and got back by the early train this morning as he said, but he could just have nipped out of his meeting unnoticed, come down in a fast car, and gotten back in time to be seen at his club later. We can't rule him out on his alibi."

"But," said Preddie, "if he knew she was seeing Dr. Angel, why did he think she went there to see Donat?"

"We have only their word for that," Faulkner reminded him. "If she *did* have a mental ailment, I'd certainly like to know what it was."

Just beyond Wheat Sheaf Inn, Faulkner directed Preddie to bypass the turn that would take them directly to Salisbury. "I've an urge to revisit the scene of the crime," he explained.

He never failed to be stirred by the approach to the old stones. One minute you were rushing down a long straight road with flat unbroken plains stretching as far ahead as the eye could see, and the next small humps appeared on the horizon, growing steadily larger till they dominated the landscape.

They left their car in the now-crowded car park, crossed the road, and bought two tickets. Walking through the crowds of sightseers milling, gaping, and taking pictures, they headed for the Altar Stone. A plump, giggling girl was posing on the spot where the corpse had lain such a short time ago while her companion busily adjusted his camera.

"Why *here*, Hugh?" Faulkner mused. "Did that poor woman have some kind of craziness that turned her into a sacrificial victim? A sick relationship with Donat—or someone else?" He shrugged. "Let's go see Carmichael. I want to know what he has to say about his wife's need for a psychiatrist."

"Surely you don't believe that, inspector?" was what he did say, in a condescending tone, when they asked him. "Felicity told me she was seeing this Dr. Angel, but it was a blind to cover her going there so often. I assure you she was perfectly sane and happy. I don't doubt that everyone who knows us will say the same."

They had, Faulkner thought, with the exception of the London pair. "She wasn't—ah—carried away by cultism?" Faulkner pursued.

"My dear man," Carmichael said with asperity, "*I* am sometimes 'carried away' by ancient mathematics. Does that make *me* crazy? No," he said, reverting to his earlier manner of listless misery, "I *know* she was seeing him. I have reasons. For one thing, she had a disguise which transformed her appearance."

Abruptly the mathematician buried his shaggy head in his hands.

"I'm sorry," he apologized after a moment, "I can't discuss it without breaking down. She was very dear to me. I wanted her back, inspector. I would have cherished her all the more for her transgression. It just showed her human frailty."

Faulkner murmured something, and they left.

"Back to the station, Hugh," Faulkner said when they were outside. "I'm almost sure, but I want to think it through. I've a good idea, too, what Dr. Angel can tell me, and I want to talk to her."

"You've solved the thing, sir?"

"We'll see." But in his long thin bones he knew he had. The data was all there for the answer, and he was finally reading it right.

It came to a head that night.

The moon was more fitful than it had been the previous evening, for dark heavy clouds were drifting across it.

She was sitting on the Altar Stone, waiting, long slim legs dangling over the side, when he arrived, a dim form at first, striding through the intermittent shadows cast by those giant hulks.

"You came," he said in a low voice, when he was close enough.

"I thought you needed my help," she said in her soft accent.

"You said you know everything. This is a fitting place to meet. Do you know why?"

"You wanted to return to the scene of your crime."

"I want to commit another," he corrected in a conversational tone. The full moon appeared in time to glint on the kitchen knife he had produced. Suddenly he jerked his head.

"What's the matter?" she asked tranquilly.

"These stones," he muttered. "It's absurd, but sometimes they seem—alive. Have you felt it?"

"You're not far wrong, doctor. Drop that knife!" Faulkner spoke briskly from the shadows, which came swarmingly to life as police poured from behind the stones. The circles seethed with them, converging on the Altar Stone.

The moon emerged brilliantly again to illumine the grey, shaggy head of the man the policemen were holding firmly.

"Got you, Carmichael!" Faulkner was jubilant.

"Amalie, you idiot." Donat was holding the analyst as firmly as, and a good deal more tenderly than, the police were holding their captive. "Darling," he said, "you were marvelous."

"I was terrified," she said, burrowing into Donat's arms.

"Damn you all!" snarled Carmichael. "You're all in it together to cuckold me, but I'll kill every one of you!"

But the police had already disarmed him, and now two burly constables led him away.

"Inspector," Donat said, "when I was working on Stonehenge, I stayed at a nice old inn in Devizes called The Bear. Could you meet us there and fill us in?"

"With pleasure," Faulkner said. "I owe the lady a lot for the risk she took, though I have a few well-chosen words to say about her taking it—calling him and telling him she knew, and agreeing to meet him. A headstrong woman, if ever I saw one."

"Amalie says you had it all figured out," a curious Donat was saying to a complacent Faulkner a short time later, around a table in The Bear's private bar.

"A lot of things didn't make sense until Carmichael gave himself away," Faulkner said. "When I reviewed everything in the light of that, it all fell into place. I thought Dr. Angel's conscience might let her corroborate what I was already prepared to act on. Especially—" he grinned "—as it would clear you. I thought she might not be completely uninterested in that.

"If there was an affair," he went on, "motive was no problem. But if you and Dr. Angel were telling the truth, I couldn't see at first why either you *or* Carmichael would want to kill her—unless her mental problem were involved in some unknown way. But once he gave me reason to think *he* had killed her, I realized there was another alternative—that *she* wasn't mentally ill, but *he was*, with a jealousy that wasn't rational, and she was getting help to cope with it. I wanted Dr. Angel's confirmation. So he really thought he was being cuckolded—and you knew it, by the way. You put on quite an act."

"It seemed prudent," Donat said.

"He sent his wife a telegram making the rendezvous at Stonehenge," Faulkner continued. "He told us later what I finally realized—though he didn't sign it, he expected her to think it came from you. When she came, that constituted the final 'proof' to his crazed mind."

"He didn't seem crazy to me," offered Preddie.

"That's true paranoia," Dr. Angel explained. "Logical within the frame of the delusion, and sane outside it. The paranoid schizophrenic thinks the world plots against him because he is Napoleon or a lost prince, but the true paranoid is most apt to think his spouse is unfaithful and weave a chain of 'proof' to support his delusion."

"Like the hairdresser," Preddie suddenly realized. "She really did have an appointment."

"That," said Faulkner, "was the giveaway. She got the fall yesterday *after* he went to London, and she wasn't wearing it when he identified her, yet he referred to how different she looked in disguise. So he must have seen her in the new fall when he killed her."

"Why Stonehenge?" Dr. Angel wondered. "He wasn't mad in a way to believe in sacrifices."

"Purely practical," said Faulkner. "His alibi required her to be found soon enough to establish time of death, and he also needed a private place to kill her. At home he risked being seen in the neighborhood when he was supposed to be in London. Stonehenge was ideal—private but accessible by night and public by day. Besides, it was another pointer to Donat. He wanted to punish him, too.

"I have a question for *you*, Dr. Angel," he added. "You believed your patient utterly. Wasn't it within the realm of possibility that she was the sick one weaving a false story?"

"Not in this case, inspector." The pretty analyst smiled. "I *knew* Gary wasn't carrying on with her because I don't give him time. You must come to our wedding, which will be soon."

And, having drunk amply to the solving of the case, they drank to that.

Call Me Nick

by Jonathan Craig

"**H**e'll see you in just a few moments, Mr. Wilson," the incredibly beautiful secretary said as she put the intercom phone back in its cradle and smiled at him across the width of the anteroom.

"Thank you," Harry said, trying not to stare at her, and failing completely. She wore no clothing. No one here did, of course; but then, not everyone here was a curvaceous movie star who had been dead only a few years. He rubbed his eyes.

"It might help if you were to say something nice about his horns," the secretary said.

"What?" Harry asked.

"His horns," the secretary said. "He's an old dear, but he *is* a little vain about his horns. It would please him if you were to compliment him on them."

"I'll do that," Harry said, still trying unsuccessfully not to stare at her. "Thanks for the tip."

The secretary smiled at him again and went back to her typing.

"Miss?"

"Yes?"

"Does he interview *all* newcomers like this?"

"Oh, goodness no," she answered in the soft, enticing voice he remembered from the sound tracks of a dozen motion pictures. "He couldn't possibly. There are thousands of arrivals every day, you know. Tens of thousands, some days."

"Then I guess, whatever it is, it must be pretty serious."

"I wouldn't worry about it," the secretary said. "I'm sure everything will work out all right."

"I sure hope so," Harry said. "I've been here only four hours, but . . . Well, they've been the happiest, the most wonderful hours of my life."

ALFRED HITCHCOCK'S ANTHOLOGY

The secretary laughed. "Well, not of your *life*, exactly," she said. "But I know what you mean, Mr. Wilson. All the newcomers feel the same way."

The intercom buzzed softly. The secretary lifted the phone, listened for a moment, then nodded to Harry. "You may go in now, Mr. Wilson."

Harry rose, walked to the black door with the initial S inlaid at eye level in fuming brimstone, and reached for the doorknob.

"Don't forget, now," the secretary whispered. "Say something nice about his horns."

"Right," Harry said, and stepped into the inner office.

The being seated at the massive executive desk smiled, got to his feet quickly, and extended his hand.

"Nice of you to drop by, Harry, and *very* nice to meet you." He had a deep, melodious voice, powerful but controlled, like the controlled strength of the hand that clasped Harry's own.

"Thank you, sir," Harry said.

"Call me Nick," the being said, motioning Harry to a chair beside his desk. "We don't stand much on formality here, Harry. Sit down and let's chat a bit."

When they were seated, Nick leaned back in his chair, folded his hands behind his head, and regarded Harry warmly.

Harry was certain the friendliness was genuine, but he sensed that despite Nick's casual manner there was something troubling him, that he had something unpleasant to say and disliked having to say it.

"Well, Harry, now that you have seen something of the place, what do you think of it?"

"It's wonderful. It's so terrific here I can hardly believe it."

"Scarcely what you'd been led to expect, eh?"

"That's putting it mildly. But to tell the truth, sir, I—"

"Nick."

"Yes. To be honest, Nick, I never really believed there was such a place."

Nick laughed. "And what about the *other* place, Harry? You didn't believe in that, either?"

"Not really. I don't know . . . I just couldn't ever seem to make up my mind one way or the other."

"Well, it's up there, all right," Nick said. "You've been here about four hours, I think."

"Yes, and what a four hours! I never had so much fun. I never enjoyed myself as much in all the thirty years I was alive as I have in the few hours I've been dead."

"You approve of our ladies, do you, Harry?"

"Who wouldn't? I mean, with the kind of ladies you have here—and with no clothes on and all."

"Ah, yes," Nick said. "And the gaming rooms?"

"I never saw anything like them. Not even in the movies."

"And the various—to use an euphemism—spectacles?"

"Oh, fabulous!" Harry said. "Absolutely fabulous." Harry paused, remembering what the secretary had told him. "I hope you won't think I'm being too forward, Nick," he said, "but that's a mighty handsome set of horns you have there."

"Why, thank you, Harry," Nick said, obviously pleased. "Actually, though, most of the credit should go to my special horn wax." He nodded toward a small round tin he was using as a paperweight. "It's a formula I developed myself—through more millennia than I care to remember."

"Very effective, indeed."

Nick smiled. "Still, Harry," he said, "as pleasant as our little place down here is, it does have a few unfortunate features."

"I can't imagine what they could be. From all I've seen so far, everybody is having a ball."

"Yes, that's true," Nick said. "But wouldn't you say it's a trifle warm?"

"Not enough to matter," Harry said. "I'd hardly noticed."

"Atmosphere, you know," Nick continued. "After all, we do have a certain tradition to keep up. The brimstone, for instance— don't you find it annoying?"

"Not a bit," Harry said. "Oh, the fumes did bother my eyes a little, right at first. But I got used to it in no time. I hardly think of it."

"Glad to hear it."

Nick fell silent for a moment, then said, "Harry . . . "

"Yes, sir? I mean—yes, Nick?"

"Harry, I'm afraid I have some bad news for you."

Harry swallowed. "Bad news?"

"Yes, Harry—very bad. You see, there's been a mistake. I'm not sure just where it occurred, but it did. We've only recently computerized the Personnel Section, you know, and so it may very well have been the fault of a machine. Or possibly someone in the Screening Section erred. And

216   ALFRED HITCHCOCK'S ANTHOLOGY

of course the Selection Committee isn't infallible, either. In any case, Harry, an almost unprecedented mistake has been made." He looked away, plainly ill at ease.

"Mistake?" Harry said.

Nick sighed. "Yes. There's no use in trying to tiptoe around it, I guess. The bald truth is that you don't qualify for admittance here."

Harry half rose from his chair. "What? I don't *qualify?*"

"I'm sorry, Harry. By rights, you should have gone up to the other place."

"But I'm already down here," Harry said. "I love it here. I just don't understand."

"You simply don't have the credentials, Harry," Nick said, reaching for a folder on his desk. "Here's your file. You weren't even a *naughty child,* for Pete's sake. In all your life, right up till you died a few hours ago, you never sinned at all. You never did anything wrong, Harry. You never even had an evil *thought*. I don't come across a life-history as spotless as yours once in a hundred years."

"But . . . " Harry began, and then compressed his lips and stared at the floor. It was all too true, he knew; he'd never sinned in his life.

"I hope you'll understand my position," Nick said. "I really have no choice in the matter."

"You're going to send me up there, you mean?"

Nick nodded sadly. "Much as I hate to do it, yes. You don't deserve to be here, Harry. You just haven't got what it takes. I'm sorry as can be, fella, but I'll have to send you upstairs."

Harry's shoulders slumped. "What's it like up there?" he asked dully.

"Oh, you'll like it fine," Nick said, trying to make his voice bright. "It's . . . well, very restful and all."

"Restful?"

"Yes, indeed," Nick said. "By the way, Harry, do you have an ear for music? A lovely instrument, the harp, and—"

"I couldn't carry a tune in a washtub," Harry said. "And besides, I've got ten thumbs. Do they really play—uh, *harps* up there?"

"Yes," Nick said, "they really do."

"And what else do they do?"

Nick shrugged apologetically. "Not much, I'm afraid, Harry. Of course, you'll have wings, so you can always flap around a bit."

"I see," Harry said. "Play the harp, and flap around."

"I admit the place doesn't swing too much," Nick said.

"Listen," Harry said suddenly. "Once I won twenty dollars in an office pool and didn't report it on my income tax!"

Nick's smile was kind. "Sorry, Harry."

Harry shook his head. "It's so ironic," he said. "Edna *wants* to go up there. She expects to. She—"

"Edna?"

"My wife."

"Oh, yes," Nick said, opening Harry's file again. "I have a poor memory for names, I'm afraid."

"It's just that *she wants* to go up there. She says she can hardly wait. And me—I'm actually going up, when all *I* want to do is stay down here."

"Hmmm," Nick said, studying the file. "Your wife seems to be quite a woman, Harry."

"Oh, she is. She is that, Nick."

"Nothing personal, of course," Nick said, "but judging from the file, she would appear to have given you a pretty hard time. Eh?"

"She's very strong-willed,"Harry admitted.

"Indeed she is," Nick said. "She wouldn't let you smoke your pipe in the house, Harry?"

"No."

"Or drink? Not even a beer on your birthday?"

"No."

"Or go bowling with the boys now and then?"

"No."

"And made you turn your paycheck over to her every week?"

"Yes."

"And gave you an allowance of a dollar and a half a day for lunch money and bus fare?"

"Yes."

"What happened to the rest of your pay?"

"She had rather expensive tastes."

"So it would seem. And did she really make you sleep on a cot in the kitchen?"

"Yes, she did."

"Yet it says here that you lived in a two-bedroom apartment."

"There's a phone between her bedroom and the kitchen. She liked to have me in there so that I'd be handy in case she wanted anything during the night—a glass of water or something."

Nick closed the file and sat drumming his manicured claws softly on the desktop, his eyes thoughtful. "It's now three forty-five in your part of the country," he said at last. "You died in your sleep about four and a half hours ago."

"Yes," Harry said.

"Your wife would still be asleep, wouldn't she?"

"Yes."

"And no one up there knows you're dead?"

"No. But what—"

"Harry, you never did an evil thing in all the years of your life. If I were to let you go back topside for a few minutes, do you think you *could* do just one evil thing?"

"I—I could try," Harry said.

"Trying won't be good enough," Nick said. "*Could* you do just one evil thing, Harry? I'm asking you straight out. Yes or no?"

"I think I . . . Yes. Yes, I could, Nick. I know I could."

"Good," Nick said, smiling. "Because if you can, I'll be able to keep you with me."

"You really mean it?" Harry said excitedly. "Golly, Nick, that's wonderful!"

"Poor Harry," Nick said. " '*Golly*'! You never even learned to swear, did you?" He laughed. "But no matter. I suppose you've divined—if you'll pardon the expression—what you'll have to do?"

"Uh . . . well, I . . ."

"No, I suppose, being *you*, you wouldn't have," Nick said. "Well, Harry, it will all be very fast and very simple. And after it's over, you'll be able to come back here, a resident in good standing for eternity."

"I'll be qualified?"

"Fully."

"What must I do?" Harry asked.

"You'll wake up in your bed—in your cot, rather—in the kitchen, very much alive. There are knives in every kitchen, Harry. You'll take one of the knives and—"

Harry gasped.

"You said your wife *wanted* to go to that place up there, didn't you?"

"Yes, but—"

"So you'll be making her wish come true. You'll be doing a very good thing, Harry."

"In that sense, I suppose I would. But—"

"No buts, Harry; you would. At the same time, you'll be committing murder—and that's a very evil thing—but it'll qualify you for admittance here, which is where you want to be."

Harry felt excitement flooding through him. "By golly, Nick, you're right!" he said. "Edna and I—we'd both have exactly what we want."

"And I'd have what *I* want, too," Nick said. "I've taken quite a liking to you, Harry. I'd very much like to have you aboard."

"I just don't know how to thank you," Harry said.

Nick chuckled. "Please don't give it another thought. Shall we embark on our little mission at once, then?"

"Gosh, yes!" Harry said, jumping to his feet in his enthusiasm. "The sooner the better."

"Just one thing, Harry," Nick said as he reached toward his intercom. "Once you're topside, you'll have only five minutes. The regulations governing unusual procedures such as this are quite inflexible, I'm afraid. Five minutes, Harry. Not a second longer."

"That's more time than I'll need," Harry said. "Twice as much."

"Of course it is. I just wanted you to be informed." Nick depressed a key on the intercom. "Please arrange for Mr. Wilson's immediate return to his body," he directed his secretary. "And alert the Receiving Section to stand by for his readmission here."

"Yes, sir," the secretary's mellifluous voice said.

"Golly," Harry said, "this is almost too good to believe."

Nick stood up, shook Harry's hand, clapped him on the shoulder, and walked with him to the door.

"Good luck, Harry, old man," he said. "You'll be back with us before you know it. Don't worry."

When Harry returned to awareness, the luminous hands of the kitchen clock stood at exactly five minutes of four. There was snow on the windowsill, and a wintry moon shone through the window, cold and bleak and remote.

Harry rose from his cot swiftly, took a butcher knife from the cabinet by the sink, and walked noiselessly down the hall to his wife's bedroom.

Beside the bed, he paused for almost a full minute, waiting for his eyes to grow accustomed to the darkness. His wife lay motionless, snoring softly, a huge, shapeless mass beneath the electric blanket.

Harry grasped the edge of the blanket and gently inched it down to his wife's waist. Then he raised the knife above his head, judged his stance and the distance carefully, tightened his grip on the knife until his wrist ached, balanced on the balls of his feet for the plunge of the blade, took a deep breath—and froze. He just stood there, poised for the thrust he could not make. Then, very slowly, he lowered the knife.

His palms were wet with sweat, despite the cold room, and he dried them on the front of his pajama jacket. There was a pain in his chest, and he realized he had been holding his breath. He sucked air into his lungs and braced his feet, trying to stop the trembling of his knees.

I've got to do it, he told himself. I've got to do this evil thing.

He raised the knife once again, and once again he set his mind and body for the single thrust that would qualify him for admittance to the place where he so desperately longed to be. Again, it was like the first time. He stood as if paralyzed, the knife held high, while the seconds slipped away and the tremor in his knees spread throughout his body.

Down in the street a car went by, a broken cross link in a snow chain clanking against a fender wall. From somewhere across the city a police siren keened suddenly, then was silent.

I can't do it, Harry thought. I simply can't do it.

Of course you can, a voice in another part of his mind said. *You must. Eternity's a long time, Harry. Do you want to spend it in a place where all you can do is play the harp and fly back and forth?*

No! Harry thought. No! I couldn't stand it—not after I've seen what the other place was like. I just couldn't stand it.

Then kill her, the voice said. *Look at the clock on the bedtable. Your time's running out, Harry. Don't you want to go back down there with Nick? Down where all the naked ladies and the fabulous spectacles and all the other wonderful fun-things are?*

Yes! Oh, yes!

Then do it, the voice said. *If you want to spend eternity there, you'll have to qualify. You've only a few seconds left, Harry. Just raise the knife again—yes, that's right—and . . .*

Harry did, and then did it again, and again.

I've done it! he thought exultantly as he withdrew the knife from his wife's body. I've qualified! I'm going to hell!

"Congratulations, Mr. Wilson," the shapely secretary said with a smile as Harry entered the anteroom of Nick's office. "You see? You succeeded in spite of yourself."

"I was beginning to think I wouldn't be able to do it," Harry said. "I don't know what got into me."

The secretary laughed. "I do," she said. "*He* got into you, Mr. Wilson. As a matter of fact, he gets into a *lot* of people."

"He does?"

"Oh, my yes," she said. "He's waiting for you, Mr. Wilson. You're to go right in."

"Thank you," and Harry opened the door to the inner office.

Nick was standing beside his desk, grinning broadly. "Nice going, Harry. Welcome back."

"It's great to *be* back, I can tell you," Harry said happily. "But for a while there, I didn't think I was going to make it."

"You were superb, Harry. Magnificent. A truly splendid performance in every way."

"It's all so wonderful," Harry said. "I've never been so happy. Is it okay if I go out and join in the fun now?"

"Well, no," Nick said. "All those happy sinners you saw gamboling about are merely awaiting final processing. They'll all soon be down in hell proper—where they belong."

"What?" Harry said. "They'll be where?"

"Down below," Nick said. "And in case you've wondered about my rather large clerical force, it's made up entirely of assistant Nicks, so to speak—beings very much like myself. The only exception is my pulchritudinous secretary, whom I keep around for reasons as excellent as they are obvious."

"I don't understand," Harry said.

Nick pressed a button on his desk. "Look behind you," he said.

Even as Harry turned, a large section of the floor suddenly slid back to reveal a yawning pit at his feet. He gasped, and cringed back, staring down at a scene of such unspeakable horror that he felt his legs begin to sag beneath him.

There, far below him, were the tortured souls in their multitudes, chained and naked, writhing in a churning sea of flame and molten rock. Blood-chilling shrieks of agony and terrible wails of despair rent the steaming air, and the sulphurous stench of brimstone mingled with the reek of burning flesh.

Harry whirled around, to find that Nick had come up behind him. The horned being was laughing so hard there were tears in his eyes.

"You tricked me!" Harry managed to say, his voice high-pitched with terror. "You were just playing a game with me all along!"

"Of course I was," Nick admitted.

"But why?"

"Why?" Nick said, his slitted yellow eyes twinkling merrily. "Why, just for the pure hell of it, Harry. We've got to have a little fun around here, after all. You wouldn't begrudge us a few laughs, now and then, would you?"

"What a fiendish thing to do!" Harry cried.

"It really is, isn't it?" Nick said and, laughing, he shoved Harry backward into the pit.

One November Night

by Douglas Farr

Lyle Beckwith was a methodical man who believed that one could organize the future as well as the present. One organized the future simply by foreseeing and being prepared for all eventualities. Even the eventuality of being assaulted and robbed in the street.

Such violence was a possibility in Lyle Beckwith's life because on one night every week he had to be out on the streets. On that night, usually Monday, he didn't go home to dinner. Instead he drove over to the other side of town where he kept the books for Garman's Market. Mr. Garman paid Lyle fifteen dollars a week for this service—pretty good pay, Lyle figured, for about three hours' work. And it was a rather important fifteen dollars because it bought music lessons for his daughters, Sandra and Sheila, plus a few other small extras—and all without disturbing the "basic Beckwith budget."

Against that tidy little weekly sum, Lyle had weighed the dangers. Garman's Market was one block off Majestic, which was a well-lighted, well-traveled thoroughfare. Lyle had to think of the safety of his automobile, too, so he thought it best to park on Majestic, preferably right under a street light. He would usually arrive at the market about seven, and he would leave between ten and ten thirty. Theoretically then, his only real risk was the one-block walk from the market to Majestic Avenue about ten o'clock at night. Surely the risk was small.

But he had a plan of action ready just the same. This plan involved his briefcase, a battered old black job with a reluctant zipper. Lyle carried the thing with him to work every day, but it was really misleading. Lyle was not important enough at his office to be required to take papers home in the evening and pore over them. The briefcase was only a camouflage for his lunch—and on Mondays his dinner, too. The savings from this little practice had bought braces for Sandra's teeth. But since he was a white collar man, Lyle thought carrying a lunch pail was somewhat degrading. Besides, he was a small man, and thin in the bargain, so the briefcase also lent a certain air of distinction.

Moreover, the briefcase was the key to his plan of defense. He had a perfect horror of physical violence. And should he be accosted by holdup men, he certainly didn't want to be on the receiving end of any of the kind of rough stuff he read about in the papers—not to mention what it would cost him if the would-be bandits broke his glasses or anything like that.

All that could be avoided, Lyle figured, by sacrificing the briefcase. When the bandit approached—and Lyle was sure he would recognize the type—he would simply throw his briefcase at him, yell, "Here, you can have it!," and run. The implication of "Here, you can have it!" would be obvious. The briefcase contained valuables of some kind, but the owner would rather surrender those valuables than try to resist. What bandit in his right mind would pursue the man and not stop for the briefcase? Lyle had read somewhere that a man who had been held up had scattered some money on the ground which his assailants stopped to pick up, enabling the man himself to escape. Lyle reckoned that the bait of the briefcase was just as good. And with that reluctant zipper, it would take somebody a long time to get a peek inside the thing, and that would give Lyle plenty of time for retreat. Besides, the briefcase was cheaper than new glasses, and maybe, too, he could get Mr. Garman to buy him a new one.

A foolproof plan, with perhaps even a positive advantage. All one had to do, Lyle figured, was to be prepared for all eventualities.

On this brisk, chilly night in November, Lyle Beckwith left Mr. Garman's premises confidently. He was dressed in a gray topcoat and a gray felt hat, not recently blocked, and he carried his briefcase. With the purposeful stride of a man who has somewhere to go, he walked toward Majestic Avenue.

As always on these Monday nights, he was alert and suspicious. He kept a sharp lookout for other pedestrians, determined to give them all a wide berth, not to let anybody get so close to him that he couldn't pull his briefcase routine.

The journey promised to be uneventful. He seemed to be alone on the sidewalks. Nevertheless, when he reached the corner at Majestic, he paused for a moment and glanced around in all directions, up and down the street, right and left. His car was parked half a block down Majestic, and the space between it and him appeared to be empty. He turned with military precision and marched in that direction.

But he hadn't taken more than a dozen steps when the whole picture changed. Twenty feet ahead of him, out of the shadows of the line of parked cars, two men stepped. Lyle halted instantly, and so did the men.

With his glasses, Lyle's eyesight was keen enough. And what he saw about the two men wakened his primitive instincts of fear and self-preservation. The men were not of a size—one was much taller and leaner than the other—but they were dressed similarly. Each wore a hat with the brim turned down. Each wore a topcoat, and each had both his hands thrust into the pockets of his coat. They both stood as still as statues, waiting for Lyle to come up the sidewalk.

It wasn't quite as Lyle had foreseen it. The men weren't supposed to be dressed like a couple of private eyes or foreign correspondents, and they were supposed to approach him more furtively and ask for a match or something like that. Yet Lyle felt no ebb of confidence. His plan of battle would adjust easily to this change of strategy by the enemy.

For a long moment, the antagonists faced one another. Lyle's flabby, civilized muscles tensed for what he knew must surely come. If he would not go to the men, they certainly would come to him. So he was ready when they took their first tentative steps.

"Here, you can have it!" he shouted, and he threw the briefcase at them.

He did not wait to see where the poor bag landed or the men's reaction to the maneuver. While the briefcase was still in mid-air, he whirled and ran down Majestic Avenue in the opposite direction.

For a second or two, his own footsteps made the only sounds in the quiet night. He had definitely taken the marauders completely by surprise. In his mind's eye he imagined the pair, first staring down at their booty so easily claimed, then seeing their victim receding down the street, finally saying, "The heck with him," and greedily stooping to examine their treasure. And that zipper—that good ol' zipper, his ace-in-the-hole—delaying them and delaying them till their quarry was safely out of reach.

Just how much of this routine the two men followed, Lyle never exactly knew. But he had scarcely regained the corner when it first began to appear that his plan had somehow gone awry. For the footsteps of those men were pounding on the sidewalk behind him.

The realization couldn't hasten him any because he was already moving faster than he ever had in the past twenty years. But the fact that he was being pursued didn't stop him, either. He flew across the street and hurtled down Majestic's next block. Still he didn't realize how far things had gone amiss until the next several events happened in quick succession.

"Stop, or we'll shoot!"

He didn't stop.

Three shots rang out, and things like bees buzzed past his ears.

Lyle knew then that his plan, however it might have comforted him for the past six months, had somehow fizzled. And from that point on he proceeded without plan, using every instinct and bit of primitive cunning that lies dormant within the mind and body of every twentieth century bookkeeper.

The echo of the third shot hadn't died when Lyle forsook the sidewalk and dived for shelter into the darkness between two parked cars. He crouched there for a second, panting, all his senses finely tuned.

Majestic Avenue was profoundly silent. He knew the men hadn't abandoned the chase. He seemed to have confused them at least. Probably they didn't know his exact whereabouts.

He raised himself a bit so that he could peer through the car windows to check on theirs.

Then he saw them. They were standing on the sidewalk about five or six cars down from the car that sheltered him. One had the briefcase. Both had guns, he was sure. He couldn't exactly see the guns, but he could tell from the way they held their right hands, waist high and thrust forward.

How long would they pursue him? he asked himself. How anxious were they to get hold of him? And why? He was no expert on the strange workings of the criminal mind, so he couldn't imagine their motivations. They had the briefcase—one of the men was carrying it. What more did they want? Him, of course. But were they angry at the way he had outsmarted them? Or were they perhaps—and this thought really chilled him—the sadistic kind of criminal who sought the pleasure of inflicting injury rather than financial gain?

He had little time to speculate on these horrible possibilities. One of the men—the one without the briefcase—was sidling over to the curb, inching cautiously between two cars, and approaching the street side of the line of parked vehicles. The pincers technique. They were trying to surround him.

Lyle reacted instantly, without premeditation. Leaving cover, and dashing out to the open of either the street or the sidewalk, would have only made him a target. So he did the only thing there was to do. He flattened himself on the ground, then propelled himself forward, face down, using his elbows and knees for traction in a way that would have delighted a marine training sergeant, and wriggled completely under one of the automobiles.

He well knew how helpless he would be if discovered in that position, but he tried not to think of it. He lay there and held his breath, his mind blank but the springs in his body still coiled to move in any direction.

He had concealed himself just in time. He heard soft footfalls from two directions. They told him clearly what was happening. One man was coming down the sidewalk, the other down the street. They were moving at the same cautious speed, like G.I.'s in movies he had seen, working as a team into a booby-trapped town. Then they stopped, still synchronized, one on either side of the car he was under. For a drawn out interval there was utter silence. "Where'd he go, Mike?" came a whisper finally.

"Thought it was somewhere about here," the voice belonging to Mike whispered back.

"Do you see him?"

"No."

"Don't think he got into one of these cars, do you?"

"We'd have heard the door."

Lyle shivered as he waited for the inevitable. All they had to do was have a different preposition occur to them, change "into one of these cars" to "*under* one of these cars." It was a switch in the thought direction of one of the men that saved him.

"Charley, take a look into that briefcase while you've got a chance."

"Can't get the bum zipper open."

Bless that bum zipper! If Charley looked into that briefcase and found only a lunch box and a thermos bottle, they'd really be mad.

"Well, hold onto it, anyway."

"I'm not letting go of it."

"He could have sneaked farther down the line on the street side, before I came around here. I think he's farther down. Let's keep going."

The voices stopped, and the footsteps continued on. Lyle waited till there was silence again. He had decided one thing. Pretty soon they'd think of looking *under* cars, and he didn't want to be where he was when they did. Using the same wormlike means of locomotion, he inched out from beneath the car on the street side. His pursuers, he saw, were eight or nine cars down the street. So it was back in the other direction for him. He straightened up and began his retreat with the best combination of silence and speed that he could manage.

When he reached the corner again he had to make a decision, whether to continue down Majestic Avenue toward his car or to turn right toward Garman's Market, hoping that Mr. Garman would still be there and let him in. Without any particular reason, trusting to luck, he chose the latter course.

He increased his pace to a run now. One block to go . . . you'd think somebody would have heard those shots and would have called the police . . . but there were mostly small stores in this immediate area . . . all shut up for the night now . . . would Mr. Garman still be at the market?

What happened next, however, made that last question of no concern. Lyle was halfway down the block, full of momentum, when he saw the two men appear under the street light at the far corner. He lurched to a stop by swerving into the wall of a building. He stayed there a moment, staring at the men.

They weren't Charley and Mike, who were, as far as he knew, still walking down the line of parked cars on Majestic Avenue. And yet these two looked just like Charley and Mike, with the topcoats and the turned down hats. And the way they held their fists forward meant they had guns.

Either coincidentally another pair of toughs, Lyle thought wildly, or part of the same gang. But it scarcely made any difference. He knew somehow that they were after him, or if luckily they hadn't seen him yet, at least they would soon be after him. And he didn't have a briefcase to distract this pair.

He hesitated only long enough to see that they were coming toward him at a fast trot. Then he turned and ran. His gray topcoat must have been light enough for the men to see him. They yelled something. He couldn't hear what they had yelled, above the sound of his own running, and he didn't stop to find out. There were two shots. More bees in the air, buzzing above his head.

He was back on Majestic now. To his left, down the block, he thought he saw movement. Presumably Charley and Mike. Lyle turned right.

As he did so, he was aware of the headlights of a car coming down the side street, not from the direction of Garman's Market and his second pair of pursuers, but from the other way. It was coming fast and it was going to turn into Majestic.

Lyle did some quick thinking. This was the only car he had seen on Majestic since the chase began, and it might be the last he would see. As it lunged into its fast turn, he darted out toward it, waving his arms like a drowning man.

The driver must have seen him, because the brakes screeched. Even so, the car was going so fast that it hurtled thirty or forty feet beyond Lyle before it quivered to a full stop.

He ran in pursuit of it.

Only to halt once again in full flight. Because he saw doors on each side of the car open and a third pair of men in topcoats and turned down hats emerge from them. Their fists were also clenched around what undoubtedly were guns.

Despair hit Lyle full in the face now. This thing had all the horror of a nightmare. A pair of gunmen in every direction he turned. Yet he knew it was real. Terribly real. And he was only a little undersized, underweight bookkeeper who couldn't do a dozen push-ups. Why didn't he give up?

But he didn't. As far as he knew, he had no ancestors at Thermopylae or the Little Big Horn. It was just the plain cussedness in him that makes all human beings of whatever size or kind want to stay alive.

He turned to his left now, steering a middle course between the second and third pairs of gunmen, the ones from the car and the ones from the direction of Garman's Market. To his far, far left, Charley and Mike might be closing in, too.

He ran across to the other side of Majestic, half-surrounded but not yet trapped. Ahead of him in the gutter lay a brick. He didn't throw the brick, but used it as a hammer against a store's plate glass front. Three smashes against the glass in a vertical line, then some shoving with his topcoat-protected shoulder, and he was through the glass without a scratch.

Inside the store, Lyle acted with the instinctive cunning of a weasel in a chicken house with the farmer coming through the door. He knew that if his pursuers had shot at him, they wouldn't hesitate following him into the store. And he knew also that he couldn't indefinitely evade a

230

gang of six armed men.

He didn't know what kind of store it was. He only knew that he toppled over several racks of some kind of merchandise as he ploughed through the place. A small square patch of darkness not as dark as the rest of the black interior beckoned him toward the rear door.

When he got there, to his surprise, he saw that the door was ajar. He pushed it wide open, but instead of going through it, he flung his body to the floor, rolled a few times, and then lay still.

He'd been just in time. From where he lay, he saw two men arrive at the front of the store, hesitate, then pick their way gingerly through the man-sized hole in the glass.

"Look," a voice said, "the back door's open. He went out that way."

They blundered through the store toward Lyle, tripping over the things that he had knocked down, cursing as they came. They passed within two steps of his prone body. They didn't even hesitate at the door, to question whether the person they were after had really gone out it. They simply ran out into the back alley and in a moment had completely disappeared.

All was quiet. Lyle lay where he was and rested. Somewhere outside the six would converge and then begin to wonder there their man had slipped by them, and then maybe they would backtrack.

So he couldn't rest where he was too long. After a minute or so, he got up and began picking his way toward the front of the store. He still had the brick somehow, dangling heavily from his fingers and dragging his whole arm down with it. And he continued to hold onto it for he might need it.

He paused at the broken glass before trying to go out through it. Majestic Avenue seemed empty, of cars, of gunmen, of anything that lived and moved. Empty and safe. Or was the emptiness deceptive? He had been surprised several times too often this evening. He'd wait a moment longer and see.

It was while he was waiting there, staring suspiciously out, that his sharpened instincts told him that some kind of danger lurked inside the store. He froze, and his fingers clenched tightly around the brick. He was no longer tired, but tense and prepared.

Holding his own breath, he became certain that he heard someone else's breathing. They'd fooled him again, he thought. He would have sworn that only two of the gang had come through the broken glass, and that two had also left through the rear door. But they'd tricked him somehow. One of them was still here, waiting in ambush.

The breathing came from his left. Lyle turned his head slowly, his eyes now well accustomed to the dark and searching the room. For a moment, he thought that perhaps there was nothing there; even the sound of the breathing seemed to have stopped.

Had it all been imagination? No, those aroused instincts had been right. There was something there. But because he couldn't see what it was he waited. After a moment or so, the breathing came again, starting with a little poof of suddenly expelled air. He had to laugh, silently within himself. The guy hadn't been able to hold his breath indefinitely. He was no superman. He could be had.

With this realization came the opportunity. One of those infrequent cars coming down Majestic Avenue moved by now, its headlights poking into every window it passed. In the gleam of those lights, Lyle saw his new antagonist.

Standing flattened against a side wall. A hat, a topcoat, a gun in his fist. Lyle didn't hesitate. He'd been on the defensive all evening, and now at last he had a chance for revenge. He hurled the brick with all his might.

Mercifully perhaps—for Lyle Beckwith wasn't the sadistic kind—the headlights passed just as the brick sailed toward his target. Therefore Lyle did not see the damage he had wrought. He only heard the thud, the stifled cry, then another thud—that of a body hitting the floor.

After that he didn't linger. He squeezed out through the broken glass, found the street still empty. He started running again, this time toward his car. He didn't see any more men in topcoats and turned down hats. He reached the car, unlocked it, got in, and drove home.

There was nothing in the morning paper, but the afternoon edition was more enlightening. POLICE DRAGNET CATCHES ROBBER, the headline said.

"The police of our city," the story went on, "acted quickly and efficiently in the location and capture of a lone bandit. The bandit, a small man in a gray topcoat, appeared at the Majestic Pharmacy, 5021 Majestic Avenue, just before closing time at 10 P.M. He pointed a gun at the clerk, emptied the contents of the cash register into a briefcase, and fled on foot. The clerk, Richard Handy, telephoned a description of the bandit, and within less than five minutes plainclothesmen from the Second District converged on the Majestic Avenue area. After a chase of several blocks, during which detectives fired five shots, the bandit was cornered in Milo's Haberdashery, 5235 Majestic. He had entered the store by smashing a display window, but injured himself. Detectives made the final capture inside the haberdashery. The bandit, who has identified himself as Roger Smith, is expected to recover from a fractured skull, and is in Marlborough Hospital. The briefcase, containing over six hundred dollars in cash, was recovered intact. . . ."

Lyle could easily reconstruct what had happened. The bandit had been calmly walking away with the loot when he heard the shots. So he'd found himself a hiding place till the excitement died down. And he'd been real cosy there, while he—poor, innocent Lyle Beckwith—had provided target practice for the law. Reflecting on this, Lyle wasn't a bit sorry about his use of the brick.

But his briefcase! The police have two briefcases. But they're not mentioning that fact, are they? Because they don't know how to explain it. Should he go down to the Second District and claim his briefcase? He could easily identify the lunch box and the thermos.

In the end, Lyle decided not to. The bandit had undoubtedly entered that store by forcing the rear door, which explained his having found it ajar. That open door was another puzzler for those cops which they weren't mentioning, either. So it might be just like that haberdasher Milo to charge Lyle for the broken window. That would cost a bit more than his ten-dollar briefcase. Lyle's accountant's mind clicked. Charge it off—ten bucks—to experience.

Arbiter of Uncertainties

by Edward D. Hoch

Arthur Urah was a tall, slender man with thick white hair and the bearing of a dignitary. He wore silk shirts with the monogram *AU* over the left breast pocket, and this was what had led some in the business to dub him the Arbiter of Uncertainties. It was a good name. It fit him perfectly.

He had never been to the Brenten Hotel before. It was in an old section of town, and in truth it was an old hotel, dating back some fifty-five years in the city's history. No one of importance stayed at the Brenten any longer, and thus it was perhaps a bit odd to see a man of Arthur Urah's obvious character entering the lobby on a Sunday afternoon.

"I'm to meet some people here," he told the desk clerk, a seedy little man chewing on a toothpick. "My name is Arthur Urah."

"Oh, sure. Room 735. They're waiting for you."

"Thank you," he said, and entered the ancient elevator for the ascent to the seventh floor.

The corridors of the old hotel were flaky with dead paint, and a dusty fire hose hung limply in a metal wall rack. Arthur Urah eyed it all with some distaste as he searched out room 735 and knocked lightly on the door.

It was opened almost at once by a slim young man with black hair and pouting lips. Arthur Urah had known the type for most of his life. The room itself was as shabby as the rest of the hotel, and its big double bed had been pushed against one drab wall to give more floor space, revealing in the process a long accumulation of dust and grime.

"Arthur! Good to see you again!" The man who came forward to greet him first was Tommy Same, a familiar figure around town.

Arthur Urah had always liked Tommy, though personal feelings never entered into his decisions. "How are you, Tommy? How's the family?"

"Fine. Just fine! Glad to have you deciding things, Arthur."

Urah smiled. "I don't play favorites, Tommy. I listen to both sides."

The other side was there, too. Fritz Rimer was a little man with a bald head and large, frightened eyes. It was obvious at once that he was out of his league. "Pleased to meet you, Mr. Urah," he mumbled. "Hate to get you down here like this on a Sunday."

"That's his job," Tommy Same pointed out. "You and me've got a disagreement, and Arthur here is going to settle it. He's an arbiter, just like business and the unions use."

Arthur Urah motioned toward the door. "I'm not used to settling cases with a gun at my back. Get rid of the kid."

Tommy Same spread his hands in a gesture of innocence. "You know Benny. His father used to drive for me. Benny's no kid gunman."

Urah eyed the slim young man with obvious distaste. "Get rid of him," he repeated. "Let him wait in the hall."

Tommy made a motion and Benny disappeared out the door. "Satisfied?"

Urah gave a slight nod, running his fingers through the thick white hair over one ear. "Now, who else is here?"

"Only Sal. She won't bother us."

Urah walked to the connecting door and opened it. Sally Vogt was lounging in a chair with a tabloid newspaper. "Hello, Arthur," she said. "Just catching up on the news."

He closed the door. "All right," he decided. "She can stay. Nobody else, though. Tell the room clerk nobody comes up till we're finished."

"I told him that already."

Arthur Urah opened the slim briefcase he carried and extracted a notepad. "We'll sit at this table," he said. "Since Fritz is the offended party, he gets to talk first."

It was only an outsize card table, with rickety legs, supplied by the hotel. Sitting around it on their three chairs, they looked a bit like reluctant poker players defeated by the odds.

Fritz Rimer cleared his throat and nervously fingered a pencil. "Well, everybody knows what the trouble is." He paused, as if suddenly aware of his smallness at the table.

"Suppose you tell us anyway," Urah prodded gently.

"There are thirty-six horse rooms in this city where a man can lay a bet on the races or the pro games. Twenty years ago, when I started in business, there were thirty-six individual owners of these places. We all knew each other, and helped each other out. When the cops closed down one place occasionally, the rest of us came to the owner's aid. We were one big family, see?"

Tommy Same moved restlessly in his chair. "I'm crying for you, Fritz. Get to the point."

"Well, about a year ago, Tommy Same and some of his syndicate friends moved in and started taking over the city's entire bookmaking operation. Some places they forced out of business and then bought up cheap. Others, they demanded a big cut of the take and sent somebody around to babysit and make sure they got it. Right now the syndicate is a partner in thirty-five of the thirty-six places in this city—all but mine."

Arthur Urah nodded. "And now he wants yours, too?"

"Right. He sent that guy Benny down last week to scare me, but I told him this wasn't like the old days. I don't scare. If he wants to kill me, he can, but that just might be the end of Tommy Same." As he talked, a certain courage seemed to flow into the little bald man. Now his cheeks were flushed and there was an unmistakable power in his words. The others had not stood up to Tommy, but little Fritz Rimer had, even though it might cost him his life.

Tommy Same cleared his throat. "When do I get a chance to talk? You going to listen to this guy all afternoon?"

Urah smiled slightly. "You can talk now, Tommy. Is Fritz telling the truth? Are you trying to take over his operation?"

Tommy Same leaned back in his chair, frowning. "It's like labor unions, Arthur. We all have to stick together, to protect ourselves from the law, and deadbeats, and occasional swindlers. With all thirty-six horse rooms in town linked together in a sort of syndicate, it's better for everyone."

"And that's your defense for this?"

"Sure. I'm not trying to force anyone out of business. I'm giving valuable services, and I just want a share of their profits in return."

"Did you threaten Fritz here?"

"Look, this isn't the old days. If I'd threatened him, do you think I would have allowed him to call you in? Do you think Capone or some of the other old timers would have sat still for arbitration?"

"You're not Capone," Arthur Urah reminded him quietly.

"No, but I can realize the importance of us all sticking together. If Rimer goes his own way, pretty soon the others will start to, and then where'll we be? Back to the old days when the cops could knock off the places one at a time."

It went on like that for another hour, with each man arguing for his side. Arthur Urah had heard it all before, in a dozen different contexts, and at these times the dialogue took on a soporific quality that dumbfounded him. Petty criminals, the dregs of society, taking up his time in a shabby hotel room while he listened to their sordid tales. He had sat, a year earlier, as mediator in a boundary dispute involving some big underworld names in Brooklyn, and it was the peaceful settlement of that potentially dangerous situation which had made his reputation as a gangland mediator. It was a reputation he had never sought and never fully accepted, and yet it stuck and grew through a half dozen other disputes. He was Arthur Urah, the Arbiter of Uncertainties, the one to call when there was bloodshed to be prevented.

"That's enough for now," he told them finally, pushing back from the card table. "I think I have enough information to reach a decision."

"When?" Rimer asked him.

"Leave me alone for a bit to ponder it all."

They went out of the room, Rimer to the hallway, and Tommy Same to the girl who waited next door. Urah stood and stretched, feeling at that moment every one of his fifty-three years. He walked to the window and looked down at the Sunday afternoon street seven stories below, ominously deserted.

Presently, as he stood there, he heard a footstep on the rug behind him. It was Tommy Same, returned for a few private words. He slipped his arm around Urah's shoulder and spoke in tones of brotherhood. "You and I know how to handle these things, don't we, Arthur? These punks like Rimer have to be coddled just so far. Imagine—sitting down at a table with the guy when I should be kicking his teeth in!"

"Times are changing, Tommy."

"Sure they are. That's why I'm taking over the horse rooms in this town. The day of the independent operator is gone forever."

"Fritz Rimer doesn't think so."

Tommy took his arm away. He was nearly a head shorter than Arthur Urah, and standing there close to him he reminded Urah somehow of the wayward son he'd never had. "Look, Arthur, be good to Rimer. Tell him he's all through and save the poor guy's life."

"You're telling me something, Tommy, and it's not something I want to hear."

"I'm telling you the facts of life in this town. I like to keep everybody happy and look respectable, so I go along with this arbitration bit. But I can't afford to lose the decision. The other thirty-five guys would all bolt if Rimer got away. They wouldn't be still a week."

"So?"

"So you rule against me, Arthur, and I gotta score on Rimer. I'm up against a wall. There's no other way."

"You'd be crazy to try it."

"Arthur . . . I already told Benny. He's waiting out in the hall. If you rule that Rimer stays in business, he never leaves this hotel alive."

Urah stared out the window at the occasional passing cars below. The afternoon shadows were already long, offering a hint of approaching night. "Get out," he said to Tommy. "I'll pretend I never heard that."

"Whatever you say, Arthur."

Then he was gone, and the room was quiet once more. Urah sat down at the card table and began to make a few notes. He'd been at it for ten minutes when another visitor entered through the connecting door.

He glanced up and smiled. "Hello, Sal."

Sally Vogt was a cute blonde trying hard to stay under thirty. Most of the time she succeeded, thanks to her hairdresser. "What have you been doing with yourself lately, Arthur?"

"Bringing people together. Making peace."

"I mean besides that. We used to see you often down at the club."

"That was a long time ago. We travel in different circles now."

"Arthur . . . "

"Yes?"

"He sent me in to talk to you. He thinks he handled it badly."

"He did."

She shifted her feet and gazed at the worn carpet. "He's up tight, Arthur. If he loses control of these horse rooms, he's all finished in the organization. They don't give anybody a second chance."

Arthur Urah shrugged. "Maybe they fire him and hire Fritz Rimer in his place."

"Don't joke, Arthur."

"I'm not. Is he really going to kill Rimer?"

"Of course not."

"Then what's Benny for? Just to scare people?"

She lit a cigarette and inhaled slowly. "Benny's left over from the old days. Tommy inherited him, along with everything else in town."

"Not quite everything."

"Arthur, Arthur! This isn't your big moment in Brooklyn with the syndicate chiefs. Nobody cares what happens here. Give Tommy Rimer's place and everybody lives in peace."

"You just said Tommy's bosses cared what happened here. That makes it important to him, at least."

"How much would you take to give Tommy the decision, Arthur?"

Urah rubbed a hand across his eyes. "First Tommy, and now you. Do I get Benny in here next, with his gun?"

She didn't answer that. Instead she said, "I suppose you'll make a decision this afternoon.'

"There's no reason to delay it. In fact, I think you can tell them to come in now."

As he waited for Rimer and Tommy Same to appear, the room clerk from downstairs stuck his head in the door. "Some of the big boys are waiting in the lobby. They want to know how long you'll be."

"Not long," Urah said, resenting the intrusion. Their presence in the lobby meant that someone didn't trust him to handle the situation.

Fritz Rimer came in alone, shuffling his feet over the faded carpet, hardly able to look at Urah. "It's going bad for me, isn't it?"

"Not so bad."

"Even if I win, I lose. He'll kill me—I know it."

"Then why did you fight him? Why didn't you just pull out?"

"That place is my life. I don't just see my whole life crumble without trying to hang on.'

Tommy Same and Sal came in, and she stood behind his chair while they waited for Arthur Urah to deliver his verdict. He cleared his throat and snapped on one of the table lamps because the room was growing dim in the afternoon twilight.

"I've studied the issues," he began, "and tried to arrive at a fair decision." He cleared his throat once more. Sally Vogt caught his eye and seemed to be telling him something, but he paid no attention. "My ruling is that Fritz Rimer has the right to remain in business as long as he desires. If he should sell his establishment, or pass away, the business should be made part of Tommy's syndicate. But until that time, Rimer is to continue as sole owner and manager."

Tommy leaned back in his chair, saying nothing.

Rimer got to his feet, shaking. "Thanks, Mr. Urah. Thanks for nothing.

That decision just sealed my death warrant."

"You can sell out to Tommy," Arthur pointed out.

"Never! He'll have to kill me if he wants my place."

"That's something I can arrange," Tommy said quietly.

"There'll be no violence," Urah told them, but even to his own ears the words carried a hollow ring.

Fritz Rimer turned and headed for the door. Tommy Same got up and started after him but then Fritz turned and showed them the little silver pistol in his hand. It looked like a .22, like something he might have borrowed from his wife. "I'm leaving here," he said. "Alive."

Then he was in the hall. Tommy bolted and ran after him, and Arthur was at Tommy's side. Fritz was halfway down the dingy hallway, heading for the elevator, when Benny appeared at the opposite end of the corridor. He saw the gun, and immediately drew his own weapon.

"No!" Sally screamed. "Don't shoot!" but it was too late for anyone to listen now.

Benny fired one quick shot without aiming, and Rimer's little gun coughed in echo. Tommy Same was shouting above the roar, and then he seemed to stumble back into Arthur Urah's arms. He tore free, lurched into the dusty fire hose on the wall, and then fell forward on his face.

"Tommy!" Sally Vogt was on the floor at his side, trying to turn him over, but her left hand came away all bloody from his back and she screamed once more.

Down the hall, Benny had dropped his gun and was running forward. Fritz Rimer simply stared, more terrified than ever, and then he suddenly darted into the elevator. Within moments the room clerk had arrived, summoned by some hotel guest lurking terrified behind his locked door. There were others on the scene, too; the big boys whom Arthur Urah knew so well—Stefenzo and Carlotta and Venice, big men in the syndicate—bigger men than Tommy Same had ever hoped to be.

"What happened?" one of them asked, staring down at the body on the floor. This was Venice, a slim, almost handsome man.

"There was a shooting," Urah explained carefully. "Benny here took a shot at Rimer and missed."

"I didn't mean to," Benny mumbled, too frightened to say more.

The room clerk looked up from the body. "He's dead."

Somebody had taken Sally aside, but her sobbing could still be heard. One of them picked up Benny's fallen gun and brought it down the hall.

ALFRED HITCHCOCK'S ANTHOLOGY

"This looks too big for the hole in him," somebody observed.

"Search everyone," Stefenzo ordered. "The girl, too."

"Rimer's gone with his gun," Benny said. "He did it, not me."

A quick search of Arthur and Benny and Sal and the dead Tommy revealed no other weapon. There was only Benny's big .38 and the missing gun with which Rimer had fled.

"We don't want the police in on this," Venice told Arthur Urah. "Not yet, anyway. We'll never convince them it was an accident."

"No," Arthur agreed.

They wrapped Tommy Same's body in a sheet and carried it into one of the rooms.

"Check everybody on this floor," Stefenzo ordered the clerk. "Make sure there's no one who'll talk."

"Most of the rooms are empty."

"Check anyway."

Arthur Urah walked past the still-stunned Benny and into Sally's room. She was over by the window, staring out at the lights coming on all over the city. "He's dead," she said without emotion to Arthur.

"Yes."

"So what good was all your arbitration? In the end, it came back down to a couple of people shooting it out in a hallway."

"I tried to avoid that."

"Tommy wanted too much. That was always his trouble. Too much. Not thirty-five horse rooms, but thirty-six. He wanted to be too big."

"Yes," Arthur agreed quietly.

She turned suddenly to face him. "What did you do before?" she asked. "Before you started to arbitrate their disputes?"

"Various things. I studied law once."

"But they trust you. Both sides trust you."

"I hope so."

After a time she left him and went in to look at Tommy's body in the next room.

Venice came in to sit with him. "We've taken Benny away," he told Arthur. "He was always a little nuts."

"I suppose so."

"Dangerous."

"Yes."

The telephone rang and Arthur answered it, then passed it to the syndicate man who listened intently. After a moment he held the receiver down against his chest. "They've run Rimer to earth. He's home, packing, apparently getting ready to skip. They want to know if we want him alive or dead."

"Alive," Arthur Urah said without hesitation. "There's been enough killing."

"I suppose so." Then, into the telephone, "Bring him down here."

Arthur Urah sighed and sat down to wait.

An hour later. they had gathered in the room again, around the rickety card table. Rimer was there, under protest, and Benny had been brought back, too. The room clerk from downstairs, and Sally, and the three big men from the syndicate were all seated, their eyes on Urah as he spoke.

"What we have here," he said, "is an interesting problem. We cannot, like the police, dig into Tommy Same's body and compare bullets under a microscope. We cannot do anything except take testimony and examine the facts. I was there in the hall myself, and I saw what there was to see. The hall, for our purposes, is about fifty feet in length from the door of Tommy's roon to the spot where Benny stood. Fritz here was about halfway between the door and Benny, at the elevator, when the shooting started."

"Benny fired toward us," Sally interrupted to explain. "Fritz fired away from us."

"And there was no third shot?" Venice asked in a puzzled tone.

"No."

"Tommy just staggered and fell," Urah said. "And therein would seem to lie the impossibility of the thing. The wound indicates to us a small caliber weapon—as nearly as we can tell without being able to dig for the bullet—yet Rimer's small caliber gun was fired in the opposite direction from where Tommy was standing. Benny's larger gun, fired toward Tommy, would have left a bigger entry hole."

Stefenzo grunted, lifting his bulk from the chair. "Yet there was no other shot, no other gun."

"Why waste time, anyway?" Carlotta asked. "Tommy's death was an accident, no matter how you look at it. The bullet bounced off the wall or something. Let's get on to splitting up his holdings."

"Well, I don't think it was an accident," Sally told them all. "I think he was murdered by Fritz Rimer."

"I didn't . . . " Rimer began, and then fell silent.

Arthur Urah cleared his throat. "I was called in to decide the matter of Rimer's horse room and Tommy Same's claim to it. In that affair, my original judgment of this afternoon still stands. The horse room remains in Rimer's control and, since Tommy is now dead, there's no question of his taking over after Rimer's possible death."

"You can talk about this all you want," Sally told them, "but I'm more interested in how Tommy died." She stormed out into the hall, seeking perhaps some sign, some scrawled revelation on the wall.

"You don't need me for anything," Fritz Rimer said. "Let me get out of here."

"Wait a bit," Carlotta told him.

"I have a business to attend to!"

"On Sunday night? Wait a bit."

Arthur Urah interrupted. "Let him go. The killing of Tommy was accidental."

Rimer left, a little man and fearful. Then they settled down to the business at hand.

In the hour that followed, Tommy Same's empire was divided. Arthur Urah listened to it all, taking little part in the discussions. This was not his job, and he would only be needed if a dispute arose. He wandered over to the window at one point, and then into the next room. It was there that Sally Vogt found him.

"I was in the hall," she said.

"Yes?"

"If you look, you can see the marks where both bullets hit the wall."

"I didn't look." He was starting to zip his briefcase. It was time to be going home.

"Arthur . . . " Sally hesitated.

"What is it, Sally?"

"Are they still in the next room?"

"Yes. The territory has to be reassigned."

"Reassigned. Tommy dies, and the territory is reassigned."

"Life must go on, Sal. You know that."

"And what about his body, wrapped in a sheet like some mummy?"

"The body will be given a decent burial."

"In the Jersey dumps?"

"Sal . . . "

"The wound was in his back, Arthur. In his *back*! He was facing the other two, but you were right behind him. He stumbled into you, just before he fell."

"I had no gun," Arthur Urah said quietly.

"No, but you had this!" She brought her hand into view and dropped the ice pick on the low table between them. "Tommy wasn't shot by a small caliber bullet at all. He was stabbed with this ice pick just as the other two fired at each other. Then, while we bent over the body, you simply pushed the ice pick up the nozzle of the fire hose in the hall—where I just found it."

"You try too hard, Sally. You look too closely. This world isn't made for people who look too closely, who find ice picks in fire hoses."

"You killed him because he wouldn't go along with your settlement, because he was going to get Rimer."

"Perhaps I killed him to save Rimer's life, Sally."

"I'm going in there and tell them, Arthur," she said. "It won't bring Tommy back, but at least it'll avenge him just a little."

She had moved toward the door when he reached out to stop her. "Not that way, Sally. Listen a bit."

"To what? To the Arbiter of Uncertainties, while he foxes out another decision? What will it be this time, Arthur? What will they give you when I walk in there and tell them? Life or death?"

"You don't understand, Sal."

"I understand. I'm going to tell them."

"You don't have to. They know."

She paused again, backing against the coffee table, staring at him with widening eyes. "They know?"

"You asked once what I did before I became the Arbiter. I did many things, Sally. Some of them with an ice pick," he admitted.

"No!"

"Tommy was getting too big. They wanted his territory. They thought Fritz might do the job for them, but Fritz was a coward. When I saw my opportunity, there in the hall, I had to take it."

"And all this talk, this investigation?"

"For your benefit, Sally. And Benny's."

"If they won't do it, Arthur, I will." She bent down for the ice pick again, but he merely brushed it away, onto the floor.

"Get out, Sally. You don't want to get hurt."

"Damn you! You're not human, Arthur! You're some sort of monster!"

ALFRED HITCHCOCK'S ANTHOLOGY

He smiled sadly. He'd been called worse things in his life. He picked up the ice pick and dropped it into the briefcase, and finished zipping it shut.

After a time, when Sally had gone, he went down in the elevator. He nodded to the room clerk as he passed, and then went out into the night.

Witness

by Lee Chisholm

For a moment the sight nearly took my breath away. The next minute I could feel my usual idiotic grin spreading over my homely face and I wondered what the cops would say. I had stopped to light a cigarette, glanced in the high, narrow window of the fashionable boutique, and there she was—she and the corpse, that is.

Francine Boucher Stafford, one of The Beautiful People, *membre extraordinaire* of the international jet-set and all the rest of that drivel they use to describe the rich and famous unemployed leisured class, was just about the richest and most famous of all. Mrs. Harold Stafford also belonged to The Beautiful People in the truest sense of the word. Her skin was creamy-white against the great mane of long auburn hair that framed her face, and her features had the strong, clean look of some ancient Celtic queen.

Well, just standing there looking at her and wearing my stupid grin, I almost forgot to peruse the corpse, but he was there, too, very much in evidence in the shadows of the closed shop, stretched out on the floor with a jeweled dagger in his back and Francine Stafford's white hand clasped around the handle. From where I stood, he didn't look half as interesting as Francine, even with the addition of a jeweled dagger, because Francine was, indeed, all woman.

I push a cab here in High City, or I did. It's a ritzy resort town a couple of good spits inland from San Francisco, all very posh and private, with a manmade lake and Spanish haciendas rimmed around a golf course—you know the sort of thing. That's just for the rich tourists, of course. We natives still cool our burning feet in Dobson's Creek and beat the heat by fanning ourselves with newspapers on the back porch, but having this high-class playland development on the outskirts has definitely made the whole town a lot more toney—fancy stores and stuff, you know.

But never mind that, where was I? Oh yes, Francine Boucher Stafford.

I knew she must be close to forty, but did she look it? No. Not a day of it—like wow, man!—which is why I wasn't all that interested in the corpse.

I knew him, same as most people in High City. He was what they call in the newspapers a flamboyant figure and this here Gold Rush Boutique was his place of business; that is, if you can call selling women a lot of leather stuff stitched together with cowhide things a business. His name was Martin Ulster. He wore his hair long, his mustache full, and his clothes colorful. Oh, man, were they colorful! Picture a tall willow-wand of a guy in a bright blue "Olde California" frontier shirt laced with leather thongs (you guessed it) at the chest and wearing brick-red (so help me) "Olde California" laced denims. This is Martin Ulster, lean of flank, hawk of nose, and dark of eye, and the women loved him. Don't ask me why. The serious study of women for most of my thirty-six years has made me nutty enough as it is. But no kidding, this guy descends on High City about eighteen months ago to open up a weirdo, overpriced boutique for the rich and favored dames ensconced in our wealthy playground outside of town, and what happens? Every local hausfrau and her daughter has to have an "Olde California" creation by Martin Ulster. When I think of the money.

Well, never mind that, but imagine this wild scene: me standing there looking in, wearing my stupid grin and wondering what the cops would say, but managing to ogle Francine Stafford plenty while debating what to do—move off and forget it or make like a good solid citizen and report it. But I grinned and ogled and lingered too long. One minute this Francine babe is on her knees bending over the body, the next she's on her feet looking right at me—and what a look! Like a tigress, body motionless like she's ready to spring right through the window; her cold, glittering green eyes bored into mine. It's enough to scare a guy. I felt like a piece of red meat framed in the window, late evening sunlight behind me etching me all too clearly, while she stood with the shadows of the darkened shop behind her, a light burning somewhere in an office to the rear. I started to back away, feeling my lunatic grin harden into something more like a grimace of fear.

What does she do but raise her hand and crook her finger at me, gesturing come here, just like some teacher in grade school and me an errant pupil. I tell you, it was too much. I remember shaking my head as if to say you've got to be kidding, but this gorgeous Francine babe stamps her foot and shakes her head at me, and points firmly to the door, meaning get in here this minute!

Like someone in a dream I went to the door. She opened it from the inside, almost yanked me in by the sleeve, and banged it closed behind me, snapping the lock and leaving the drawn shade flapping against the frame.

I stood there stupidly, feeling outsized and out of place in the narrow, feminine surroundings. Although I'm not that big a guy, that's how you feel with your feet sunk ankle-deep in carpet, surrounded by racks of dresses and half-draped female forms wearing bits and pieces of leather. It wasn't my bag, as the saying goes.

I stole a look at the long, still form lying kitty-corner to the display window and felt my forehead break out in a sweat. Swallowing, I looked away, realizing that what might seem like a Hitchcock movie from the outside, scary but not without its humor, was nothing like being in the act for real.

Francine Boucher Stafford's clipped, cool, finishing-school voice broke through my wavering confusion. "This is not what you think it is," she said crisply.

"No, of course not," I agreed, and put my sweaty hands in my jacket pockets. It was very hot in there and it occurred to me that the air-conditioning had been turned off, which was natural, I suppose. It was after hours and the shop was closed, but with a corpse lying there—I gave myself a mental shake.

"Do you know who I am?" Francine Stafford had come around to stand directly in front of me, hands on the hips of her leather midi-skirt, her firm, full bosom pulsating in a knit, leather-trimmed top.

Five hundred dollars' worth of leather, I estimated, looking at her, at the same time faltering out an answer, "Yes—" She was definitely in control, this babe, and I let her be, already regretting my impetuous move into the shop.

"I was afraid of that," she said, staring at me with something next to loathing. "I could tell it by your riveted glance through the window. One gets to know when one is recognized."

"Sure," I said again; anything to be agreeable. Licking my lips, I shot another hasty glance at the body.

"I told you this is not what you think it is, and I told you the truth."

I noticed she kept her head turned away from the late Martin Ulster and I guessed that under her highbrow calm she was a little shook up herself.

"I came in here not three minutes ago and found him myself," she continued. "Then you looked through the window and saw me. Naturally, I had to motion you in to explain before you set off some kind of unnecessary and ill-advised alarm."

Unnecessary and ill-advised alarm—I looked at her and some of my usual cynicism must have showed in my face.

"Martin Ulster is dead," she said quietly. "Quite dead. I ascertained that for myself. There is nothing anyone can do for him now. But there is something you can do for me. Say nothing about this, nothing at all. Don't report it. Go your way as if nothing had happened."

"In other words, forget I saw you here?"

"Exactly. I can make it worth your while, not to buy you off as witness to a murder but to convince you I had nothing to do with it. Martin and I were friends, better than friends. Partners, you might say. I knew him when and he knew me when. I helped set him up in this shop, but our association was secret. You do understand how these things go?" She pinned me with a cool green glance that spoke volumes about how these things went between her and Martin Ulster.

"Sure." I gave her my worldly taxi-driver's grin. Pushing cab at night for ten years makes you a third party to lots of "secret associations" and soon teaches you the high profit in tips for keeping your mouth shut. I stood there sweating in the heat of the closed shop, perspiration rolling down my back while I angled myself into the shadow of a dress rack for cover since people were still going by in the fading light outside, knowing that the biggest tip of my life was coming up. It wouldn't be a crumpled ten or twenty either, pressed into my hand with a conspiratorial wink. This time I had hit the jackpot and I aimed to make the most of it. I cared nothing for Martin Ulster, dead or alive, but money—well, man, that's something else again.

"Good. I see you're a man of the world, Mr.—?" Francine Stafford joined me in my shadow and, stepping close to me, looked up into my face, or maybe I should say across into my face. She's a big babe, that girl; an amazon with a pearly overlay of culture, if you know what I mean. She waited for me to give my name.

"Let's call me Mr. Anonymous," I said. "I don't want you to look me up sometime and make me Victim Number Two."

"Oh, you idiot! You're stupid!" The green eyes flashed and I could see she was on the verge of having one of her famous tantrums, but with a sudden lapse into coldness she controlled herself. "So you still don't believe me?"

"Look, what's it matter if I do or I don't? From where I stand, it looks like a woman's crime. Stabbing somebody in the back with a pretty little jeweled dagger is just the kind of thing some wildly jealous female might do. This guy Ulster was a mover and a shaker. Lots of jealous dames would be glad to see him breathe his last, for the simple reason that he got tired of 'em and went on to greener pastures. Hell hath no fury like a woman scorned and all that jazz."

"So you quote poetry, too?" She looked me over coolly, an expression of studied insult on her face and a flash of contempt in her eyes for my shapeless old tweed jacket and the bag in the knees of my drip-dry slacks. "What are you, a poor man's philosopher of some sort?"

"No, ma'am," I said, giving her my idiotic smile which always reassures 'em I'm harmless, to a point. "Just a poor man."

I heard the relieved release of her breath, which said quite plainly that slobs like me she could deal with. We could be bought and sold, something she was very adept in. I waited, like the good slob I was, for my payoff while she opened the deep pouch slung over her shoulder and took out her wallet.

"Here," she said, almost emptying the wallet of bills and plunging them into my hand, "this is all I have. Take it."

In the glimmer of light from the back of the store I could make out five one hundred dollar bills, a couple of twenties, and a ten. My unhappy silence conveyed my disappointment.

"Please," she said earnestly, "that's all I've got with me. I have to keep these—" she showed me two twenties still in her wallet—"to get back to town. There's a big party there tonight, a major social event thrown by some boring social climber. I was planning to skip it, have already begged off, in fact. But now I've got to make it somehow. Have my picture taken. Be seen—" Her voice wandered off, and her anxiety to get away from High City and make a very big scene far away in the big city just sort of hung there between us; embarrassing, in a way, for someone like Francine Boucher Stafford to be in a spot like this.

"You might get back in time," I volunteered, "but you're sure to be recognized at the airport."

"I'm not going by air," she said. "I'm driving my maid's car."

So, I thought, learning something new every minute. This is how these high-society ladies get around on the sly. Drive the maid's car and probably carry all the maid's ID as well, just in case. Maids, like taxi drivers, can be very understanding, too—for a price.

"Well?" she said impatiently, her voice going a little shrill.

"Well, what?" I replied, shuffling my feet and folding my arms across my chest like someone prepared to stay a while, although by now the place was stifling hot and my own nerves were strung out like so much piano wire on a Steinway. I knew I had her and I was in a priceless position to wheel and deal *if I* could just keep my own mind and eyes off the shadowy hunk of corpse over by the window.

"Well, is it a deal? Will you take the money and say nothing, and let us *both* get out of here?"

I guess she pretty well saw through my pose of assumed nonchalance, but it was still my ball game and she knew it.

"No, not quite," I said, as if giving the matter a good deal of thought. "There's a lot at stake here: your lily-white reputation as Mrs. Untouchable Harold Stafford, fine old family name, et cetera, et cetera, above and beyond the rest of us humankind; and my own reputation as a solid citizen."

"What do you do for a living?" she interrupted harshly.

"I drive a taxi, ma'am," I said with as much pride as I could muster under the circumstances, we cab drivers being put down far too much for our supposed unscrupulous dealings and lack of human sensitivity.

"I should have known," she said coldly, and her scorn would have shriveled the skin on a crocodile's back. "What do you want, then?"

"I think my silence in this unfortunate situation is worth a lot more than five hundred and fifty dollars. A *lot* more, if you get what I mean." I gave her my special taxi-driver leer. It had loosened up a few pockets before.

"Leech," she said conversationally. "Parasitic leech."

"Whatever you say," I replied, prepared to be amiable and gentlemanly to the end. "So, for openers, how about that hunk of ice on your third finger, left hand? Looks like the Foxworth diamond that all the publicity was about. Fenced through certain channels that I happen to know of, and probably having to be cut, it wouldn't bring the cool million clams your loving hubby paid for it, but even so the pittance it would bring could keep me on easy street for the rest of my life. Not your brand of easy street, Mrs. Stafford, but mine. I'm a man of simple needs."

This time it was her turn. "You have to be kidding," she said derisively. "This is a paste copy, but even if it were the genuine Foxworth diamond, even *if it were*—" she paused to give the stressed words extra special effect—"I wouldn't be able to give it away or sell it on my own initiative. Harry—my husband—would wonder immediately why I wasn't wearing it. The world would wonder!"

"Why couldn't you just go along wearing the paste job? Who would know the genuine article was gone? The fake is a fine copy."

"It would be known," she said, "almost at once." With that, she lapsed into a kind of contemplative silence and I realized that there must be security measures taken by the rich and famous to guard their precious baubles that we ordinary folks know nothing about, and I was too far down on the social scale in the human anthill even to try to guess. What did she do? Flash her hand in front of an X-ray machine every night before beddybye to make sure the hunk she was lugging around was still the real McCoy? Or did a jeweler in residence, bent and obsequious like some kind of paternal gnome, creep into her bedroom every night and check each bijou and baguette through a loupe glued in his eye? Whatever it was, I knew it was beyond me and, I could tell by her silence, beyond her, too.

I sighed, said goodbye to the quarter of a million I might have garnered from this caper, and gracefully settled for second best.

"But that is the real Foxworth diamond you're wearing, isn't it?"

She nodded her head yes, her face tight.

I'll say one thing for her, she was on good terms with the truth, and even in a tight spot she didn't try to kid anyone. I guess she knew she didn't have to.

"The ring is out," she said flatly.

"No, the ring is in. You will lose it. In other words, leave it with me for safekeeping. Then, desperate and distressed over your great loss, you will offer a huge reward, and who should come forward to claim it but a poor-but-honest taxi driver who finds the ring when sweeping out the back of his cab? I suggest the reward be commensurate with the value of your loss and *not* a few miserly thou, or the poor-but-honest cabbie might not have enough inducement to come forward. Which means, make it good. That way everybody wins. You get the ring back, I get the hefty reward money, and no one is any the wiser."

"No, it won't work," she said, and I could see that she was breathing a little heavily because she was really pouring on the brainpower, too. "I'd have to report the loss by tomorrow. Your coming forward would place me here in High City today, the very thing I'm trying to avoid. 'Officially' I haven't been here in the last two months."

Gloomily I saw her point.

"You'll have to trust me on this," she said briskly. "I'll fly in unannounced this weekend to visit friends at the resort. Since no one will be expecting me, I'll take a cab out there. Your cab. We'll go through with the ring plan then."

I looked at her with admiration. She was cool. She was desperate, but she was cool, and I trusted her; but just to keep the edge on her I said, "Okay. I'll meet the Friday night eight thirty flight—and you'd better be on it. I'll take off on a fishing trip early tomorrow morning, so I won't hear the news about your friend Martin Ulster's death. I'll come back Friday for the weekend trade, which is prime time to us cab pushers. If you're not on that plane I will drop by the police station and tell 'em how shocked I am about poor old Martin, but I just heard, see, since I've been out of town fishing. But it seems to me I remember seeing a certain famous jet-set dame hanging around Martin's store Monday evening—"

"You don't have to spell it out," she said coldly. She cast me another withering glance that, under different circumstances, would have made me feel real bad, but I figured that since this was business she didn't mean anything personal by it.

"Friday night I'll be wearing a brown belle epoch wig—that's an upsweep style to you—and an orange pantsuit so you'll recognize me. I don't think anyone else will, but make it quick, just in case."

I nodded, glad I was dealing with a woman with a mind for detail, but then I guess this incognito thing was old stuff to her.

"Now, let's get out of here," she said, once more in full command. "You go first. Crawl along the floor to the back door so you won't be seen in the light from the office. I'll do the same after I get this black wig on."

She was already dragging a curly Afro-type thing out of the depths of her handbag and, instead of moving, I stood there fascinated at the transformation. Wigs, I decided, were damned handy gadgets.

"Go," she snapped, flashing those green eyes at me one last time under a new head of curly dark hair. "Get out! And don't run when you get outside or make yourself conspicuous."

"No, ma'am," I agreed, and dropping to my knees I crawled away from her and the late Martin Ulster just as fast as I could. Easing myself out the back door, I stood a minute in the shadows of the alley, gulping deep breaths of fresh air. Then, following orders to the end, I resisted the urge to run like hell, forcing myself instead to walk casually down the alleyway and blend, just as casually, with the rest of ordinary humanity on the street beyond. In my right coat pocket was the comforting bulge of five hundred and fifty dollars I hadn't had before, and apart from the fact that my shirt was wringing wet with perspiration I went on my way none the worse for my little brush with murder.

The fishing was fine. I found myself some back-country up in Nevada near Tahoe and I stayed there like the good boy I had promised to be, dipping my old rod in the water and dreaming of the fat reward money to come, thanking my lucky stars all the while for rich women and secret involvements which had to be kept hidden—at any price.

The price turned out to be one hundred thousand dollars. Not bad, huh? Maybe you read about it? HONEST CABBIE WINS FAT RE-WARD! the papers screamed. Or saw me being interviewed on television? I didn't say much, just kept shaking my head and wearing my idiot smile, mumbling about how I couldn't believe it. Again and again I kept repeating that it was just by accident that I dumped the plastic car tidy bags in the garbage at home where the pickup is just once a week instead of in the trash at work that gets picked up and carted off every other night. Looking stunned at my own brilliant thinking, I allowed as how with all the publicity about the missing ring and it coming out that I had actually taxied Francine Stafford to the resort (although I didn't know who she was at the time), I got to thinking about the car tidy bags that I hang on the window handles in the back of the cab and what had happened to them that night. And how I'd gone poking through my own garbage can and saw this thing sparkling in the sunlight.

Francine Boucher Stafford, interviewed on network TV as she and her aging, aristocratic husband boarded a plane for an extended European holiday, allowed as how she'd blown her nose and stuck the used tissue in the car tidy bag, never dreaming that her ring had come off at the same time. She almost wept out her gratitude to me, that unknown taxi driver back in High City who had returned her most precious possession, seeing as how it had come from "her darling Harry." If you don't think that wasn't something to see, you missed a good show. She should have had her name inscribed on an Oscar for that piece of acting.

But never mind. Live and let live, I always say. I'm not one to cast brickbats, seeing as how I'm a wealthy man myself now (in a manner of speaking) and have an "Olde California" shop of my own. No, not leather fashions for ladies. That's still not my bag. I've got a wig shop, would you believe it? Wigs for gentlemen as well as ladies; handy gadgets that can cover up more than a bald spot, if you know what I mean. It's doing well, too, although opening it up was kind of a sentimental gesture on my part, seeing as how wigs played a role in my good fortune. I'm pretty well versed in wiggery talk now, know a belle epoch from a fall and a pixie from an Afro. But I'm not in the shop too much. I leave that to the hired hands.

Mostly I travel with my wife, Mary. She always wanted to see the world from the back seat of a taxi, not the front, if you get the connection. Now I can afford to give it to her and leave the cab-pushing to someone else. Besides, Mary was pretty shook up over Martin Ulster's death, it being High City's lone unsolved murder and all. It does her good to get away, especially since she was planning on going anyway—not with me, of course, but with Martin.

Yep, my own Mary, small and slender with soft mousy-colored hair and big blue eyes; she, not any of those sleek well-preserved society dames, was the big thing in Martin Ulster's life. He told me that himself just before he died. And as I told him (just before knocking him out with one well placed blow to the solar plexus and another to the side of his head as he went down) it was just too bad he happened to fix on my wife because I wasn't the easy-loser type. It's a wonder someone didn't look in and see us fighting there in the front of the closed shop; then the witness to be paid off would have been someone else and I would have been doing the paying.

But things work out for the best, I always say. When he went down, I saw that dagger doodad on a display and finished him off. It looked like the sort of thing a jealous woman might do and, knowing his reputation, I aimed to extricate myself as best I could. But whatever his faults, I was certainly grateful to his masterly sense of discretion which kept his association with Mary a deep dark secret.

It was only dumb luck that in returning to my cab later, stopping to light a cigarette to pull myself together, I'd glanced in to see someone else bending over the body—someone who couldn't afford to be seen, someone who had to pay off a witness. But that's me; dumb and lucky and the only witness to the same murder, twice on the same night.

Breakfast in Bed

by Maeva Park

Alfred paused outside the door of room 321 and smoothed his black curly hair before he knocked. While he waited, he stared critically at the cart with Mrs. Galbraith's breakfast laid out neatly on the white, gleaming cloth, the silver-covered dish of scrambled eggs, the toasted English muffins, the little pot of jam. And the red rose in a silver vase. That was his touch.

Mrs. Hortense Galbraith liked Alfred, and Mrs. Galbraith was rich. Several times, in the three years in which he had been serving her she had given him a twenty-five dollar tip. But now, at last, she was working up to something really big, something which would take him away from this life of subservience, put him where he belonged. Alfred was a young man who appreciated the finer things in life.

Yesterday, when he had brought Mrs. Galbraith's luncheon, she had been in bed still, her preposterously red hair flaming against the white pillow case. Mrs. Galbraith had a heart condition and had to take life easy these days.

"Well, Alfred!" she'd said fondly. "How young and bright you look!" She'd glanced at the little nosegay of flowers which he had put on her table. "You spoil me, but I love it."

She had made him sit and listen to more of her rambling stories of the old days when she and her twin Horace were young. He had heard the same stories ever since Mrs. Galbraith came to live at the Hotel Blystone, but he always listened attentively.

"We did everything together," she mourned. "We felt things together. When I was first married and living in San Francisco I had appendicitis. Twenty-four hours later Horace was operated on for acute appendicitis. What do you think of that?"

She smoothed the soft taffeta coverlet with her old, ringed fingers. "When I feel a bit better I'm going to Chicago to visit Horace. He's all

I have left in the world now that Francis, my husband, is gone. And I'm all Horace has except for a young niece and nephew of Isabel's."

Then she had brightened and looked at Alfred with the little sidewise glance of merriment which made him realize the old gal must have been quite a charmer in her day.

"I'm not giving you any paltry little tip when I leave this hotel," she had said mysteriously. "I have something better in mind. A bright young man like you should have a good start in life. Today I made my will. I shall read it over once again tonight, and mail it to my attorney in the morning."

Thinking of this, Alfred straightened his tie and knocked again. There was no answer, so he opened the door and wheeled the cart inside. Sometimes Mrs. Galbraith had to be awakened for breakfast in bed.

He tiptoed over and began to put the breakfast things on the bed tray on which Mrs. Galbraith had her morning meal. He set the tray across her legs and shook her gently.

"Wake up, Mrs. Galbraith," he said. "It's time for breakfast."

Her grotesque red curls toppled over onto the white pillow. Alfred's breath whistled through his teeth.

"She's dead," he said to the empty room.

Feeling the bony old wrist for a pulse, he let his eyes wander around the opulent hotel bedroom. There was Mrs. Galbraith's solitaire deck on the little piecrust table, her purple shawl, very fine and silky, across the chair, and on the bureau the photograph of her brother Horace, a distinguished looking man in rimless glasses.

The desk was covered with letters and magazines. Alfred took one more look at Mrs. Galbraith's still face, with the death pallor on it. Then he moved quietly to the desk and began to look through the little stack of stamped letters, ready for mailing.

In less than a second he had found it, a long envelope addressed to her attorney, Silas Benton, but not yet sealed. It was Mrs. Galbraith's last will and testament, made out in her own trembling hand, dated the previous day and witnessed by two of the chambermaids. Couched in legal language, it seemed very formal to Alfred. First, her jewelry, photographs, and family heirlooms to a distant cousin; then, "Everything else of which I die possessed to my kind young friend, Alfred White, who has served me so faithfully during my residence at the Hotel Blystone."

His heart thumping wildly, Alfred stood with the document in his

ALFRED HITCHCOCK'S ANTHOLOGY

hands. Mrs. Galbraith was dead, and he was rich!

He looked over at the bed. Mrs. Galbraith was staring at him.

Shaking, Alfred laid the will back on the desk and went over to the bed. It was true; her blue eyes were wide open, and she was looking at him. He bent close to her trembling lips.

"Almost didn't make it this time," she whispered. "Get a doctor, Alfred. Quickly."

He said obediently, "Yes, Mrs. Galbraith," and started to pick up the telephone on the bedside table. He looked down at Mrs. Galbraith. Really, she was a remarkable woman. Even without the doctor's assistance, the color was starting to come back into her cheeks. In a few minutes, he could see plainly, the "dead" woman might be very much alive; and Alfred White would be a penniless waiter with a few uncomfortable gambling debts and a great taste for the good things of life. It might take Mrs. Galbraith some time to die. In that time, if the whim took her, and she was a woman of caprice, she might very easily change her will in favor of some other kind, deserving young man.

Alfred stood behind and above her, looking down at her eyes, shut now. Her face really did look almost like a death mask. It was only a question of days or weeks or months, even with good care. It would be a kindness to her, actually.

Alfred took one of the bed pillows and pressed it over Mrs. Galbraith's face for a little while. It took a very short time. He consoled himself with the thought that she had been nearly gone anyway, only a few minutes ago.

This time he made certain, checking the lack of pulse and heartbeat, the coldness of her skin, using the mirror test about which he had once read. There was not the faintest hint of mist on the little hand mirror that he held to Mrs. Galbraith's lips.

Alfred left the breakfast tray where it was and went over to the desk. Wiping his fingerprints from the things he had touched, in case there should be any suspicion surrounding Mrs. Galbraith's death, he put the will back into the long envelope and sealed it. Then, checking to make certain no one saw him, he dropped the little packet of letters down the chute beside the elevator.

Smiling a little to himself, he thought there wouldn't be any question now of an unscrupulous attorney suppressing that will. Also, Maisie and Sara, the two chambermaids, weren't likely to let anyone forget they had witnessed Mrs. Galbraith's last will and testament, even if they had no inkling of what was in it. He'd give them each a nice little present when he came into his money, Alfred decided. Then, after checking Mrs. Galbraith one last time, he went to the telephone and called the desk.

"This is Alfred, in room 321," he said. "I'm afraid Mrs. Galbraith is either sick or dead. You'd better send the house doctor."

When Dr. Hoffman arrived, Alfred was standing protectively beside the bed, as if to guard Mrs. Galbraith's body from the curious or insensitive.

"Poor old lady," he said to the doctor. "I brought her breakfast just like always, but she never did wake up to eat it."

The doctor nodded and went about his examination.

"She's gone all right," he said a few minutes later, as he put the stethoscope back into his bag. "I knew that heart of hers couldn't hold out much longer. I'll get in touch with her personal physician and her attorney."

After they had taken Mrs. Galbraith's body away, Alfred continued about his work until it was time for his afternoon break. He had three hours off in the afternoon; then he had to be back and work the dinner hour.

Today he dressed carefully in his best sport jacket and slacks, his carefully polished, slightly pointed shoes, and went out into the world, ready for living.

Passing an automobile dealer's showroom, he paused to look at the glistening new cars, powerful autos whose very lines suggested speed and luxury. He decided the first thing he would buy after the estate was settled would be a car. He had walked and bussed long enough. Every time he had a little money ahead toward the down payment on a car, he lost it on the horses or at cards. No, for a person like him, the answer was spot cash, and for the first time in his life he'd have it.

He saw himself in the plate-glass mirror of the showroom, young, audacious, handsome. Soon he would possess the things a man like him deserved.

Herbie's Cigar Store, as always, presented a secretive, closed appearance. The man sitting on his stool behind the glass counter was like a fat unsmiling Buddha, a big cigar in his mouth, his eyes little slits. He was only Herbie's henchman, the fall guy whom the police arrested every now and then as the "keeper" of a gambling place. Herbie paid his fine, and Biff was released, only to be arrested again a few months later with monotonous regularity.

Recognizing Alfred, he let him into the back room, where the bets were taken. This room, with not a cigar in sight except in the mouths of gamblers, was a smoke-filled room with radios blaring and a half dozen telephones in use.

"Hi, Herbie," Alfred said. "What's good today?"

Herbie, with his deceptively genial face, favored Alfred with a cold look. "I'll tell you one thing that's not good. Your credit's not good. You're into me for five yards, kid. It's time to pay up."

Alfred looked around carefully, but no one was paying any attention to him; each man was fiercely interested in his bets and nothing else.

"Look, Herbie," he said quietly. "I can level with you, because you have a reputation for being close-mouthed."

Herbie's expression was bored, and he poured a little funnel of cigar smoke into Alfred's nostrils.

"I mean it, Herbie! An old lady I been waiting on at the hotel—she died today and I know for a fact I figure in her will. She was rich; she lived like a queen. All I gotta do is wait for the reading of the will to make it legal, and if they don't pay up right away I can borrow on my prospects."

Herbie shrugged. "I'll gamble," he said laconically.

Alfred made his bets, then left Herbie's establishment and continued his walk downtown. He felt wonderful. If he had any luck today he might make enough to tide him over until the will was probated. Pretty soon, when the money was his, he'd be able to leave here for a more exciting city—Vegas, maybe—where he'd be able to spend money on beautiful girls and the other things which made life worth living, and of which he'd merely dreamed before.

For just a moment, he thought of Mrs. Galbraith's pleading eyes as she lay panting against the pillows, then he pushed the memory away. He had done her a favor, really. She was very old and sick and all her friends and relatives were gone, save for her twin, and he, obviously, must be as old and tired as she had been.

Besides, he thought, feeling rather self-satisfied, he had made the last three years very pleasant for Mrs. Galbraith, with his flattery, his little gifts, his willingness to listen to the repetitious stories of her long-ago youth and beauty, her travels, her conquests.

When Alfred strolled back to the hotel for his early supper, before going on duty, he was feeling pleasantly affluent, even though he had little money in his pocket.

The atmosphere at the hotel was a bit subdued tonight. Old Mrs. Galbraith had been a well known figure in the hushed, luxurious lobby and on her good days in the discreetly lighted dining room.

Alfred answered the murmurs of patrons and help alike with his own murmured, "Yes, she was a wonderful woman. Yes, it was a terrible shock, serving her breakfast in bed, before I realized she was gone."

He felt almost like the bereaved son of a rich woman, receiving the condolences of friends and acquaintances. The similarity was faithful, right down to the point of the inheritance.

By the next morning it was plain that Mrs. Galbraith's death had been taken for what it very nearly was—a heart attack. Alfred presumed that the will must have reached Mr. Benton's office so it scarcely surprised him, in the early afternoon, to receive a telephone message from Silas Benton's secretary. Would Alfred stop in that afternoon, between two thirty and four P.M.?

As soon as he had worked the luncheon hour, Alfred changed his clothes and hurried over to the Ames Building five blocks from the hotel. It was an impressive office building and Mr. Benton's office was even more so, with thick Oriental rugs and heavy, polished desks.

Mrs. Galbraith had spoken of the attorney as "the man who handles my affairs." Alfred rather liked the sound of that. He wondered if it might not be possible to have Mr. Benton handle *his* affairs.

The secretary escorted him into Mr. Benton's office. The distinguished, whitehaired man behind the desk said, "Ah yes, Alfred White. I've seen you at the Hotel Blystone when I've been visiting Mrs. Galbraith."

"Yes, sir," Alfred said politely. "I've seen you, too, sir."

He was profoundly grateful that no one had an inkling Mrs. Galbraith's death had been—premature. He would hate to have this man with the piercing grey eyes and the severe mouth suspect him of any sort of wrongdoing.

"Now, Alfred," Mr. Benton said, tapping a pencil against the desk blotter, "I received this will in the mail today. It was made out personally by Hortense Galbraith and apparently is entirely legal. It is dated day before yesterday and has been witnessed by two women employees of the Hotel Blystone.

"Normally I wouldn't be ready to talk to you about this, but we have here a special case."

He paused to offer Alfred a cigarette.

"Apparently Mrs. Galbraith thought a lot of you, Alfred."

Alfred said gently, "I thought a lot of her." And it was true, he realized with surprise. He'd gotten used to the old girl.

Mr. Benton considered. "In fact, Mrs. Galbraith thought so much of you that she left you everything she had."

Alfred allowed himself to look startled and humble.

Mr. Benton held up a hand. "Before you say anything, I must explain something. Mrs. Galbraith had nothing to leave beyond the jewelry and trinkets she bequeathed to an ancient cousin."

Alfred's heart began to pound with slow, sickening thuds.

"It is true that she was once a very rich woman. She and her twin brother Horace were left fortunes by their parents. But during his lifetime, Mrs. Galbraith's husband gradually dissipated his wife's inheritance. For several years now, Horace Wainwright has been sending Mrs. Galbraith a very comfortable allowance, which I have administered. I'm not sure whether advancing senility made her forget this or whether she liked to pretend to herself that she was still rich. But she had nothing of her own."

Visions of the sleek automobile, expensive new clothes, and most of all Herbie's menacing face swam before Alfred. Mr. Benton's smooth voice came to him as a distant drone, scarcely louder than the hum of traffic many floors below.

"It's a strange thing. Mrs. Galbraith always said she and her twin did things together, that they experienced the same joys and sorrows even when they were separated by many miles.

"Horace Wainwright died last night, less than twelve hours after his twin sister passed away. If she had outlived him, she would have inherited everything he possessed. As it is, his entire fortune will go to his dead wife's sister's children, a young man and woman who live in California."

The odor of the single rose in the silver vase on Mr. Benton's desk made Alfred feel ill.

Summer in Pokochobee County

by Elijah Ellis

The sun was right in our eyes as we drove east along the dusty county road. It wasn't much past seven o'clock. But already the August morning was hot and sticky. The fields on either side of the road were baked as hard and brown as overdone pancakes. Hell would be a relief, after a summer in Pokochobee County. The muggy heat, day after day, was enough to drive a man to anything. Including murder.

Now the car rattled across a wooden bridge that spanned a dry creek-bed. "Not much farther," Sheriff Ed Carson said.

I grunted. The third occupant of the car, Dr. Johnson, the county coroner, leaned forward from the back seat and asked me, "You know these people, Lon? The Englands?"

"No," I said curtly. I didn't like the fat, supercilious doctor, and this morning I was in no mood to pretend I did. I'd had very little sleep the night before. And the thought of what lay ahead made me sick to my stomach.

Dr. Johnson was saying, "Then you won't get the irony of this business. See, old man England and his wife are the terror of this part of the county. So upright and upstandin' that—well, any time some farmer comes home drunk, or some little girl gets in trouble, the first thing people worry about is, what'll the Englands say? England's own daughter—"

"Knock it off, doc," Ed Carson snapped. "What the girl and the Tice boy were doing in the barn there don't matter a bit any more. What matters is that they're both dead. Murdered."

"Oh, certainly, certainly," the doctor agreed. We rode in silence a few seconds. Then Dr. Johnson gave another whinny. "But it does have its amusin' aspects."

I said, "You have *some* sense of humor."

The doctor muttered something, then subsided.

I took off my glasses, massaged the bridge of my nose between thumb and forefinger. I felt lousy. I wondered how I'd manage to get through the hours ahead. But, as my wife had told me earlier that morning, I was the one who wanted to be Pokochobee County Attorney; no one had forced me into the office. Far from it. Now I was stuck with it.

And, on this hot Sunday morning, I was also stuck with what promised to be a very messy case of double murder, messy in more ways than one.

I glanced to my left at Ed Carson. His hawk-like face was pale and drawn. There were big half-moons of sweat at the armpits of his faded khaki shirt. He looked about like I felt. He'd had even less sleep than I had the night before.

Ed took his eyes from the road long enough to give me a weary wink and a shrug. "Sometimes it don't seem to be worth the trouble, does it?"

Dr. Johnson horned in from the back seat, "Well, if you fellers done your job—caught this fire bug before he had a chance to kill . . . "

"Oh, shut up," I said angrily. "Just shut up."

Carson again glanced at me, shook his grizzled head. I swallowed my temper. "Sorry, doc," I said. "It's this heat."

But the coroner wasn't about to let me off that easy. "No, now, Lon, admit it. You two ain't cut the mustard in this case. Eight fires in a month's time, all of them in the county, within a twenty or thirty mile radius of Monroe, and you ain't been able to get a clue, much less stop this monster."

I blurted, "Monster, my—"

"Now, doc, you got to give us time," Sheriff Ed Carson cut in quickly. "We'll get him."

Dr. Johnson gave an unconvinced snort.

And he wasn't exaggerating too awfully much. Actually, during the past seven weeks, there'd been six fires of incendiary origin on farms that formed a rough semicircle around the county seat at Monroe.

The fires were similar in detail, springing up in the middle of the night without warning, blazing furiously, with the telltale scent of gasoline. All had been set in barns.

In farming country, if you want to hurt a neighbor, you don't burn down his house. You put a torch to the real center of the farm, the barn.

Until last night there hadn't been any human casualties, though a good deal of livestock had gone up in flames. But last night was different. Last night Nancy England was entertaining a boyfriend named Jack Tice, in the hayloft of the barn on her father's place.

When fire struck, the two were killed, whether intentionally or not remained to be seen. Either way it was murder. Both the boy and the girl were eighteen years old.

So it looked like Pokochobee County's barn burner had become a killer. Only there was one thing wrong with it.

Early yesterday afternoon, Sheriff Ed Carson had caught the arsonist, some thirteen hours before the fire at the England place. That was what had kept Carson and me up most of the night, sweating a confession out of the firebug.

A simple-minded farmer, named Frazier, finally admitted setting the series of fires. Why? He thought it would make an excellent cover-up to burning down his own barn, which he'd insured for $1000, a few months ago. It was through the insurance company that Carson and I had got on his track, and nailed him.

When Frazier at last talked, he gave us enough details to make it certain he was responsible for five out of the six fires. ("What the heck, man's got to make a dollar somehow," he told us. "Sure ain't no money in farmin', what with this drought and all.")

But there still remained the sixth fire. That was the one last night, in which the two young people had died.

Frazier certainly hadn't set that one. He was in a cell.

For the time being, Carson and I had decided to keep it to ourselves that we had the barn burner in jail. It gave us at least some kind of a hole-card.

Last night, as every night during the last couple of weeks, a volunteer group of firemen, farmhands from the vicinity, had been cruising the county roads in a radio-equipped fire truck borrowed from Monroe.

They were only minutes away from the England farm when the flash came over the radio. They'd arrived in time to save a good portion of the barn. The lower part was a burned-out shell. But the hayloft, where the boy and girl were, did not receive much damage.

No one had known the kids were there, until dawn this morning. Then a guard left on duty had explored the upper reaches of the barn, looking for hidden embers. Instead, he had found the bodies of the boy and girl, huddled together on a blanket in a corner of the hayloft. He had called the sheriff, the sheriff had called me. After the brief discussion, I had called the county coroner, Dr. Johnson.

And now here the three of us were.

Me, I wished I'd stayed in bed. Carson braked the car, turned off the county road and in through a gate. Beside the gate was a tin mailbox on a post. On the mailbox was "England," painted in neat black letters.

The farmhouse itself was set back about a hundred yards from the road, amid a grove of dusty, dried-up trees. We reached the house and parked. There was no one in sight. But there were a couple of cars and a pickup parked helter-skelter under the trees.

Neighbors come to extend sympathy, or perhaps eagerly to eye the remains of violent death. I shook my head hard, trying to clear away the cobwebs. It didn't do much good.

As I said, after a Pokochobee County summer, hell itself would be a relief. But I didn't get paid to be human. If I was as miserable as everyone else in the county, driven half-crazy by the day-after-day heat, not to mention a night of one hour's sleep, that was too bad. I was still County Attorney Alonzo Gates.

The three of us got out of the car. We walked along the side of the big white house toward the back yard. Dr. Johnson waddled along beside me, his medical bag in one hand, a large handkerchief in the other. "I bet it's ninety-five degrees a'ready," he grumbled. He mopped his heavy jowls.

Sheriff Ed Carson said, "It's goin' to get hotter than that."

We turned the back corner of the house. People stood in little groups about the broad back yard. They were talking and looking toward a fire-blackened structure that was some hundred feet on beyond the yard.

Now a voice said loudly, "Here's the sheriff."

The chattering stopped, and all eyes turned our way. A man in blue overalls and stained workshirt bustled toward us. "About time you all showed up," he said. His eyes were red and swollen. "Awful thing here!"

The farmer's beard-stubbled face worked, as if he might start crying.

"We got here quick as we could," Ed Carson said. "You're Robert Tice, aren't you? Is that your boy?"

"Yes, and yes. And that's my boy layin' dead up yonder. . . ."

The middle-aged man began to weep now. It wasn't pretty. To make it worse, Tice was obviously about half drunk. His breath smelled like a backwoods still. Suddenly he turned and walked away.

"Let him go," Carson muttered. "We can see him later."

As we headed on across the yard, the crowd milled around us, several of them talking at once. Carson raised his voice, "All right, all right, folks.

Please. Where's the Englands?"

A broad-beamed woman eyed us severely. "Better yet, just where were you, Ed Carson? Last night when this awful thing happened? If you'd done your job . . . "

"Had time enough, I'm thinkin'," a crusty old man added from the edge of the crowd. "Durn near two months these fires been goin' on—and what've you all down at the courthouse done about it? Nothin', that's what."

The sheriff sighed patiently. I noticed that Dr. Johnson had edged away from us and stood now among the crowd of farmers, nodding and mopping his red face with his handkerchief.

Then a tall, gaunt man with deep-set eyes pushed through the press and said, "Good morning, sheriff."

In the sudden silence, Carson said, "Mr. England. This is County Attorney Gates."

England nodded at me. His eyes were fixed on some spot in the far distance.

I had the idea he didn't like what he saw there. I wouldn't either, in his place.

Now Dr. Johnson scuttled over. "Your dear wife—is there anything I can do for her?"

"What? Oh. No, she's all right. She's in the house. She has her Bible, and her friends around her." England ran a calloused hand back over his thin gray hair. "I'll show you—"

"No, that's all right," Carson said. "We can find our way to the barn. You'll want to be with your wife."

The old man nodded vaguely, and turned back toward the house. The sheriff, Dr. Johnson, and I crossed the yard to the barnyard. We entered through an open gate.

Some of the crowd started to follow, but Carson said sharply, "You folks stay here, please."

As we went on, I heard the broad-beamed woman mutter, "Just wait till next election. We'll see who's so high and mighty then."

"Why don't we tell them?" I asked Carson.

"Not yet." He gnawed at the fringe of his mustache. "Not quite yet."

"Tell them what?" Dr. Johnson wheezed.

"That you're a fat slob," I said.

The coroner sputtered.

A man I knew slightly stepped out of the open barn door ahead and came to meet us. He was the one who'd found the bodies. At Carson's orders, he'd stayed on guard, not allowing anyone to enter the barn.

"What about it, Bob?" I asked him.

He shook his head. His young face had a sickish tinge under its layer of suntan. "Rough. Man, I never want to go through anything like that again. Findin' those kids . . . "

"Yeah. Well. Anybody been in there since you called me?" the sheriff asked.

"No, I did just like you said. 'Course, old man England gave me a hard time. But I finally convinced him there was nothing he could do, and he went on back to the house."

By now the four of us were inside the gloomy interior of the barn. There was a strong smell of charred timbers. The section off to our left was a jumble of blackened rubble, and a part of the wall and roof had caved in. To the right we saw the damage wasn't so bad.

Bob pointed to a wooden ladder down at the far end of the less damaged part of the barn. "Up there. Lucky that old hayloft wasn't full of hay, or there wouldn't be a thing left. There ain't anything up there now but a clutter of old tools. And . . . those two kids."

We climbed the ladder, Dr. Johnson having a hard time of it, and looked around. The big door at the end of the loft was open, and through it I could see the barn lot, and the house in its grove of trees in the distance.

The bodies were lying on a blanket at the side of the loft, some distance from the ladder. Dr. Johnson waddled that way. The rest of us slowly followed.

"Oh, I opened the hay door there, sheriff," Bob said. "It was shut and barred when I first came up here."

Carson nodded. "Don't seem to be much damage up here."

"Just a couple of places where the fire came up the insides of the inner walls," Bob said. "No, it was smoke that killed them. You'll see, their bodies ain't burned at all. No, it was the smoke. Got 'em before they had a chance to . . ."

The coroner was kneeling beside the bodies, his bag open on the scorched floor beside him. I looked down over his shoulder. The boy and girl were lying on their backs, the girl's head resting on the boy's upper arm. They looked relaxed and peaceful as if they were asleep. Beside them lay an empty pint whisky bottle.

Bob abruptly turned away. He moved toward the open hayloft door. After a moment, Carson and I went to join him. Dr. Johnson continued his probing and pulling, mumbling to himself the while.

Bob leaned against a side of the door and stared down at the hard-packed earth of the barn lot twenty feet below. "Damn this heat," he said. He suddenly blurted, "I knew them, Nancy and Jack. They were only a couple years behind me in high school." He looked up, gave a wry smile. "Heck, I even tried to date Nancy. But her old man—he wouldn't let her date anybody. Strict, he was. . . . And now, this."

I lit a cigarette. I said quietly, "I'm sure Mr. England is wishing he'd played things a little differently."

Ed Carson gave an uneasy cough. "What can you tell us about last night, Bob?"

"What's to tell? Old man England woke up about two, and saw the barn was on fire. He called your office, sheriff, and your man there got on the radio and gave us the news. We were only three or four miles from here. We got here in a hurry, and got the fire out, though a few more minutes and the place would have all gone up. Anyway, we got it out. Rest of the boys went on home, then. I stayed on to keep an eye on things. A little after dawn, I came up here to the loft for a look-see. I found them. That's it."

"What about the fire itself, Bob?" I put in. Carson and I exchanged glances.

Bob made an angry gesture. "Just like the others. Gasoline sloshed around; we could still smell it when we got here. The so-and-so started it down at the far end of the barn. If you guys don't get him pretty soon, there won't be a barn left in the county. Then he'll start on houses . . . "

"No, he won't," I said. "Keep this to yourself. The sheriff picked up our firebug friend a little before one o'clock yesterday afternoon, at least thirteen hours before the fire here. And he's been in a cell ever since Ed brought him in. Get it?"

Bob's eyes widened. "Then who—"

"You tell us 'who.' But not the character that's been putting the torch to places these last weeks."

Carson said, "Maybe somebody else just liked the idea of what the feller was doin', and decided to copy him. Or maybe there's more to it than that. We don't know, yet. There could be two of them."

ALFRED HITCHCOCK'S ANTHOLOGY

We turned to look toward the coroner. Dr. Johnson was leaning back on his haunches, wiping his hands on a cloth. For once his fleshy face had lost its usual fiery color. He looked pale. And frightened.

"What is it, doc?" I called. "What'd you find?"

He levered his bulk to his feet. "They were killed," he said wonderingly. "Both of them. Shot." We hurried to join him beside the bodies.

"I—I almost missed it," he went on. "I thought it was asphyxiation. But I noticed a lump, here, at the base of the boy's skull, see? And there's a similar lump in the same place, on the girl." He gulped, mopped his face. "They've been slugged with something that didn't break the skin, a sandbag, something like that. Then when they were unconscious, they were shot."

Carson and I were bending over the bodies. "I don't see any blood," I said.

"No," Dr. Johnson said. "You wouldn't. They were both shot through the roof of the mouth, the bullet traveling up into the brain."

The sheriff's hand was trembling as he gently pried open the boy's mouth, bent to look inside.

"You see, both are lying on their backs, so that any blood would course down their throats." The doctor looked sick. "Terrible. Just terrible. Who'd do a thing like that?"

Carson got up. He slowly brushed his palms together. "Have to be a very small caliber gun, since the bullets didn't come out. Light-loaded .22 fired from a snub-nosed pistol, maybe."

By now I'd steeled myself enough to take a look at the victims. One look was plenty. Shakily I rose to my feet. "If the fire had got to them, chances are a million to one it'd never have been discovered they were shot," I said. "Even as it is—"

I turned to the county coroner and held out my hand. "Doc, I apologize for anything out of the way I ever said about you."

The doctor was regaining some of his color. He shook my hand briefly, then gave one of his rumbling whinnies. "That's what the county pays me for—if you can call it pay."

Carson was looking around. "Say, where did Bob Hofner go?"

Except for the three of us, and the two silent forms at our feet, the hayloft was empty. I said, "Maybe he couldn't take this."

"Maybe," the sheriff said soberly. Then, "Well, we'd better go talk to the Englands."

I nodded. The heat up here was making me dizzy. I headed for the ladder.

Behind me, Carson asked the doctor to stay there until the ambulance arrived to carry the bodies into Monroe.

"But what happened here?" Dr. Johnson complained. "This certainly don't look like the work of some out-at-the-elbow half-wit who gets his fun out of burnin' barns."

When Carson and I were outside, walking toward the house, I echoed the doctor: "What did happen?"

The sheriff sighed. "Somebody went to one heck of a lot of trouble to pull off a perfect crime . . . and nearly did it. Except for a couple of bad breaks, from his point of view, he'd be home free. Heck, he might make it yet."

I grunted, lit a fresh cigarette I didn't want, from the stub of the last one—that I hadn't wanted either.

The crowd had grown considerably during the time we were in the barn. Carson and I shoved through, ignoring their questions—and their condemnations. I saw Bob Hofner off to one side, talking to the seedy-looking father of the dead boy. As I watched, Tice straightened up, lifted a hand as if to ward off a blow, and yelled something.

The people nearest him turned to stare curiously. Tice began waving his arms and shouting.

"Looks like Bob is passing the word," I said to Carson.

The sheriff shrugged. "Don't matter now. And maybe it'll get these folks off our backs for a few minutes."

We reached the big white house and went inside. In the kitchen we found a gaggle of farm women, brewing pots of coffee and chattering. One of them told us the Englands were in the living room. She pointed down a hallway toward a closed door at the far end.

There Carson tapped on the door, then opened it, and we went in. The Englands were alone, sitting side by side on a couch beneath closely-drawn shades. England rose wearily. His wife just stared at us, and through us.

The next few minutes were terrible. When Carson told them their daughter had been intentionally murdered, and how, the woman began to scream in a hoarse, choked voice. The old man squeezed his eyes shut a moment. When he opened them, they were a dead man's eyes, blank and unfocused. "It was the will of the Lord, that they should be punished," he said unsteadily. "But not like this."

Suddenly his wife was up. She was shaking violently. "Will of the Lord. Don't ever again mention that name in my house."

She stumbled across the room and out. Carson closed the door behind her. He put his back to it, gave me a nod.

I went to the old man, eased him down on the sofa, and stood in front of him, trying to think where to start. My mind felt like a congealed mass of gelatin.

I took off my glasses and sleeved the sweat from my face. The old man was looking down at his clenched fists.

"Mr. England," I finally said, "we're going to have to ask you some things about your daughter."

"What do I know about her? What've I ever known?"

I said, "Where was she last night? I mean . . . "

"She left here about six," England said dully. "She was going to spend the night with a school friend of hers, in town. She's done it several times this summer."

"Who is the friend?"

"What? Oh. The little Lambert girl—you all probably know her father, Judge Lambert."

I nodded. "You had no idea that Nancy was—uh—seeing the Tice boy?"

England looked up. His bluish lips pulled back from his clenched teeth. "If I had—if I had, the swine would have died a lot sooner than he did."

I blinked. Here was a man quite capable of murder, under the right circumstances . . . maybe even the murder of his own child. I glanced over my shoulder at Carson.

Then I came back to the old man. "Do you know of any enemies your daughter might have had?"

England shook his head. "No. Everyone liked her. She was—she was . . . "

He broke off. His face crumpled like wet paper. There was no point in going on with this. I walked over to the sheriff. He nodded, and we left the room, shutting the door softly behind us. I muttered, "You thinking what I am?"

Carson didn't answer for a moment. "I don't know. He's always been a hard-nosed, unyieldin' man, a little too unyieldin', maybe. But this? I don't know."

We went along the hall, out through the kitchen. In the back yard we saw Dr. Johnson waddling toward us. When he arrived, he wheezed, "The ambulance got here. They're loadin' the bodies now. I'll ride into town with them. Get at the autopsy right away."

"Fine," the sheriff nodded. Then he turned to talk with his two deputies, who had finally managed to get out of bed and get here. "You fellers have a good breakfast?"

The deputies shifted their feet uneasily. "What the heck," Buck Mullins said. "We didn't know—"

The sheriff cut him off. He snapped orders and the two hurried away toward the barn. The dusty black ambulance passed them as it came slowly along the lane from the barn. It stopped long enough to pick up Dr. Johnson, then moved on past the house, to the county road in front.

The crowd stopped chattering long enough to watch the ambulance out of sight. Then again they descended on the sheriff and me. "Let's get out of this," I said.

We made our way to the sheriff's car in the driveway and got inside. The leather seat was blistering hot to the touch. It was like getting into an oven, but at least it gave us some protection from the swarm of people.

Carson leaned his head out the window beside him, and spoke to the nearest man, "Say, would you find Mr. Tice and ask him to come here a minute?"

The man nodded and walked importantly away. Moments later Tice came to the car, and, at the sheriff's invitation, climbed into the back seat.

"Thought we'd give you a lift home, if you don't have your car with you," Carson told him.

Tice shook his head vaguely. He was sober by now, and obviously not liking it. "No, come across the fields this mornin' when I got the news. Only about a mile that way." He swallowed, and went on, "Jack—he took the pickup last night. Don't know where he left it."

"Well." Carson started the car, turned it, headed for the road. "My deputies are looking around back there in the woods beyond the barn. There's a lane back there a piece that connects with the county road. More'n likely they'll find your pickup parked in the lane."

The beard-stubbled, red-eyed farmer said, "Huh? Oh yeah, I expect so. It don't matter."

We drove in silence a few seconds. Then I asked, "Mr. Tice, did you know your son was spending time with the England girl?"

274

Tice shrugged. "He told me, but I didn't believe him. Nancy was such a hoity-toity gal. Just like her paw. All them Englands think they're so much better'n anybody else." He snorted. "Guess the old man'll change his tune now."

The sheriff cleared his throat, and said, "Did Jack have any enemies around here?"

"Why, any young feller full of spunk and vinegar, he'll make a few enemies—but nobody that'd do a thing like this." Tice scrubbed shaky hands over his face. "I feel bad. This heat, and now this about my boy gettin' killed—it's enough to drive a body crazy."

A few minutes later we dropped him off in front of a ramshackle farm-house that obviously hadn't seen a paintbrush in thirty years. He got out of the car and walked away toward the house. He didn't say goodbye.

Probably all he could think about was getting to the house, and a bottle of moonshine.

We drove on toward Monroe. When we were about halfway there, the radio under the dashboard crackled to life. It was Carson's deputy, Buck Mullins, calling from the England farm. "Ed? Listen, we found the pick-up truck right off, parked in a little old lane in the woods, about a quarter of a mile behind the barn. Nothin' in it, though. Nothin' but what you'd expect."

Carson told him, "All right. Keep looking. I want you to go over that barn with a fine-tooth comb." He replaced the mike on its hook under the dash and chuckled grimly. "Course, they ain't about to find the gun in the barn, but they'll sure get sweaty and dirty enough."

I nodded, yawned widely. "I could sleep for a week."

The sheriff gave a disapproving grunt. "You can sleep some other time. Right now, we got work to do."

When we got to town, we stopped by the Lambert house on Third Street, the home of the girlfriend of Nancy England. The Lambert girl had heard about the murders. By now everyone in the county had, of course. She was extremely nervous and upset, but she couldn't help us at all.

Several times during the summer, usually on a Saturday evening, Nancy had asked her to tell Nancy's father, if he should call, that Nancy was with her. That was all she knew.

With a little prodding, she broke down and admitted she knew that Nancy was spending the time with Jack Tice. "They were in love," the girl told us, twisting a handkerchief between her fingers. "Very, very much in love. And this was the only way they could be—be together. Because of Nancy's father. They were going to run away, soon as Jack had enough money together."

That was all. If she knew any more, she wasn't telling. Carson and I got up to leave. She came with us to the front door. "What I don't understand is why Jack didn't protect them," she said then.

"How's that?" Carson asked.

"Why, he always carried a gun, Nancy told me. She said it was a little-bitty thing, you could hide it in the palm of your hand, but it was a real gun."

We stared at the girl. Then Carson said, "Well, thank you, Miss Lambert. Give our best to your father," and we left.

As we walked down the broiling sidewalk to the car, I whistled softly. "A 'little-bitty' thing you could hide in the palm of your hand."

"Yeah," said the sheriff. "How about that?"

It was still only about nine o'clock when we got to the courthouse. But it had been a very full two hours. We went in the back door of the ancient building, and along the echoing corridor to Carson's office on the ground floor. There, the deputy on duty shook his head at Carson's inquiry if there'd been any news. The sheriff and I went on into his private cubbyhole, which opened off the rear of the big, dingy main office.

Carson turned on the fan. He sank into his chair at his desk and sighed wearily. I dragged a chair up to a corner of the desk and sprawled down. "Yeah, I agree with you. This is some way to spend a Sunday."

Carson snorted. "You know old Farris, has that hock-shop on Main. I had a little dust-up with him a while back. Seems he'd been sellin' watch-pocket-size .22 derringers to the kids around town here. Little two-barrel jobs that fired low-power .22 shells . . . "

"Uh huh. And evidently Jack Tice owned one, and carried it with him," I said. "But it wasn't on his body. So, where does that leave us?"

"It leaves us with a good idea of where the gun came from that killed those kids. The killer found it on Tice, after he'd knocked the two of them out. And bang."

I stared thoughtfully at the flyspecked window beyond the sheriff's desk. "That could mean he hadn't planned to kill them at all. Or, more likely, he just substituted Tice's gun for whatever he'd meant to use as a weapon."

276

"Uh huh." The sheriff slapped a palm down on the battered surface of the desk. "I don't care if it is against all my principles. I'm goin' to have a drink."

"I'm with you," I told him.

He opened a bottom drawer, came out with a bottle and two paper cups. He filled the cups, handed me one. I was glad to see it. I took a long sip, then said, "You know, I just can't see ole man England doing the killings. Not like this. I get the idea he'd be more likely to take a shotgun and blow someone's head off, then tell all the world about it. He wouldn't try to cover up."

Carson nodded.

"Yeah, I'm inclined to agree. He just don't fit at all."

"I think somebody must've followed the kids. Maybe he saw Jack pick up Nancy here in town, or wherever they met, and followed them, clear out to the England place, and then to the barn. He waited till they went to sleep. He sneaked up to the loft, slugged them, found the gun—and killed them. Why? Who knows? A psycho, maybe. Or one of the kids might have got a look at him before he could knock them out. Or he hated one or both of them for reasons unknown. Whatever, he killed them. Then he set the fire, believing it would destroy the barn, and the bodies with it. But the patroling fire truck got there too fast. . . ."

The sheriff considered in silence. He took a drink, wiped his mustache on the back of his hand. "Well, I can't think of any better theory, that's for sure. but, damn it—"

The phone rang on his desk. He picked it up, growled, "Carson here." He listened a few moments. His shaggy eyebrows pulled down in annoyance. Then he said, "Oh, for—all right, all right. I'll come over." He banged down the phone, turned to me. "That was the jailer. Like we ain't got enough trouble, now Frazier is over there in the cellblock, raisin' hell, and the jailer can't do anything with him."

I leaned my head back and laughed, almost hysterically. "What next?"

"The black plague, probably," Carson said, getting up from his desk. "Want to come along?"

I nodded, finished my drink, and we left the office. The jail is separated from the courthouse by a wide, dusty parking lot. By the time we arrived, we were both streaming with sweat.

Back in the cellblock, Frazier yelled at the sight of us, "About time you got here."

We looked through the bars at the overalled arsonist. He didn't look any better this morning than he had last night. "What do you want?" Carson snapped.

"Listen, listen here! I got a right to know," Frazier gabbled. "That durn old jailer, he won't tell me nothin', won't even say hello to me. But I got a right to know."

Carson breathed deeply, then said, "What is it?"

"Why, about the England barn, of course." Frazier's round, mottled face leered with expectation. "Did it go up?"

For a long minute, Carson and I just stared. Then I managed to ask, "What're you talking about?"

"England, the England barn," he said impatiently. "I had 'er timed to go up about two o'clock last night . . . "

Carson shot an arm into the cell, grabbed the man by the shirt and dragged him up against the bars. "What do you mean, you had it timed?"

Frazier struggled free of the sheriff's grip. He backed away across the cell, giggling happily. "Oh, I fooled you. I fooled you all. You all thought I set those fires the same night they happened, didn't you? Oh, I fooled you last night. Went along and agreed with you, about as how I was supposed to of poured gasoline around, and then set a match to it." He did a grotesque capering dance.

The jailer had the cell door open. Carson plunged inside, again grabbed Frazier, and shook him. "Talk, or I'll break your lousy neck."

"Simple," Frazier laughed, when Carson had released him. "Just a little old twenty-four hour fuse, attached to a can of gasoline." He was eager to tell us about it now. "See, see, I'd go in a place one night, and hide the gas and the fuse attached to it. Then next night, boom! Up she'd go. But me, I'd be to home, or in town, see. I had me a perfect alibi."

Slowly Carson came back out to the corridor. The jailer re-locked the door. Half-formed thoughts and wild conjectures were tumbling around in my brain.

Just before we left, Frazier said, "Did it go up?"

"Yes," I told him. "It went up."

"Ah," he breathed happily. Then his face clouded. "If it hadn't been for that one piece of bad luck . . . "

"Mister, you bein' where you are right now, is the biggest piece of good luck you'll ever have in your lousy life, believe me," Ed Carson snapped.

Neither of us spoke during the walk back to the courthouse and Carson's office. We sat down, and still in silence, Carson brought out the bottle and refilled the paper cups. I lifted mine. "Well, here's to—nothing."

"Not quite," the sheriff mused. "Not just quite."

He picked up the phone, called Dr. Johnson's office. When he had the coroner on the phone, he said, "What've you got?" He listened, nodded, then for my benefit he said, "Each body had a .22 slug buried in the brain, resting against the inner side of the skull. Uh huh. Yeah. Doc, just one thing."

I noticed that he was gripping the phone so tightly that his knuckles were white. Suddenly it hit me what he'd meant. I leaned forward in my chair.

He asked the question I'd expected: "Doc, was there any trace of smoke in their lungs?"

A moment later he hung up. He nodded slowly.

"Let's go get him," I said. We left.

While the county car ate up the dusty miles on the way to the England farm, we worked it out, the way it had to be, the only possible way that would fit in with what we now knew. The key fact, of course, was that Frazier had, after all, been responsible for the fire at England's place.

The volunteer firemen arrived, put the fire out, and left, all but one, who had stayed behind as a guard.

Bob Hofner. And, by his own admission, no one else had entered the barn except himself after that. Mr. England had tried, but Hofner had talked him out of it. No one else had been inside.

"Bob did it, all right," the sheriff said. "Heaven only knows why. But he did it. Doc findin' traces of smoke in the lungs of those kids proves they were there in the loft, and alive, durin' the fire. Probably the smoke knocked them out, but it didn't kill them. A .22 slug apiece did that. Remember, there was that empty whisky bottle up there beside the bodies. They'd both been drinkin', likely enough. Then they went to sleep, sometime before the fire."

I took it up, "Yeah. It makes a chain. They have enough booze to keep them sleeping, until the smoke comes along to make them really unconscious. Then, sometime afterward, Hofner makes it permanent."

The England place was just ahead now. Carson slowed, made the turn into the long driveway.

"And, too, that's why they were killed like they were. Shot through the roof of the mouth, and laid out on their backs, so there wouldn't be any outward sign of blood," I said. "Hofner figured there wasn't a chance of a medical examination thorough enough to find the wounds, since it was supposed to be obvious they were asphyxiated by smoke from the fire. . . . Hadn't been for Doc Johnson, it might have worked."

"Might have," Carson agreed. "Well. Here we are."

There was even more of a crowd milling around the England property now than there had been before. We left the car, found Carson's deputies.

Ten minutes later, we found Bob Hofner.

He was with a group of young people, down by the charred barn, telling them about the things that had happened there last night. Though not quite everything. The sheriff caught his eye, beckoned to him.

Hofner came over. He looked at us questioningly.

"Let's go, Bob," the sheriff said quietly.

"Go? Go where?"

"Into town, Bob. Come on. Don't give us any trouble, or attract attention to us. Lots of these folks would be glad to hang the murderer of those kids. And we know who that is, don't we?"

Hofner's knees buckled. He would have fallen if one of the deputies hadn't taken his arm, held him up. His mouth opened, shut, opened again. But nothing came out.

We got him to the car and into the back seat, with Buck Mullins sitting beside him. The second deputy would follow in the other county car.

Hofner bent forward until his head rested on his knees. He began to sob. "I don't know why I did it. Don't know what happened."

"Where's the gun?" I asked him.

"Gun? I—I dug a hole there beside the barn; buried the thing. I wish I hadn't found it in Jack's pocket . . ."

Again his hunched shoulders shook with sobs.

Slowly the story came out of him, as we rode back to town through the late morning heat. It was about as Carson and I had thought. Not long before dawn, Hofner had heard the sound of coughing, coming from the hayloft of the barn. He went up. He had a flashlight, and by its gleam he had found the boy and girl.

"Jack was stirring around, tryin' to sit up. He was still about half out. I walked over, and I hit him. You know, a judo chop, across the back of his neck, hard as I could. By then Nancy was moanin' and her eyelids were flutterin', so I raised her up and I hit her, too. The same way."

Hofner retched. At last he went on, "So they were both layin' there, out cold again. I went through the pockets of Jack's pants. I thought maybe he had some money. I don't know. It was all like a dream. I found this little gun in the pants. I saw it was loaded, two shells. I turned around and looked down at them. Everything was whirlin' around and around. All I could think about was that Nancy had been too good to have anything to do with me, but here she was, like this, with a jerk like Jack Tice. . . All of a sudden somethin' exploded inside me. So I—I killed them. I didn't think there was any chance at all of anybody findin' out."

The sheriff said, gently, "You cared for Nancy quite a bit, didn't you? More than you've told us?"

Hofner raised tear-filled, swollen eyes. "Yes, I loved her. I loved her. I wouldn't have hurt her for anything. If only she'd have—just once—been nice to me." He shook his head violently. "But I wouldn't have hurt her for anything. I must have been crazy.'"

We pulled up in the parking lot behind the courthouse. For a moment Ed Carson stared out at the heat-dancing ground before us. "Summer," he said, "in Pokochobee County."

Variations on an Episode

by Fletcher Flora

"This one," said Marcus, "is fancy." Bobo Fuller, deliberately spaced the maximum distance away on the seat of the police car, stared gloomily out the window at the passing buildings. They were moving through sparse traffic at an almost leisurely pace, and the siren was silent. This, to Fuller, was a violation of proper procedure, almost an offense against propriety. Two cops going to a murder, in his opinion, should be going at high speed with siren howling. But Marcus, unfortunately, believed that should be left to the ambulances and the fire trucks. After all, there was no great rush. The scene of the murder was secured in status quo by uniformed patrolmen, sent early to the scene, and it was certain the corpse wasn't going anywhere. High speeds made him nervous, Marcus said, and sirens made his head ache.

"Fancy how?" Fuller asked.

"As I get it," Marcus said, "this guy named Draper was asleep in his bed this morning, and someone walked in and stabbed him."

"That doesn't sound fancy to me. It sounds simple."

"I didn't mean fancy that way. It happened to a fancy guy who lived in a fancy place. That's what I meant."

"Thanks." Fuller's voice was tainted just enough by bitterness to register his animus while sustaining diplomacy. "It's nice to be informed. Was this Draper married?"

"He was."

"Where was his wife when he was getting stabbed?"

"A good question, Fuller. At the first opportunity, let's ask her."

They had turned, meanwhile, onto a broad boulevard split down the middle by a raised median strip that was planted with bluegrass and evergreens, in an area devoted largely to apartment buildings and hotels. They stopped in front of a hotel, the Southworth, and got out. In spite of a bronze name plaque and a canopy from curb to entrance, the place was not really so fancy. What Marcus had meant was that the Southworth was undoubtedly expensive. This conviction was in no degree weakened by the resplendent doorman who held the door open for them.

"It's on the fifth floor," Marcus said over his shoulder as he crossed the lobby to the elevator, with Fuller trailing. "We'll go right up."

Getting out on the fifth floor, they went down the hall and around a corner to 519. Marcus opened the door, already slightly ajar, and entered a short hallway created by the protrusion of a bathroom, which was immediately on his right. A few feet farther on, he came into the bedroom of a two-room suite. Again to his right, headboard flush against the interior wall of the bathroom, was a double bed. Beside the bed, staring down as if bemused by death and the prospects of heaven, was a gray, dehydrated little man with a stethoscope hanging out of his side coat pocket. The stethoscope was just dressing, a kind of professional emblem in support of the caduceus. The gray little man had not needed it, for the man on the bed, the object of his bemused stare, was as clearly dead as a knife driven into the soft hollow at the base of his throat could make him. He had bled a lot, and the blood had soaked the front of his white silk pajamas and spread in a great stain over white cotton sheets. The gray little man looked up at Marcus with curiously angry eyes.

"Hello, Marcus," he said. "You're running late."

Marcus walked around the bed and stopped beside it in the narrow clearance between the bed and the wall. Fuller remained on the other side, behind the medical examiner, and surveyed the carnage with a forced air of detachment. It was Fuller's secret shame that the sight and smell of blood made him queasy.

"Sometimes I do." Marcus, returning the stare of blind eyes, resisted a desire to close them. "He certainly bled a lot, didn't he?"

"You generally do when your throat's cut."

"How long has he been dead?"

"Since seconds after he was stabbed."

"When was he stabbed?"

"Not long ago. Say around nine o'clock. Shortly before he was found."

"Who found him?"

"Should I know? I just pronounce them dead, Marcus. You're the cop."

"Right. He was sleeping when it happened, sleeping on his back. How did whoever did it get in here? These hotel doors lock automatically when they're closed. You can't open them from outside without a key. Don't bother to answer, doc. You've already told me that I'm the cop."

Marcus, sacrificing a handkerchief, reached down with a faint fastidious feeling of revulsion and extracted the knife, carefully preserving in the process the fingerprints which he was convinced would not be there.

The knife was a common kitchen paring knife. It was of poor quality, but plenty good enough and sharp enough, for all that, to peel a potato or trim a steak or cut a throat. You could buy it, or one like it, in thousands of hardware stores or department stores or dime stores. In brief, it was impossible to trace or to identify as the property of any person. Were knives like this available in the hotel kitchen? If so, it would be at least a beginning, but Marcus, the perennial pessimist, bet bitterly that they weren't.

He had been aware all the while of voices and movement in the room behind him, the second room of the suite. Now, abruptly, carrying the knife in the handkerchief, he went through the communicating door. A couple of technicians were working expertly at their scientific hocus-pocus. One of the pair of patrolmen who had arrived first on the scene was standing by the hall door. Marcus, with a wave of a hand to the technicians, approached the patrolman. The latter identified himself and, at Marcus' request, gave a report so brief and orderly that it had apparently been arranged and edited in his mind beforehand for the purpose of making a high efficiency rating. It did, in fact, do so and Marcus mentally noted it.

The patrolman and his partner had received at nine twenty the radio message which had sent them to the Southworth. They were cruising nearby and had arrived at nine twenty-seven. They had found the hotel manager, a Mr. Clinton Garland, fresh from the chamber of horrors, maintaining a resolute guard in the hall outside the bedroom door. The body had been discovered by a hotel maid who had come in on her regular routine to put fresh towels in the bathroom. The maid had set up a howl that had reached in relays to the manager's office, and he had come at once in the company of the captain of the bellboys, who had been dispatched to summon the police. The patrolmen, arriving, had relieved the manager of guard duty. Nothing, subsequently, had been touched until the invasion of investigators.

"Where," asked Marcus, "is his wife?"

The patrolman looked stricken, realizing at once that he had, in his orderly report, been guilty of an egregious omission. "Wife, sir?"

"Right. Wife. He had one, you know."

"As a matter of fact, sir, I didn't know."

"I take it, then, that she hasn't been in evidence since you got here?"

"No, sir. No wife."

"No matter. We'll turn her up in good time. Where's the manager now?"

"Waiting in his office on the ground floor. He was pretty badly shaken up. I thought it would be all right to let him go."

"You did everything fine. Now you and your partner better get back on patrol."

Marcus turned back into the room and put the paring knife in its cotton nest on a table near a technician who was methodically dusting for prints.

"You can check the handle of this," he said, "but you won't find anything."

He walked back through the communicating door into the bedroom. The medical examiner had gone, but Fuller lingered.

"Have a look around, Fuller, and see what you can come up with. Odds are you won't find anything that means anything, but I guess we ought to try." Marcus, speaking, reached the hall door. "I'm going down to see the manager. I'll be back up pretty soon."

He went out, and Fuller began looking for something that meant something.

Marcus, however, did not go directly down to the manager. He was delayed, almost before he started. In the hall, he was arrested by a sudden sharp hissing sound, rather like the warning of a startled snake, and he saw that the door across the hall had opened far enough to allow the passage of what appeared to be the decapitated head of somebody's grandmother. It had white hair parted in the middle and drawn back on both sides of the part into a bun; an avid little face, full of wrinkles, with a tight little mouth that looked very much like another wrinkle with teeth; rimless glasses slipped down the bridge of a pointed nose, and behind them, peeping over the rimless glass with an effect of slyness, a pair of alert, inquisitive eyes.

Marcus thought wildly of a wicked wren.

"Did you hiss?" he asked politely.

She nodded briskly and darted a glance both directions in the hall, seeming thereby to invite Marcus into a conspiracy. "Is it true?" she whispered.

"It may be," Marcus said. "Is what true, precisely?"

"Is Mark Draper dead?"

"He is."

"Murdered?"

"Unfortunately, yes."

The white head nodded again. The bright eyes glittered over glass. "Small wonder."

"Oh? You think so? Why?"

"Some people are born to be murdered." The whisper was now barely audible. "And some people are born to be murderers."

"That's an interesting theory. I'd be pleased to hear you develop it."

"I know a thing or two. I do indeed."

"I shouldn't wonder."

"I have an instinct. I feel things."

"Madam, instinct is not allowed in a court of law. However, when supported by adequate evidence, it may prove useful in an investigation. May I come in?"

"Please do."

She widened the crack in the door just enough for him to slip through, then quickly and quietly closed it behind him. The conspiratorial atmosphere, Marcus thought, was really becoming a bit absurd.

"Permit me to introduce myself," he said. "Lieutenant Joseph Marcus."

"I'm Lucretia Bridges. Won't you sit down?"

They looked at each other across five feet of green carpet in a room which betrayed itself by the presence of many small additions of whatnot, obviously personal, as a place of permanent residence. Lucretia, clearly, was no transient. She was one of a swelling company of hotel dwellers.

"You have a theory," Marcus said. "Also an instinct. I'm interested in both."

Her white head bobbed, and again Marcus was wildly reminded of a wicked wren.

"Mark Draper," she said, "was no better than he should have been."

"Most of us aren't."

"He drank and he gambled and he kept late hours."

Marcus, who was guilty of the first and the last, although not the second, clucked disapprovingly. "Is that so?"

"It is. Moreover, he was a wastrel, and he didn't work."

Marcus' cluck was somewhat more genuine now. He himself was not guilty on either of these counts, being far too poor to afford them. "If he didn't work, how could he afford to maintain residence in a place like this? It must be very expensive."

"It is. He had money. He inherited it, more than he could spend in a lifetime, wastrel though he was. Why else do you imagine that sly little baggage married him?"

"Baggage?" Marcus made a rapid mental adjustment. "Oh, yes. His wife, of course."

"She's much younger than he was, years and years. Disparity in ages makes for a bad situation. It invites trouble."

"How so?"

"I was never unfaithful to Mr. Bridges. Never!"

"That's commendable, I'm sure. Mrs. Draper, you think, was unfaithful to Mr. Draper?"

"I know what I know."

"Instinct?"

"I have eyes. I see what's going on."

Marcus didn't doubt it. Witnesses, however, to be of value, must be somewhat more specific.

"What did you see? When did you see it?"

"Comings and goings. Mr. Draper was gone much of the time, you see. He didn't work, but he was forever off somewhere, and she was always having callers. In the daytime, mind you. I always think it's so much more shameful in the daytime, don't you?"

Marcus had no preference, day or night, but he repeated his useful cluck. "So flagrant," he said.

"Exactly. I could drop a few names that would surprise certain folk." She waited for Marcus' cue.

"Surprise me."

"That young Mr. Tiber who lives on the floor above, Jerome Tiber. He was most brazen of all. As you said, so flagrant. I'm certain that she had given him a key."

"To her room?"

"She must have. I've seen him enter, bold as brass, without knocking."

"That's interesting. That's very interesting, indeed."

"He wasn't the only one, however. There are those, so to speak, who have keys by right of position."

"Such as?"

"Well, I'm sure that Mr. Clinton Garland visited her far more often than was necessary."

"The hotel manager?"

"There is simply no occasion, I mean, for a hotel manager to go to a guest's room so frequently. And that bell captain, Lewis Varna. One would think Dolly Draper spent half her time thinking up one pretext or another to get him to her room."

"Her tastes, if I understand your implications, were remarkably catholic."

"It's more to the point to conclude that she had no taste at all."

"She seems to be missing this morning, incidentally. Do you happen to know where she is now?"

"I'm sure I don't," Lucretia Bridges said, then added with a monstrous improbability that took Marcus' wind away, "I am one who strictly minds her own affairs."

The shock of it brought him to his feet. He had acquired enough food for thought, in any event, to tax his mental molars. He looked around and tried to think of a graceful exit line. "You have a pleasant room," he said. "Do you live here as a permanent guest?"

"Yes. I find residing in a hotel so convenient. I've been here nearly ten years, since shortly after Mr. Bridges died."

"He must have left you well off."

"Indeed he did. Winston was a wonderful man, poor dear. He died so suddenly. No warning whatever. We were just beginning dinner, and he fell right over into his soup. There was not time even to fetch a doctor."

"Well, thank you for your help, Mrs. Bridges. It's possible that I may want to talk with you again."

"I am at your service," said Lucretia, and followed Marcus to the door, where he said goodbye. As he passed through, she had, woman-wise, the last word.

"When you find Dolly Draper," she said, "you must be on your guard. She is quite deceptive, and appears to be what she is not. I tell you she's a bad woman. She's *evil.*"

The ancient and ominous adjective seemed to hang in the air and repeat itself in whispers. The hall, as Marcus walked down it toward the elevators, seemed suddenly colder and darker than it was.

Mr. Clinton Garland, surrounded by walnut paneling, was waiting behind his walnut desk. He was impeccably dressed, his hair was all present and sleekly brushed, and his face, properly composed for a tragic occasion, was handsome enough to qualify him as the moderator of a TV quiz show, although a bit long in the nose. As he rose and extended manicured fingers, Marcus could detect that Mr. Garland had taken a very large drop for his nerves.

After introductions Marcus said, "This is bad business."

"Indeed it is," Garland said, retrieving his hand after token contact. "It will do the Southworth no good, lieutenant. No good at all."

"It didn't do Mark Draper any good, either."

"It's dreadful. Simply dreadful. Whoever could have done such a monstrous thing?"

"We'll try to find out. I'm hoping you can help."

"I'll do what I can, of course, but I'm afraid it will be very little."

"Perhaps," said Marcus, "you will just tell me about your own part in the affair."

"Certainly. I was right here in my office, discussing several routine matters with Lewis Varna, the bell captain. When the news reached the lobby, one of the bellboys reported it to the desk clerk, and the desk clerk brought it immediately to me."

"What time was that?"

"I'm not sure. I was naturally so distraught by the news that I failed to make proper note of things. It was after nine. Before the half hour, I think. Sometime between."

"Never mind. Go on, please."

"Well, Lewis and I rushed up, of course, and I went into the room and verified the report." Garland repressed a shudder. "So much blood! It was dreadful. Simply dreadful."

"Which room did you enter?"

"Which room? Why, the room in which Mr. Draper had been stabbed, of course."

"I thought you might have entered the adjoining one."

"No, no, I went directly from the hall into the bedroom."

"Was the door closed and locked?"

"If it were closed, it would automatically be locked. It wasn't. Poor Mrs. Grimm, the maid, had rushed into the hall screaming and had left the door standing open behind her. What a dreadful experience for the poor soul!"

"Draper was apparently sleeping when he was stabbed. Do your maids enter the bedrooms of your guests when they are sleeping?"

"Certainly not. However, Mrs. Grimm had encountered Mrs. Draper on the floor below about half an hour earlier, and Mrs. Draper had told Mrs. Grimm that Mr. Draper was sleeping late, but that it would be quite all right to slip in quietly and change the towels. As a matter of fact, Mr. Draper was chronically a late sleeper, and it was understood that the maid could slip into the bathroom when necessary. After all, our maids must perform their services."

"Where was Mrs. Draper going when she encountered the maid on the lower floor? Do you know?"

"She was in the company of Mrs. Bryan Lancaster, who occupies a two-room suite on that floor with her husband. Mrs. Draper and Mrs. Lancaster met the maid just as they were descending the stairs. They had been up in Mrs. Draper's suite and were walking down to Mrs. Lancaster's. The maid saw them enter."

"You seem to have a fair number of permanent guests in this hotel."

"That's true. We rather cater to them. Our rates are not excessive for the comforts and services offered."

"Naturally. Anyhow, I'm delighted finally to have crossed the trail of Mrs. Draper. I've found her rather elusive."

"Elusive? Not at all. She has been in Mrs. Lancaster's suite all this while. After she heard the news about her husband she was prostrate, of course. Simply prostrate. What a dreadful thing to happen to the poor little thing! Mrs. Lancaster has been taking care of her."

"What's the number of Mrs. Lancaster's suite?"

"421. I trust, if you must talk with Mrs. Draper, that you will be considerate."

"I am always," said Marcus. "considerate of everyone." He fished for a cigarette, found one, and lit it. "What did you do after seeing the body?" he continued.

"I sent Lewis Varna to summon the police, and I remained in the hall outside the door until the police came. Then, with their permission, I came back here. I was limp. Simply limp!"

"I know. It was a dreadful experience. Where is the maid now? I'll need to talk with her."

"I have her standing by. Lewis Varna, too. I was certain that you'd want to see them sometime."

"Good. I'll see them together. Two birds, you know, with one stone."

Clinton Garland left the room, and was back in less than two minutes with Lewis Varna and Mrs. Grimm. The former was a slender, swarthy young man with black curly hair, courteous but not deferential, who undoubtedly would be attractive to the ladies. The latter was a small woman, almost dainty, neatly uniformed in crisp white. Her hair was going gray, but her face still retained a smooth, youthful quality, and her throat, in the vulnerable area beneath the chin, its taut elasticity. Marcus was surprised. He had expected, somehow, someone canted sidewise from carrying a mop bucket.

Lewis Varna, at Marcus' request, reported first. His report was concise, and it supported in all significant details the prior report of Clinton Garland. Which might mean, Marcus realized with the detached skepticism of his race, that the pair had told separately the simple truth, or that they had, on the other hand, plotted their stories in the ample time that had been allowed them. Marcus was invariably skeptical of any pair who alibied each other so neatly, especially, in this case, a pair who carried passkeys. Still, the alibi was not airtight. There was, after all, the crucial time *before* Garland and Varna met in the office for their discussion of hotel matters.

"Let's see," Marcus said casually. "You and Mr. Garland were right here together when you first heard the report of the murder. How long would you say you had been here?"

Varna got the point. So did Garland. Their eyes met, struck sparks, and passed, but Varna's expression did not otherwise alter. He remained a perfect picture of candor, as one who was willing to accept the digressions of a police investigation, but recognized, nevertheless, the basic absurdity of them.

"It's hard to say. We were not, of course, particularly conscious of time. What would you say, Mr. Garland? Half an hour?"

"There was quite a number of things on the agenda," Garland said. "Half an hour would be a conservative estimate. Nearer forty-five minutes, I'd say."

"I see." Marcus turned to Mrs. Grimm. "Madam, you had a trying experience."

"It was a shock. A terrible shock."

"Have you sufficiently recovered to talk about it?"

"I'm all right now, thank you."

And she did, indeed, seem quite composed. She stood erect with her feet together and her hands folded in front of her. Her eyes, with the proper deference of a servant before masters, were fixed on an imaginary spot somewhere over Marcus' head.

"You entered the bedroom shortly after nine, I understand. Is that correct?"

"It must have been. I'm not positive."

"The medical examiner estimates that Mr. Draper was murdered around nine. You must have just missed a scene more shocking than the one you saw."

"I try not to think of that, sir."

"Right. Nothing to be gained from magnifying horrors. Did you see anyone near the door before you entered?"

"No, sir."

"Anyone in the hall at all?"

"No one."

"You went in to change the towels in the bathroom, I believe. Were you also going to change the sheets on the bed?"

"No, sir. Mr. Draper was sleeping late. I had seen Mrs. Draper on the floor below, and she told me it would be all right to slip into the bathroom quietly."

"Did you, indeed, change the towels?"

Mrs. Grimm thought for a moment, then slowly shook her head.

"Now that you put the question, sir, I don't believe I did. It was the shock, you see. I'm rather confused in my mind about things."

"Understandably so. Just tell me briefly what you did after seeing the body of Mr. Draper."

"I screamed and ran from the room and down the hall. I must have screamed several times, and my head was spinning. At the elevator, I ran into a bellboy who had just come up from the lobby. He helped me to a vacant room and put me on the bed there. The guest had checked out early, you see, and the door was standing open. A few minutes later, when I was not so faint, I thought that I had better see Mr. Garland at once, but when I went into the hall again, I saw Mr. Garland standing guard outside Mr. Draper's door. I didn't wish to go near that room again, so I came down here and waited. That's all, sir. That's all I can remember."

"Very good. Thank you, Mrs. Grimm."

"Are you finished, lieutenant?" Garland asked.

"For the present, yes."

ALFRED HITCHCOCK'S ANTHOLOGY

Garland nodded at the bell captain and the maid. "You're free to go."

They left, and so, after a polite word of parting with the manager, did Marcus.

He rapped lightly beneath the neat chrome numbers: 421. A mnemonic gem, second number half the first, third number half the second. Remember the first, you got them all.

The mnemonic gem retreated as the door swung inward, revealing a young man wearing a gray cardigan. He had thick brown rebellious hair, a slightly crooked nose, and an expression that was, all in all, inordinately cheerful for the circumstances.

"Mr. Lancaster?" Marcus queried.

The young man grinned and shook his head.

"No such luck. Old Bryan's off doing his daily stint. Tiber's the name. Jerome Tiber."

"Oh? I'm Lieutenant Marcus. Police. I'm looking for Mrs. Mark Draper."

"This is as far as you go, lieutenant. Dolly's here, safe and sound, although, as you will understand, a bit upset. I must say that you've been an unconscionable time getting to us. We've been waiting for you."

"Well, here I am at last. Now where is Mrs. Draper?"

"Come in. I'll get her for you."

Marcus entered. On a low table before a sofa stood a silver pot that emitted the aromatic odor of hot coffee. Beside the pot, a cup, half full, sat in its saucer. Marcus sat on the sofa, smelled the coffee, and coveted a cup.

Jerome Tiber, at the communicating door, spoke cheerfully into the adjoining room. "Dolly, my darling, your sins have found you out. You had better emerge and face the consequences."

In response to this airy summons, two young women came into the room. One of them was rather tall, with bright red hair, and had about her the firmly benevolent attitude of one who is determinedly giving aid and comfort to someone else. This one, Marcus guessed rightly, was Mrs. Bryan Lancaster.

The other, then, was Dolly Draper. Marcus, rising to meet her, was aware instantly of a feeling to which he should have, at his age, developed immunity long ago. Tenderness? Affinity? The faint siren singing of "September Song"? Say, for decency's sake, fatherliness. For Dolly Draper, who was surely at least in her middle twenties, looked to be in her late teens. And she was small; small and slim with an innocently seductive body now poured into a white cashmere sweater and a pair of red slacks. Her hair, the soft yellow color of ripe field corn, was little longer than a contemporary male folk songster's. Her eyes were grave and gray. She sat down on the edge of a straight chair and folded her hands on her knees. She did not seem grieved. She seemed only infinitely sad.

"Damn it, Jerry," said the redheaded Mrs. Lancaster, "please don't be quite so cheerful. It's absolutely obscene."

Tiber, undaunted, waved a hand and made a little bow. "Gloom accomplishes nothing. 'The Moving Finger writes; and, having writ . . .' You know the bit, darling. One must have a philosophical attitude, I say. Besides, I must add, someone, however reprehensible his method, has done me a service. He has, in brief, removed my competition."

During this remarkable speech, Dolly Draper sat quietly with her grave gray eyes turned on the speaker, and the faintest shadow of a sad and tender smile touched her pink lips. "Darling," she said, "I know you mean well, but you mustn't say such things. It isn't proper."

"It's obscene, that's what it is," said the redhead. "Jerry, mind your manners."

"What? Oh, yes. Introductions are in order. Mrs. Draper, Mrs. Lancaster, Lieutenant Marcus. Lieutenant Marcus, as we have anticipated, is of the police. Since we are clearly to be on familiar terms in this business, I suggest that we abandon formality at once. If you choose, lieutenant, you may call these alliterative ladies Dolly and Lucy."

Marcus did not choose.

"Mrs. Draper," he said, "this is a grim affair, and I understand that it must be very difficult for you. I'm sorry."

"I feel much better now." She smiled sadly at her folded hands. "I suppose, now that the shock has worn off, that I'm not even particularly surprised."

"Oh? What do you mean by that?"

"Well, to be truthful, poor Mark was really a rather disagreeable man, and he was always running around to all sorts of places and associating with all sorts of undesirable persons."

"What places? What persons?"

Dolly Draper lifted her hands in a helpless little gesture, and immediately folded them again. "I don't know, actually. Just places and persons."

"Didn't he ever take you with him?"

"Oh, no. I don't care for such places and persons."

"Mrs. Draper, men are seldom murdered simply for being disagreeable."

"On that score," said Jerry Tiber, "you can make an exception of old Mark."

"Shut up, Jerry," Lucy Lancaster said. "Lieutenant, why do you keep looking at the coffee pot? Would you like a cup?"

"No, thank you," Marcus lied.

"Nonsense. Of course you would. I can tell by the way your nostrils twitch. Jerry, get a cup for the lieutenant."

"There isn't a clean one. Room service only sent up three, and we've used them all."

"Well, I'm sure there's no insurmountable difficulty. Go and rinse a cup in the lavatory."

Jerry went obediently, with reasonably good grace, and Marcus, feeling uneasily that he was somehow not controlling the situation, turned his attention again to Dolly Draper to revive the case at hand.

"Are you suggesting," he said, "that an outsider slipped into the hotel and murdered your husband?"

"Perhaps a guest. A transient. I suspect he's checked out and gone by this time."

"That's possible, of course. But how did he get into the room?"

"I suppose he came through the door. Isn't that how one usually gets into a room?"

"Usually. In this instance, I don't see how. Mrs. Draper, the door of the bedroom was locked. So was the hall door of the adjoining room. How would a transient guest, not possessing a key, get into either room of the suite?"

"Is that a problem? I would say, offhand, that Mark let him in."

"Your husband was sleeping when he was stabbed."

"Was he? How do you know?"

Marcus started to respond and stopped suddenly before making a sound, his mouth open in the middle of a rather foolish expression. Which was, for Marcus, extraordinary.

"He looked as if he'd been sleeping," he said finally, and the words limped in his own ears.

"If you care for my opinion," Dolly Draper said, "you have started off with a very large assumption that may be wrong. Anyone could arrange a body on a bed so as to make it appear to have died sleeping."

"Have you heard that he was stabbed at the base of the throat from the front?"

"I've heard that, yes. It was a cruel thing to do to poor old Mark."

"How in the devil could someone have approached your husband with a knife and stabbed him neatly in such a spot when he was awake and erect and aware of what was going on?"

"Did I say he was erect? I don't believe I did. When Lucy and I left my suite this morning, Mark had a terrible headache. He was so beastly about it, grumpy and all, that he was simply intolerable. That's why Lucy and I decided to move down here to her place. Before we came, however, I gave Mark a sedative and sent him back to bed. If someone came to the door soon after we left, before the sedative had taken effect, Mark would have let him in, and then, if it was someone he knew well, he would have lain back down and closed his eyes. It's quite possible, you know, to carry on a conversation while lying on your back with your eyes closed. As a matter of fact, he has often done it with me. He was always having severe headaches in the morning, often from hangovers, and he frequently lay in bed while I was up and about, and we would talk, and all the while his eyes would be closed. It's better for a headache, of course, if you keep the light out of your eyes."

Marcus, who was not without experience himself, was forced to concede the point. He looked at Dolly Draper with a kind of growing wonder.

"It's a reasonable explanation," he said. "Do you have any idea who may have called on your husband this morning after you left?"

"Oh, no. It was quite impossible to know who might call on Mark, or when, or why."

"We must at least conclude that the purpose this time was murder."

"Must we? Maybe not. Maybe it was something that was incited and done on the spur of the moment."

"I doubt it. I doubt if anyone, unless he plans to use it, goes calling with an ordinary kitchen paring knife in his pocket."

"Was that what poor Mark was stabbed with? Imagine it, Lucy, an ordinary kitchen paring knife!"

Thus summarily challenged, it remained unknown if Lucy Lancaster's imagination was equal to the occasion. At that moment, carrying a rinsed cup on a saucer, Jerome Tiber came back into the room. He poured coffee into the cup and handed it to Marcus.

"There you are, lieutenant. Compliments of the house."

"Thanks," Marcus acknowledged, then turned to Lucy. "Why did you go upstairs to Mrs. Draper's suite so early this morning?" he asked.

"It wasn't particularly early. It was just after eight o'clock. Do you imagine that we are all the indolent rich or something?"

"Excuse me. Why did you go?"

"Because Dolly called me on the telephone and asked me, that's why. She wanted to show me a silver cigarette box she bought yesterday afternoon. It plays 'Smoke Gets in Your Eyes' when you open the lid."

"I thought it was rather clever," Dolly said. "Cigarettes and smoke in your eyes and all that, I mean."

Marcus was not diverted. "And shortly afterward you decided to come down here?"

"We were practically forced to," Dolly said. "We were going to have our coffee there, but Mark behaved so abominably and kept shouting at us to keep quiet and everything, that we left."

"On the way here, I understand, you met the maid in the hall."

"Yes. The maid who always does our rooms."

"And you told her that it would be all right if she slipped in and changed the towels in the bathroom?"

"I didn't think it would disturb Mark. He'd had the sedative, as I said, and I was sure he'd be asleep again by the time the maid got around."

"I've talked with the maid. She says she saw no one near the bedroom. If your husband admitted someone to the room, he was gone before the maid got there."

"Well, murderers seldom stick around after committing murder, do they?"

Marcus was compelled to admit that they seldom did. He decided also that he had stuck around as long as it was profitable. He drained his cup, set it aside, and rose to his feet. "Thank you very much," he said. "It's time I was getting on to other things. I'm sorry to have intruded."

"Are you going back upstairs?" Jerome Tiber wanted to know.

"That's right."

"I'm going that way. I'll just drop you off if you don't mind."

Marcus didn't mind. In fact, he welcomed the chance to get the remarkable Jerome Tiber a few minutes alone. Having said goodbye to Dolly and Lucy, they departed together.

"I understand," said Marcus, "that you and Mrs. Draper are what some may call good friends."

"I'm working at it," Tiber said cheerfully.

"It has even been suggested that you have a key to her door."

"A key? Nonsense. Why should I need a key? If the coast was clear, as they say in the cheaper thrillers, Dolly could always give me a ring and extend an invitation. I had no wish, believe me, to wander in on old Mark with a hot key in my hand." He stopped and shot Marcus a startled glance. "Are you by any chance implying, lieutenant, that I could have admitted myself this morning and done old Mark in?"

"One has to explore the possibilities."

"Well, you may have guessed that I wasn't exactly one of old Mark's fans, but on the other hand I wasn't his mortal enemy either. Dear as little Dolly is, she isn't worth the risk. Suggested by whom?"

"What?"

"Who suggested that I might have a key?"

"Someone who claims to have seen you enter without knocking."

"Never mind. It must have been the old witch across the hall. When Dolly invited me down, she sometimes left the door slightly ajar. It expedited matters."

"I see."

They had climbed the stairs to the upper floor, and now they paused for a breather before Jerome Tiber continued his ascent.

"Well," he said, "I suppose we must part here. Friends, I hope. I don't suppose you'd be willing to let me come along and poke about the murder scene a bit?"

"No."

"I thought you wouldn't. Well, no matter. It's just that I have such a morbid curiosity. Good sleuthing, lieutenant."

Jerome Tiber went on up the stairs, and Marcus, lingering, heard him begin to whistle softly as he went.

Fuller was at a window with his head out. He pulled it in and turned as Marcus entered. Marcus, however, veered off into the bathroom.

Mrs. Grimm's memory, he saw, had served her well. The towels in the bathroom had been used, and there were no fresh ones in evidence.

On the wide surface into which the lavatory was sunk, among a variety of jars and bottles, was a clear plastic container of capsules. Marcus, examining it, satisfied himself that the capsules contained the sedative which Mark Draper was reported to have taken, then went into the bedroom. Fuller was still standing by the window. The police ambulance had come and gone, and the body of Mark Draper was no longer on the bed. Marcus, who was not fond of bodies, was relieved.

"There's a narrow ledge," Fuller said. "Outside, a narrow ledge below the windows. It would be a risky trick, but a man could conceivably inch his way along it. The window was unlocked."

"Oh." Marcus seemed abstracted. "I don't think so."

"Why not?"

"As you said, too risky. Not only of falling, but of being seen from the street. Besides, how could anyone coming in that way be sure that Draper was in bed and asleep at nine o'clock in the morning? For that matter, how could he be sure that Mrs. Draper wasn't here?"

"I didn't say I had all the answers." Fuller's voice was abrupt, almost harsh. "It's just something to think about."

"Oh, right, Fuller. Any signs of a search in the room?"

"Nothing apparent."

"Anything seem to be missing?"

"Nothing obvious. We'd have to ask Mrs. Draper to be sure."

"I don't think it will be necessary. Draper wasn't killed by any burglar. That's plain."

"It is? I admit it doesn't look likely, but how can you be so sure? The ledge isn't *that* narrow."

Marcus' air of abstraction still pertained. He stood by the bed and pinched his lower lip and stared at the floor. He seemed for a moment not to have heard.

"I'm sure," he said after the moment has passed, "because *I know who did kill him.*"

Fuller, trained by experience in stoicism, said quietly, "That's very interesting. Maybe you wouldn't mind telling *me.*"

"Not yet, Fuller, not yet." Marcus perked up, as if he were brushing the whole vexing business from his mind. "Because I don't know *why.* I can't for the life of me see *why.*"

He turned toward the door abruptly. "Come on, Fuller. We might as well get out of here. There's nothing more at the moment to be done."

In Fuller's opinion, there was, on the contrary, a lot to be done. There was, for example, a murderer to be arrested. If, that is, Marcus actually knew the murderer's identity. Personally, Fuller doubted it. To put it kindly, Marcus was merely trying to measure up to some exaggerated image he had of himself. Behold the great detective! To put it less kindly and more honestly, Marcus was a liar.

Fuller didn't venture the accusation, but his conviction was supported by what happened in the next six days. Indeed, so far as Fuller himself was involved, nothing happened at all. Marcus, for two days, was around headquarters. He had a session with the chief and another session with the chief and the district attorney together. He spent quite a lot of time on the telephone discussing with someone something that Fuller wasn't privileged to know and couldn't get into position to overhear. Then Marcus disappeared. He simply dropped out of sight. To all appearances, Mark Draper had been judged expendable. His murder, apparently, incited no concern.

Then, after four days, Marcus reappeared. He simply turned up again. Fuller, invading his office in the afternoon of the fourth day, found him sitting slumped behind his desk looking across it silently at Mrs. Grimm, who was sitting erect in a straight chair with a purse gripped in her lap. The knuckles of her hands were white. Her face was like a stone.

"Oh, Fuller, there you are," Marcus said. "I've been asking for you."

"That's considerate of you," Fuller said. "Where have you been?"

"Why, I've been all over, Fuller. Both coasts and back. On the Draper case, you know. Incidentally, you remember Mrs. Grimm, I'm sure. Or did you ever meet her?"

"I didn't."

"You know who she is, don't you? Well, meet her now. Mrs. Grimm, Sergeant Fuller."

Fuller nodded at Mrs. Grimm. Mrs. Grimm did not nod or speak. She did not move.

"Mrs. Grimm," said Marcus, "is the murderer of Mark Draper."

Fuller sucked in his breath, held it until his chest hurt, and then released it in a long sigh, barely audible. Taking a step forward, he leaned heavily against Marcus' desk. "Is that so?" he said.

"Unfortunately, it is. Isn't it, Mrs. Grimm?"

Mrs. Grimm didn't answer. She did not move.

"I would be interested in knowing," Fuller said slowly, "how you reached this conclusion."

"Oh, it was plain enough, Fuller, from the beginning. You were right, you know, when you said this case didn't sound so fancy. It wasn't. Mrs.

Grimm had a passkey. Mr. Draper was sedated and presumably asleep. Mrs. Grimm simply admitted herself to the bedroom, stabbed Mr. Draper in the throat, and then, after a brief delay which permitted Mr. Draper to get good and dead, rushed out into the hall screaming murder." He smiled benevolently.

Fuller looked with wonder at Mrs. Grimm. Mrs. Grimm did not move or speak.

"How," asked Fuller, "did you know?"

Marcus sighed and built a little tent of fingers on his stomach. "Mrs. Grimm came, presumably, to change the towels. But the towels had not been changed. Mrs. Grimm explained it by saying that she was naturally too distraught by what she found on the bed. Good enough. But what would most women do if, carrying an armload of towels, they came suddenly upon the body of a murdered man? I submit that they would throw the towels all over the place. Anyhow, as they screamed and ran, they would at least drop them. Did you see any towels on the floor, Fuller?"

"No," said Fuller, "I didn't."

"Let it go. That wasn't the big point, at any rate."

"What," asked Fuller, "was the big point?"

"You saw the room, Fuller. You saw how it was shaped. The bathroom is constructed in the corner, next to the outside hall, leaving between the bathroom and the opposite wall a short, narrow hallway. In the bedroom, the bed was placed against the interior wall of the bathroom. Around the corner, that is. *Mrs. Grimm could not possibly have seen the body of Mark Draper unless she walked on into the bedroom.*"

"So," said Fuller, "she couldn't."

"And there was absolutely no reason why Mrs. Grimm should have done so. She was merely going to change the towels. She had been instructed, moreover, to slip in and out quietly so as not to disturb Draper. Instead, she went right on into the bedroom. Does that sound sensible to you, Fuller?"

"No," said Fuller, "it doesn't."

"Neither did it to me. I decided that Mrs. Grimm could bear investigation."

Again Fuller looked with wonder at Mrs. Grimm. Still Mrs. Grimm did not move or speak.

"Why?" said Fuller. "Why?"

"Why indeed? As usual, Fuller, you come directly to the heart of things.

Unless Mrs. Grimm was a homicidal maniac, which she wasn't, there had to be some kind of reasonable motive. Had Draper fleeced her at one time or another? Had he, perchance, ruined her daughter or destroyed her husband? I was led, you see, to all sorts of melodramatic speculations. Anyhow, that's where I've been the last few days, Fuller. I've been on the backtrail of Mrs. Grimm, and I dug up, I must say, a couple of rather, ah, enlightening episodes."

"What episodes?"

"Out on the west coast three years ago, Mrs. Grimm, then calling herself Mrs. Foster, worked as a maid in the private home of a well-to-do young couple. One afternoon, while the wife was away, the husband was shot and killed at close range with his own rifle. Mrs. Grimm, who was present, reported that he had been preparing to clean it and had shot himself accidentally. Circumstances aroused some suspicion, but the case, for lack of evidence to the contrary, was eventually closed as accidental death.

"But as you know, Fuller, I have a littered mind. There was one element in the case that reminded me vaguely of another case I'd read about, and after a while I remembered just what it was. On the east coast some six years ago, a wealthy young husband was knifed to death in his home, presumably by a surprised prowler. The wife was spending the night with a friend, but the maid was in the house and testified to what had happened, prowler and all. Again suspicion was aroused, but the bulk of the evidence seemed to support the story. Case closed, and you are right as rain, Fuller. The maid, I discovered, although she called herself Mrs. Breen, and later called herself Mrs. Foster, was no one but the woman who now calls herself Mrs. Grimm."

Whatever her name, she was made of stone. If she heard, she gave no sign. Whatever she felt, she felt in secret.

"And still," said Fuller, "I don't see why."

"Don't you, Fuller? Neither did anyone connected with those two cases. But I do. I see and I understand because all three cases, those and ours, have a common denominator. In each case, *the young wife was away and securely alibied.*"

Abruptly, almost angrily, as if he wanted suddenly to be done with the matter as quickly as possible, Marcus stood up and walked to the door that opened into the next office. He pushed the door open and stepped back. "Come in, Mrs. Draper," he said. "Your mother needs you."

"A mother and daughter team of professional murderers!" Fuller exclaimed.

"That's what they were. Daughter, damnably attractive, marries a reasonably rich man. Mother, in good time, is hired as a maid. Later, exit husband. Still later, much money inherited, including insurance. Later still, reunion of mother and daughter in another place far removed. Plush living, bright prospects of many husbands to come, routine repeated. In our case, there was a slight complication. Draper insisted on living in a hotel, so Mother had to get a job on the staff and work herself onto the right floor. She managed. Mother was clever."

"They were making a career of it!"

"Well, don't let it shake you too much, Fuller. It's been done before by others. Most of them have been poisoners. One of them, you may recall, was a chronic husband who kept drowning his wives in bathtubs. This time, at least, we had some refreshing variations."

Fuller looked at Marcus with surprising, if somewhat grudging, respect. You must, he conceded, give the devil his due.

"Tell me something," Fuller said. "The simple truth?"

"Nothing else. It is my code."

"You suspected Mrs. Grimm from the beginning. That's clear. Did you also suspect Dolly Draper?"

"I did."

"Why?"

"Because she's evil."

"Oh, come off. How could you possibly have known that?"

"I knew because a woman named Lucretia Bridges told me so. To everyone else she was poor little thing, sweet little thing, dear little Dolly. Not to Mrs. Bridges. You know why? Because like reacts to like, and one dog always smells another."

"If you want to know what I think, I think that's crazy."

"Nevertheless," Marcus said, "I'd give a pretty penny to know what was in old Winston's soup."

Finders-Killers

by Ed Lacy

I admit it sounds childish but I was pretty excited about the Frankie Sun murder. It wasn't because it happened on my post and I knew—by sight anyway—about everybody connected with the case. Nor was it taking me out of uniform and placing me on fly assignment with Homicide. It was just . . . well, frankly, being a cop gets dull and boring. There were big things doing like the armored car robbery in Brooklyn. the chorus girl murder downtown, the drug raids over in Queens. And me, I was still trying locked store doors up on Washington Heights, running in a drunk now and then.

Understand, I don't go looking for trouble, but in the ten months I'd been on the force there *had* to be more to law enforcement than a pair of tired feet.

So now I sat in the precinct detective squad room and politely listened with the others as the Homicide inspector from downtown outlined the case. I was up with the big wheels; I thought I was living.

"Here's what we know," the inspector said, his voice soft for a guy his size. "A thug named Frankie Sun is found stabbed in front of a private house. Frankie has a long yellow sheet: rapped for assault, armed robbery, stolen cars, forced entry, carrying a gun, did time for pimping—the works.

"I don't have to tell you that when a hardened criminal like Frankie is knocked off, it isn't a simple murder. Not to mention that he was first sapped, then deliberately knifed while he was out cold. I want this case solved fast because it isn't only a killing, it will give us a lead on other crimes. So far all we've been able to learn from stoolies is that Frankie was in on something 'big,' but nobody knows exactly what." The inspector paused, looking at me, seemed satisfied when I didn't ask any jack questions but waited for him to finish.

"Frankie," the inspector went on, "seems to have been working with an out-of-town hood named Marty. We haven't a thing on this Marty, except his first name. Get the picture: Frankie was killed in a low-income block on Washington Heights. Only two people live in the private house—the landlady, a Mrs. Austin, and her only roomer, a nineteen-year-old girl named Ruth Thomas. Both deny knowing or ever having seen Frankie Sun." The old inspector jerked a thumb at me. "This is Patrolman Stewart, the block is part of his post. He'll be on assignment with us for a while. Stewart, what sort of neighborhood is this?"

"Well, sir," I said, standing up, feeling like a schoolboy among all these vets, "as you said, sir, it's an average low-income area. And crimewise it's . . ."

"What?" the inspector asked.

"I said crimewise it's also an average block."

"Come on," he barked, "talk English, we haven't time to waste!"

Some of the others chuckled and I couldn't stop my face from turning red.

"Yes, sir. I meant as far as crime goes it's a respectable area. Some minor numbers playing, a few penny-ante crap games, maybe a small bookie; but no big or organized crime, certainly nothing that would interest a crook like Frankie Sun.

"About the two women. I think we can forget about Mrs. Austin. She's an elderly lady who only leaves her house to buy groceries. Most of the time she's puttering around her back yard garden. I don't know much about the younger woman except that she's been rooming there for the past three months, works as a sales girl in a five-and-dime store over on Amsterdam Avenue. In my opinion she hardly looks the type that would associate with a punk, a—"

"If she's nineteen," a snappily dressed detective cut in, "sounds like the kind of quail who would interest Frankie. He went for young stuff."

The Homicide inspector said, "This Miss Thomas—she isn't exactly a glamor gal. Plain, scrawny kid, fresh from a hick town. Tell them what else you found out, Stewart."

"Yes, sir. Naturally a murder is big talk in the neighborhood. There's a shoemaker named Jake Cook who has a small shop across the street from Mrs. Austin's house. He's never gotten over the fact he was an M.P. sergeant during World War II, He likes to talk about police methods with me. He claims he's seen Frankie Sun watching the house, tailing Miss Thomas for the last few days. He positively identified a picture of Frankie as the man he thought was a jealous boyfriend."

"This Cook sounds like a crime-happy jerko to me," another detective said.

"It's a fact that Jake is a frustrated cop," I said, "but I would hardly call him a jerk. He's . . . "

The inspector held up a heavy hand for silence. "Now you know everything we have. I've talked to this Cook, he's positive about seeing Frankie hanging around. We've wired Miss Thomas's hometown for any info on her. Stewart and I will talk to her this morning. I want you," he nodded at two of the detective squad dicks, "to shake down Mrs. Austin, dig into her past. Rest of you are to work the bars, keep after your stoolies. I want to know where Frankie Sun lived, what he was doing that far uptown. Keep in touch with me. That's all."

We didn't get much from Miss Thomas. She was a shy kid, obviously afraid of the police, despite the inspector's fatherly voice; a little angry at being called from her job, losing a few hours' pay. She'd come to New York from a tiny upstate village three months ago to find a job, moved into Mrs. Austin's, and found work in the five-and-dime the first day she was in the city. No, she didn't know a soul here except Mrs. Austin and the girls in the store. Oh no, she certainly didn't have any boy friends. She looked pathetically thin and young in her worn, plain dress. I always thought farm kids were sure of plenty of food, if nothing else, but Ruth Thomas sure looked as if she'd missed a lot of meals.

The inspector kept asking if anything unusual had happened recently, but she insisted nothing unusual ever happened to her. All she did was work, cook on the one burner stove in her room, spend her evenings reading books on stenography and office work. No, she never went out, not even to a movie; she couldn't afford to and besides, wasting money was almost sinful. She hoped to attend a business school when she had saved enough money. She proudly showed us her bank book. She'd been putting away five dollars a week since her first pay day. She also sent five home to her folks every other week.

When she left I was told to tail her. The five-and-dime was eleven blocks from the precinct house and she saved bus fare by walking, doing a little window shopping. It struck me as odd, though, that for a kid so desperately poor she only looked into the windows of the expensive stores.

I left her at the five-and-dime, spent the rest of the afternoon talking to storekeepers. They all examined Frankie Sun's picture and said they'd never seen him before. At four I returned to the squad room. Seemed like we were running in circles A team of detectives had traced Frankie to a cheap room near Penn Station. There wasn't much of anything in his room—he'd only moved there in the last week. They also found a waitress Frankie had been running with; she said he'd talked about making a "big score soon," but she had dismissed that as big talk. Frankie acted like he didn't have money, was tight with a buck. She had never heard of any Marty, nor did she know where Frankie lived, or anything about him.

Stoolies hadn't come up with anything new, and there wasn't anything interesting about old lady Austin, as I had known there wouldn't be.

I shadowed Ruth Thomas the following day. I took her to the store and back home at night. I asked routine questions of the other salesgirls, found only that they considered her a "real square," and she was not very popular because she nursed her pennies, never talked about dates. When I returned to the station house and made out my report, it seemed to me downtown had lost interest. The inspector was off the case and I was told to report back in uniform the following day, on the four o'clock tour. I was sore about the sudden change in tours because I had a movie date with my girl for the following night.

The next day I walked my beat and after phoning into the platoon sergeant, stopped to talk with Jake Cook. I asked him if he was still positive about seeing Frankie Sun following Miss Thomas about. That seemed to me to be the odd point in the case. Jake went into a lecture about how he could spot a tail and while we were talking in the doorway of his shop there were screams and shouts from around the corner. It was a few minutes after six, growing dark, as Jake and I sprinted around the corner into an hysterical group of women standing about Ruth Thomas. She was on the sidewalk, unconscious, her dress torn at the shoulder, her mouth and right eye bleeding.

Two women said they'd heard Ruth shouting, "No! No!" and saw a heavy-set man slugging her. He had run when the women shouted at him. I told Jake to call an ambulance as I tried to get the women to calm down, give me a description of the guy. But it was too dark for them to tell me anything except he'd been beefy, wore a hat and grey top coat, and ran fast. A squad car came about the same time the ambulance arrived. The doc said Ruth Thomas was okay, was suffering from shock more than anything else. He gave her a sedative and the squad car drove her home.

When I phoned in, the sergeant told me to keep a post in front of her house. Jake lived above his shop and after supper he came out to ask what was new. I told him about Ruth being given a sedative and taken away before I had a chance to question her.

Jake puffed on his pipe and said, "It's clear what the guy had in mind." His tone told me what he meant.

"At this time of night, on a street full of people returning from work?"

"Look, I had a case something like this when I was in the army," Jake said patiently. "A joker tried to attack a girl on a busy street in broad daylight. After all, a guy like that must be a moron to start with. Everybody heard her shouting, 'No! No!' What else could it be?"

I said, "There has to be a tie-up with the Frankie Sun killing, that's what else."

Jake didn't agree. He bent my ear for about an hour, then Mrs. Austin came out to give me a cup of coffee and talked for another half hour on how she didn't know "what the neighborhood was coming to. When I first moved here thirty-two years ago it was an elegant . . . " and so on. When I could get a word in, I asked her to let me know the second Miss Thomas came out of the sedative.

About midnight a prowl car drove me back to the station house. Seemed they were taking away the guard but would have the night beat man keep an eye on where she lived. When I said I was surprised at their removing me from the front of her house, the midnight tour sergeant made a few sarcastic remarks about eager-beavers.

I got into my old roadster and drove back to Mrs. Austin's. I let the beat cop believe I had been sent back. Mrs. Austin opened the door in a nightgown and a comical lace cap. When I asked if I could speak to Ruth Thomas, the old biddy snapped, "At this time of night? That's what you got me out of my bed for? Let me tell you, young man, the neighborhood may have changed but I still run a respectable house and—"

"Mrs. Austin, this is a police matter."

"She's awake, go up if you wish. But remember, keep the door wide open."

Ruth Thomas was sitting up in this plain metal bed, her face various shadings of blue and purple. I asked, "Miss Thomas, can you tell me exactly what happened?"

"A man stepped up and suddenly punched me in the face. That's all I remember."

Her voice was frightened, and sullen.

"Didn't he say anything?"

"No. And I never saw him before, either. Hardly had a good look at him when—"

"Miss Thomas, I don't know what you're mixed up in, but I'd advise you to tell me all about it. You're playing with a killer. What were you yelling, 'No! No!' about?"

She seemed to shrink against the pillow for a moment, become even more childlike. Then she let it go. "All right," she said, "I'll tell you. I'm afraid. He asked for the money and I told him no. He just came up and asked, 'Where's the money? Give it to me!' "

"What money?"

"I . . . I found a wallet with two one hundred dollar bills in it a few days ago, as I was coming home from the store."

"Where's the wallet now?"

She hesitated a second, her puffed eye glaring at me; then she pulled this battered wallet from under her pillow. It was an old, beat-up brown leather wallet, not a thing in it but a couple of one hundred buck bills.

She said, "It's mine, I found it," and tried to grab the wallet. She was wearing a thin nightgown and her arm and shoulder were so skinny I wondered how Frankie or any man ever could get interested.

I pushed her hand aside. "Have you told anybody about finding this?"

"No. Give it back to me!"

"You should have told us about this yesterday," I said, a lot of bells ringing in my head. I started to put the wallet in my pocket. Her thin, sharp face grew hysterical. "That's *mine!*" she said, her voice almost a scream. I started to tell her a citizen was supposed to turn over found money to the police, but she wasn't in any shape for a lecture. I took down the serial numbers and gave her back the bills and wallet.

"Miss Thomas, I don't want you to tell anybody else about this money. No one. Not even Mrs. Austin."

"I won't. It's mine, nobody's business but mine." Her hand was clenching the wallet.

"Now you try to relax, get some sleep. I'll be back to see you early in the morning. Don't you leave the house, for any reason, until I return. Do you understand?"

She said she did, shoved the wallet under her pillow, closed her eyes. I went downstairs. Mrs. Austin was standing there. I was pretty sure she'd been listening. How much she could have heard I didn't know.

I drove back to the precinct house. The detective in charge of the night tour of the detective squad was a fat fellow with a big grin and full of laughs. When I started to tell him about Ruth finding the dough, he laughed, told me, "It'll hold until morning, son. I know how it is. Your first big case and you see clues all around. I'm busy. In the morning take it up with the lieutenant. It'll keep." He leaned back in his swivel chair. I thought his weight would take it over. "You're new on the force, Stewart, so here's some advice—when you're off duty, stay that way. Just patrol your beat, don't play like a movie dick; we got detectives for detective work."

Sure, I thought, getting their pants shiny on the mahogany.

At the desk I phoned downtown to Homicide. When I asked for the inspector's home phone I was told, "Sonny, are you sure this is important?"

"Well, I have a theory about—"

"A theory? Bust up his sleep for a crackpot idea and he'll beat your brains out. For your own sake, wait until morning . . . after he's had his second cup of coffee."

I phoned Central Bureau and at least they had somebody who didn't object to giving me a couple of facts on the armored car robbery. I scouted around the locker room, got two empty shoe boxes and wrapped them in a newspaper. Then I got in my car and parked in front of Mrs. Austin's house for the balance of the night. I didn't make out anyone else watching the house, but then there were too many parked cars and other rooming houses where a guy could safely take a plant on the place. At seven I took my shoe boxes-package through the back of an apartment house, and over a couple of fences until I landed in Mrs. Austin's fancy garden.

I gave the old lady a start, coming in the back way, and she bawled me out for stepping on her flowers. Ruth Thomas was dressed, having a cup of coffee in the kitchen. Her face wasn't puffed but her lips were still bruised and her eye purple. I told her, "I want you to do me a favor, Miss Thomas."

"I was thinking about going to work. Otherwise I'll lose a day's pay."

I hesitated, decided to gamble.

"I'll take care of it."

She looked at me, as if wondering how a cop could cover the day's pay even of a five-and-dime girl. If I was right, I knew that the department would pay.

She said, "I suppose my eye looks pretty bad. What's the favor?"

"Take this package and walk to the library, then walk back here. Walk slowly."

She gave me what she must have thought was a shrewd glance, asked, "Why?"

"Let me worry about the why. Just do it. There'll be an extra five added to the day's pay," I threw in expansively, telling myself that I was right as I talked.

"Sounds like foolishness to me," Mrs. Austin said. "You want some coffee, young man?"

"No, thank you. Will you do it, Miss Thomas?"

"What will happen?"

"Nothing—maybe. But if the guy comes up and grabs for the box, let him take it. Don't put up a fight or say a word." I started to tell her to drop to the ground if Marty showed, get out of the way, but I needed a pigeon and it had to be Ruth.

She asked, "If I do it, can I keep the . . . what I showed you last night?"

I said, "Yes," as Mrs. Austin's ears perked up like they were wired for sound.

Ruth Thomas left the house at eight, the package under her arm. I followed her in my car, my gun out on the seat beside me. She walked the three blocks to the library, which was closed, and not a damn thing happened. Then she started back.

As she turned into her street, this beefy guy in a baggy brown suit jumped out of a doorway, grabbed the package, and took off. Happily he ran in the direction my car was pointed. I overtook him and shouted, "I'm a police officer! Stop or I'll fire, Marty!"

It was like shooting deer from an automobile, which I've read about. Still running, he tucked the package under his left arm and went for his shoulder holster with his right. I dropped him with a slug in his shoulder, anchored him with another shot—a lucky one—in the right leg.

We were all in the detective squad room again, and by all I mean everybody: all kinds of brass from downtown, and even little Ruth Thomas looking very pale and scared. I was feeling swell. I was a cinch to be made Detective, 3rd Grade. Also I was enjoying telling them, all these police vets, how I did it.

"When Miss Thomas told me about finding the two one hundred bills, Frankie Sun's following her made sense to me. Last week when the armored car guard was slugged and two men made off with a bag of hundred dollar bills . . . well, my idea was that the two men had to be Frankie and Marty. As we know now from Marty's confession, Frankie crossed him, took off with sixty grand in hundred dollar bills. Okay, now two things were worrying Frankie Sun—his partner finding him, and whether the money was 'good.' By that I mean Frankie had to know if he was carrying bait money, a few bills whose numbers are known, or since these are large bills, whether *all* the serial numbers were known, hence . . ."

"All the numbers were known, written down before the money was shipped," the detective squad lieutenant cut in. "The money wasn't any good to Frankie. Nor was checking the package at Penn Station smart; he should have known that a routine check, once we knew he was the bank robber, would have . . . "

The Homicide inspector said sharply, "Let's hear the rest of this before going into details. Continue, Patrolman Stewart."

"Yes, sir," I said proudly. "Well, there was only one way for Frankie to learn if the money was good—spend some. Better yet, let somebody else spend it and see what happened. So he put two bills in a wallet and dropped it on the street. Miss Thomas 'found' it and Frankie tailed her to see what broke when she spent the money. As it turned out, she didn't spend it and Marty caught up with Frankie while he was watching Miss Thomas's house. Obviously Marty thought Miss Thomas was Frankie's girl, must have the sixty grand, so with her help I set a trap . . . and collared him."

"Fine work, Stewart," the inspector said, "although you were lucky, too." He turned and smiled at Ruth Thomas. "Why didn't you spend the money?"

"*Spend* two hundred dollars?" Ruth asked, awe in her thin voice. "Why that would be downright silly. I never saw so much money before in my life. I was going to put it in the bank, toward my schooling, but I kept putting it off. Those two bills looked so terribly pretty I just couldn't stand letting them out of my sight."

"That reminds me," the lieutenant said, holding out his long hand, "let me have them. They belong to the bank."

Ruth looked at me, her eyes big with alarm. "But you promised I could keep . . . ?"

"Give him the money, Miss Thomas," I told her. "And don't worry;

there's either all or a good part of a five-thousand-dollar reward coming your way, depending on how the inspector sees it."

"Half and half," the inspector said.

That was all right with me, even minus the five bucks. I couldn't have done it without her.

The Pin-Up Boss

by Georges Carousso

To tell you the truth, I don't know much about these things. I mean, I'm scared. What do I know about voodoo? That's stuff for Haiti and those dark islands.

But I couldn't resist the doll. Honest. Sitting in the corner of the window all limp and dusty, it looked just like her. Not that she's limp and dusty. Believe me, when she goes limp it's a glamorous kind of limp, like lounging. The dust part is like gold dust floating around her, she's so bright and blonde. Also, she was my husband's boss, and I hate her, as one woman hates another.

I mean I saw the doll in the window of the novelty shop that's only a block from Tim's office and I went in and bought it. Two ninety-five plus tax—with the pins thrown in.

Honest, I didn't know about the pins when I went in. I guess I just wanted to buy the doll and maybe give it to Thelma as a gag or something, because it looked so much like her, especially the silver-blonde hair and the silky strand that always gets loose and hangs down by her left eye so she has to keep brushing it back. That motion sure draws attention to her beautiful face, with her green, almond-shaped eyes. So I went in and bought the doll. I didn't know it was a voodoo doll. Honest, I mean it. The man told me.

"That's a real voodoo doll," he said. "Made in the dark islands of Haiti by witch doctors."

For two ninety-five? I thought to myself. Plus tax?

"The pins go with it," the man said. "You name the doll after your enemy or your rival or somebody, say the magic word, and then stick a pin where you want her to hurt. A pin here, she gets a bellyache. A pin here, or here, or—"

"Funny man," I said and dug into my bag. "What's the magic word?"

"What? Oh, uh, you just say Popocatepetl!"

"That's in Mexico."

"These dolls get around," he said. "I got a nice clean one in the store-room just like it, only the hair is different."

But I wanted the one in the window and he grumbled because he had to reach out to get her. He finally pinched her between his thumb and forefinger and golly! Her limp arms sort of jerked up as if he was hurting her. I mean I know that if you squeeze any rag doll, her arms— Well, anyway!

I didn't give the doll to Thelma. Thelma isn't exactly the kind of gal you give dolls to, unless they're men dolls, and of these she gets plenty by herself.

Well, like I said before, she was Tim's boss. She owns the advertising agency Tim worked for. Tim was her number one man. Just on the job, I mean. I mean, I hope. You see, this agency specializes in industrial and scientific accounts, which sounds crazy for an agency run by a beautiful blonde, no matter how smart or shrewd she is. But it worked out fine, as long as Tim was there.

You see, Tim is a graduate engineer, with a rare knack for writing about technical stuff and making it sound so clear and simple even I can almost understand it. After he graduated and we were married, the electronics firm he went to work for found out about this knack of his and set him to writing all kinds of manuals and stuff. I guess some of Thelma's clients must have turned green with envy or something because she traced him down and then one bright evening she breezed into our apartment and offered to double his salary if he'd work for her. I thought that was pretty clever, her coming to our place instead of having him go to her office, don't you?

"I'd rather be doing research," Tim said, because that's what he's been saying ever since they put him to writing. Only he never before said it all mealy-mouthed and bug-eyed like he was looking at a vision or some-thing. Let's face it, double the salary or not, this boss looked like she'd stepped out of a magazine cover, and me in a pair of Bermudas and my sleeves rolled up from the dishpan, and—I mean, I knew he'd take the job.

After he had this job a while, Tim changed his tune. He began saying, "I'd rather be doing research but we can't afford it, can we?" I agreed with him. Like Tim, I try to be adaptable. I mean, what's so hard about getting used to a mink jacket for Christmas? You know what I mean?

Oh, yes, the doll. Well, of course I didn't believe in that voodoo bit. And I wasn't jealous of Thelma, you understand. I will admit that I got annoyed with Thelma sometimes because after a while Tim got to be her number one man and she never offered him a partnership or anything. After all, it was Tim who wrote all the presentations. Thelma just presented them to a bunch of old bug-eyed directors of industrial firms and came away with these juicy accounts for her shop. I mean, wouldn't you be a little annoyed?

I guess that's why I did it. I guess I just have to admit it since I'm supposed to tell the truth and everything. Also, I've got a temper, like most redheads—natural redheads, I mean.

I really had put the doll away in the back of a closet and never told a soul about it. Then one night Tim had to stay at the office half the night to finish a presentation for Thelma so she could make a pitch for a new account instead of taking me to a show like we'd planned. I mean Tim was going to take me to the show—not Thelma. See what I mean about my temper? Just talking about it I get so mad I can't talk straight. Well, anyway, you know what I mean. I was *mad!*

So I went into the back of the closet and took that limp doll with its strand of limp blonde hair, and yelled, "Popocatepetl," and stuck one of the black-headed pins into her shoulder.

For Pete's sake, it was just a doll, wasn't it? And I had a right to be mad, with tickets to a show and a new dress and everything, didn't I? Well, anyhow, that's how it happened.

The next day Tim called and said everything was a mess. He had finished the presentation, but Thelma was sick so he had to go to Arizona where this research outfit is and make the presentation himself. "I never made a presentation in my life," he tells me as if I didn't know it. "I'm an engineer, not a supersalesman like Thelma!"

Thelma? Oh, she had bursitis in her right shoulder so that she could hardly stand the pain. Tim would be in Arizona all week maybe, and "happy birthday" to me because chances were he'd miss that, too, but there was a present for me in his top drawer.

I was *boiling* at Thelma. I mean my birthday and all, who wouldn't be? So I got the doll down off the closet shelf again and gave her a piece of my mind and stuck pins all over her.

I even put one through her head, like that blonde hair was a hat or something. Man, was I ever frustrated!

Next day I got a call from Tim from Arizona. He'd been stalling the presentation, hoping Thelma would feel better and come out and do a real snow job. But he'd just called the office and Thelma was real sick, so sick she was in the hospital and near-paralyzed. They thought it was a brain tumor or something. Arizona was great. His sinuses were all cleared up. I'd love it in Arizona. The lab this company had was fabulous. And could I drop in at the hospital and see Thelma? Tell her he'd make the presentation himself.

Three minutes—"Your time is up." He loved me—click! That's Tim, a real scientist. We never get overtime charges on *our* phone bills!

I mean, I hate Thelma and all that, but she is a human being and it's the least I can do for Tim, right? So I went to the hospital and her husband Ralph was there. Sure, she has a husband. What would Thelma do without a man around? Ralph is a real nice guy for a rich stockbroker. He bought the agency for Thelma like another man would buy his wife a—

Well, anyway, Thelma looked terrible, groaning and everything, and being demonstrative with her blonde hair all messed up on the pillow and no makeup on. You could see Ralph was half out of his mind with worry. I'd met him a couple of times and he's a real sweet guy. I mean a lot of fun even for a rich stockbroker. We sat around listening to Thelma groaning and after a while they chased us out. Ralph was so upset he needed a drink, so we went downtown to a nice cocktail lounge. I mean, I couldn't leave him all alone with his worry, right? A man has to have *somebody* to talk to at a time like that.

He was so grateful he asked me to go to the hospital with him again the next day. We did, and the day after that. The third day it was raining when he took me home and I asked him in for a drink to warm up a bit. The fourth day it wasn't raining but it *was* chilly. Just before he left he took me in his arms real tight and said, "I'm scared, Betty. I'm really scared," like a sister almost. Also, it was my birthday.

The next day Tim came back. The presentation had gone badly and the account had been given to another agency. Ralph was there, just picking me up to go to the hospital, and the three of us went to see Thelma. The tests still didn't show anything wrong, but she wasn't any better. She listened to Tim telling how he didn't get the account and all the time those green eyes kept looking at Ralph and her face was all twisted up like a pain was digging inside of her where no drugs could reach. When Tim was finished talking, her eyes drifted away from Ralph and passed slowly over me like I wasn't even there. Then they turned to Tim.

"You're fired," she said.

"I know," Tim said. "I got your wire just before I left. I haven't had a chance to tell Betty. They didn't like my presentation, Betty, but I guess they liked me. They offered me a job with them—research."

"Research!" I screamed. "Out in the desert?"

"There's a town forty miles away," Tim said. "I signed a five-year contract." He grinned like I haven't seen him grin since he stepped into that wall-to-wall money office of Thelma's. He handed me a legal-looking paper. "Belated happy birthday, darling," he said. "This contract is what you always wanted—for both of us."

I looked at Ralph. He looked at me. Like I say, I try to be adaptable. I guess maybe that happy grin on Tim's face helped to clinch it.

When we got home, I took all the pins out of the doll and threw it in the garbage and started packing, I mean I was real *happy* for Tim. I guess I was happy for me, too. I wouldn't tell this to anybody but a doctor, but I hated that mink jacket. Believe it or not, I'm allergic to mink. Thelma? Oh, she got better, got out of the hospital feeling kind of tired, but with nothing the doctors could pin down.

ALFRED HITCHCOCK'S ANTHOLOGY

Rainy Wednesday

by Thomasina Weber

When the siren split the air like a witch's shriek, Mae leaped out of bed and pulled her robe around her. The cold floor sent shivers through her body as she hurried to the front door. By the time she got the door unlocked, unbolted, and unchained, the ambulance was gone.

It was always that way, she thought peevishly as she secured the door once again. She simply was not fast enough. You would think that to a poor old lady with no excitement in her life the Fates would be kind once in a while. As it was, there would be nothing to tell Pauline about at lunch today, and that meant Mae would have to listen to a long dreary account of Pauline's latest dream.

Mae went back to bed, but she didn't sleep. It was nearly four o'clock and she lay on her back staring into the darkness. Four o'clock was an unlikely hour for an automobile accident, she reasoned, so it would be safe to assume the ambulance had been called for a different reason. Heart attack? Possibly, especially if the victim were a man. Just like a man to inconvenience his wife in the middle of the night.

Or it might be some young woman about to have a baby. Mae wrinkled her nose in the dark. Miserable creatures, babies, self-centered little monsters, and the women who bore them were not much better, carrying on like that. There were times Mae Krone was glad she had never married.

The room grew lighter and Mae decided she might as well get up. It was while she was boiling water for tea that the rain began. Mae pulled the curtain aside indignantly. Rain on *Wednesday?* Didn't everyone know Wednesday was her only day off, the day she always met her sister Pauline in the park for lunch, where they shared a thin sandwich and an afternoon of talk? Mae dropped the curtain in disgust. "Wouldn't you know," she said aloud, "it would have to rain when it was Pauline's turn to bring the sandwich!"

Mae couldn't remember a time when she had ever loved her sister.

Pauline had been the pretty one with the coquettish manner, but behind the sparkling blue eyes reposed a weak, vacuous mind. Flirtatious though Pauline was, her deficiency of brains must have been too noticeable for any of her numerous boyfriends to propose marriage, so she and Mae, husbandless, approached their forties, Mae stoically, Pauline with an ill-concealed desperation—until Arthur had come along.

Arthur was a forty-five-year-old bachelor, innocent in the ways of women, having reached that foolish age intact. Perhaps that was one reason he had appealed so to Mae, but his main attraction had been his fine mind. Mae had met Arthur when he came to join the library soon after his arrival in town. As head librarian, she issued him a card. There was an immediate rapport between them and Arthur began to visit the library nearly every night. Pauline heard about it, of course, and when Mae would tell her nothing, she contrived to confront them one evening, forcing Mae to introduce them. That was the end for Mae. The flesh took over and Arthur succumbed to Pauline's obvious charms. To this day Mae couldn't understand how a mind such as Arthur's could be discerning enough to recognize a kindred soul in Mae and yet be stupid enough to overlook Pauline's lack of one.

Mae had been dreadfully hurt and humiliated by this treachery, but she hid it well; well enough, in fact, to give Pauline her first bridal shower after the engagement announcement. It was only natural, therefore, for Pauline to turn to Mae for comfort when Arthur was killed in that unfortunate accident a few nights later.

"They'll find the one responsible," Mae had said soothingly. "They always find a hit-and-run driver."

"No, they don't," wailed Pauline, "but what does it matter who hit him? Arthur's *gone!* My Arthur's gone!"

He was not your Arthur, Mae wanted to tell her. You were not married yet. She would also have liked to tell Pauline that good never results from wrongdoing, and if Pauline hadn't stolen Arthur from Mae, chances are the tragedy would never have happened. Mae, however, said none of these things, but provided a shoulder for Pauline's tears. Figuratively, Pauline had never stopped crying. It would not occur to her, Mae thought bitterly, that perhaps Mae was mourning Arthur's death, too.

After Arthur's death, the two women were never far apart. Each lived alone, Pauline in an apartment, while Mae stayed on in the small family homestead after the death of their parents. Somehow the question of joint tenancy never came up, for which Mae was grateful. Although she kept telling herself that she ought to break away completely, Mae couldn't bring herself to do it. She liked to look at Pauline, rounder and frumpier now, and remind herself that Arthur had really been saved from a miserable life.

At half past ten a knock came on the door and Mae called, "Who is it?"

"It's Pauline."

Now what was she doing here? Mae unlocked and unbolted the door, opening it only as far as the safety chain would allow. When Pauline smiled in at her, Mae frowned and shut the door to unhook the chain.

"I hope you don't mind my coming over like this," said Pauline in a tremulous voice, "but it is our day and—"

"You're puddling on the floor."

"Oh, I'm sorry." She held the dripping umbrella out at arm's length, as if that would stop the water.

"Come into the kitchen and put it in the sink," said Mae, leading the way.

"We could hardly sit in the park in the rain," said Pauline, "and I brought the sandwich."

"We don't usually meet when it rains," said Mae, reaching for the umbrella to open it.

"I know, but I had to see you," said Pauline, tightening her grip on the umbrella. "Leave it closed, Mae! Don't you know it's bad luck to open an umbrella in the house?" She placed it in the sink.

"You've had another dream, I suppose?"

"Yes, and this one is too terrible for words."

"Good. Then I won't have to listen to it."

For a moment Pauline seemed surprised, then she laughed. "Oh, Mae, you always act so grumpy about my dreams, but you'd never let me rest if I didn't tell you about them."

Mae sighed. "I only let you tell me because if I didn't you'd blab them all over town."

"You don't have to put it in the icebox, Mae. It's only peanut butter." Peanut butter! All Pauline knew how to make was peanut butter sandwiches, and she made them so thin you could see through them.

Mae knew Pauline was impatient for her to sit down so she could begin telling her about the dream, so she perversely discovered nonessential tasks to keep her on her feet. She wouldn't have been so reluctant had she been able to report something definite on the ambulance that had wakened her. Although Mae considered herself far above Pauline in intelligence, maturity, and perspicacity, Pauline always had the most to talk about. That was depressing to Mae until she remembered what they say about an empty barrel and she felt better.

Pauline was rattling on about a vacuum cleaner salesman who had called on her the previous day. "Really, Mae, he was such an adorable man I simply couldn't say no."

"You mean you ordered a *vacuum cleaner?*"

"Well, I didn't want to disappoint him. He seemed so eager and he said I was his very first prospect."

"But you don't even own a rug!"

Pauline wrung her hands.

"That's just it, Mae. I see now how foolish I was. But what am I going to do?"

How Mae despised weakness! She couldn't understand how Pauline had lived this long on her own with no one to do for her and make her decisions. "Did you give him any money?"

"No."

"Then just refuse to accept it when he makes delivery."

"All right, but I'm sure that will bring him bad luck, his very first prospect backing out like that."

The mention of bad luck reminded Mae of the ambulance and her misfortune in not being quick enough to see it. To forestall Pauline's narration of her latest nightmare she asked quickly, "Did you hear the ambulance this morning?"

"No, I didn't, and it's a wonder, too, because I slept so poorly, what with that dream and all."

"Four o'clock it went by. It shot me right out of bed."

"I awoke at two o'clock and tossed and turned—"

"It went right by the house, its siren wide open—"

"Arthur was in the dream and he was walking down that dark street alone, except that you could see his white jacket. You remember the white jacket Arthur used to have—"

"It went by so fast I could only catch the merest glimpse of any—"

"That's the funny thing about it. That jacket showed up in the dark. Wouldn't you think that driver would have seen—"

"It looked like a man in the ambulance and he was quite a big man.

I could tell because—"

"So whoever ran Arthur over was either drunk or he did it on purpose."

"You would think an ambulance could go to the hospital a little more quietly in the middle of the night."

"*Mae!* You haven't heard a word I said!"

Mae looked in surprise Pauline's flushed face. "Of course I heard you, just as much as you heard me. I think I had less than your undivided attention."

"How can you talk to me like that?" said Pauline, fishing for a handkerchief to dab at her eyes. "Arthur comes to me in a dream and you aren't even interested enough to listen!"

"I was listening, Pauline. Arthur was wearing his white jacket."

"But that isn't all!"

"That's all you said."

"You wouldn't shut up long enough for me to finish!"

Mae pulled a chair out and sat down, her hands folded on the table before her. "Very well, Pauline, you may continue. I'll sit here quietly and listen with all my ears."

Pauline sniffled several times and smoothed her skirt. With a final dab at her eyes, she went on. "I think Arthur was trying to tell me something. That's the reason he came to me in my dream."

"Really, Pauline! Do you expect me to believe that Arthur finally got around to communicating?"

"Well, we don't know how things are on the other side. Maybe a year is only a day to them. An hour, even."

"And what was this earth-shaking thing Arthur wanted to tell you?"

"You'll never believe it! I hardly believe it myself. If it was anyone but Arthur—"

"And of course it couldn't be anyone but Arthur."

"Of course. I ought to know Arthur when I see him. After all, we were—"

"You seem to forget that it was only a dream, Pauline."

"It was as real as life. He was standing there with his white jacket all bloody—"

"You mean he hasn't found a laundry on the other side?"

"Mae, you're making fun of me. Now this is a very serious thing, as you'll see if you ever let me finish telling you."

"So sorry."

"Very well. He was standing there all bloody, holding out his arms, or trying to because the left one was broken in three places, and his legs—"

"*Pauline!* I don't care to listen to a clinical description of the body. Now either you spit out what you're trying to say or pick up your peanut butter sandwich and go home."

Pauline's eyes narrowed. "For two cents I'd do just that, Miss High and Mighty, but Arthur's communication happens to concern you and I think you should be the first to know."

"It concerns me, does it? And just what did Arthur say?"

"Well, he pointed to his white jacket."

"Yes?"

"As if he wanted me to notice it."

"But what did he say, Pauline?"

"He said—well, actually all he said was 'Mae,' but I could tell from the way he said it that it meant something."

"Oh, without a doubt."

"It was your name, Mae."

"So?"

"Don't you have anything to say for yourself?"

"About what?"

"About what Arthur said!"

" 'Mae'?"

"Of course! He was trying to tell me that you were the one who killed him!"

"You are nuttier than a fruitcake, Pauline."

"I see it all just as plain as day. He was trying to tell me it was no accident because anyone could have seen his white jacket in the dark. If it hadn't been for that dream, I would never have remembered he had been wearing that jacket the night he was killed. And when he said 'Mae,' he was naming his murderer."

"Now I have heard everything."

"No, you haven't. That isn't all Arthur said."

"Oh?"

"He said, 'Beware!' "

"*Beware?*" Mae burst out laughing. "How corny can you get? I suppose he was trying to tell you I'm going to kill you next."

"Exactly."

Mae stared at her sister. "You've got to be kidding."

Pauline shook her head.

"Would you mind telling me the whole plot then? First, why did I kill Arthur? And second, why am I going to kill you?"

"Because Arthur used to be your beau before I came along."

Mae sighed. "Pauline, if that were the case do you think I'd have waited until now to kill you?"

Pauline's smile faded. "Oh, I hadn't thought of that."

"Now if I were you, Pauline, I wouldn't spread a story like that around town."

"But you did get rid of your car right after the accident," said Pauline.

"A coincidence. I had been planning to get rid of it for some time."

"And you've never driven a car since."

"I never did like driving."

"And you had that nervous breakdown a month later."

"I was working too hard. We were short of help and I put in a lot of overtime."

"You used to love Arthur."

"That, too. His death affected me deeply, even though I didn't weep and wail all over town as you did."

"I was engaged to him!"

"How well I know."

"A week later and we would have been married."

"He was a louse."

"Mae! How dare you say that?"

"Just because you swung your skirt more than I did he lost all perspective."

"Are you insinuating that—"

"He was blinded by sex. We could have had a good life together with our mutual interest in books and philosophy, and then you spoiled it all!"

"There is more to life than books and philosophy, Mae dear, but of course you wouldn't know anything about that!"

"He wouldn't have been happy with you. His life would have been empty and futile, leading nowhere."

"You don't know what you're talking about! I would have made him happy. I would have given him love and care and children. And now because of you I have no children!" Pauline jumped to her feet.

"Because of *me?*"

"You killed Arthur, I know you did! And you haven't killed me yet because it gives you more satisfaction to watch me grow old and fat and lonely!" Pauline was at the sink, groping in the folds of her wet umbrella. "When I came over you got me all confused by asking questions and arguing and I thought maybe I was wrong after all, but now I know it's true. I see you for what you really are, Mae Krone, and I don't know how I could have been so blind all these years." Pauline, having freed the knife from the folds of the umbrella, whirled around—just in time to see the iron skillet descending on her head.

The morning had grown older and Mae was sitting on a kitchen chair, the iron skillet in her lap. Pauline was lying on the floor. It was very rude of Pauline to come visiting and then curl up on the floor and go to sleep like that. Oh well, Pauline was an idiot, an empty-headed idiot. Some time ago, Mae didn't know how long, she had heard the milkman's truck in the driveway. He had knocked on the glass of the door—and then he had gone away. She wondered if he had left the milk on the step.

Suddenly a siren shattered the silence. Instinctively Mae leaped to her feet and ran to the front room. Her luck was changing! She was not too late this time. It sounded like a police car and it was coming closer. Then she saw it. It was stopping in front of the house. How nice! They had finally taken pity on a poor old lady and were going to stop and tell her what was going on. She would make them a nice cup of tea for their trouble. And just wait until next Wednesday! She'd make Pauline green with envy.

ALFRED HITCHCOCK'S ANTHOLOGY

The Short and Simple Annals

by Dan J. Marlowe

I'd just come out from under the welding hood and was inspecting a silver seam intended to staunch a leak in a battered radiator when "Fat" Carson, the welding shop hack, touched me on the arm. "You're wanted in the warden's office, Toland," he said. He led the way to the door, unlocking it and then carefully re-locking it behind us, observing the regular procedure.

We marched down the echoing stone corridor while I tried to think where I could have put my foot down wrong. I was no stranger to such summonses, but I hadn't been up before the mast in some time. Carson left me at the door of Warden Wibberly's office, and I went in and braced in front of his desk, standing stiffly at attention. To the left of the chunky, grayhaired Wibberly, a big man in a dark business suit sat off to one side. It took a second look from the corner of my eye before I recognized Tom Glick, the precinct police captain from my home town who'd sent me up. I'd never seen him out of uniform before.

"Have a chair, Toland," Wibberly said. "Smoke if you like." He actually sounded pleasant.

"Thank you, sir." I lit up quickly. You can't smoke under a welding hood. I sat at attention in the designated chair.

Wibberly opened a file folder on his desk. I knew it was mine, because one of the mug shots taken when I arrived at the prison was pasted to the outside of the tan folder. It showed a blackhaired, rugged-looking type with big shoulders and a to-hell-with-you look in the eyes. I hadn't seen much of that look lately in my shaving mirror.

"I've been looking over your record here," Wibberly began. "Upon arrival you were close to being an incorrigible, but I note that in the past thirty months no disciplinary action has been necessary. Except for your choice of friends, I'd say that you made a good, if belated, adjustment." I didn't say anything. I wondered what he was leading up to. Off to the side, Glick was elaborately studying the lighted tip of his cigarette.

Wibberly closed the folder, cleared his throat, and looked directly at me in my chair. "I have news for you, Toland. A professional thief named Danny Lualdi was shot and critically wounded by a policeman. Before he died, he gave the police a list of the crimes he'd committed. The Gurnik Baking Company safe job was on the list, and bullets fired from Lualdi's pistol matched the one fired at the Gurnik watchman in the getaway, and which was later removed by the police from a door. There's no question Lualdi did the job."

I could feel the old adrenalin coursing through me. I couldn't sit still; I bounced upright, pinching out my cigarette and automatically dropping the butt into my pocket. "Then where does that leave me?" I demanded. "I've done three years, two months, and seventeen days for that job on the strength of a positive identification by Spider Haines, the Gurnik night watchman."

"It leaves you a free man." Wibberly gestured at his desk. "The governor has signed a pardon for you that takes effect at noon tomorrow. When it does, you'll be walking out that gate down there." He pointed to the steel doors in the forty foot gray wall that could be seen from his office window.

A buzzer sounded, signaling the four thirty P.M. end of the prison work day. "In that case," I said, "if you've nothing more to say, I've got people to see and things to do."

I'd stopped saying "sir," and he'd noticed it. His mouth drew down at the corners. "Captain Glick has a word to say to you before you leave this office, Toland." Wibberly got up and left, closing the outside door behind him.

"I suppose you're already spending the money you're going to get for suing the state and the department for false arrest and imprisonment?" Glick rumbled at me.

"I hadn't had time to think of it yet, but thanks for the idea."

"Don't do it," he said. His tone was flat and unemotional.

"I'd like to see you stop me." I warmed to the subject. "I'd like to see you try. Even with a pardon, what kind of a job can I get when employers know where I've been? You bet your life I'm going to sue! Julie and the baby can use the money, too."

"Don't do it," he said again. "There are people who wouldn't like it." He rose from his chair. I'm no midget, but he outbulked me in all directions. "You're no rose, Toland. You had a previous record—"

"Misdemeanors!" I burst out. "A couple of fights . . . "

"The rap sheet says the charges were reduced from assault. And on the Gurnik job, Haines identified you."

"With you twisting his arm!"

Glick's rocklike expression never changed. "I picked up Marsh Wheeler the other day," he said. "Used to be a friend of yours, didn't he?" He was watching my face. Fear nibbled at me, sharp as a rat's teeth. "Old Marsh is going up this time. Open and shut case. He got careless." Glick was still watching me. "Didn't seem to be any point in it before, but maybe I ought to lean on him and ask him who his partner was in the days before you went away?" He waited, but I didn't say anything. I couldn't have said anything. Glick seemed satisfied with the impression he had created. "You're a machinist, or were," he said. "Work at it. Stay out of my sight. And forget the suing." He strolled to the door.

Wibberly re-entered immediately. "All right, Toland," he said briskly. "See you tomorrow."

I got out of there, so mad I could hardly see. They thought they had me nailed down, did they? Well, I'd show them.

I had the guard who picked me up at the door take me down to the gym, where I usually went after work. Benny the Weasel Krafcik and Trigger Dunn were sitting on stools beside the lifting mat, talking. They were my closest friends in the prison—the choice of friends of which Wibberly had disapproved—but I didn't know how to break the news to them. I stripped to the waist and loosened up with the fifteen pound dumbbells, shifted to the thirties, and worked up a sweat. I hoisted a barbell over my head a few times, then let it drop to waist level and did a few curls. It's good for the arms. I'd gone from a medium to a large size in shirts since I'd been on the weights, and I was only another layer of muscle away from extra-large.

Finally I broke into the low-pitched conversation. "I'm leaving tomorrow, fellas," I told them.

"That's too bad, Igor," Benny said. He called everyone who lifted weights Igor, his idea of a joke.

"Yeah," Trigger chimed in. "What'd you do to get yourself transferred out? An' where they shippin' you to?"

"OUT," I emphasized. "On the bricks. Clean. A pardon."

Their smiles were both quick and genuine. It's not hard—in fact, it's extremely easy—to dislike the man getting out ahead of you, but these were my friends. Benny was a safe mechanic, and a good one. Trigger was a gunman. Nobody except a few intimates called him "Trigger" to his face. Benny lifted weights, too, but not Trigger. "How strong do you have to be to pull a trigger?" he'd ask, and laugh.

"How to go, man," Benny said softly. "This change your plans any?"

"It's going to speed them up considerably."

Trigger smiled. "Hope you remember everything Benny's pounded into you," he said.

The conversation died. I couldn't think of anything to say. I knew what they were thinking: *here's a guy making it to the street. By tomorrow this time he'll be doing all the things we'd like to be doing out there.* Anything I said would be so much rubbing it in. "You sure you got it all straight?" Benny asked finally. I rattled off names, addresses, and telephone numbers. They both nodded. Benny had a few special questions. I answered them. He smiled, satisfied. The buzzer sounded for the end of the recreation period, and I exchanged a cross-handed handshake with them, both at the same time. They each said the one word: "Luck!" and we went off to our cells.

That night I wrote Julie a long letter. I told her about the pardon. I didn't tell her I was getting out the next day; I told her I loved her and the baby. Baby? Lucy was four years old now. And that I'd be seeing them the first of the week. The first part was certainly true, and I hoped the last part was just as true.

I was processed out by one o'clock the next afternoon. The prison clothing shop outfitted me with slacks and a sport jacket that fitted reasonably well. The warden handed me my pardon, a copy of my release papers, a one-way bus ticket to the city, my wallet, and $86.14, the money I'd earned in prison. I went out through the steel gates, walked to the bus terminal, and caught the one thirty bus, settling down in it for the ten-hour ride.

En route, during a stopover, I bought a cheap briefcase, shaving gear, a toothbrush, a shirt, and a couple of changes of underwear. I'd left all my things behind me in favor of a fresh start. The briefcase was my only luggage when we reached town. I took a cab up to the Hotel Carlyle, where no one questioned my skimpy luggage or hatless, crew cut head. I signed the register with my right name. When they came looking for me, I wanted to make it easy for them.

Despite my late arrival, I showered and shaved. Then I went out to a nearby steakhouse and savored every bite of a $6.50 porterhouse. After strawberry shortcake and three cups of coffee, real coffee, I went to a pay phone and made two calls. Both parties assured me they'd had the word and would expect to see me the next day. I went back to the hotel, and after half an hour's tossing and turning on the strange bed, I finally fell asleep.

The first address in the morning turned out to be a barber shop in a rundown neighborhood. "I called here last night," I said to the baldheaded barber who was alone in the place.

"You're Trigger's friend who just got out?"

"That's right. I'd like to borrow a .45 Colt automatic and a clip-on holster."

"Borrow? That's not what makes the world go round, mister."

"Trigger said you owed him a favor."

He shrugged, and went to the front door and bolted it. He led me to another door in the back and up two steps into a narrow hallway that opened on what looked like an apartment in the rear. "Wait here," he said in the hallway. In five minutes he was back with the automatic, the holsters, and a dozen rounds of ammunition. I wrapped the bullets in my handkerchief to keep the grease off my pants, and dropped the handkerchief in my pocket. I clipped the holster on my belt and holstered the automatic. It felt heavy, but it felt right.

Back out in the barber shop, I pointed to the large mail slot in the front door. "I'll drop these things back in here tonight," I said. "Wrapped." He opened the door and let me out.

The second stop was a cab ride across town. It was a barroom. I introduced myself to the bartender as a friend of Benny the Weasel, and he pointed out to me Benny's friend who was waiting for me.

"I want to borrow Benny's vest," I told him, "and the kit. I'll return it tonight and you can put it away for him again."

"I'll bring it across the street to the diner in half an hour," he said.

He was ten minutes late. I was on my second cup of coffee when he showed. He put down a heavy, brown paper-wrapped package on the counter beside me. I hefted it. It must have weighed twenty pounds. "I'll have it back by midnight," I said.

"Good enough," he said, and took off.

In a nearby pawnshop I bought a used suitcase. At a hardware store

I bought a small can of paint remover, a large sheet of heavy brown wrapping paper, and a ball of twine. I put everything into the suitcase and moved on to a drugstore. I bought two dollars' worth of stamps at a stamp machine. I added the stamps to the collection in the suitcase and took another cab back to the hotel.

At the front desk I bummed an address label from the clerk. Up in the room I addressed the label to a fictitious address in a nearby town. In the upper left hand corner of the label I put Julie's name and return address. When the parcel turned out to be undeliverable, eventually it would be returned to Julie's apartment.

I opened up the brown paper package and examined Benny's canvas vest. It was an adjustable type, and I had to loosen the straps before it fitted snugly under my sports jacket. It had twenty-two large and small pockets, and I took a careful inventory of the contents. Everything seemed to be there. Because of a small drill motor in a pocket on the right hand side, I had to unclip my holster and refasten the pistol on my left, to avoid a suspicious bulge. With the weight of the kit distributed around the trunk of my body, I hardly felt I was carrying anything.

I looked at my watch. Two o'clock. I took off the vest and stretched out on the bed for a nap. At six I got up and put the vest back on, re-clipped the holster, and buttoned the jacket over everything. I was ready to go. I wouldn't eat until after the job.

I walked the two and a half miles to Gurnik's. I had plenty of time, and no desire to test cab drivers' memories for faces in a police roundup. The bakery covered most of a block, and I came up on the rear of it, passing a mailbox on the corner. The watchman's shack was just inside the four foot stone wall, behind the closed gate. I passed it on the wrong side of the street, and I could see the whitehaired Spider Haines at his desk in the shack, the same wizened Spider Haines whose testimony had sent me up.

When he left the shack on his eight o'clock rounds, I vaulted the wall. Benny's information was that Haines made a tour of the plant every two hours. At the back door of the main building I unloaded the suitcase; I put paint remover, twine, address label, and stamps in my pockets, and folded the wrapping paper and carried it under my arm. When Haines came back out the door after punching his clocks, I met him halfway through it. He took one look at the gun in my hand and another at my face and went right down on his skinny knees. "Don't do it, Toland!" he begged. "Glick *made* me testify!"

He had nothing to worry about, but he didn't know it. I wanted him very much alive. I prodded him upright with the pistol and hustled him down the corridor to where the cashier's office should be, according to Benny's information. It was there, all right, and so was the safe, a large double-door model.

I tied Haines into a chair. His eyes rolled up at me; he was shivering as though with an ague. I pulled the chair into a corner out of sight of the safe, and left him there. He wasn't about to make any noise; he had to figure he was a big winner. Besides, after sundown in that warehouse neighborhood, not even a good-sized explosion would have had an audience.

On my way to the safe I took the can of paint remover from my pocket. I opened it, and spread a four inch border of it around the upper half of the door containing the combination dial. I gave it time to soften the paint, and then scraped it off with a putty knife I took from the vest. The bare metal of the safe door was now exposed. Working quickly, I took a two pound lead block from the vest and screwed a steel handle into it. Using it as a mallet, I struck the face of the door sharply several times. Cracks appeared around the heads of previously invisible rivets that had been machined flush with the surface of the door.

Successful safecracking requires specialized knowledge, skill with tools, and physical strength. I centerpunched each rivet, and then drilled off the head of the dial. I took the pry-bar from the vest. It consisted of four six-inch steel lengths that screwed together. One of them had been the mallet handle, and it had several interchangeable tips. I used a flat tip first to loosen the front plate, and then switched to a hook shape to bend the plate down, exposing the concrete lining. After shifting again to a pointed tip, I knocked out the concrete to get at the bolt works.

It was hot, dusty work. A fine film of cement dust settled over everything. When I had the bolt works exposed, all I had to do was remove one pin from the main bolt arm. The bolts retracted easily. The doors opened smoothly. This was no safe with another steel door behind the first one. The cash was right out in plain sight.

I scooped it out and piled it on the floor. The denominations on the packages of bills made pleasant reading. I found some cardboard for a stiffener, made a neat stack of the whole business, and wrapped it all up in the heavy brown wrapping paper I'd brought along. I tied it securely with the twine, using double knots, applied the previously prepared label and over two dollars' worth of stamps, and was ready to drop it into a mailbox. In the post office's own good and sufficient time, the package would arrive at Julie's marked RETURN TO SENDER.

I slipped out of the vest and wrapped it, too, and I made two small packages of the gun and the holster. I went over everything in the place carefully with a damp rag, erasing possible fingerprints. I didn't forget Benny's tools. With the same rag I cleaned my shoes. After brushing off my slacks, I picked up my packages and went out the way I'd come in, stopping at the back door to pick up the suitcase and take that with me, too.

I dropped the money package into the mailbox at the end of the block. The suitcase I shoved into a doorway after wiping it for prints. I walked rapidly away from Gurnik's. When Haines didn't make his ten o'clock round, someone was going to investigate. My nerves were screaming for transportation, but I made myself walk a mile before I hailed a cab. I made my first stop the barber shop, where I pushed the wrapped pistol and holster through the mail slot. At the diner I left Benny's kit with the short order cook. Back at the Carlyle I took a long shower, dressed again, and stretched out on the bed to wait.

I knew it wouldn't be long, and it wasn't.

When the pounding started on the door, I was sure it was Glick, even before I opened it. "Let's go," he ordered without preliminary.

"What's the charge this time, captain?" I asked him. "Spitting on the sidewalk?"

He refused to answer. We rode downtown with a detective on either side of me on the back seat, and Glick glowering up front beside the driver. An assistant district attorney was waiting when they brought me in. "Gurnik's safe was burglarized tonight, and the watchman said you did it," he started in on me. "You must be out of your mind, even if you think you did get a bum rap before. Now, if you turn over the money and make a full statement, I'm sure the judge will take it into consideration when he hears all the facts in the case."

I laughed in his face. "Mister Whatever-Your-Name-Is, I don't know what happened at Gurnik's, if anything did, but I'll tell you something. Spider Haines's testimony will never convict anyone again, let alone me. Didn't he already identify me once in error? You think a jury's going to believe him again?"

It wasn't that easy, of course. There was brow-beating and breast-beating, and telephone calls, and hurried, whispered consultations. They rushed me from room to room, fingerprinting me, and taking my picture. And at two A.M. they gave up and threw me out on the street. Glick's face was like a thundercloud. I walked along, laughing to myself. It was beautiful. I'd really put it over on them. All I needed now was to get rid of the load of tension that had built up in my stomach like a tight, hard ball. I ducked into a bar for a couple of quick ones, liquid tranquilizers.

I had three. I felt fine. I ordered a roast beef sandwich. I'd forgotten I hadn't eaten, and I was ravenous. I could feel the tension oozing away and being replaced by a wonderfully expansive feeling. I counted my money. I wouldn't have much left after settling up at the hotel, but Julie wouldn't mind the drought before the payoff. It would take me a while to catch up on home living. I was looking forward to it. I didn't expect to mind a bit, waiting for the package to be returned by the post office.

I cabbed back to the Carlyle and went up in the elevator. I'd check out in the morning, but first I needed a good night's sleep. At the room I had trouble with the key in the lock, and for a second I wondered if Glick had turned nasty and ordered the lock plugged to keep me out. Then the door opened and I walked in. I couldn't believe my eyes when I saw Glick inside my room. With him was a big sergeant and a bigger patrolman, and an assistant manager-looking type with a passkey. "An afterthought," Glick said, moving between me and the door. "Sergeant Bonar here is going to take a specimen of the dirt under your fingernails to see if any of it matches the cement dust down at Gurnik's. So hold out your hands."

The long hot shower should have taken care of that, I thought hopefully.

"And he's going to vacuum the cuffs of your slacks," Glick continued.

All I could think of was the fine layer of powdery dust filming everything in front of the Gurnik safe.

It must have been the three drinks that made me bolt for the door. I tried to run right over Glick. The next thing I knew, I was on the floor, looking up at him from my back. "Put your little vacuum on him, sergeant," he was saying. I heard the bzz-bzz-bzz of a small electric motor. "Looks fine," Glick announced. "Mooney, you can babysit with our friend here, while I check this out."

When the rest of them left, Mooney and I sat there like two bumps on a log.

After a while the phone rang, and I took another ride downtown.
They're still after me about the money.

I haven't told them anything, and I won't. I'm sure of that.

The insurance company is making the most noise. The district attorney's office is embarrassed by the newspaper publicity going back to the first Gurnik safe job, and they'd like to forget the whole thing. They as much as said that if I'd come up with the cash, they'd see to it I was eased out the back door of wherever I was sent as soon as the headlines died down.

But there's Julie and the baby. I'm a real loser now. When I get out, I'll be good only for more of the same, or the ash heap. Either way, it doesn't leave much for them.

So I'm leaving it up to Julie.

When the package is returned, she'll know where it came from. If she wants to return it, and get me a lessened sentence, that's fine. If she doesn't, that's all right, too. She doesn't owe me anything except one small vow, and I figure I tarnished the brass on that a good while ago.

If I don't hear anything in another week, I'll be pretty sure of the answer.

Bite of Revenge

by James McKimmey, Jr.

Erwin—his father would never have called him that, it was his late mother's selection—walked slowly across the field away from the old stone quarry, hoisting the chunks of wood he'd gotten from the pile sawed there and not yet stored in the tool shed near the house.

It was midsummer, but the air was raw and chill in this early California morning and Erwin wished his father had borrowed the pickup truck from the main house on the ranch and had transferred the wood so that he wouldn't have to carry it a half mile by hand the way he was doing. But his father hadn't, and his father would still want a fire when he got up on this Sunday morning.

Thus Erwin, a tall skinny boy in worn and dirty bluejeans and brown wool jacket, trudged along toward the small aging frame house, the metal-framed spectacles on his nose steaming over from the exertion.

He moved slowly but steadily, avoiding the reddish tri-leafed growths of poison oak; his fair skin was very susceptible to rash. He also watched the stubble of grass where there might be rattlesnakes. Erwin would be twelve years old next August, but he knew his way around this ranch where his father worked as a hand.

And so had Bolo. Thinking of that, Erwin's throat got tight all over again, and the blurring of his glasses seemed to get worse as his eyes got hot. He'd had Bolo for over four years; they'd been companions day and night.

Erwin passed the pump shed now, listening carefully to the rhythmic grind of the pump inside. He'd repaired the belt yesterday and it was still holding together. They really needed a new belt, but his father wouldn't buy one. He left it up to Erwin to see that the old one kept working. And when it didn't, there was a cuff on the ear, a blast of cursing.

Erwin carried the wood inside and put it by the stove in the large kitchen. The house was very old. It had served as quarters for a long line of ranch hands and their families for some fifty years now. But it had looked very neat when Erwin's mother had been alive. It had been warm and clean and always smelled good from freshly baked bread. Now it was all different, including the smell. It smelled now of cheap wine, even though Erwin had thrown away the empty bottle earlier.

Erwin put old newspapers into the stove, then some kindling, and then the larger wood. He lit the paper just as his father appeared from the bedroom, eyes red-rimmed, a black stubble of beard on his face, still wearing the clothes he'd finished work in the late afternoon before. The smell of wine became stronger.

"About time," his father said, walking heavily and unsteadily across to the kitchen sink. "You'd get up when you're supposed to, you'd get your chores done on time." His father filled a glass with water from the tap, drank it greedily, then drank another. His father was large, hulking about the shoulders, dark and weather-burned.

"I got up early," Erwin said.

His father drank another glass of water.

"I got up soon's it was light," Erwin said, "so I could bury Bolo."

His father turned around finally, looking at him with disdain and an anger caused unreasonably by the aching of his head, the insatiable thirst. "You're not so prompt," he said, "with chores that need to be done."

Erwin looked down at his hands through his spectacles. "What'd you have to go and kill him for?"

His father frowned, knitting his black bushy eyebrows. "Why'd I want to kill that worthless dog? Why wouldn't I?" He stopped speaking, eyes shifting a little, and Erwin thought he was remembering how he'd kicked the dog again and again, until—

"I still don't know why," Erwin said. "Why—why'd you do it?"

His father stared at him for a moment, then turned and splashed water from the tap into his face. He didn't answer. He wouldn't, Erwin knew. If it was something he didn't like, he just wouldn't talk, ever. It had been like that after his mother had—

Erwin compressed his thin lips, the vague shadows of memories returning. His mother had died three years ago, and those memories kept coming back: that night, the black voice of his father growing stronger, angrier, while Erwin curled tighter in his bunk on the porch, pulling Bolo close in beside him. They had gone long distances that day, he and Bolo, and fatigue was strong. The black voice turned thunderously mean and then there had been the scuffling sound, but Erwin had seen his father stumble drunkenly before. He'd slept despite all of that, drifting away.

And then morning had arrived and there had been his father coming into the house, just at dawn, face grey, eyes red-rimmed. His father had telephoned immediately, without telling Erwin what had happened, and afterward Erwin thought about how happy his mother had been to have that telephone she'd always wanted and pleaded with his father for, and how it was that same telephone that his father used to say that his mother was lying at the foot of the stone quarry, dead.

He'd tried to talk to his father later, to ask him why his mother would have been up at that time of day walking by the quarry where that slide of crumbled rock had smashed into her and nearly buried her—why, when she almost never went over there. But his father shut him up quickly and would never talk about it.

The men in the uniforms had asked his father the same kind of questions about how Erwin's mother had been over there, but all he would tell them, over and over, was, "I don't know—she was a good woman, a good woman." Erwin wondered how his father could seem to mean that so much when he'd seen his father, with the smell of sweet wine strong from his lips, turn mean with her, ugly.

Erwin put those memories out of his head. He straightened his thin shoulders a little.

His father turned around, another glass of water in his hand. "Better check that belt on the pump. I don't want that thing breaking down again. And don't be fooling around with that car, do you hear?"

The pump breaking down and the consequent interruption of the house's water supply had become almost a mania with his father; it was something to build new angers with, to spark new rages. Erwin checked the fire in the stove, pausing just long enough to half close his eyes and remember how it had been once.

There was a bare spot on the small shelf where the telephone had been, and once again Erwin remembered how happy his mother had been when that telephone had been installed. "Four miles from anybody out here, and it makes me feel comfortable, safe—"

Now it was gone. His father didn't want to waste any money on it.

"Hurry up," his father said, drinking water again.

Erwin got his pair of old pliers from a pantry drawer, shoved them into his hip pocket, and walked outside.

He didn't go straight to the pump shack because there was a storm of resentment building inside him that morning. Instead he walked across the dirt drive, past the dusty 1950 sedan, brushing his fingers over the metal of the hood. Erwin liked mechanical things, and when his father wasn't around he would pull up the hood and check over the engine, loosening and tightening nuts, removing the spark plugs and wiping them clean and replacing them. He would have liked to have made his own mechanical things, but he didn't own the materials or any tools, with the exception of a pair of pliers.

He walked on back of the tool shed—it wasn't really a tool shed, it was just called that; all there was in it was a rake and a spade and an old rusty saw—and stopped some forty yards beyond, where he kneeled down beside a mound of fresh earth. He'd put a large stone at the head of that mound, and now he placed his hands gently on the stone and once again his glasses blurred and his eyes got hot.

Bolo hadn't been all beagle—just a part—but he'd looked mostly like a beagle, even if he was bigger and his nose was too long.

He could run terribly fast and he had just as good a sense of smell as any hunting dog. Erwin didn't own any kind of gun, but he could have shot all of a thousand rabbits if he had, because that was how many Bolo had tracked down. Mr. Kindler, who owned the ranch and lived in the main house four miles away, had said Bolo was as good a hunting dog as any he'd ever seen. And four times he'd taken Bolo out to hunt and got a rabbit each time.

Erwin's glasses were all steamed now and tears were streaming hotly down his cheeks. He kept thinking about how Bolo had looked when he was running, kicking out those short muscular back legs, pumping with them, and as fast as the wind. Now Erwin wanted to forget how Bolo whimpered when the first kick had struck him.

Erwin stood up blindly, not able to see anything for a long time, until he'd finally admitted that he was really crying and got out a dirty hand-kerchief and wiped his eyes dry and put the spectacles back on.

Then Erwin walked back past the tool shed and toward the pump shack. The pump was silent now and Erwin hoped it was because enough water had been temporarily pumped into the pipes and not because the belt had broken again. He didn't know if he could fix that belt again or not, it was so worn.

He opened the door of the weather-grey structure that held the pump and looked inside. It was muddy in there from water leaking and it smelled musty. The belt, Erwin saw, was all right. It was just that enough water was in the pipes.

And then Erwin saw something else. His eyes widened a little, and he stepped back suddenly, but softly and carefully. He stared inside for a moment, then he turned and ran part way to the house.

Then he stopped. He stopped abruptly, a flush of excitement in his face. He stood there through a long pause, frowning a little. His mother had always said that Erwin had a good quick brain and despite the fact that his father disliked the skinny look of him she'd always said you couldn't beat Erwin's quick thinking.

Erwin turned and walked rapidly to the car. He glanced toward the house, released the hood, and got out his pliers. He worked swiftly, replaced the hood, and went to the tool shed where he got the rake.

He carried the rake to the pump shack, looking back at the house once more, then he looked in the shack. The pump was running once more. Carefully, Erwin turned the rake backwards and extended the handle inside slowly until the tip of it touched the switch handle on the wall. He pushed down and the pump stopped.

Erwin stepped back, drawing the handle of the rake out, and returned to the tool shed. There he waited, back from the door in the darkness. He waited, hopefully.

Minutes went by, one by one, and then his father, dark and angry, burst out of the house. "That pump's off again!" his father shouted. "Now get it fixed! Hear me? Get it fixed!"

Erwin didn't move. He didn't answer.

His father stood there, eyes blazing, looking around the yard, then he marched to the road and down to the pump shack, muttering angrily. He kicked at the door, stomping inside. Erwin waited, tense. The blood was pounding in his eyes and ears.

A second later, there was a scream and his father was crashing out, eyes wide in disbelief. He stood there for a moment, one hand grabbing the calf of his right leg, then he whirled, stumbled and fell, picked himself up, and ran back toward the house, yelling and swearing.

A dozen yards from the house he stopped, turning, throwing his arms out wildly and shouting, "Erwin! Erwin!"

Erwin had never heard his father call him by his name—it was always kid or some sort of swear word or nothing at all. Erwin was interested in the way his father was calling him Erwin now. But he didn't answer. He didn't move. He waited.

He waited until his father suddenly ran to the car, got in, and ground his foot against the starter.

The starter whirred strongly. It whirred over and over.

But the car didn't start. And his father was screaming once again, face blanched with panic and fear. Erwin was also surprised that his father was reacting this way. He was just wild, and he wasn't even attempting to cut the bite with X's and suck the poison out. All he did was keep that starter whirring over and over, all the time yelling, "Erwin! Erwin!"

Erwin didn't know exactly how long he waited in the shed. He waited quite a long time, however. The starter wasn't whirring any more when he did step out into the sunshine. And his father wasn't yelling any more.

It was very quiet when Erwin walked back to the car, reached around the still form of his father, and released the hood once again. Erwin was surprised at how quiet it was.

But he was used to solitude. Still, when he'd replaced the spark plugs, locking them tight with his pliers, and started out on the four-mile walk to the main house to tell them about his father and that rattlesnake, he was feeling lonely again. He wished that Bolo were running up ahead of him, those strong short legs pumping. Erwin's glasses blurred all over again, but still he felt better now. A lot better.

ALFRED HITCHCOCK'S ANTHOLOGY

The Pearls of Li Pong

by W. E. Dan Ross

Mei Wong carefully shut the door that led to the outer office and showroom of his Bombay Art & Curio Co. and snapped its lock against any unwanted visitors. His huge frame padded across to the wide window overlooking the street. He listened for a moment to the monotonous chant of a snake charmer's reed and gourd far below; then with a deft movement he closed the venetian blind. Satisfied, he lowered his great body into an oversized chair behind a littered mahogany desk. He fitted a cigarette into a long holder, lighted it, drew several casual puffs, and studied the once famous artist, Gilbert Rendell, who, dirty and dejected, sat opposite him.

The artist shifted uneasily in his chair, rubbed his beard-stubbled chin with a trembling hand. "You weren't expecting me, I suppose," he mumbled and regarded the floor with red-rimmed eyes.

"I remember I advised you," the old Chinaman said tonelessly, "that you were not to come to this establishment again."

Rendell lifted his blotched face and leaned forward. "I'm here only because I'm desperate. I've got to get away. It means my life. Let me have a thousand dollars to get back home."

Mei Wong shook his head. "It wouldn't do any good, my dear Mr. Rendell. Surely you remember the other sums I have let you have—each time to pay for your trip home. You've destroyed a great talent. Once I had hoped to save it, but I hope no longer."

The young man sneered. "I see. Now that there are no more canvasses in prospect, you're not interested. Surely you made enough on my work in the old days to—"

"I paid you well," Mei Wong interrupted calmly, "And since you have ceased painting I have continued to give you large amounts of money. But I am finished."

At this pronouncement, Rendell's bravado disappeared. "I must have a thousand dollars," he pleaded.

"You will not receive it from me, my friend," the old Chinaman smiled, "It seems you have lost your last shred of pride. I believe that now you would do almost anything for a price."

"I want to quit drinking—get right with myself again."

"Idle words, Mr. Rendell, idle words. You are past saving. Drink means everything to you. You'd even kill to get money for it."

There was a moment of silence. Then Rendell said: "Possibly I would."

Mei Wong watched him with expressionless eyes. "Yes—yes, you would. So perhaps we may come to an understanding, after all, you and I. You may be able to undertake a delicate mission for me. One that does involve killing a man."

The old Chinaman puffed easily on his cigarette and studied Rendell, who had slumped back in his chair.

Finally the young man spoke in a tired voice. "What will it pay?"

"Three thousand dollars."

"A neat price for murder."

Mei Wong spoke coldly. "This is not a joke. I am willing to pay for a man's death."

For the first time Rendell looked him in the eye. "And I am willing to accept your money," he said. "Who is the man?"

"A stranger to you. It will be like eliminating a symbol. His name is Han Lee. He lives in the mountains on the mainland of Hong Kong. He has in his possession the Pearls of Li Pong. I have tried to bargain with him. His last word was that he would not part with them while he lived. So, he must cease to live, Mr. Rendell." Mei Wong put aside the cigarette holder. "You shall have help in your task. I have a good friend in Hong Kong, an Englishman, John MacDonald. He lives close to Han Lee and will give you my final instructions. He is trustworthy and will be of great assistance to you."

Gilbert Rendell stood up, nearly sober now. "I want to make sure of the details," he said, "I take a boat to Hong Kong. Go to the mountains on the mainland and look up this MacDonald."

"John MacDonald. And he will have your orders in a sealed box." Mei Wong pulled out a drawer and extracted a small key and passed it to him, "This key will open it."

"Following your orders, and MacDonald's, I locate this Han Lee. And when I find him, I kill him. It shouldn't be too difficult."

Mei Wong shrugged. "Han Lee is wily, he is strong. But you were once a fine, talented man, Mr. Rendell."

"I have an added advantage. Han Lee will not be suspicious of me. A shot in the back—sounds easy." The young man chuckled without mirth and went over to the window.

"There are other means," Mei Wong lifted a small enamelled case from his desk and with a quick pressure released a blade that converted it into a dagger which he sent hurtling across the room to a vibrating stop in the wall a few inches above Rendell's head. "I suggest you take my little weapon with you," he said. "Become familiar with it. It is a weapon of surprise and silence and more suited to your task than the vulgarity of firearms."

"Murder should not be vulgar!" Rendell replied mockingly and removed the beautiful yet sinister instrument from its resting place. He snapped back the blade and put it in his coat pocket. "And what about the three thousand?"

"I will have the money for you when you bring back the Pearls of Li Pong. And I must have them within nine weeks."

"Nine weeks. Should give me time enough. But suppose I decide to keep them for myself?"

"It would be too risky, Mr. Rendell. You wouldn't be able to dispose of them to your advantage." Mei Wong's smile was bland. "You will do best to place yourself entirely in my hands."

Rendell remembered this scene four days later as he roused himself from a drunken stupor and sat, head reeling, on his dirty, sagging bed. The room was small and hot. The only other furniture in it was a washstand and an *elmirah*, the Eastern substitute for a clothes closet. He reached in his pocket for a cigarette and instead brought out the evil little enamelled dagger case. It reminded him of his bargain. It was a killer's weapon.

He released its blade and raised himself to a standing position by steadying his body against the foot of the iron bedstead. The washstand was at the other end of the room, perhaps eight feet from him. He raised the dagger and aimed it. But the washstand wavered in a blurred mist. His hand trembled. He tried to control it, and failed. If he threw the thing he knew he would miss his target. He was in no shape to look after himself. Han Lee could easily kill him before he could kill Han Lee.

Disturbed by this truth he put the dagger back in his pocket. He made his way out of the room and into the street. The blazing sun temporarily blinded him and his lips burned. It was time to begin the day's serious drinking. The bar around the corner would be crowded. There were always some American tourists who could be cadged for drinks.

He stumbled down the narrow street, elbowing through the crowds. An ancient and watery-eyed beggar blocked his path with a whining, "*Baksheesh*, master, *baksheesh!*" He pushed him aside without hesitating but then as he neared the entrance to the bar he stopped. The ornate gilded clock over the doorway gripped his attention. Time was passing for him—he had only a little better than eight weeks left. He remembered the enamelled case and his shaking hand. He couldn't chance drinking now. It was time to ready himself for his meeting with Han Lee.

Back in his room he paced restlessly till darkness came. Now came the struggle against gnawing thirst. He spent a tormented, sleepless night. He dreaded the dawn when he knew his thirst for a drink would be unbearable. But he knew he would have to suffer in soberness until his hand was steady and his brain alert. He must be fit, fit to murder without risking his own life.

He suffered on for another week, his throat burning and his body aching. But he stayed sober. And all the time, his hatred of the art dealer Mei Wong grew. He pictured him as a satanic schemer, an ugly monster who had cheated him of the last shred of his decency. When the day arrived to board the vessel for Hong Kong his face was lined with pain. Since the morning he had turned back from the bar he had drunk nothing stronger than coffee.

He had gained enough strength to bargain a place for himself on the ship's crew to pay his passage. He pitched into the heavy new work with a strange eagerness. It exhausted him and gave him the pleasure of sleep once again. Sleep that would build his strength further for the murder of Han Lee.

He spent his free time reading quietly in his bunk. He wanted no friends among the crew. Several times a convivial bottle was passed to him. Just once there had been a long second's lapse between the offered drink and his refusal.

After a while the days became a stimulating and pleasant experience. But the nights were suddenly filled with troubled dreams. Dreams of death as the dagger became an expert and precise weapon in his steady

ALFRED HITCHCOCK'S ANTHOLOGY

hand. He practiced with it until his control was perfect.

He tried to picture what Han Lee might be like. Always he conjured up a vision of an ancient, white-bearded Oriental. Perhaps a gentle man, a man of great culture. And each day brought him nearer to Hong Kong, nearer the day when he would become a paid assassin. With his cleared brain and returned health, Rendell's whole being was revolted by the idea. How had he sunk low enough to be willing to kill a man?

He stepped ashore at Hong Kong sick with fear. There were only three weeks left to complete his mission. And now he had no wish to murder this stranger. There must, he felt, be some way out.

He soon located the whereabouts of Mei Wong's confederate, John MacDonald, and began the journey up to the mountains. After a day he arrived at a luxurious bungalow and John MacDonald, hearty and gray-haired, gave him a boisterous greeting. "Deuced glad to see a new face," he exclaimed, pumping his hand vigorously. "Mei Wong sent word you were coming last mail. I have a box for you."

Rendell studied him as they went into the house. It was hard to imagine this pleasant man as a criminal. But the plan was taking shape. The box had arrived.

As soon as they were inside MacDonald went to his desk and brought the box to him. Rendell took it carefully. It was of medium size and not too heavy. "You know what is in this?" he asked.

MacDonald shook his head. He said: "Haven't an idea. Came just a few days ago."

Rendell put the box under his arm. But you have heard of Han Lee?"

"Han Lee? Yes, everyone here has heard of Han Lee."

And you know that Mei Wong has sent me here to settle things with Lee and bring back the Pearls of Li Pong?"

MacDonald stared at him. "Han Lee is a term the village people here use when they refer to the evil spirit

"Yes, I suppose we can admit, you and I, that Han Lee is evil."

"A local superstition, goes back centuries. That's why . . . The Pearls of Li Pong? Come out to my back verandah."

Rendell followed the man outside There stretched before them a breathtaking view of three tiny lakes at the base of a range of stately gray mountains. A scene of such perfect balance and splendor as to excite any artist—and in Rendell grew an excitement he had forgotten, almost entirely lost.

MacDonald chuckled. "*Those* are the famous Pearls of Li Pong. You might be able to settle your differences with the evil spirit, Han Lee. But as for taking back the Pearls of Li Pong, you will admit that would be quite some task. I'm afraid Mei Wong has been having one of his little jokes. He's been making a fool of you, my good man."

Rendell's eyes remained on the magnificence before him. "Just the opposite," he said quietly. "He's been making a man out of a fool." He remembered the box underneath his arm. He laid it on the bamboo table at his side, found the key, and opened it. He saw tubes of paint, a palette, brushes, and canvas. He looked up at MacDonald, his eyes bright and eager. "And you're wrong about the Pearls of Li Pong. I will take them back with me."

ALFRED HITCHCOCK'S ANTHOLOGY